CREATIVE
CAPITAL

CREATIVE
CAPITAL

Georges Doriot and
the Birth of Venture Capital

SPENCER E. ANTE

Harvard Business Press

Boston, Massachusetts

Library of Congress Cataloging-in-Publication Data
Ante, Spencer E.
  Creative capital : Georges Doriot and the birth of venture capital /
Spencer E. Ante.
     p. cm.
  Includes bibliographical references and index.
  ISBN 978-1-4221-0122-3
  1. Doriot, Georges F. (Georges Frederic), 1899-1987 2. Capitalists
and financiers--Biography. 3. Venture capital--History. I. Title.
  HG172.D67A58 2008
  332.6092--dc22
  [B]

                                        2007036142

The paper used in this publication meets the minimum requirements of the American National Standard for Permanence of Paper for Publications and Documents in Libraries and Archives Z39.48-1992.

CONTENTS

ACKNOWLEDGMENTS

This book relies predominantly on a number of primary materials: Georges Doriot's voluminous notes on American Research and Development Corporation's operations and meetings; the annual reports of American Research and Development, European Enterprise Development, and Canadian Enterprise Development; U.S. military documents from the Library of Congress and National Archives; and manuscript collections, oral histories, letters, diaries, memoirs, newspaper and magazine stories, newsletters, pamphlets, DVDs, VHS cassettes, interviews, and personal observations of Doriot's homes and workplaces.

Several sources merit special mention. First and foremost, this book could not have been written without the personal papers of Georges Doriot, which are housed at the M.I.T. Entrepreneurship Center Library (and on loan from the French Library and Cultural Center of Boston). Doriot was an extraordinary record keeper who seemingly documented every moment of the history of American Research and Development. The papers comprise more than twelve hundred pages from eight different books. I owe considerable thanks to my first research assistant, Tess Oliver, for her diligence in corralling these papers and sending them to me. They helped jump-start my research, serving as a touchstone throughout the entire process.

I also owe a special thanks to Roanne Edwards and Elaine Uzan Leary of the French Library for introducing me to many of the men and women who knew General Doriot. Roanne, in particular, was a huge help and inspiration in the beginning of this journey, and generously shared with me many of her contacts.

Besides Doriot's papers, the most important source of information were the dozens of interviews I conducted with the people who worked at American Research and Development, the entrepreneurs who were financed and nurtured by the firm, the men who studied under Doriot at Harvard Business School, and the large circle of Doriot's friends and colleagues. I conducted interviews with these individuals between October 2005 and July 2007: James Aisner, Vernon Alden, Steven Anders, Harlan Anderson, Gordon Bell, Brian Brooks, George H. W. Bush, Philip Caldwell, Patricia A. Clark, Charles Coulter, Wilbur Cowett, Alexander d'Arbeloff, Arnaud de Vitry, Nicholas DeWolf, Catharine-Mary Donovan, William Elfers, Sumner Feldberg, Frederick Frank, Art Goldstein, Richard H. Groves, Jean Gueroult, F. Warren Hellman, Winston Hindle, Molly Hoagland, Ralph P. Hoagland, Ray Hoagland, Daniel J. Holland, Francis Hughes, Eileen P. Jacobs, Claude Janssen, Ted Johnson, Michael Koerner, Arnold Kroll, Josh Lerner, David L. Luke, Derek Mather, Dina McCabe, Robert McCabe, Parker G. Montgomery, James F. Morgan, Gib Myers, Kenneth H. Olsen, Thomas J. Perkins, Eveline Poillot, Marie-Helene Poillot, Isabelle Pounder, James P. Robinson, Andrew G. C. Sage II, John A. Shane, Robert Shapiro, Jack Shields, James M. Stone, Lewis H. Strauss, Gerald D. Sutton, Janet Testa, Marvin Traub, Jimmy Treybig, Donald T. Valentine, Charles P. Waite, William Welsh, and Peter Wilson.

I spoke to every one of these people at least once, and some of them I interviewed two, three, or more times. Without their cooperation, this book would not have been possible. I owe an especially deep gratitude to Robert McCabe, one of Doriot's closest friends. Bob stepped up from the beginning, answering every one of my phone and e-mail queries, as well as opening many doors within the Doriot network.

I also would like to give a special, warm thanks to Marie-Hélène Poillot and Eveline Poillot, the surviving members of the Doriot family. Eveline is Georges Doriot's niece, and Marie-Hélène is her daughter. The Poillots were very supportive from the start of the project, and were gracious hosts to my wife and me when we visited Paris for a week to research the roots of Doriot and his family. They invited us to visit them at Doriot's ancestral home in Courbevoie, where Eveline still lives today. There, she gave us a tour of the home, hosted an outstanding lunch featuring a rack of lamb, and shared scrapbooks, photo albums, and other family memorabilia. Afterward, they continued to lend a helping hand whenever I needed it, answering questions and providing me with many family letters, documents, and photos, which were crucial elements of my research.

During our trip to Paris, we also met with two other individuals who deserve special mention: Arnaud de Vitry and Claude Janssen. Arnaud and Claude were also surrogate sons of Doriot. They both were extremely supportive of the project, inviting us into their homes and sharing many wonderful stories. Afterward, they both continued to answer every question I threw their way, whether by e-mail or phone.

I owe a debt of gratitude to several other research assistants who scoured through various collections of papers scattered across the country. The papers of Lewis Strauss, which are housed at the Herbert Hoover Presidential Library in West Branch, Iowa, proved an invaluable window into Doriot's first two decades in the United States. Many thanks to Dwight M. Miller for discovering a treasure trove of letters in the Strauss papers. Kudos to Jason Godin, a PhD student at Texas A&M University, for digging up some jewels in the archives of the George Bush Presidential Library in College Station, Texas. And thanks also to Monica Corbin, who translated the Poillot family letters and other French-language materials.

The files of Deans Wallace B. Donham and Donald K. David at the Harvard Business School's Baker Library provided another invaluable source on Doriot's teaching career, from the 1920s all the way up until the late 1950s. I owe a big thanks to Rachel Wise and Laura Linard of the Baker Library reference staff for pinpointing the relevant files in a mountain of material.

The papers of Georges Doriot housed in the manuscript collection of the Library of Congress provided an extraordinarily detailed account of Doriot's military career, during and after World War II. Spanning six linear feet and containing eighteen boxes, including one box of classified material (which I was able to declassify), the register contained a total of thirty-six hundred items. Many, many thanks to Manuscript Division staff members Lia Apodaca, Jennifer Brathovde, Jeffrey Flannery, Joe Jackson, Patrick Kerwin, and Bruce Kirby for helping me navigate through this collection during my week-long stay.

The papers of Ralph Soda were another critical source. One of the most well-known journalists of his generation who broke stories about Iran Contra and other government scandals for the Gannet News Service, Soda was commissioned in 1988 by the trustees of Doriot's estate to write a biography of Georges Doriot. Soda never finished the project, and he died in 2004. But some of the research that Soda did for the book survived in his estate. Many thanks to Soda's close friend Robert Dubill, former executive editor of *USA Today* and the executor of Soda's estate, for sending me a large box of papers filled with these materials.

Several items in Soda's Doriot papers deserve special mention. Soda's interviews and notes on Doriot's early years were especially valuable, as well as copies he made of Doriot's pocket diary and hundreds of private journal entries, which Doriot referred to as "reveries." Moreover, I was able to access hundreds of classified, secret, and confidential government documents, mostly from the U.S. military, that Soda declassified from the U.S. National Archives and Records Administration. Soda's hard work saved me countless hours of toiling in government archives, and his insights into Doriot's character were illuminating.

Another important source was the Ken Olsen papers, which are housed at Gordon College in Wenham, Massachusetts. I believe I am the first person to access this collection. For that honor, I owe a special thanks to Daniel B. Tymann, the college's vice president for Advancement of Science and Technology. When I called Dan, he immediately offered to help, and followed through by combing through the collection and sending me a dossier of letters, interviews, photos, and other primary materials.

A videotape of a 1995 reunion of members of the Military Planning Division of the Office of the Quartermaster General hosted by the Lemelson Center at the Smithsonian Institution provided another critical source of firsthand recollections of many World War II veterans no longer with us today. Many thanks to Dr. Stephen Anders, the Command Historian of the U.S. Army Quartermaster Center and School in Fort Lee, Virginia for sending me a copy of the tape and a slew of other relevant files and materials on the history of the Quartermaster Corps.

Although in writing this book I consulted dozens of books, reference volumes, and research papers, I wish to cite a few sources that stood out. *Sustaining the Venture Capital Firm* by Patrick R. Liles provided an indispensable overview of the history of American Research and Development. *The First Venture Capitalist*, a collection of interviews, newspaper articles, essays, and lectures by Doriot, and commentaries on Doriot, edited by Udayan Gupta, provided a superb introduction to the ideas and world of Doriot. I especially relied on *The Ultimate Entrepreneur: The Story of Ken Olsen and Digital Equipment Corporation* by Glenn Rifkin and George Harrar, for a vivid retelling of the rise of Digital. *The Manufacturing Class Notes of Georges F. Doriot* supplied an important window into Doriot's legendary class at Harvard Business School.

The academic literature on venture capital was surprisingly sparse, but I found two research papers that were especially insightful: "Organizing Venture Capital: The Rise and Demise of American Research and Development Corporation, 1946–1973," by David H. Hsu at the Wharton School of the

University of Pennsylvania and Martin Kenney at the Department of Human Community Development of the University of California at Davis; and "Creating Modern Venture Capital: Institutional Design and Performance in the Early Years," by Caroline Fohlin of Johns Hopkins University's Department of Economics. Another academic source that provided essential background and context was the unpublished dissertation of Martha Louise Reiner of the University of California at Berkeley's Department of Economics, "The Transformation of Venture Capital: A History of Venture Capital Organizations in the United States."

On the publishing end of things, I would like to thank my agent Christy Fletcher for her steadfast support of this project. Without her persistence, this book would never have seen the light of day. Christy was willing to take a chance on a first-time author, and I am forever grateful to her for that vote of confidence. I would also like to thank my editor Jacqueline Murphy. Before I started this project, I had been warned by many authors to not expect any editing from my "editor." Book editors are all about selling and marketing, friends and colleagues told me. Jacque, however, is keeping alive the tradition of book editing, striking the perfect balance between providing helpful feedback while not micromanaging the manuscript. Jacque delivered excellent advice that sustained me through a long and complicated task. I am also grateful to my colleagues at *BusinessWeek*: Jon Byrne, especially, for approving my book leave; Steve Adler, Frank Comes, and Dan Beucke for backing me all the way; and Steve Hamm, Steve Baker, Heather Green, Peter Elstrom, Peter Burrows, Arik Hesseldahl, and Catherine Holahan who kindly offered their counsel and supported me in so many ways.

My parents, Leslie Schoengold and Dr. Hermenegildo Ante, and my two sisters, Nicole and Allison, were always encouraging and inquisitive. I owe extra thanks to my father, who taught me a love of learning and of books, which goes back to the time when I was around seven years old and he bought me the entire collection of the 15th edition of the *Encyclopaedia Britannica*. My grandparents expressed enthusiasm throughout the project, which lifted my spirits. I trace my love of words and language in large part to the epic games of Scrabble I played with my grandmother when I was a youngster. Big props also go to my close friends Jamie Bernardin, Marc Ench, Darren Gordon, Alan Siegel, and Steven Taub, for making me laugh and keeping me sane during the inevitable spells of doubt and darkness that accompany the writing of a first book.

I owe the biggest thanks to my lovely wife, Erin, for bringing her sensitivity, thoughtfulness, and intelligence to this story. I constantly bounced ideas off of her and she always offered a constructive and helpful suggestion. And whenever I needed to spend an extra day or two cranking out some copy, she would always help me carve out the time and space to get the job done. Finally, I want to thank my beautiful daughter, Justine, who was nice enough to let me keep my computer and voluminous research notes in her bedroom while I finished the book. I will never forget when I put her on my lap and she started banging away at the keyboard.

INTRODUCTION

Venture capital has existed in one form or another since the earliest days of commercial activity. The Spanish monarchy and Italian investors who financed the transatlantic voyage of Christopher Columbus were, in a sense, venture capitalists. But it wasn't until the second half of the twentieth century that venture financing became a professional, large-scale industry. And the man who led that transformation was Georges Doriot.

I can't recall exactly when I first came across the name of General Georges Frederic Doriot (pronounced door-ee-*oh*) but I do know that in 2002, when I looked into the sparse literature on the history of venture capital, his name kept popping up. I found a bunch of newspaper and magazine profiles, a chapter on him in a book or two, and a short film, but no full-length biography.

"He is the founder of the modern VC industry, but there's been remarkably little written about him," says Josh Lerner, a professor at Harvard Business School who specializes in the study of private equity. "He is the first person who basically ran an institutional venture capital fund. And he played a lead role in getting the VC community to see itself as a real industry."

The venture capital industry began to take shape after World War II on the northeastern seaboard when in 1946 Doriot became president of the first public venture capital firm: Boston-based American Research and Development Corporation (ARD). The famous inventor Charles F. Kettering predicted ARD would go bust in five years. But Doriot proved him wrong over the next twenty-five years, as his firm financed and nurtured more than one hundred start-ups, many of which became huge successes that pushed the frontiers of technology and business. ARD companies led the way in developing computers, atom smashers, medical devices, and new machines that desalinated brackish water. Doriot even backed George H. W. Bush's first company, Zapata Off-Shore Company. "He was very important because he was the first one to believe there was a future in financing entrepreneurs in an organized way," says Arnold Kroll, an investment banker at Lehman Brothers who worked with ARD.

Doriot was not a physically imposing fellow but he exuded a magnetic aura. "It was almost like knowing someone like Beethoven or Einstein," says Charles Dyer, a pilot for Eastern Airlines and Harvard Business School graduate who became close to Doriot in the General's later years. A wiry man with ramrod posture, Doriot was about 5'10", with a thin moustache, elegant bearing, and piercing blue eyes. He spoke with a charming French accent that some associates referred to as the "velvet glove." And he brought a unique style to everything he did—even when smoking his trademark pipe. "As with everything else, he was an artist in selecting tobacco and filling his pipe," said James F. Morgan, an executive at ARD. "He had a custom-tailored blend of tobacco in the office." Always impeccably turned out in a suit and tie, Doriot required all of his students in his class at Harvard Business School to dress accordingly. "Sport coats are for newspaper boys and college boys," he would chide his pupils.

The more I researched Doriot's life, my fascination with an idea transformed into a fascination with the man behind the idea. Doriot was one of the most charismatic characters I had ever come across. Though I had never met the man, I fell under his spell.

Born on September 24, 1899 in Paris, Doriot was the son of an engineer who helped build one of the first automobiles for the Peugeot Motor Company. When I visited Doriot's surviving relatives in Paris, I learned that Doriot's father, Auguste, was also an entrepreneur himself who, in the early twentieth century, launched Doriot, Flandrin, Parant, an innovative car company.

In 1921, Doriot came to America on a steamship. Even though he had no friends or family in the United States, never graduated from college, and dropped out of graduate school, the Frenchman became, arguably, the most influential and popular professor at Harvard University's Graduate School of Business. Over three generations, Doriot taught thousands of students, many of whom went on to become executives at the world's top corporations. He called his course Manufacturing, but it was really his philosophy of life and of business. At Harvard, Doriot became a Yoda-like figure, dispensing wisdom to an ever-growing group of disciples. "Doriot was arresting," says Ralph Hoagland, cofounder of the CVS Corporation, who took his course in 1962. "He was a person you couldn't take your eyes off for a minute. He got me motivated to start a business."

His lectures were so memorable and controversial—he once lectured his students on how to pick a wife—that many former students who have forgotten most of what they learned at business school still remember Doriot vividly. He stressed common sense themes such as self-improvement, teamwork, and contributing to society, while spicing up his philosophy with practical and pithy words of advice:

"A real courageous man is a man who does something courageous when no one is watching him."

"If any information is to be exchanged over whiskey, let us get it rather than give it."

"An auditor is like a tailor; he can make a fat man look thinner or taller or younger."

"You will get nowhere if you do not inspire people."

"Always remember that someone somewhere is making a product that will make your product obsolete."

Doriot was one of the century's most visionary thinkers. He was early to recognize the importance of globalization and creativity in the business world. And decades before economists appreciated the value of technology, Doriot realized that innovation was the key to economic progress. "A lot of the things that were attributed to Peter Drucker were Doriot's ideas," says Charles P. Waite, a former student who went on to work at ARD for many years.

In his classes, Doriot often spoke about the railroads, air conditioning, and air travel, and how those technologies opened up new worlds and increased the productivity of business. "The general's view of the world as one of constant competition, led to his belief that innovation, continuous innovation, never relaxing, was the only way to stay ahead of the competition," says Robert McCabe, a close friend and former investment banker at Lehman Brothers.

During World War II, Doriot played a critical role in the Allied victory—and learned how to become a venture capitalist. As the head of research and development in the Office of the Quartermaster General, Doriot led a revolution in the military by applying science to the art of war. Under his command, the U.S. Army found substitutes for critical raw materials, and developed dozens of innovative items such as water-repellent fabrics, cold weather shoes and uniforms, sunscreen, insecticides, and nutritious compact food, including

K-rations. In one confidential project, Doriot oversaw the invention of Doron, lightweight plastic armor that was named in his honor. For his achievements, Doriot was promoted to the rank of Brigadier General and won the Distinguished Service Medal, the highest U.S. military medal given to a noncombatant, as well as being decorated a commander of the British Empire and awarded the French Legion of Honor.

Doriot's wartime experience proved his exceptional talent: he was not only a visionary but also a man of action, someone who had the energy, discipline, and charisma to bring his big ideas to fruition. Indeed, during the postwar period, Doriot went on to found a number of important institutions. In 1954, his vision of a peace-time research organization for American GIs was born with the opening of the U.S. Army Soldier Systems Center in Natick, Massachusetts, a research lab dedicated for the last sixty years to providing America's soldiers with the world's best equipment. In 1959, his dream of a European business school came to life with the Institut Européen d'Administration des Affairs (INSEAD), today's leading European business school.

Scaling each of these peaks, Doriot bucked the prevailing system. Although he helped implement the Business School's famous case study method early in his teaching career, after the war Doriot transcended this approach. Instead he lectured students with his philosophy of business and life, and gave them practical experience by sending them on consulting assignments with real companies. In the military, he ruffled feathers by resisting orders so he could make sure soldiers had the equipment they needed to survive in the trenches. And in the financial world, he upset the conventional wisdom by proving that there was big money to be made from patient investing in and the nurturing of small, unproven companies.

In hindsight, it is Doriot's work running ARD that truly distinguishes him as a twentieth century giant. In 1946, Doriot was recruited to run ARD by a cadre of New England elites—Massachusetts Investor Trust chairman Merrill Griswold, MIT president Karl T. Compton, and Vermont Senator Ralph E. Flanders, the first Congressman to publicly upbraid Joseph McCarthy.

Fresh from the U.S. victory in World War II, these luminaries conceived ARD as a vehicle to revive New England and the U.S. economy. In their minds, ARD would solve a major imperfection of modern U.S. capitalism: new companies were starved for money and professional management. It's hard to imagine these days, with billions of dollars swimming around the globe, but after the war, entrepreneurs had a difficult, if not impossible, time raising capital. Banks were ultraconservative, reluctant to lend money to unproven ventures. Sure, rich families like the Rockefellers invested in new companies but they were few and hard to reach. ARD promised to break down the walls of an elitist, insular world, reviewing ideas from thousands of companies across the country.

In his personal life, Doriot was cautious to a fault at times. But in his professional life, Doriot realized venture capital was all about taking huge but calculated risks. "He always thought ARD should have a major goal or undertaking that could be worked on as a Holy Grail," says Daniel J. Holland, an ARD staffer during the late 1960s. "But he wouldn't write a check until all the risks were understood."

ARD's beginnings were modest—its first venture fund was a mere $3.4 million. A few of its initial investments failed, and Doriot spent a lot of time in ARD's early days responding to angry and impatient sharcholders. But under the General's leadership, ARD created the paradigm of entrepreneurial success. The dozens of prominent companies nurtured under ARD were the most obvious proof of Doriot's achievements. Yet Doriot also exerted an influence through his writings, speeches, and ARD's annual meetings, in which its investment companies set up booths and enjoyed an opportunity to network and talk to potential investors. "He gave a dignity or a substance to the process, and that always attracts imitators," says Lehman's Kroll, who attended many meetings over the years. In the late 1960s, Doriot's influence persisted through the work of his disciples, as various ARD alumni founded and ran the second generation of successful VC firms, including Greylock Partners and Fidelity Ventures.

Doriot achieved success by staying true to his patient investment philosophy. He believed in building companies for the long haul, not flipping them for a quick profit. Returns were the by-product of hard labor, not a goal. Doriot often worked with a company for a decade or more before realizing any return. That is why he often referred to his companies as his "children."

"When you have a child, you don't ask what return you can expect," Doriot was quoted in a 1967 *Fortune* magazine story. "Of course you have hopes—you hope the child will become President of the United States. But that is not very probable. I want them to do outstandingly well in their field. And if they do, the rewards will come. But if a man is good and loyal and does not achieve a so-called good rate of return, I will stay with him. Some people don't become geniuses until *after* they are 24, you know. If I were a speculator, the question of return would apply. But I don't consider a speculator—in my definition of the word—constructive. I am building men and companies."

One child, an ambitious little outfit called Digital Equipment Corporation, grew to become a giant, cementing the legend of ARD and Doriot. In 1957, ARD gave $70,000 to the two young MIT engineers who cofounded Digital—Kenneth P. Olsen and Harlan Anderson—in exchange for 70 percent of the start-up's equity. Olsen, who was Digital's president and undisputed leader, wanted to build smaller, cheaper, and easier-to-use computers that would challenge the glass-encased mainframes of IBM, the dominant computer manufacturer and only one making money.

It was a perfect match. In Olsen, Doriot found the archetypal engineer-cum-entrepreneur who was dedicated to making his company a success. "A creative man merely has ideas; a resourceful man makes them practical," said Doriot. "I look for the resourceful man." Olsen embodied that ideal. In Doriot, Olsen found a comforting father figure always ready to offer words of encouragement or some bit of wisdom. The fates of these two men would be forever intertwined.

When ARD liquidated its stake in Digital, the company was worth more than $400 million—yielding a return on their original investment of more than 70,000 percent. It was the young venture capital industry's first home run, and it helped make the Route 128 area outside Boston a technological mecca. "ARD led the advent of technology companies being financed by venture capital firms, which ultimately became important factors in our economy," says F. Warren Hellman, a former president of Lehman Brothers, which took many ARD start-ups public, including Digital. "Doriot was very much at the forefront of fundamentally changing our economy."

Just as important, ARD's support of Digital and dozens of other unproven little companies ushered in a new era of corporate culture. At Digital, the engineer was king. Hierarchy was out. Controlled chaos was in. Like Jack Kerouac and the Beat Generation, Digital was a petri dish in which the counterculture was spawned in the late 1950s. "He was definitely part of a social revolution that loosened things up," says Parker G. Montgomery, founder and chief executive of Cooper Laboratories, a successful health care products company that ARD financed during the 1960s. "There was such support, his presence, his philosophy, his belief in new enterprise was an inspiration."

Doriot did not act alone. His wife Edna Allen supported him every step of the way, allowing him to focus obsessively on his intellectual and commercial pursuits. A pretty, intelligent, and caring American woman, Allen was a research assistant at the Harvard Business School when she first laid eyes on Doriot. For the next forty-eight years, Edna was his devoted wife and closest friend, and the couple enjoyed a lifelong storybook romance. Doriot would often write love poems about Edna. And the favor was returned. "When he went on a trip he'd find a love note in his pajamas," says Olsen.

Despite Doriot's singular talents, he was far from perfect. ARD should never have been incorporated as a publicly traded company. Doriot never groomed a successor to take over the firm. And Doriot never figured out a way to appease government regulators, who repeatedly threatened to put ARD out of business. The Securities & Exchange Commission (SEC), to cite one example, ruled that ARD officers could not hold stock options in client companies, which meant Doriot could not attract the best and brightest talent. The tension grew so great that in 1965 the SEC even raided its offices to conduct a "surprise audit." Doriot was so enraged at the SEC that he kept a file of vituperative letters addressed to the agency that were stamped: "Not sent—on advice of counsel."

Despite a somewhat tragic ending to his career, all of the strands of Doriot's life connect to form something quite profound. In the second half of the twentieth century, the United States experienced a historic transformation, in which a society dominated by large corporations such as Standard Oil, U.S. Steel, and General Motors shifted to a nation driven by venture-backed start-ups such as Digital Equipment Corporation, Intel Corporation, Microsoft, Starbucks, and many others. Ever since, those small, innovative companies have created new markets and millions of high-paying jobs while also forcing old industries to become more efficient and productive. A recent study by the National Venture Capital Association found that U.S. venture-backed companies between 1970 and 2005 accounted for ten million jobs and nearly 17 percent of the nation's gross domestic product.

Doriot was the prophet of this new "Start-up Nation," the leader of a social and economic crusade that democratized the clubby world of finance. More than any other person, Doriot—through his teaching, writing, and leadership in the military, academic, and financial worlds—pioneered the transition to an economy built on entrepreneurship and innovation. For playing this role, Doriot should be revered as much as other well-known business titans such as J. P. Morgan, John D. Rockefeller, or Andrew Carnegie. Hopefully, you'll agree with me after reading the book.

ONE

ROOTS

(1863–1898)

O N A SUNNY AFTERNOON in the spring of 1913, Georges Frederic Doriot ran as fast as he could all the way to his home on the outskirts of Paris. Young Georges and his family lived in Courbevoie, a bustling town twenty miles north of France's capital nestled along the eastern bank of the Seine River. Thanks to its proximity to the wide ribbon of water, Courbevoie had established itself as a manufacturing center. In factories sprinkled around town, companies produced automobiles, perfume, and other products in their more affordable environs, and then shuttled their handiwork down the river to the big city.

It was the end of the school year and thirteen-year-old Georges was running home because he had good news to share with his family. A student at Coubert 7, Courbevoie's public secondary school, Georges disliked school because he was always afraid of not doing well and saddening his parents, particularly his demanding father.

But today was different. Georges had excelled in his classes, and had the paper to prove it. He excitedly careened around boulevard corners and short cut across intersections, nearly colliding with several *flâneurs* strolling down the street. It was only when he reached Rue Franklin, a block from the walled garden of his family's home, that he paused long enough to savor the honor embossed on the scroll he cradled in his sweating palm: Georges had placed second in his class at the École Communale.

It was an award certificate—the first such honor he had ever received. Beaming with pride, he couldn't wait to share the good news with his family. Educational achievement was prized highly in the Doriot household. His father and mother would be pleased with him, he was sure. And so he resumed his dash for home.

Camille, his doting mother, responded as Georges had expected. An educator herself, she knew the value of supporting the achievements of young, insecure children. She embraced the radiant Georges with a warm hug, gave him a laudatory pat on the head, and set out a generous serving of home-made cookies that marked special family occasions. But Auguste, his stern father, had quite a different reaction. In stark contrast to Camille, Auguste seemed unimpressed with his son's award. He acknowledged the certificate with only a cursory glance, nodded perfunctorily, and then fixed his son with one of those chilling stares of appraisal. "And why not first?" asked Auguste.

Auguste's voice was calm but his words were a blow to Georges's heart. And his father's cool stare was more painful than any punishment Georges had ever received. Staggered, Georges didn't know what to think, or how to react. He had expected congratulations. He had expected his father to be proud. Instead, he was knocked back on his heels, put in his place. Bewildered and humiliated, he fled to his room, tears welling up in his eyes. His glorious triumph had ended disastrously. Why, Georges wondered? Why did I disappoint father?

It was an experience that could have scarred him for a long time. But as Georges calmed down and reflected on the situation, he began to understand the reasons behind his father's behavior. His father, he would tell a friend years later when recalling the incident, was not concerned that Georges had failed to achieve first place honors in his class at École Communale. No, he was concerned that Georges was *happy* placing second. To Auguste, a famous automobile engineer who had raised his children to strive for excellence in everything they did, celebrating anything less than the best possible result smacked of contentment. And contentment, Auguste believed, is a state of mind that recognizes no need for improvement. As Georges came to realize, his father's seemingly cruel question was actually a well-meaning parent's method of challenging their child to reach the stars.

It was a challenge he never forgot, and an experience that some friends theorize was responsible for driving Georges Doriot to extraordinary accomplishments later on in his life. Georges Doriot would never again be satisfied with being anything less than the best. Not in himself. Not in others. Not in anything.

⁓

When Auguste Frederic Doriot was discharged from the French Army in the fall of 1889, he was a young and ambitious man who harbored great hopes and dreams. Up to this point, however, they had been dreams deferred. Doriot was unfortunate in that he had to devote five years in the prime of his youth to the military. And yet he was also lucky. He happened to serve in the Army during one of the few periods in nineteenth century France that was not racked by war, revolution, or civil unrest.

In 1889, France was in the middle of its most peaceful period of the modern era—still stinging from its defeat in the Franco-German War of 1870–1871, when it relinquished European hegemony to the newly constituted German Empire. The terms of the Treaty of Frankfurt were harsh: an indemnity of five billion francs, plus the cost of maintaining a German occupation army in eastern France until the indemnity was paid. Most distressing, Alsace and half of Lorraine were annexed to the new German Empire. Then, a few days after the Treaty was signed, France tore itself apart when a civil war broke out during the rebellion of the Paris Commune.

Still, after its war with Prussia, France would not see another conflict or revolution until the early twentieth century. There would be no more "Bloody Weeks" for a long time. So after putting in his required years of service stationed in the armory of Bourges and Versailles, then the seat of the French government, Doriot left the army, all of twenty-six years old, in good health and spirits, with his homeland getting back on its feet.

Auguste had something else going for him: he had lined up a job for himself at the prestigious Peugeot Company. After his discharge from the Army, Doriot headed back home to Valentigney, a beautiful village in northeastern France near the borders of Switzerland and Germany, and the home of the Peugeot Company's factory and cooperative store. While the majority of the villagers in Valentigney were farmers, many residents also worked in the factory. Indeed, most members of the Doriot family worked there at one time or another, including Auguste and his father Jacques Frederic Doriot.

Originally part of the Holy Roman Empire, Valentigney sits on the western bank of the attractive Doubs River. In the late seventeenth century, Louis

XIV acquired the province in which Valentigney resides, Franche-Comte, following the Dutch War of 1672–1678. Louis XIV coveted the province because it provided the ancient regime with a buffer on its eastern border, helping to secure the safety of Paris. Turning eastward, Auguste could look over the crumbling Roman aqueducts and green forests and rolling hills of the Doubs district. And as he gazed over the horizon, he could marvel at the low, crenellated ridges of the Jura Mountains ranging across the Franco-Swiss border like some giant humpback whale.

Though it was a classically picturesque French village, Valentigney was unique in at least one respect. While nine-tenths of the French population was Roman Catholic, Valentigney was one of the few areas in the country that was completely Protestant. In fact, the district was so devoid of Catholics there was not even a single Catholic Church in the village. Later on, Georges, Auguste's first and only son, fondly recalled his hometown and the industriousness of its people: "I remember it with a great deal of feeling. It was a wonderful world. People were not rich; they had to work for everything they had. They went to church very regularly and the Protestant minister was a kind and very respected man with a good education."

The architecture of the village reflected the area's working class roots. In the late nineteenth century, the typical house in Valentigney was a simple but sturdy structure built of stone and red roof tiles, and was encircled by a low stone wall, allowing passersby to peek over, luxuriate in the lush gardens and chirping birds, and smell the flowers.

This was the bucolic yet busy setting that Auguste returned to after five years in the Army. Auguste, the next-to-youngest child of a family of eight children, was born on October 24, 1863, in Sainte-Suzanne, a village in the Franche-Comte province about a dozen miles northwest of Valentigney. Auguste's father Jacques, who had been a farmer in the early part of his life, worked his way all the way up to become the foreman of the Peugeot factory. In 1878, when Auguste was fifteen, Jacques arranged for him to become an apprentice fitter, or metal worker. Auguste worked in the factory for six years before he was called to join the Army. Now, back in Valentigney, Auguste could not have been more eager to return to the Peugeot Company.

If there was one thing that brought joy to Auguste, it was the pleasure of a hard day's work. Photographs of him in his middle age show a man of medium height and solid build with a very serious look on his face. His most notable features were a strong Gallic nose, large ears, and a thick black moustache that was popular during the day. "My Father was a very wonderful person, extremely quiet, very thoughtful, very kind, but very strong," recalled Georges. "He was a terribly hard worker. When he was young—I know this from my mother—he had worked as many as twelve to fourteen hours a day and he had still kept on doing that."

By going back to work for Peugeot, Auguste showed wise judgment. The Peugeot clan had first settled in the east of France in the fifteenth century and, like most elite clans of that time, drew its wealth from vast tracts of land. In the eighteenth century, the Peugeots expanded into windmills and textile mills. In 1810, the brothers Jean-Pierre and Jean-Frédéric Peugeot converted one of those mills into a steel foundry for manufacturing saw blades, thereby creating the Peugeot Company.

By the late nineteenth century, the brothers had created one of the most well-known and successful companies in France. Building on their textile and steel plants, the family transformed their namesake into a diversified manufacturing concern with expertise in producing household tools such as kitchen utensils, coffee grinders, sewing machines, and various other items. But much of the Peugeots' wealth came from a more unusual source: they cornered the market in women's corsets, because they alone possessed the secret of manufacturing the special steel needed to stiffen these Victorian Age garments. Through hard work, a keen sense for spotting opportunity, and a flair for innovation, Peugeot forged a reputation for making quality products.

The Peugeot brothers were fortunate in that the family business was large and profitable enough to finance their expansion into new industries, for in the nineteenth century, financial markets were crude and entrepreneurs had a difficult, if not impossible, time raising money for new ventures. After all, the concept of the entrepreneur was relatively new, having been first introduced into economic theory by the underappreciated philosopher-economist Richard Cantillon in his remarkable treatise *Essai sur la Nature du Commerce en Général*, written between 1730 and 1734. In the nineteenth century, entrepreneurs virtually disappeared from classic economic and political thought thanks to the lack of financial support for their undertakings and awareness of their importance to the economy.

The idea of venture capital was even less developed. In fact, it was not until the early twentieth century that the term *venture capital* was first popularized. Sure, there were a multitude of individuals throughout the eighteenth and nineteenth centuries who were small saver-investors. They typically congregated around large European port cities and were prepared to take modest risks, such as sending a few goods on a departing ship. But by and large their meager savings were invested more readily into government bonds.

Banks, which had existed since antiquity, were also of little to no help to a struggling entrepreneur. It wasn't until the Bank of England was founded in 1694 that banks began offering loans and advances of credit. Until that time, large public banks such as the Bank of Barcelona or the Bank of Genoa only handled deposits and transfers. Still, banks were not in the business of providing equity financing. It was too risky.

The most powerful bank of the nineteenth century, the House of Rothschild, is a case in point. In the first part of the century, the Rothschild family rose to power, transforming a small merchant bank in Frankfurt and a clothes exporter in England into a multinational financial conglomerate by lending money to war-torn, cash-strapped European governments. Later on, they created the biggest bank in the world by pioneering the creation of the modern bond market, enabling British investors to buy internationally tradable bonds of other European nations with a fixed interest rate. The Rothschilds made a colossal fortune by making these loans and by speculating on their rise and fall.

Occasionally, the Rothschilds invested their capital into a new business. But when they did it was to help finance major infrastructure or natural resource development projects. In the middle of the nineteenth century, the Rothschilds used their ample resources to become a dominant force in the finance and construction of European railways. Between 1835 and 1846, the Rothschilds contributed nearly 38 percent of the capital invested in thirty-two French railway concessions.

By and large, though, early European financial enterprises like the House of Rothschild were attached to their privileges, thoroughly conservative, and not interested in the future or fomenting change. In other words, they had nothing to do with venture capital as we know it today. "A commercial bank lends only on the strength of the past," said Doriot in one of his favorite maxims about the venture capital business. "I want money to do things that have never been done before."

The earliest instances of the initial financing of groundbreaking enterprises were primarily found in America. The first major modern communications technology, the telegraph, was financed by a small group of wealthy investors. In 1845, Samuel Morse hired Andrew Jackson's former postmaster general, Amos Kendall, as his agent for locating potential buyers of the telegraph. Kendall had little trouble convincing others of its potential for profit. By the spring of 1845, he had found a small group of investors who committed $15,000 to form the Magnetic Telegraph Company.

One of the most famous inventors of all time also got his big financial break from two wealthy individuals. In the early 1870s, Alexander Graham Bell, a Scottish immigrant who developed an early fascination with the science of acoustics, became a professor of Vocal Physiology and Elocution at the Boston University School of Oratory, a school for mute children. In addition to teaching, Bell was driven by a desire to cure his mother's deafness and thus continued his research in an attempt to find a way to transmit musical notes and speech.

During the fall of 1874, Gardiner Hubbard and Thomas Sanders, parents of two of Bell's students, found out that Bell was working on a method of sending multiple tones on a telegraph wire using a multi-reed device. Sanders, a successful leather merchant, began to underwrite some of Bell's expenses. After hearing about Bell's experiments, Hubbard, a wealthy patent lawyer always looking for opportunities to improve things and make a dollar in the process, saw the opportunity in developing an "acoustic telegraph"— in other words, a telephone. He drafted a partnership agreement between Bell, Sanders, and himself and began to financially support the inventor's experiments.

On March 7, 1876, the U.S. Patent Office issued a patent to Bell covering the "method of, apparatus for, transmitting vocal or other sounds telegraphically . . . by causing undulations, similar in form to the vibrations of the air accompanying the said vocal or other sound." Bell and his backers Hubbard and Sanders offered to sell the patent to Western Union for $100,000. William Orton, Western Union's cigar-chomping robber baron president, balked, countering that the telephone was nothing more than a toy. But after Hubbard organized the Bell Telephone Company in June of 1877 and hundreds of businesses began leasing the phones, the unscrupulous Orton ignored Bell's patents and began to manufacture a telephone that incorporated the inventions of Thomas Edison and other inventors. Western Union had the considerable advantage of piggybacking on the company's already existing telegraph network, easily stringing telephone wires to the telegraph poles.

By this point, Thomas Sanders had poured $110,000 into Bell's work and had not seen a cent in return. And Bell Telephone was facing a serious cash crunch and a vicious illegal competitor. So Hubbard did the only thing he could to save the company: he launched a lawsuit against Western Union, accusing the company of patent infringement. It was a classic David and Goliath battle, the first major lawsuit of the age of modern communications. "The position of an inventor is a hard and thankless one," wrote Bell to his wife during the middle of the trial. "The more fame a man gets for invention, the more does he become a target for the world to shoot at—while no one thinks the inventor deserving of pecuniary assistance."

After company lawyers finally convinced Bell to provide his expert testimony, Western Union lawyers knew they stood no chance of winning the case. On November 10, 1879, Western Union signed an out-of-court settlement transferring at cost all telephones, lines, switchboards, patent rights in telephony, and any pending claims to Bell Telephone. In return, Bell Telephone agreed to stay out of telegraphy and to pay Western Union 20 percent of all telephone receipts until Bell's patents expired. Now that Bell Telephone owned a monopoly on telephone service, its stock zoomed from $65 per share before the suit to more than $1,000 following the settlement. The humiliating defeat led Orton to admit that if he could snare the Bell patent for $25 million it would be a bargain.

In late-nineteenth-century Europe, another innovative new technology was poised to explode—the horseless carriage. With the backing of the family fortune, a young member of the Peugeot clan seized on the opportunity—a move that would ultimately catapult the family's company into the ranks of the world's leading conglomerates. Born in 1848, Armand Peugeot exhibited an interest in machines from an early age and went on to study engineering at the prestigious École Centrale Paris. After graduating from the École, Armand visited Leeds, then the heart of manufacturing in Britain, and came back convinced that the future of horses as a means of transport was not very bright.

In the early 1880s, Armand first pushed the family into bicycle manufacturing. Later in the decade, he teamed up with Leon Serpollet, a young engineer who had built a reputation as an expert in steam engines. In 1887, Serpollet had caught Armand's attention when he built a single-cylinder steam engine almost entirely out of scrap parts and fitted it to a pedal tricycle. Armand subsequently provided financing to Serpollet to create the world's first steam-powered tricycle. In 1889, at the World's Fair in Paris, Serpollet introduced his invention, making Peugeot one of the pioneers of the proto-automobile.

At the same World's Fair, Armand noticed the debut of another new machine that he thought showed even greater promise than the bicycle. The German engineer Karl Benz had introduced his Motorwagen Model 3—a carriage with wooden wheels and a gasoline-powered engine. Today, thanks to the 1886 Motorwagen patent, Benz's machine is officially recognized as the world's first automobile.

This was the hothouse of innovation that Auguste Doriot stumbled back into in 1889 when he returned to civilian life and the Peugeot factory. Every successful man can usually point to a mentor that helped guide his career. For Auguste Doriot, that man was Armand Peugeot. Armand recognized Auguste's mutual fascination with machines and with the future, and, shortly after his return to the factory, sent Auguste on a series of apprenticeships in order to learn the latest techniques in automobile design and engineering and gas-powered "explosion" engines, as they were called at the time.

In 1891, Auguste finished his apprenticeships and returned to a new Peugeot factory in Beaulieu. He immediately set about working with the top engineer of the company, a gentleman named Louis Rigoulot, and began installing Daimler engines into the first Peugeot cars. "The beginnings were rather arduous," said Auguste. "We had no machines except for those which served the manufacture of bicycles." But despite numerous obstacles, the two men built several successful prototypes of a four-wheeled "quadricycle." Armand rewarded Auguste's hard work and ingenuity by promoting him to foreman of the factory. But Armand had another important assignment for Auguste, one that would elevate his stature and name to an even more formidable plane.

In September of 1891, Pierre Giffard, editor-in-chief of *Le Petit Journal*, a well-known French newspaper, staged the first Paris-Brest et Retour—a grueling 750-mile bicycle race that took riders from Paris all the way to Brest, at the tip of Brittany, and back. The race was a media coup for *Le Petit Journal*, generating a significant circulation increase.

Inspired by the success of this event, Armand Peugeot struck upon a brilliant idea. To create a successful business, car makers had to first prove that these strange machines were a reliable, safe, and effective means of transportation. The best way to prove such matters, Armand realized, was through a car race. So Armand asked Giffard if he could enter his quadricycle into the next retour. Giffard agreed and instructed the race agents to record the trip of the quadricycle as well as those of the bicycle racers. This ensured Peugeot would have independent proof of his car's passage—and reliability.

Charged with the success of this mission were Rigoulot, the engineer, and Doriot, the foreman who doubled as the driver of the quadricycle. In these days of global jet travel, the difficulty of such a journey is hard to imagine. A trip of this length in a car had never before been attempted. The previous distance record was set by Serpollet who had traveled about two hundred miles from Paris to Lyon. Rigoulot and Doriot were attempting a fifteen-hundred-mile journey across a much more varied and challenging expanse of terrain. It was a bold and risky test that could easily backfire, ruining their reputations.

At ten o'clock in the morning, Doriot and Rigoulot set out for the first leg of their trip, from Valentigney to Paris. It was about a three-hundred-mile drive. They filled their car with tools, luggage, and a few water tanks. The Type 3 was powered by a two-and-a-half horsepower engine from Daimler and had four gears with a reverse gear.

Trouble struck early. Because the gas tanks were placed too low, the wicks of the headlamps were not receiving enough gasoline, and they were burning up. The two devised the "especially ingenious idea of covering the [gas tank] with fresh grasses in order to maintain it at the lowest possible temperature." This solution helped gasoline reach the lamps more easily and it improved the flow of the fuel throughout the engine so the gears worked more smoothly.

Although the car reached speeds as high as thirteen miles per hour on flat stretches, it slowed down on hills. Auguste would throw the car into first gear, which reduced the speed to a near crawl. On very steep hills, while Doriot drove, Rigoulot followed the car, ready to push it if the motor stopped. But, happily, the motor chugged along.

Over the next few days, the two continued their journey. Along the way they slept in small French towns with charming names such as Coutrey, Bar-sur-Aube, and Provins. Three days later, after reaching Paris at one o'clock in the afternoon, the two men "made a triumphal entry" at the factory of Panhard-Levassor, another innovative French car-maker. Armand Peugeot greeted them with a big smile. Their average speed during the first leg was a respectable eight miles an hour.

A few days later, full of confidence, the two set out to establish the Paris-Brest record. At the time, there was no such thing as a gas station. So as a precaution, Doriot and Rigoulot had Peugeot employees place fuel supplies in advance of their arrival with railroad stationmasters every sixty miles or so. As it turned out, the stationmasters were often afraid to keep the gas for the racers for fear it would catch fire. In those cases, Auguste approached dry-cleaning establishments and asked to borrow or buy the liquid used to clean their customers' clothes.

Rigoulot and Doriot covered one hundred twenty-five miles the first day. The following day they drove another one hundred miles without serious trouble. But while they were headed toward Brest, a problem in the differential delayed them twenty-four hours just outside of Morlaix. They had to make use of all their ingenuity in order to repair the damage, borrowing tools from the shoemaker of the hamlet and using a schoolyard offered up by a kindly teacher to repair the car.

That evening, after dark, "in the midst of the indescribable tumult of a curiously enthusiastic crowd," the quadricycle arrived at Brest. The two men drove along the Rue de Siam, where they were greeted by M. Magnus, the Brest representative of Peugeot. After a night of rest, they set forth on their return voyage. The trip was filled with many comic moments that illustrated the radical and frightening nature of this new machine. Throughout the entire race, telegraphs alerted people of the advancing racers. In many villages, trumpeters sounded the approach of the rumbling vehicle. In one town, villagers "in strange and scanty garb" rushed out of their houses and inns to marvel at the oncoming vehicle.

"Thus it happened one Sunday morning, in Brittany, a worthy gentleman . . . surprised by the sound of the clarion just at the moment when he was changing his clothes, rushed out on the sidewalk holding his trousers in his hands, one leg in and one leg out of the trousers, while there came rushing out to stand beside him another curious individual from a barber shop, with the towel still at his neck, one half of his face shaved while soap suds covered the other half! Moreover, as the dogs were not yet used to automobiles, they often bothered us the first days. Therefore, having found near Dreux a wagon whip, we took possession of it and when a dog disturbed us by jumping and running about us, we had only to raise the whip to get rid of him. This method, which should still be useful in many countries, rendered us a real service."

Other onlookers were less amused. When Doriot and Rigoulet pulled into one village where people were going to church, "we saw women fall to their knees and [cross] themselves at our passing." They thought the car was the sign of Satan.

The return to Paris was accomplished without any major problems. While there, they took "several Paris personalities interested in this new form of locomotion" for rides in their car. The two then returned to Valentigney without a hitch. All in all, it was a stunning success. Rigoulot and Doriot had covered fifteen hundred miles in 139 hours at an average speed of nine miles an hour without a serious accident other than the differential glitch. Instead of ruin, the Paris-Brest et Retour had made their reputations. That year, thanks to the race, Peugeot sold five cars, and boosted its output to twenty-nine cars the following year.

The year 1894 brought Peugeot and Auguste Doriot another level of fame. In July, Pierre Giffard and *Le Petit Journal* decided to hold the first race exclusively for automobiles. There would be no bicycles riding alongside Auguste this time—the car had earned the right to its own contest.

The contest was called the Paris-Rouen Trial of 1894 and was run from Paris to Rouen, a city about eighty miles northwest of the French capital. It was not truly a race but rather a point-to-point contest during which the reliability and performance of the vehicles were judged. The intrepid drivers competed without crash helmets, protective clothing, or barriers, racing over, as the great English driver Charles Jarrott put it, "the never-ending road that led to an unobtainable horizon." The string of epic motor racing contests that subsequently took place prior to World War I were regarded with as much awe, excitement, and alarm as putting a man on the moon, and it all started with this 1894 contest.

The race organizers declared Auguste Doriot the winner. He had finished the course at an average speed of 11.5 miles per hour, slightly faster than the pace he set three years earlier. Doriot shared the seventy-thousand-franc purse with a car from Panhard-Levassor, which came in second. A famous picture taken after the race shows Auguste sitting in the car beside Giffard. Two other men sit across from them. A crowd of children and men surround the car, staring at the men and their bizarre contraption. Giffard and the two other men look back at the camera, smiling, while August looks straight ahead with a stern and focused expression, as if he was still surveying the road, racing toward that unobtainable horizon.

To Auguste, 1894 was a momentous year for a far more personal reason. While Auguste was living in Valentigney, he met a young woman named Berthe Camille Baehler. Berthe, known as Camille to her family, came from Voujeaucourt, another village in Franche-Comte, just east of Valentigney. Camille was born on August 16, 1870 to a Swiss father and French mother. Her father, Jean Baehler, came from Uetendorf, a Swiss village outside of Bern. Baehler supported his family through trading wood between Switzerland and France, and settled in Voujeaucourt, where he met his wife. Since Camille's mother died when she was a child, she was raised by her grandmother and three older sisters.

A family photo taken when Camille was thirty-eight shows a fit, attractive woman with a heart-shaped face wearing a long white dress. In the photo, Camille tied her voluptuous mane of brown hair behind her head, which accentuated her short, straight nose, wide-set eyes, and pretty thin lips. Camille was advanced for her time. She spoke English and graduated from a French lycée, earning a living as a schoolteacher. Like Auguste, Camille was an adventurous spirit. Once, around 1890, she even traveled to Canada where she worked as a nurse and teacher for the children of a wealthy family in Montreal. Camille came back from Canada to marry Auguste, a marriage that was encouraged by their respective parents.

On September 27, 1894, Auguste and Camille were married in Valentigney. He was a relatively old thirty, while she was a fetching twenty-four. The couple shared a deep bond and created a loving home and atmosphere for their two children. After the wedding, Armand Peugeot sent Auguste to Paris to serve as the director of its factory and technical director of Peugeot's first showroom on L'avenue de la Grande-Armée. Cars were so new that people did not know how to operate these machines, so Auguste taught customers how to drive, and took care of the repairs and maintenance of the growing fleet of Peugeot vehicles.

As a sign of his affection and loyalty to Auguste, Armand invited Auguste and Camille to live in a home owned by the Peugeots in the 17th arrondissement in the western part of Paris on 83 Boulevard Gouvion-Saint-Cyr. Mr. and Mrs. Armand Peugeot lived on the first floor, and Auguste and Camille took the second floor. Armand transformed the stable adjoining the house into a garage.

Later on, Georges would retell the many stories about his father and mother driving around Paris. "Peasants would chase them with whips, chickens would get killed, which made the peasants very mad," recalled Georges. "One day Father was driving around Paris with Mother and her car got stuck. Well, they thought that they would be lynched, but somehow they finally convinced people and they saved themselves from a complete lynching. In other words, one could say that cars were not at all welcome. They are noisy, dangerous, and even horses didn't like the cars. However, as more cars were made, as we know, all of that has changed."

TWO

THE STUDENT

(1899–1920)

GEORGES FREDERIC DORIOT WAS born in the Peugeot house in Paris. The birth announcement sent out by Auguste and Camille could not have been more cute or clever. It pictured a cherubic baby boy enthroned in the open cab of the newest mechanical marvel to astound mankind: the horseless carriage. The car was a Peugeot, of course, a two-seater with a rear engine and penny farthing wheels. Attached to the front of the car was a sign saying "No. 1". The bare-bottomed boy—one arm placed firmly on the steering column, the other raised in a buoyant wave—smiles while driving the car. The card read: "Mr. and Mrs. Doriot are happy to announce the birth of their son Georges." A wind-whipped banner hitched to the back of the car proclaimed details of the joyous occasion: "Arrivée Paris, 24 September 1899 at 3:45 pm."

Congratulatory letters began arriving. Marianne Peugeot, one of Armand's three daughters, sent Camille a note with a playful picture of a baby enwrapped in a cabbage patch. "I am delighted that you finally have a good cabbage in your garden that has produced a little boy," wrote Marianne. "I rejoice at seeing his eyes shrouded under the fat of his cheeks. Goodbye dear Madame. I send coos to you, as well as to your little baby." Two of Marianne's children also sent Camille congratulatory notes. "I hope your hens can manage now that there is a new mouth to eat their plentiful eggs," wrote her ten-year-old daughter Germaine. "I'm so happy you have a little boy!" rejoiced

Madeleine, Marianne's twelve-year-old daughter. "Be careful when he starts eating donuts!"

In October, a Peugeot customer and friend of Auguste sent the new father a letter in which he pointed to his son's promising future:

My dear Doriot,

I was enchanted to receive the little car #1, from the race of 1899, steered by the worthy representative of a very brave father and of Mrs. Doriot, who although I do not know very well, has made an impression that can be assured by his good nature, a life of happiness. When little George[s] is 20 years old, what will be the amazing speed, what will be the car that will victoriously win in the Tour de France? I hope that Mrs. Doriot and little George[s] are in the best health.

By all accounts, Georges lived a charmed life during his childhood. Indeed, the young Doriot was lucky to be born into such a comfortable and loving household. At the time of Georges's birth, Auguste was thirty-five years old, the right-hand man of one of France's most prosperous industrialists. A picture taken in July 1900, when Georges was almost a year old, shows signs of that good fortune: a smiling baby boy ensconced in a poufy white dress and large bonnet while perched on a small, ornate wooden high chair.

From his father, Georges inherited a sturdy Protestant work ethic, a fascination with technology and the future, and a confident yet humble personality that was at ease both with plutocrats and peasants. From his mother, Georges was bequeathed the gift of Gallic volubility, a sense of compassion, and a firm grasp of the importance of education.

Then, on August 15, 1902, Auguste made a decision that must have thrown the Doriot clan into a state of turmoil: he resigned from Peugeot. Walking away from the company where he had worked his whole professional life of twelve years, where he had made his name, must have been excruciatingly difficult. The specific reason for Auguste's departure from Peugeot was not clear at first. This much we do know: according to his family, he went to work for another car company in Paris for a few years. However, he left the Peugeot Company—and Armand—on good terms. In fact, Armand wrote him a glowing letter of reference when he left the company: "For the many years I have known him as a collaborator, I've had the occasion to appreciate his intelligence and devotion to the work given to him. I consider him a man you can trust and an excellent mechanical engineer. He has exceptional technical aptitude and knows by heart the fabrication of automobiles and the explosion engine."

Armand had ample reason to praise Auguste. When Doriot left Peugeot, the company had established a leading, if not the top, position in the budding French car industry. In 1902, the year Auguste left, Peugeot introduced another line of cars that transcended the company's heritage of the horseless carriage. The innovations that were rolled out that year included electric ignition, steering wheels (which replaced the tiller), pressed steel frames, honeycomb radiators, and engines covered with bonnets, or hoods.

Even though the Doriots had moved to Paris, they did not forget their roots. After all, the Doubs district was still home to most of the Doriot clan. Often, young Georges journeyed back to Valentigney for family vacations. These were carefree days filled with warm memories of the fading pastoral life. He spent most of his time with his cousins, mostly girls, because they had more free time. They were older and were all very sweet to him. Some of Auguste's brothers moved away from the village but his sisters married and stayed there. Georges had a particular affection for his aunts, especially Tante Lucy and Tante Juliette. Tante Lucy's husband was the local captain, a sort of leader of the working people, who was a portly yet industrious man.

"In the summer," recalled Georges, "men requested permission to be able to start work at four or five o' clock in the morning so that they could spend the afternoon taking care of their fields and gardens. Then, at night we would all sit quietly together, talk peacefully, and be grateful for what we had."

One of the most pleasant memories of Georges's life was the time he spent at the Fraternelle, a cooperative store owned by the Peugeot Company. Every morning, a member of the family would take one of their pushcarts and visit the Fraternelle to shop. "When you got within a few hundreds yards there was a wonderful smell of freshly baked bread, coffee, and many other things," recalled Georges. "Everyone knew each other and everyone was very kind and helpful to each other. Whenever anyone was in need, there would be always some neighbor to come and help." During these early years, in the fields and gardens and factories of France, Georges learned the values of mutual aid and cooperation, values that helped him unite people in constructive action as a professor, military leader, and venture capitalist.

Although Auguste worked for another car company for a short time, he was preoccupied by other dreams. In 1906, the true reason he left Peugeot became clear: he wanted to design and manufacture his own cars. In today's world of "serial entrepreneurship," where failure is considered honorable, practically a required rest stop on the path to success, the boldness of this decision is hard to appreciate. In Europe, during the first half of the twentieth century, business failure was looked upon as a personal and professional calamity that one could never recover from. "In those days bankruptcy was a catastrophic event," says James F. Morgan, a former executive of American Research and Development who studied the history of European business. "In several European countries you were deprived of your right to vote and own property. It was a real black mark on your character and your family."

To create his own automobile manufacturing company, Auguste would be taking an enormous risk. Failure would ruin his reputation, his finances, and his family. But Auguste took the chance anyway, betting on his impressive track record and knowledge of a burgeoning industry. This was not a solo ride, however. Auguste teamed up with a colleague, Ludovic Flandrin, who worked at Clement-Bayard, another successful French car manufacturer founded in 1903 and known for making especially fast automobiles. The two men bootstrapped the venture out of their own pockets and opened a factory in Neuilly-sur-Seine, an area in western Paris along the Seine River, just a few miles west of the Peugeot house. They started simply, producing single cylinder cars sold under the name Doriot, Flandrin.

By the early twentieth century, early-stage venture financing remained stuck in a relatively undeveloped state. Most entrepreneurs still got their start by raising money from friends and family, wealthy associates, or, if they were fortunate like Auguste, they were able to take money out of their own savings. Some large American banks occasionally took a chance on a new and unproven technology, but they only put their capital behind established figures with a proven track record. And they rarely, if ever, took a hands-on role and helped to nurture a company. In his later years, Georges Doriot realized how critical such nurturing was in determining the success of a new venture. "I don't know anyone on Wall Street who ever built a company," said Doriot. "They simply furnish money, and that's the least important part of it."

In 1878, for example, J. P. Morgan and members of the Vanderbilt family helped finance the creation of the Edison Electric Light Company in New York City. By that time, Thomas Edison was arguably the world's most famous inventor, having sold the patent rights of his quadruplex telegraph to the Atlantic and Pacific Telegraph Company for the princely sum of $30,000. Edison used the money to expand his research laboratory in Menlo Park, New Jersey, considered the world's first industrial research lab.

For the most part, though, banks refused to finance innovation. Instead, more often than not they ended up reinforcing existing power structures. Nowhere is that more apparent than in the evolution of the House of Morgan, which in the late nineteenth century took over the title of the world's most powerful bank from the House of Rothschild. Like the Rothschilds, Morgan made his bones by lending large sums of money to governments.

The ultraconservative strategy of J. P. Morgan started during the Panic of 1873, when European investors lost $600 million in railroad stock investments. Petrified by all of the railroad bankruptcies, Morgan decided to limit his future dealings to only the most established and safest companies. He despised risk, wanting only sure things. "The kind of Bonds which I want to be connected with are those which can be recommended without a shadow of a doubt, and without the least subsequent anxiety, as to payment of interest, as it matures."

The conservatism of modern banking deepened during the recession of 1893. And it was J. P. Morgan who led that transformation. Overwhelmed by massive debt and overbuilding, more than a third of the nation's railways fell into bankruptcy. The collapse of the railroads triggered a depression that wiped out fifteen thousand commercial firms, leading to class warfare and a bloody round of strikes. Over six hundred banks failed and capital dried up when people started hoarding their precious dollars. English investors implored J. P. Morgan to save their shirts and bring order to the chaotic industry.

Morgan's solution was to consolidate the industry under his control. Virtually every bankrupt railroad east of the Mississippi—including the Erie, Chesapeake and Ohio, Reading, New York Central, Southern Railway, and many others—passed through such a reorganization, or *morganization*, as it was dubbed. One-sixth of the nation's trackage was morganized, allowing J. P. Morgan to ascend to a plateau higher than any other businessman had ever known. The amount of power accrued by Morgan is hard to overestimate. After all, railroads were the primary blue chips of the stock market, then accounting for 60 percent of all issues on the New York Stock Exchange. Utilities and industrial companies were considered too speculative an investment for insurance companies or savings banks.

As a further protection of his interests, Morgan transferred a majority of the voting stock of the railroads into "voting trusts." Of course, trusts were merely a camouflage for an unprecedented concentration of power, usually equating to Morgan and a few of his cronies running a railroad for a five-year period.

Bankers across the United States embraced Morgan's consolidation of the railroad industry as the business model of choice. In the first great wave of American mergers, consolidation was propelled by the shift from a domestic-oriented economy toward international expansion. The number of mergers jumped from sixty-nine in 1897, to more than twelve hundred by 1899. By 1901, a new class of corporate giants dominated a long list of industries, including sugar, lead, whiskey, plate glass, and coal.

But the most impressive (or impressively frightening) act of consolidation was the formation of U.S. Steel, led by J. P. Morgan. Fearing a repeat of the railroad debacle, with overcapacity and price wars, Morgan proposed a steel trust that would control more than half of the business. Pulling an all-nighter in his library, Morgan convinced some of the industry's leading players, including Andrew Carnegie and John D. Rockefeller, to agree to the deal. The new corporation was capitalized at a staggering $1.4 billion—the first billion-dollar corporation in history. Morgan's lesson was clear: competition was a destructive, inefficient force that could be cured through large-scale combinations. Venture financing had no place in this increasingly anticompetitive picture.

⌒

On August 11, 1906, in their new home in Neuilly-sur-Seine, Auguste and Camille's second child, Madeleine Georgette Doriot, was born. A photograph taken in 1908 shows an adorable girl standing on a lawn chair in front of a hedgerow, posed beside her smiling nine-year-old brother Georges, who has his arm wrapped around her waist. Georges and Madeleine, nicknamed Zette by her family, formed a close bond. By age nine, when that photo was taken, Georges had grown up to be a healthy boy, skinny yet tough. "I remember my youth, so to speak, as being very close to my family," recalled Georges. "I loved my sister and had complete devotion and admiration for Father and Mother."

In 1908, Doriot and Flandrin brought in the brothers Alexandre and Jules Rene Parant as their new partners. The triumvirate of families was set. The company was officially renamed D.F.P., standing for Doriot, Flandrin, and Parant. For their icon, they chose a greyhound dog galloping in full stride. For their slogan, they selected two simple yet strong words: *fidele* and *vite*, which translates to Trust and Speed. By highlighting those words, D.F.P. declared its strategy: D.F.P. cars would be fast and reliable.

The partners moved the factory farther west to a growing industrial town called Courbevoie, on the other side of the Seine River. And they began selling bigger cars, including two cars with 2.4 and 2.8 liter four-cylinder engines from Chapuis-Dornier. On March 20, 1908, D.F.P. held a public offering of stock in their new company. This was likely a significant milestone for such a young company. In those days, most new companies took five to seven years before raising money from the public. With an IPO after just three years of operation, its reputation, finances, and growth prospects must have been solid if not superb.

By 1911, D.F.P. began to manufacture cars with even bigger six-cylinder engines. But 1912 was when everything came together for this young group of entrepreneurs. That year, the company started making their own engines. More importantly, D.F.P. secured a major distribution and marketing deal when Walter Owen Bentley, known as W. O., and his brother, H. M., acquired the rights to sell D.F.P. motor cars in the British Commonwealth. An apprentice railway engineer who would become one of the most well-known racers of his day, W. O. founded Bentley & Bentley with his brother to market the French cars. The Bentley brothers imported the chassis of the cars and farmed them out to coachbuilders in London to gussy up their finish.

The Bentley brothers' timing was propitious. In 1912, D.F.P. introduced what turned out to be its most popular seller, the D.F.P. 10/12 model. Quickly after that came the 12/15 model. Its pressure lubrication, three-bearing crankshaft and four-speed gearbox produced a car that could zoom up to 55 miles per hour. The Bentley brothers entered this car into competitions, and by the end of 1913 a customized version was timed at nearly ninety miles per hour. But the Bentley brothers were not satisfied.

In 1913, working with their French mechanic, they designed a new engine that contained aluminum alloy pistons, a tuned camshaft, twin-spark ignition, and an efficient V-shaped radiator. In 1914, D.F.P. launched a car with the new engine called the 12/40 "Speed" model, built exclusively for Bentley & Bentley. This car marked a major advance in auto technology, allowing the car to top out at sixty-five miles per hour.

The 12/40 D.F.P. Speed model brought D.F.P. and the Bentley brothers commercial and competitive success. In 1913 and 1914, the Bentley brothers captured twelve of the Class B Speed Records at Brooklands, the first oval-style race track, which was built to race cars in 1907. W. O. described these achievements "as representing the very highest point that motor car efficiency had ever reached."

While Auguste learned the ropes of entrepreneurship at D.F.P., Georges was getting his own education. He benefited from the modern French education system, which had just been developed in the late nineteenth century by Jules Ferry, a lawyer-turned-politician who held the office of Minister of Public Instruction in the early 1880s. During his term, Ferry passed two laws that revolutionized French primary education, making it free, nonclerical, and obligatory for all children under the age of fifteen. The laws sparked an outcry, though, as they wrested the right to teach from the unauthorized religious orders.

In September of 1905, when Georges was six, he entered one of the newly formed elementary schools in Neuilly-sur-Seine. There, for the next five years, Georges learned how to read and write French and received a broad introduction to a number of core subjects including mathematics, natural science, and geography, as well as civics courses that taught children about La République, its function, its organization, and its famous motto, "Liberté, Égalité, Fraternité." Since the clergy was separated from French education, Georges attended church to receive religious instruction.

In 1910, when Georges was eleven, he left his home country for the first time to study English for a year at Lynton College in England. At such a young age, the experience must have been a formative one, expanding his horizons immeasurably. In France, it would have been difficult, if not impossible, to study English since Minister Ferry had outlawed the instruction of non-French languages in public schools. Auguste not only had the money to send his son abroad, he also felt comfortable in England. Since launching D.F.P., he traveled many times to the United Kingdom to sell his cars. When Georges returned, he spoke accent-free English. Moreover, his interest in the opposite sex —and his sense of humor—apparently had awakened. "When he came back from England he said to his mother he would never marry an English woman because they wouldn't sew and instead would use safety pins," says Eveline Poillot, Georges's niece, who was very close to Camille.

After the summer of 1911, Georges entered secondary school in Courbevoie, the town along the Seine where his family had recently moved. It was at that school that Auguste delivered his infamous "And why not first?" retort to a young Georges.

Pressed by his father, Georges learned the value of studying and hard work. He began school at half past eight in the morning, came home for lunch for an hour, and then went back to school until five o'clock. The evening was then filled with a great deal of homework. "I remember vividly sitting in at night in our living room, father and mother, my sister Zette and I," recalled Georges. "Father reading and working, mother knitting or repairing clothes, and my sister and I working on our homework. We usually had at least two hours of homework every night."

In 1912, with D.F.P. doing well, Auguste built a new house for his family in Courbevoie. It was a solid brick and stone two-story, four-bedroom home surrounded by a walled garden on 7 Rue Franklin. Auguste and Camille's master bedroom was on the first floor, along with the kitchen, dining room, and living room, where Georges and the family spent their evenings. Upstairs, Georges and Zette had their bedrooms, along with a small kitchen and bedroom for the housekeeper. Attached to Georges's bedroom was a small side room. Georges converted this chamber into his own personal sanctuary, where he played with his chemistry set and pretended to be a mad scientist. No one was allowed to enter this room. So adamant was he about this rule that one day he rigged the door so that if his mother tried to enter it would set off a small explosion.

When Georges had no schoolwork to do, Auguste would let him visit the D.F.P. factory. There, strolling the aisles of the factory, observing the men in their overalls welding steel and handling complex machines such as lathes, mills, boring fixtures, and drill jigs, Georges instinctively absorbed his father's obsession with machinery—and his appetite for taking risks.

Over time, Georges became a decent mechanic himself and a fairly good draftsman. He also developed a taste for reading American magazines that dealt with machine tools and factory problems. Georges liked two magazines in particular, *American Machinist* and *Machinery*. These new trade magazines were like a headlight illuminating the automotive revolution brewing in the United States. In 1910, when demand for automobiles exploded, cars could not be produced quickly enough for the massive American market. New production methods had to be invented. Until that time, automobile manufacturing had been pioneered by Europeans, mainly the French, German, and English carmakers. But now the United States was poised to take over the automobile market, led by an engineer named Henry Ford who, in 1903 at the age of forty, incorporated the Ford Motor Company. A few years later, in 1908, Ford rolled out the Model T, the best known motor vehicle in history. It was a "car for the great multitude," durable enough to withstand the rough American roads, economical to operate, and easy to maintain and repair.

When the car proved a hit, Ford and his associates turned to the problem of producing a vehicle in large volume at a low unit cost. The solution was found in the moving assembly line. In 1913, after more experimentation, Ford unveiled to the world the first complete assembly line mass production of motor vehicles. The system hinged on several basic elements: the conveyor belt, standardized parts, synchronization, and the limitation of each worker to a single repetitive task. In the spring of 1913, it took almost thirteen hours to build a "T." By the end of the year, when a complete assembly line was in place, it took only ninety minutes to produce a car. The price of the Model T dropped from $950 in 1909, to $360 in 1916, to $290 in 1926. By that time, Ford Motor was producing half of all the motor vehicles in the world. Europe may have pioneered the development of the automobile, but mass production was a U.S. innovation.

When Georges cracked open the pages of *American Machinist* and *Machinery* this whole new industry of machinery and mass production was unveiled before his eyes. After all, automobile manufacturing was like the early twentieth century's version of Silicon Valley. It was an industry transforming the world, and creating vast riches for the select few who mastered the new techniques of mass production. Flipping through the pages of *American Machinist*, Georges read about the latest technologies and production methods: "Machining the Ford Cylinders," "Interesting Milling and Grinding Operations," and "A Thousand Carburetors a Day," were just a few of the stories that captured his imagination. Undoubtedly, flipping through the pages of these magazines gave Georges an appreciation for the dynamic nature of technology and the emerging power of America.

In the summer of 1914, the peace and prosperity that France had enjoyed for the last twenty years was shattered by the outbreak of World War I. Europe was engulfed by violence once again. The war radically altered the fates of millions of people in Europe and around the world. This was as true for the Doriot clan as for any other family that suffered through the profound tragedies of the Great War. In fact, many of Georges's cousins were drafted as part of France's countrywide mobilization.

The Doriot family chose to stay in Paris despite Germany's declaration of war on France in August of 1914. But this war would require Auguste to make an extreme sacrifice. He had risked his family's finances and reputation on D.F.P., and had worked tirelessly for ten years to get it off the ground. Now, just as D.F.P. had established itself as an up-and-coming car manufacturer, Auguste had to turn over the keys of the factory to the government. The factory was turned into a shell-making plant. Although these had to have been very trying days for Auguste, no one could question his patriotism. He had served in the Army and was just as repulsed as any Frenchman by the idea of German hegemony. So Auguste devoted himself and his business to the cause. "At the time, people worked 24 hours a day, and I think my dear father worked 24 hours a day as well," recalled Georges.

Georges was lucky. In 1914, he was only fifteen and not old enough to be drafted. Instead, he continued his studies at a lycée in Paris (not at the University of Paris, as many previous accounts of Doriot's life have noted). In the French education system, a lycée is roughly equivalent to a U.S. high school. Students attend a lycée for three years from the ages of fifteen to seventeen, receiving a baccalaureate degree upon graduation. This degree allows students to enter a university, such as one of the grand Écoles. While high school students in the United States can choose most of their own courses, French lycée students follow a more regimented curriculum with a large number of required core courses and fewer electives. The baccalaureate is divided into three streams of study, called *séries*. The *série scientifique* is concerned with natural sciences, physics, or mathematics; the *série économique et sociale* with economics and social sciences; and the *série litéraire* focuses on French and foreign languages and philosophy. In the lycée, Georges's appreciation for science and technology continued to grow. And so, Georges naturally sought a degree from the sciences, studying many hours of math, physics, chemistry, and biology.

Attending school during a war with Germany—a war that threatened to overrun Georges's home city—must have been terrifying to say the least. To help him relax, Georges got his driver's license about a week after he turned fifteen, the youngest age one could receive a license at the time. The license, which was referred to as a "patrol," permitted Georges to drive a car of up to 220 horsepower, a privilege that Georges enjoyed on a regular basis.

While Georges drove around the city, he encountered many unusual sights. In the first weeks of September in 1914, Paris was hunkered down for battle. Thousands of French and Moroccan troops, called the "Armies of Paris," entered the city and were placed under command of the military governor of Paris, Joseph Gallieni. Bridges were mined, the Eiffel Tower was prepared for demolition, and reconnaissance patrols scoured the city.

As the war dragged on for six more years, the French Army suffered profoundly. In the Battle of Verdun in 1916, the French military alone suffered 351,000 losses. If one of Georges's cousins saw action in Verdun, they entered a netherworld resembling Dante's inferno, a hell on earth consisting of almost continuous and thunderous noise, of chemical warfare and flamethrowers choking and burning men and horses, of the appalling stench of rotting flesh.

Beginning in early 1917 and continuing sporadically through 1918, France's civilian population was convulsed by massive strikes and raging bouts of inflation. By the time July came around, a "veritable prices explosion" took hold as prices for a group of basic food products more than doubled since the beginning of the year. Like an army of termites, inflation ate away at the savings of Auguste Doriot and every other French family.

Then came the strikes. In January 1917, strikes broke out in several munitions factories, including Panhard-Levassor. In total, one hundred thousand workers from seventy-one industries in the Paris region took to the streets, but minimum wage scales and cost-of-living allowances ended the stoppages. Then, in May 1918, a major wave of strikes slammed the Paris region. Although it is not known if D.F.P. was hit by a strike, "most factories in Courbevoie, Suresnes, Puteaux and Levallois were working with 30% to 60% of their full complement."

By 1917, it was also time for Georges Doriot to play his part in the Great War. Georges enlisted in the French Army, signing up for the three-year service requirement. A photograph taken that year shows Georges outfitted in his new military uniform. Instead of the laughable blue and red uniforms that offered no camouflage protection, Georges wore the new beige ensemble, similar to the uniforms worn by the better-equipped German soldiers. Rifle slung over his shoulder, black leather boots laced up to his knees, hands stuffed in his pockets, and pants hitched up high over his thin waist, Georges stands in front of a barracks, a young untested soldier, prideful but looking a bit unnerved, fear peaking through the slits in his eyes. Lord knows, he had ample reason to be terrified. The war exacted a horrible toll on his family. All of Georges's first cousins on both sides of his family who had entered the war had been killed.

But Georges was lucky once again. Now that he was old enough to serve, the war was finally winding down. Georges joined the R.A.L.T., a motorized heavy artillery regiment. His regiment maintained 145 millimeter long-range guns, one of the most powerful guns in the French Army. Instead of horses, the regiment towed its guns with tractors. Soon after joining the 81st R.A.L.T., Georges was asked to replace the engineering officer in charge of artillery. His superiors believed that his experience in the motor vehicle industry made him a logical candidate for the job.

It was the first major test of the young man's leadership ability and Georges, still a teenager, was intimidated. Most of the soldiers who worked under him were experienced repairmen from the top companies in Paris. They resented the young man's promotion and tested him by asking for detailed repair orders. By conceding to their superiority, however, Georges won over the men and ended up forming a good relationship with them. "We understood and respected each other, and I can say that it was a useful time, and, in many ways, a happy time," recalled Georges. "I made some friends there that I kept in contact with for many years."

On November 9, 1918, as it became clear that Germany could not withstand the Allied counteroffensive, the Germans entered into armistice negotiations in a railroad carriage at Compiègne in France. The conflict persisted for another seven months, until it was finally declared over on June 28, 1919 with the signing of the Treaty of Versailles.

By the time the war ended in November 1918, Europe's liberal civilization was destroyed. But among the Allied Powers, it was France that suffered more than any other nation. The heaviest battles of World War I were fought on French soil, and the French deployed the greatest number of Allied troops and suffered the heaviest casualties. More than 1.3 million French soldiers were killed in the war, or two out of every nine men who marched away, while more than 3.2 million were wounded.

Although none of the great French offensives allowed France to wrest control of Germany, French soldiers prevented German victory on the most important land front of the war, the Western Front. The courageous performance of the French Army during World War I led Winston Churchill to famously refer to them as "that sorely tried, glorious Army upon whose sacrifices the liberties of Europe had through three fearful campaigns mainly depended."

After the war ended, Georges returned to the lycée. One of Auguste's friends had suggested that since Georges was interested in machinery and production, he should give serious thought to sending his son to America. France was no place for a bright young man, agreed Auguste. The country had lost millions of its best men. Its gross domestic product had shrunk by nearly 40 percent, and by January 1919, the national debt exploded more than five-fold. France, to put it mildly, was devastated by the war.

Auguste's pessimism was grounded in personal experience. The war was a major setback for his company. Reconverting the D.F.P. factory back to making cars would have been hard enough. But that year Auguste suffered another blow: he learned that his most important partner, the Bentley brothers, decided to end their deal with D.F.P. so they could create their own car company.

Auguste knew what he had to do: he had to send Georges to the United States. In 1920, after receiving his baccalaureate science degree from the Paris lycée, Georges prepared to come to America. Father and son agreed upon a plan: Georges would study machines and manufacturing in America, and then, after a short while, would return to France to get a job. Now, it was Georges's turn to take a big risk.

THREE

COMING TO
AMERICA

(1921–1925)

O N JANUARY 4, 1921, when Georges Frederic Doriot stepped aboard the S.S. *Touraine* of the French Line, one of the grand old European steamships, he left France with two important items. In one pocket, he kept a letter of introduction to a gentleman named A. Lawrence Lowell, which had been given to him by a friend of his father who was an expert in technical education in France. In his other pocket, Georges carried a small French coin, a symbol of his father's fortune, which had been destroyed by the war. The letter, which would radically change the course of Georges's life, represented the bright light of the future; the coin embodied the dark weight of Doriot's recent past.

"One of things that profoundly affected [Georges] was his father getting wiped out financially," says James F. Morgan, a former executive of American Research and Development who became close to Doriot near the end of his life. "It affected his attitude toward risk. He was very, very cautious."

At least Doriot knew where he was going, or so he thought. The same friend of Georges's father who suggested he should come to America also recommended that Georges should attend the Massachusetts Institute of Technology (MIT). So Doriot and his parents contacted the American University Union and arrangements were made for Georges to attend MIT.

Not knowing much, if anything, about America, the school seemed like a good choice. Established in 1861 in Boston, then the industrial center of the United States, MIT was a well-known regional engineering school that aspired to become a national research university.

As twenty-one-year-old Doriot cruised across the Atlantic Ocean at a steady pace of around 19 knots, he had more than a week on that beautiful ship to ponder his fate. *La Touraine* was built in 1890 by Compagnie Générale Transatlantique, one of the great French maritime companies. She was 522 feet long with two funnels and three tall masts, and held about fifteen hundred passengers. It must have been an exhilarating if not frightful journey. America was emerging as the world's most powerful nation. And since the United States had escaped the Great War without any serious damage to her people, economy, or terrain, the opportunities offered by this vast country seemed limitless.

Up until the moment that he stepped on that ship, Georges's parents had done all they could for their son. But he was now on his own, an inexperienced young man who had never left home for more than a few months, under immense pressure to do well in school so he could find a good job that would help him take care of his family. He had no family or friends in the United States, nor much money to fall back on. He was facing the most difficult challenge of his life. Standing on the deck of *La Touraine*, looking out into the deep dark void of the sea, Georges must have wondered: What does my future hold? What am I going to make of myself? And what happens if I fail?

The S.S. *Touraine* pulled into New York Harbor on January 15 at noon. In the 1920s, New York's harbor was as busy as Broadway during rush hour. Half of America's exports and imports moved through the bustling piers that lined Lower Manhattan, Brooklyn, Staten Island, and the New Jersey banks of the Hudson River. Oceangoing steamers entered or left the port about every twenty minutes. Doriot stepped off the boat, took in the armada of coastal freighters, harbor tugs, river steamers, and other ships bobbing in the water, and proceeded to the Hotel Pennsylvania across the street from Madison Square Garden and Pennsylvania Station.

One of the largest hotels in New York, Hotel Pennsylvania was built by the Pennsylvania Railroad in 1919 and was operated by the successful hotelier Ellsworth Statler. Doriot checked into room 1721A. During his first night at the hotel, he was amazed by the double door that allowed men to put newspapers and packages in front of the second door, which he could then open from his room. It was a Sunday morning and in that space between the two doors Doriot was delighted to see several pounds of newspaper.

"I thought that, America being a very kind country, people realized that I had been at sea for a week and, therefore, had very nicely kept a week's newspapers for me to read upon my arrival," wrote Doriot. "Much to my amazement, I discovered that those pounds of papers were just the Sunday edition of the American newspaper."

At one o'clock on January 20, Doriot hopped onto a train in Pennsylvania Station bound for Boston. He pulled into town just after six o'clock and checked into the Hotel Tremont. Soon after, he went to Cambridge to register at MIT. But before classes began, he decided to look up Mr. Lowell, the gentleman to whom his letter was addressed. "I decided that I should be considerate and polite, as my father and mother would have told me to be," recalled Georges. "So, I looked for him and found that he was president of a university called Harvard."

The Doriot clan had never heard of Harvard, though it was the most well-known and prestigious college in America. Georges called on Mr. A. Lawrence Lowell on the second floor of University Hall, with barely a clue as to the significance of the man. A well-known lawyer who was the son of one of Boston's most prominent families, Lowell was president of Harvard University from 1909 to 1933, during which time the school flourished.

Albeit imposing, Lowell was kind to Doriot. When he asked the young man what he wanted to learn, Doriot shared his dream of one day running a factory. Lowell smiled at this response and informed Doriot that he had chosen the wrong school. Instead of MIT, he explained, Doriot should attend a place called the Harvard Business School, whereupon he took Doriot downstairs in University Hall and introduced him to Wallace B. Donham, the dean of the Business School. Having helped found the Business School over a decade earlier, Lowell remained an energetic advocate of the institution. Donham concurred with Lowell that Harvard Business School was the ideal place for Doriot, and without further ado, Georges's papers were transferred over to Harvard.

Placing his trust in these wise men, Doriot enrolled at Harvard Business School in the spring of 1921. Doriot was the first Frenchman to attend the school, and one of only a handful of foreign students, the others hailing from the Philippines, Greece, and China. He studied the basics of business education: industrial management, factory problems and systems, accounting, labor relations, statistics, and corporate finance. He enjoyed the experience very much and was impressed by his teachers. As part of his course in factory systems, Doriot took a few field trips, including a visit to the Rolls Royce factory in Springfield, Massachusetts, during which he inspected the plant and reviewed its cost accounting system.

A photograph taken in March of 1921 that Doriot sent to his parents revealed that Georges had matured considerably since his days in the Army. The soft, timid face of a teenager had hardened into a portrait of a serious young man with penetrating blue eyes and a short, trimmed moustache. The military dress was replaced by the armor of an enterprising young business-man: a sharp, three-piece suit, crisp white shirt, and well-knotted tie, accented by a white handkerchief peeking out of his suit pocket. These years gave birth to the formal look that Doriot favored until the last years of his life, always wearing suit and tie in public.

During his second semester, Doriot was listed as a "special student" in the Official Register of Harvard University, along with thirty-seven other young men. In those early days of business education, an MBA degree was a brand-new concept and had yet to acquire the cache it has today. So many students, including Doriot, only took the basic core curriculum of the first year, and then left to seek their fortune.

Near the end of 1921, Doriot met some financiers in New York from the well-known investment bank Kuhn, Loeb & Company. They offered him a job, which he gratefully accepted. Comforted by the security that came with such a position, Georges decided to settle down in America. During an earlier trip back home to France, he had discussed the decision with his parents. "I had come to France to visit the family and they decided that it was probably best for me to stay in the United States because people there were very nice to me and I could probably earn a living," recalled Georges. "Things were not very happy in France at that time. We were still suffering from the after-effects of World War I."

Things were very happy in New York City, though. When Doriot walked around New York over the next few years, he marveled at a city on the cusp of greatness, a city of immense vitality, of great "stone buildings that the human mind has not had the vision to conceive nor the power to build until

New York stimulated mankind with its magic," as Rebecca West described it. It was the time of great dance halls, where throngs of city dwellers crammed into hundreds of joints, drank moonshine, took in cabaret shows, and danced the night away.

These were the sights and sounds Doriot saw as he walked to and from his office in Lower Manhattan. His position at the bank was a cautious yet smart choice for a first job. Founded in 1867 by Abraham Kuhn and Solomon Loeb, two German-born brothers-in-law who had run a successful merchandising business in Cincinnati, Kuhn, Loeb moved to New York to take advantage of the nation's economic expansion. In the late nineteenth century, Kuhn, Loeb made its name by selling securities for many of the early railroads. Kuhn, Loeb was the only Jewish banking house that had the temerity to challenge Morgan in the big money game of financing railways and governments. While the House of Morgan focused on railroads east of the Mississippi, Kuhn, Loeb mostly targeted railways in the south and west, including the Chicago and North Western Railway, Norfolk and Western, and the Southern Pacific.

Kuhn, Loeb was also in the vanguard of international finance. It tapped European capital to fund the railroads, made the initial dollar placements in the American market for leading European firms such as Royal Dutch Petroleum, and helped Japan defeat Russia in the Russo-Japanese War in 1904 and 1905 by loaning Japan $200 million. During World War I the firm aided the Allied cause by making a series of crucial loans to the cities of Paris, Bordeaux, Lyons, and Marseille, which used most of the proceeds to prop up the finances of the French Government.

Under Jacob Schiff, the senior partner who led the firm until the early twentieth century, Kuhn, Loeb came to rival J. P. Morgan & Company as the leading investment bank in America. Schiff was instrumental in pushing the bank to finance industrial enterprises. While the traditional investment banks of Morgan and Brown Brothers Harriman underwrote shares for blue chip companies such as U.S. Steel and General Electric, Kuhn, Loeb and other German-Jewish bankers such as Lehman Brothers and Goldman Sachs brokered securities for companies that were spurned by gentile firms as too lowly—retail stores and textile manufacturers. Among them were Sears, Roebuck, R. H. Macy, and Gimbel Brothers. Beginning in the 1890s, Kuhn, Loeb helped to secure loans for a number of pioneering enterprises such as Westinghouse Electric and Manufacturing Company, Western Union

Telegraph Company, and the United States Rubber Company. "Let the Jews have that one," was a familiar refrain on Wall Street.

Even though Kuhn, Loeb and other Jewish banks expanded the reach of financial markets, they were not in the business of betting their own capital on new enterprises. These banks were mostly middlemen, restricting their activities to selling government bonds or the securities and bonds of large, established companies to pools of investors that they rounded up—a safe though still lucrative business.

The House of Morgan, by contrast, remained even more conservative. It sometimes took small stakes in the companies for which it raised money as a commission. But it did not broker stocks, only underwriting railroad bonds, government bonds, or corporate bonds of the biggest firms such as U.S. Steel, General Electric, General Motors, and AT&T.

Young, unproven companies were still the stepchildren of capital markets, overlooked and neglected. That left entrepreneurs with the same old miniscule set of options: raising money from friends, family, or rich individuals. The only other financing option for new enterprises was to merge. By combining their financial resources, several small companies could increase the pool of capital that was necessary to help grow their businesses. Mergers could also raise the financial profile and health of a firm to a level where it could secure debt financing.

This was exactly the case with one of America's oldest and most prestigious technology companies: IBM. In 1911, the Computing Tabulating Recording Corporation, the predecessor company of IBM, was formed through the merger of three separate firms: the Tabulating Machine Company, the Computing Scale Corporation, and the International Time Recording Company. The combined companies manufactured a wide range of products, including employee time-keeping systems, meat slicers, scales, and, most importantly, punch card machine technology—an innovation which ultimately led to the development of the computer. The three companies were brought together by financier Charles Flint, who helped the firm raise a $6.5 million bond offering.

According to existing records, Georges Doriot did not actually work for Kuhn, Loeb, but rather for a closely affiliated firm named New York &

Foreign Development Corporation. In fact, Kuhn, Loeb and the New York & Foreign Development both shared the same address in lower Manhattan: 52 William Street. Although Doriot would only work for the company for four years and the period is barely mentioned in discussions of his life, his time here was significant in several ways.

In working for a Kuhn, Loeb affiliate, Doriot entered the rarified atmosphere of high finance, receiving his indoctrination into the world of power. He learned how to behave around power, how to be comfortable in a world of hidden influence. The connections he made at Kuhn, Loeb would serve him well the rest of his life. Doriot also received first-rate training in the craft of finance and investment banking, and gained an appreciation for the importance of technology. In fact, Doriot's main job was to help evaluate new technologies for possible investment. His ability to judge men and their ideas, which were formed during these early years, would remain a signature talent throughout his life.

One of the more fascinating characters that Doriot befriended during this time was Sir William George Eden Wiseman, the president of New York & Foreign Development. A descendant of English royalty, Wiseman worked as a banker at Herndon's in London before World War I. During the war, he served in the infantry, later coming to the United States as chief of the British Military Intelligence. After the war ended, he acted as a liaison between the British government and President Woodrow Wilson, and then became an advisor at the Paris Peace Conference. Following the peace accords, Wiseman, along with several other fledgling diplomats, joined Kuhn, Loeb.

More significant was Doriot's relationship with Lewis L. Strauss—another statesmen-cum-banker who joined Kuhn, Loeb after the war. Over the next thirty years, Doriot and Strauss would become the best of friends. Doriot, eager to form new ties as an unmoored immigrant, became so attached to Strauss and his wife Alice that he considered them part of his family just a few years after striking up a friendship. For a newcomer trying to make his way in a foreign land, Strauss's Horatio Alger tale must have struck a chord with Doriot.

The son of a Jewish shoe salesmen from Virginia, Strauss rose above his meager beginnings to become a rich investment banker and chairman of the U. S. Atomic Energy Commission. Valedictorian of his high school class, Strauss was offered a scholarship to the University of Virginia but turned it down to sell shoes for his father's struggling business. Strauss later saved up $20,000 to pay for college, but guided by his mother's desire for her son to serve the nation during war, Strauss instead miraculously landed a job as private secretary to the industrialist-turned-statesman Herbert Hoover.

President Woodrow Wilson picked Hoover to take charge of the Food Administration, which provided a steady supply of food to the American and Allied Armies. While in Europe, Strauss distinguished himself by helping Hoover direct America's post-war relief effort, and by coming to the aid of the Jewish Joint Distribution Committee, which alleviated the suffering of thousands of oppressed European Jews. Strauss parlayed his relief work into a job offer from the partners of Kuhn, Loeb, many of whom were Jewish and impressed by the way he helped move emergency supplies to Jews living in Vienna, Warsaw, Prague, and the surrounding war-torn areas.

Doriot came to know Strauss because he was a director at New York & Foreign Development. In Doriot, Strauss saw a younger version of himself: a young, smart man full of energy, brio, and a desire to make his mark on the world. The two worked together on a deal in the fall of 1923. On September 24, 1923, members of Kuhn, Loeb organized an entity called the International Gear Company, Incorporated to investigate an innovative new method of commercial gear production known as the Anderson Rolled Gear process. The process of forging gears under heavy heated pressure in a rolling action was "unquestionably the outstanding achievement in modern methods, for not only is a much lower cost of production realized, but the gears produced are stronger, tougher, and more accurately formed than the best types of gears produced by the machining processes of this generation," according to the leading machine experts of the day. Even though he had turned only twenty-four on the very day the company was incorporated, Doriot was elected as one of seven directors of International Gear. It would be the first of many directorships for Doriot, who learned much about the world of business through his participation on the boards of dozens of companies.

In the spring of 1924, Strauss asked Doriot to compile a list of French industrial firms, along with their financial backers. On March 18, Doriot wrote a letter to Strauss describing his findings. The letter illustrates Doriot's emerging iconoclasm and his penchant for holding strong opinions that he wasn't afraid to share, especially opinions about his native land. In his analysis of the links between French banks and industrial firms, Doriot informed Strauss "there is no definite connection, and when there is a connection it is very often a useless one. My experience has been that from the standpoint of a Company, it is perfectly useless to do business with the Bank of France." Over the years, long after Doriot left New York & Foreign Development, Strauss continued to turn to Doriot for his expertise in evaluating new technologies and investment opportunities.

In the fall of 1924, Doriot tried his hand at something entirely new: writing for the public. Doriot never took writing seriously but his efforts signaled the beginning of his evolution into a public figure, offering pointed commentaries on the world's most important issues. Under a one-word pseudonym, Beaulieu, a cheeky reference to the village near his home in France, Doriot wrote two contrarian essays for *The New Republic* criticizing the Dawes Plan, an agreement designed to keep the lid on growing post-war tensions in Europe. After Germany defaulted on its steep reparations payments of nearly twenty billion marks in the summer and fall of 1922, the French and Belgian governments occupied the Ruhr region. The occupation of the center of the German coal and steel industries both outraged Germany and put further strain on its economy.

To defuse tensions and get Germany back on a payment plan, the Allied Reparations Committee asked the businessman and politician Charles G. Dawes, who soon after became vice president to Calvin Coolidge, to find a solution. After a long and difficult negotiation, Dawes unveiled his plan in April of 1924. It called for a reparations schedule of one billion gold marks in the first year, rising to DM2.5 billion in the fifth, providing some room for changes if the price of gold went up or down more than 10 percent.

In Doriot's first story, "The Dawes Plan Myth," published in the September 24, 1924 issue of *The New Republic*, he argued that the plan "is mainly and primarily a myth" because it was an unrealistic intrusion into Germany's affairs. "The plan does provide for an initial truce," wrote Doriot. "That is all to the good. It holds out the hope of reparations payments. That approaches fraud. As will appear, no substantial reparations can be paid under it."

In the second essay, "The Dawes Plan and the Peace of Europe," published in the December 10, 1924 issue, Doriot stepped up his attacks. No longer would reparations be paid, but now Doriot argued that "the administration of the plan in accordance with the concept of its framers constitutes a standing threat to the peace of Europe." The reason? He believed that high reparations payments would come from the hide of the German "workman and consumer which must in time lead to an anti-Allied outbreak."

Doriot was ultimately right, but his analysis was too premature for anyone to notice it. In fact, the Dawes Plan initially succeeded beyond expectations, leading to a wave of foreign loans that gave Germany enough money to pay reparations to France and Britain until 1929. The plan also helped keep the peace in Europe, as war did not break out again until Hitler invaded Poland in 1939.

Doriot's use of a pseudonym betrayed a deep-seated fear: he hated writing. It is a strange admission, revealed years later in his personal notes, from someone who became a professor and was actually a very good writer, a tireless composer of thousands of pages of prose that was clear as a windowpane. The confession underscored Doriot's lack of self-confidence, which dogged him throughout his twenties as he struggled to find his way. "I never liked writing," he confessed. "I do not do it well. My sentences do not "sound" well. Also, I never thought that I had anything to say that had lasting characteristics or value, nor would it have any interest for other people. When I had to make a speech (which I never enjoyed), I always asked for no publicity. The speech was designed for a particular audience and had no value for others."

The two *New Republic* stories were an interesting diversion from Doriot's time at New York & Foreign Development. Back at the firm, Doriot was earning a reputation as a savvy, hard-nosed evaluator of investment opportunities. In one instance, in the winter of 1925 Doriot helped investigate and broker a deal for a new ice-making machine with the American Radiator Company. "There is no doubt as to the fact that the outside arm can make any amount of ice that you may wish, and this is in much shorter time than ordinary machines on the market," wrote Doriot to R. R. Santini, the head of American Radiator, after seeing a demonstration of the machine. The following year, at Sir William's request, Doriot visited the Prince George Hotel, north of New York's Madison Square Park, to investigate an invention made by a Mr. de Northall, who was demonstrating a model saw in an apartment in the hotel. In a subsequent memo, Doriot revealed a talent for cutting to the heart of a matter.

"I found that Mr. de Northall had contracted very heavy debts and owed money to friends and his relatives. It then became apparent that unless a certain sum of money could be set aside to take care of Mr. de Northall's indebtedness, it would not be possible at the time, to spend anything merely on the development of the invention. Sir William Wiseman and his friend, being bankers, and not promoters of doubtful enterprises, also not being primarily interested in the lumber industry, I did not hesitate to recommend Sir William to state that he was not interested."

Then Doriot ripped into the saw, displaying his razor-sharp analytical skills. Inspecting the machine in the hotel room, Doriot found that it was not in working condition, and that the inventor had no idea how much power the saw needed, nor did he have a clue as to the cost of its installation. "There were several other mechanical difficulties which I pointed out to Mr. de Northall," wrote Doriot. "I would not have advised anybody unfamiliar with the lumber industry to spend any time or money on that invention."

Doriot demonstrated an ability to make more subtle judgments as well. One of the more unusual projects that Doriot was asked to evaluate was an Ecuadorian natural resources venture. The plan, which forecast a very high rate of return, was to cut exotic trees in the mountains of Ecuador and then float the wood down to the coast, where a mill on the shore would then transform the logs into furniture veneer. Doriot told the bankers that when he was young boy in France he learned that some wood, being heavier than water, did not float. The bankers quickly discovered that the wood they wanted to float down the river sunk like a stone. New York & Foreign Development never invested in the program. "He had a very candid and open-minded approach to all of the problems," says Doriot's close friend Arnaud de Vitry. "Great businessmen on Wall Street missed this factor in their analysis."

In the future, Doriot's boldness, powers of judgment, and technical fluency would help him pioneer the venture industry. Before he was able to step up to that level, though, he had to answer some of the more basic questions of his young life. True, he had found a home in America. But he was still without a career, a soul mate, or any guiding purpose.

FOUR

THE PROFESSOR

(1925–1930)

DEEP DOWN, WHEN DORIOT thought about it, he knew that he did not have a future at the New York & Foreign Development Corporation, or Kuhn, Loeb, for that matter. Kuhn, Loeb had always been a family-based business, with almost every partner linked by birth or marriage. By 1911, the firm had admitted only one unrelated partner. In March of 1923, Lewis Strauss obviated this problem in regard to himself when he married Alice Hanauer, the daughter of Kuhn, Loeb partner Jerome J. Hanauer. Strauss, who met Alice while joining the Hanauer family for occasional dinners, became a partner in 1929. As late as 1933, Otto Kahn, an infamous Kuhn partner whose mansion on Long Island served as the inspiration for Xanadu in *Citizen Kane*, would say of Kuhn, Loeb, "We are a family affair."

Doriot had no blood relation to the family and never fell for a member of the Kuhn, Loeb clan. His outspoken temperament did not fit well within the staid environs of an investment bank, and he was never obsessed with accumulating extreme wealth, the chief lure of the investment banking game. So it was not all too surprising that when the dean of the Harvard Business School asked Doriot to come back to Massachusetts and become an assistant dean, Doriot accepted the offer.

Since Doriot had left the Harvard Graduate School of Business Administration, its reputation had continued to flourish under Dean Donham's leadership. A Harvard Law School graduate and vice president of the prominent

Old Colony Trust Company in Boston, Donham was perhaps the most important leader in the school's history, and a man under whom Doriot himself would eventually flower.

Dean Donham wrestled with all sorts of growing pains. The school's curriculum lacked direction. The faculty was small and classes were scattered all over Harvard Yard. In addition, the school had little money and its business connections were weak. And since graduate-level business education was a relatively new field, there was a scarcity of experienced teachers. To ameliorate the shortage, Donham looked partly outside academia, hiring businessmen, lawyers, and other white-collar professionals. But he mostly raided the faculty of other related schools, hiring professors of accounting, economics, finance, and law. Doriot was one of several nonacademics hired by Dean Donham. Even though Doriot had been appointed an assistant dean, the Frenchman had less experience than most if not all of the people Donham had recruited.

Assistant deans were like the junior varsity team of the Business School. They typically handled administrative duties, while some of them were groomed to teach at a later time. Doriot shared an office with Donald K. David, another assistant dean, in the room next to Dean Donham's office. Doriot lived in what was then called the Colonial Club, an intellectual nirvana, filled with distinguished scholars. Doriot loved sharing meals and rubbing shoulders with these grand old professors: "I enjoyed living there because outstanding people like Dean [Chester] Greenough and others in the Department of Economy and the Department of History would come there for lunch or dinner and it also gave me the opportunity to meet officers in different parts of the university," he recalled. "I also presided over meetings of the junior faculty, which was very interesting."

Doriot's academic career did not get off to a spellbinding start. His first job as assistant dean was to bring a higher degree of coordination to the school's ever-changing curriculum. In 1920, Dean Donham began a program of "study groups," focusing on basic areas of business. By 1923, those groups evolved into the standard first-year program, requiring students to take courses in several cores areas of business: Finance, Industrial Management, Marketing, Accounting, and Statistics. It was not terribly exciting work but Doriot tackled the task with vigor, setting out to "find out what was being taught and how it fitted in the students' minds."

That job led Doriot to create a "Committee on Terminology"—a group that hashed out keywords used by the faculty in an attempt to bring scientific rigor to the field of business. "It was very useful because at that time business words and expressions were not as well known as they are now," he recalled. The truth was, the Committee didn't make much sense, and it was soon forgotten.

Doriot tried to use his French connections to help Dean Donham ease his faculty recruitment problem. On November 9, 1925, Doriot wrote a letter to Professor Andre Siegfried of the prestigious École Libre des Sciences Politiques, asking him if he would like to come teach a course at the School on "Foreign Trade, Transportation and allied subjects, such as Economic Geography," holding out the opportunity "that your appointment could be transformed into a permanent one."

Their correspondence continued through December of 1926, touching several other subjects, but Doriot never convinced professor Siegfried to leave France. It was another minor setback for the young administrator. Sooner or later, though, Doriot knew he would have to come through for Dean Donham, or else he didn't have much of a future at Harvard Business School.

During the fall semester of 1925, Doriot was given another shot to prove himself. In as diplomatic a manner as possible, Doriot suggested to Dean Donham that the School's second-year course in "Factory Problems and the Taylor System" was not up to par. Much to Doriot's surprise, the Dean removed the teacher and told Doriot to teach the course. Luckily, Doriot knew a fair bit about the subject, having worked in several factories and studied them as a student at Harvard. It is one of the great ironies of Doriot's life that one of the most popular and influential teachers in the history of Harvard Business School, a man who carefully planned out every step of his professional and personal life, launched his teaching career with an offhand, almost accidental remark. Haunted by visions of failure, Doriot worked overtime to ensure his teaching debut would be a success. "Well, I didn't know if I could teach or not," Doriot admitted later. "At least it was a subject that I felt close to and had studied it very hard. So, I spent hours and hours at night studying and I took a further course in factory problems and systems."

The class drew about twenty students. In the second semester, Dean Donham tapped Doriot to teach yet another class, a second-year research course on management.

Doriot's profile at Harvard rose higher after the U.S. military sought out his expertise. In March, Major H. K. Rutherford of the U.S. War Department asked Doriot to review the content of an industrial enterprises course taught in the Army Industrial College. The purpose of the College was to train officers "in the procurement of all military supplies in time of war" and to provide "for the mobilization of material and industrial organization essential to war time needs." Doriot, as was becoming his style, did not mince his words with Major Rutherford. In his letter to the Major, Doriot criticized the course outline and its assigned problems.

"With reference to the problems," wrote Doriot, "I wish to say that I was quite surprised to see how weak they are. In a general way, they are long, do not cover the subject, and seem to have been taken out of books which were not the best in that field. The problem on standardization and changes in design seems to show that the gentlemen who were in charge of it have not very well understood what the problem was. In speaking of the problem on trusts, I must admit that I never heard of 'intergraded trusts.' I presume what was meant was 'integrated,' which means something."

Contrary to many accounts of his life, Doriot did not help found the Army Industrial College. U.S. War Secretary John W. Weeks, a successful Boston banker before entering government, backed the creation of the college after the abysmal performance of the United States in mobilizing for World War I. Doriot was one of a number of outside teachers who, working for free, helped establish the school's reputation by teaching a course nearly every semester until the start of World War II.

The War Department assignment marked the beginning of a long and fruitful relationship between Doriot and the U.S. military. In a letter to Secretary of Defense Robert McNamara written later on in his life, Doriot confessed, "I have always considered Priority 1 on my time is the Army, and Priority 2 is my teaching." Given Doriot's myriad accomplishments, this revealing remark illustrates the deep respect and love he held for the stars and stripes. With this simple request for advice from the Major, Doriot embarked on a thirty-year relationship with the military as a teacher, soldier, and officer.

The stress of learning to teach on the fly began to take a toll on Doriot. On April 7, 1926, Doriot wrote a letter to Strauss in which he complained about his workload, which had grown since the fall. "I am rather tired and half sick," he wrote. "I am teaching practically every course in the Business School, but hope to survive and arrive in New York in perfect health two weeks from yesterday."

In the letter, Doriot also asked Strauss for his advice in the matter of John S. Bartlett, a second-year student, whom Doriot had been trying to help obtain a job in the field of transportation. Over the next four decades, Doriot would go on to mentor thousands of other students, giving them advice, finding them jobs, guiding them in their careers, and taking an extraordinarily personal interest in each and every one of their futures. In fact, throughout his forty-year teaching career, Doriot kept detailed files on many of his students, which he updated on a regular basis.

The most interesting part of the Strauss letter, however, was contained in a humorous p.s. note, which revealed Doriot's first interest in a woman:

> Your nice letter just came . . . I am not in love and do not expect to be.
>
> Homer Vanderblue very much wishes to be remembered to you. Last Saturday, he and I became reckless and we actually took two girls to dinner. The School has not recovered from the shock as yet; this because Homer and I are looked upon as the two most unsociable bachelors in Cambridge.
>
> Anyhow Lewis, should anything as extraordinary as that happen, Alice and you would be the first ever to know about it.
>
> Your friend,
>
> [Georges]

When the school year ended that May, it brought huge relief to Doriot. He had survived his first year of teaching. Doriot still did not know if university education was his calling but he seemed to be getting the hang of it. He also dabbled in that wretched field of writing. Teaming up with Homer B. Vanderblue, a professor of business economics who was Doriot's roommate and friend, Doriot compiled the school's first bibliography of essential business reading material.

That summer, Dean Donham handed Doriot a treat by asking him to serve as Harvard's official representative at the International Congress of Accountancy. Held from July 5–10, 1926 in Amsterdam, Holland, the Congress was a scholarly conference organized by several financial groups in the Netherlands to promote the exchange of information and comparison of accounting methods across the world.

The trip was a welcome relief from the pressures of the classroom. Ensconcing himself in the Victoria Hotel in Amsterdam, Doriot spent a week attending sumptuous dinners, visiting the Amsterdam port and various industrial firms, and hob-knobbing with important financial figures such as G. H. M. Delprat, the Secrétaire Générale of the Netherlands Bank. Soon enough, word got back to Harvard that Doriot had represented Harvard with distinction.

When Doriot came back from Europe after the summer of 1926, Dean Donham awarded his hard work with a promotion: Doriot was now an Associate Professor of Industrial Management. Doriot was one of the few assistant deans to make the leap from administrator to academic. The promotion buoyed his spirits but it also carried more responsibility. Dean Donham asked Doriot to expand his teaching schedule, so Doriot started his own course in Manufacturing Industries, which was geared toward the study of factories and production. This class attracted ninety-six students, four times the number drawn by his first class.

Doriot's promotion could not have come at a better time for the Doriot clan. In 1926, D.F.P. went out of business. The company had never recovered fully from the one-two punch of World War I and the Bentleys' decision to manufacture their own cars. When the Bentley brothers abandoned D.F.P., Auguste had lost his largest export market. Auguste looked for additional financing to support the company but he failed to dig up any money. So Auguste and his partners sold their factory to the Lafitte concern, another new French carmaker, and Auguste retired at the age of sixty-three. He spent the remainder of his days tending to his garden in Courbevoie and taking leisurely walks. "I have these very unpleasant headaches," said Auguste. "I have a mechanic friend and occasionally go to see his very modern engines. I also read a lot."

Doriot's promotion coincided with a major new development at the Business School: in 1923, George F. Baker, president of the First National Bank of New York, made an extraordinary $5 million donation to the school, opening up the opportunity to finally solve the school's space problem. Baker's gift was gratefully accepted, and the University chose a site across the Charles River in Boston for the construction of the new facility. When it was finally opened in September 1926, 750 students moved into the five dormitories across from Soldiers Field. The expanded plant was a monumental coup for Dean Donham. Doriot was one of several staff members who helped oversee the construction of the new buildings. It was mostly project management duties, making sure materials were delivered, making good on contracts, and overseeing the construction of residences and other facilities.

Back in the classroom, Doriot began to develop a novel educational approach. Whereas most professors kept a chilly distance between themselves and their students, Doriot believed strongly in forming a close bond between student and teacher. From the start of his teaching career, he felt that every student deserved personalized attention. He studied each student's history and college grades, and was very attentive to the difficulties in transitioning from undergraduate to graduate work. Five weeks after Doriot's class started, he had seen every one of his ninety-six students at least twice.

A second tenet of his early philosophy, absorbed from his father, was drilling the value of hard work into his students. In a letter to a friend of a colleague, Doriot described with a palpable sense of glee the importance of imparting a strong work ethic. "At least 25 of my students have given me this year an average of 15 to 20 hours of work on one course alone," boasted Doriot. "I have seen several of them working steadily from 9 a.m. up to an advanced hour of the morning. I do believe when those men leave the school they have a definite notion of what an honest day's work means."

The third tenet was an emphasis on pragmatic management, on the nitty-gritty realities of day-to-day decision making—not highfalutin' theories. In the second-year courses, Doriot and other faculty split up their classes into smaller subgroups that tackled real problems in order to give them insight into "how business problems come up and are solved by business executives." Doriot was trying to teach his students what he called a "sense of operation, a sense of movement, a sense of setting goals and moving toward those goals with great strength, great determination, and energy."

As the semester drew to a close, Doriot could not wait to take a break and visit his friends in New York. In a letter to Strauss written on December 15, Doriot told him to expect him in New York early on the 24th, and that he planned to stay for three or four days. "As you know, I haven't had a day's rest for four months and am beginning to feel the need of a few days away from Cambridge," he wrote. "Just now, on top of teaching and administrative duties, I still have a great deal to do in the new buildings."

While Doriot was in New York, he took a meeting on December 28 with Paul Mazur, a partner at Lehman Brothers. Mazur offered Doriot a job, his first offer of new employment since returning to Harvard. But he declined the offer. Doriot did not address the reasons for his refusal in his personal files or letters. Still, the decision seems to make sense. He had already worked for an investment bank. Plus, things seemed to be going well at Harvard. He had just been promoted, and perhaps his new job promised a greater sense of job security. Most important, teaching seemed to represent a more gratifying profession.

In fact, Doriot was hatching a plan that would push business education in an entirely new direction. At the end of 1926, Doriot came to believe that it was time to create a business school in Europe, with the same philosophy guiding business education at Harvard. Naturally, he thought that such a school should be based in France. "Other nations respected France for her history, her culture, her arts," he argued. "They respected French architects, French dresses, parfum, art . . . but when it came to business, work, organization, they respected Germany, England . . . At the time Anglo-Saxons were superior! It seemed, therefore, that France had much to gain internally and externally if it became known as a nation teaching business the 'right way.'"

During his annual summer break in France in 1927, Doriot set up a meeting with Maurice Bokanowsky, the French Minister for Commerce and Aviation, to discuss his idea. Bokanowsky must have been impressed by Doriot because the following month he took time out on his trip to the United States to see the young professor. On September 4, Doriot invited Bokanowsky out to dinner at the Ritz Carlton in Boston. They spent a long evening together in deep discussion. The next morning, Doriot invited Bokanowsky, his son James, and Gareau Dombasle, the French Commercial Attaché to the Embassy, to breakfast at the Colonial Club on Harvard's campus. They spent the rest of the day together, brainstorming their plan. "The decision to teach business with the case system, in France, was made that day," recalled Doriot. "It remained to carry it out."

At the time, Harvard was not very interested in Doriot's half-baked scheme. Although he had an interesting idea, and the promise of support from a low-level French minister, he still had no money, no powerful backing, and no real plan. This lack of enthusiasm and support from Harvard meant that Doriot could not work on the French business school while teaching at Harvard. So he and his supporters decided to take up the matter next summer when Doriot vacationed in France.

When the Harvard semester began that fall, Doriot was greeted with two surprises, one scary and one pleasant. Shortly after the dedication ceremony of the new campus in June 1927, Dean Donham was afflicted with a serious heart ailment. So for most of the 1927 to 1928 school year, while Donham recuperated, Professor Oliver Sprague served as Acting Dean.

The pleasing news was that a pretty young woman had joined the Business School staff as a research assistant. Her name was Edna Blanche Allen. A twenty-eight-year-old graduate of Simmons College and a native of Brockton, Massachusetts, Miss Allen had just returned from California where she had been a research assistant to the director of the Food Research Institute at Stanford University. Her mother, who had lost her husband, was living nearby in Glendale, California. Edna became interested in the work of the Business School, and applied for a job there. Before long, Edna became Doriot's research assistant.

Contemporary testimonials to Edna's beauty are nearly as frequent as those in praise of her charm and brains. She was a "very nice person, sweet, bright"; she was "very intelligent" and "spoke French fluently"; she was a "magnificent woman." The imagination, stoked by these accounts and various photos, can picture Edna strolling through the rolling green lawns of the Business School campus: a pretty brunette, smiling shyly, moving with the grace of an educated and fit young woman. Peering onto the lawn from his office, Georges would see that she is tall, about five foot seven, with toned shoulders, a thin waist, and shapely legs. Her hair is brown and thick and she wears it short, which has the pleasing effect of accentuating her warm, pretty, heart-shaped face.

Given her beauty, charm, and sense of independence, Edna proved to be as elusive a prize as Doriot had ever sought. On the surface, Doriot was far from a woman's romantic ideal. While some thought him handsome, he was no Valentino. He spoke with a strong French accent that was hard to understand, and when it came to affairs of the heart, he was more the student than the professor.

Yet Edna could not help but be intrigued by Doriot. He was surely very different than the typical Boston Brahmin! Her curious mind delighted in his intellect and quirky sense of humor, and she surely appreciated his fine French manners and down-to-earth personality. Even if Edna held doubts about Doriot, she could not put him out of her mind. As Doriot's newly hired assistant, she had to work with him on a daily basis.

Indeed, Doriot was becoming one of the school's most popular teachers. For the fall semester of 1927, his Manufacturing class attracted 140 students, a 50 percent jump over the previous year's enrollment. By this time, he had devised a simple but ingenious teaching technique. Every other week, he required each student to read a newspaper or magazine article that covered an event of a particular industry, or a new technology, such as aviation, automobiles, or machine tools. Then Doriot asked the students to comment on the stories and recommend a detailed course of action.

In one example, Doriot asked the students to read an advertisement in the *Wall Street Journal* for the initial public offering of a new car company, American Mathis, Incorporated. Then Doriot told the students to answer these three questions:

1. Give, with reasons, your own opinion as to the desirability of this undertaking, including some discussion as to the size and price of the car, probable output, and class of customers to whom the appeal should be made.

2. What competitive advantages will this co. have over other companies manufacturing cars in the US?

3. What is your opinion of the:

    i. location of the plant

    ii. desirability of importing Mathis cars

    iii. adequacy of capital proposed

The approach was straightforward, yet inventive for the time. Whereas most professors taught business descriptively from the perspective of an economist or an academic, Doriot forced his students to *think* like businessmen. The technique had the effect of "infuriating students into positive brilliance."

In the spring of 1928, Doriot received a call from his new friends at the War Department. Major H. K. Rutherford asked Doriot to send him his teaching notes, and Doriot complied. On April 5, Doriot was invited for the first time to give a lecture at the Army Industrial College on the subject of "Industrial Research." Three weeks later, Doriot received a letter from Major C. A. Schimelfenig, of the Ordnance Department, whom Doriot had met on his recent visit to Washington. The War Department was trying to get control of its expenditures and the Major sought "the benefit" of his advice.

Doriot's growing prowess as a teacher culminated with an extraordinary bang at the end of the school year. On May 17, 1928, Doriot walked into Pierce Hall to give his last Manufacturing class, but instead of teaching, his 140 students asked him to take a seat. After he sat down, a student walked up to the front of the class and began reading from a scroll. The students wanted to thank Professor Doriot for a pleasurable experience, and for giving them the perspective required to solve the problems of an ever-changing world of business. Then they praised Doriot for something special.

You have given us something of far greater value than case books or assignments—yourself. As you paced back and forth on your quarter-deck before us, you looked upon our group not as a class, but as individuals needing guidance. You gave, as needed, advice, encouragement, criticism. Always you have urged us into original and constructive thinking upon difficult problems, and developed powers of analysis and understanding of infinite value in days to come.

Beneath all the levity of this afternoon lies a deep and sincere appreciation of what you have done for us this year. We hope that you will always remember our happy associations together, and understand something of the feeling of indebtedness we bear to you. You have made an important segment of the business world alive before us, in your inspiration we have had a new realization of our own possibilities.

It was a remarkably poignant moment for Doriot, a major milestone in his young teaching career. The heartfelt note from the students proved that

Doriot, despite all his doubts, was hitting his stride as a teacher. Doriot was so touched that he sent Lewis Strauss a handwritten letter that described the experience. "This past year may have been hard," wrote Doriot, "but yesterday, my 140 men made me feel that what little I had done for them was appreciated . . . I am sorry to see these men go; we worked hard together and they were always more than willing to do what I suggested. Today, I wish I could be with you but I cannot leave Cambridge now. I feel tired, rather sad, wishing to be away from Cambridge and also wishing I had done more for my class."

Doriot began the summer of 1928 with a new skip in his step, traveling to France to revive his dream of creating a French business school. On July 23 at ten o'clock in the morning, he met Maurice Bokanowsky again, and had lunch with him and his son. Earlier that January in New York, Bokanowsky told Doriot that the Paris Chamber of Commerce could make an ideal patron for the project. Unlike the U.S. Chamber of Commerce, the Parisian counterpart was a semipublic organization that enjoyed a prestigious reputation as well as a tradition of founding top-notch undergraduate business schools, such as the École des Hautes Études Commerciales and the École Supérieure de Commerce de Paris. So at four o'clock that afternoon, Doriot and Bokanowsky visited the Paris Chamber of Commerce and met four officials, including its president, vice president, and director of education, Pierre Jolly. They seemed quite interested in the idea and promised Doriot they would commence a study of the project. Maybe this idea would work after all.

When Doriot returned to Harvard for the 1928–1929 school year, Dean Donham asked him to put out another fire. The Dean, who had returned from his sick leave, told Doriot that there was something amiss with the class on Business Policy, a required second-year, full-year course. Over the past few years, students had complained about several teachers, and had even taken to stamping their feet "during lectures they considered boring or irrelevant." Like he had done before with the class on factory problems, Dean Donham told Doriot to take over the course and recast his Manufacturing lectures as a Business Policy course. Doriot accepted the assignment even though he did not want to teach a required course with an enormous enrollment. His boss was relying on him, and he had to come through.

As Doriot feared, the strain of teaching a class with 330 students disturbed his usually unflappable demeanor. Indeed, the challenge of teaching Business Policy was so great that it shook Doriot's confidence to the core, reviving his past feelings of incompetence, and forcing him to again question his choice of profession. It was a shocking reversal of emotion after ending the spring semester on such a high note. On October 2, Doriot vented the frustration in a letter to Lewis Strauss.

Dear Lewis,

I have started teaching. It takes an enormous amount of energy to teach 330 men. Trained teachers having for the past years made a mess of that course, I quite realize that the odds are against me. I shall do my best anyway even if I have to pass out doing it.

Frankly, I am looking forward to going back to N.Y. as soon as possible. While I do enjoy impossible jobs, I think that I should have left Cambridge last June at the end of my manufacturing class which I think went rather well last year. If this new class of mine goes well, I have nothing to gain and another year will be lost; if it does not go, my star will start fading as a poet would say!

Homer [Vanderblue] came back from N.Y.C. with his usual story that I am certainly married and probably have children. But, then, he enjoys such things and believes them to be very amusing. On the 8th I shall go to the National Metal Exposition in Philadelphia where I will also have to call on W. W. Ayer and Co. The following week I may go to Ford's in Detroit. When you have two minutes to spare, drop me a note telling me how you and Alice are.

With love to both,

Georges

Later that semester, Doriot's spirits were lifted after he reestablished contact with the military. On October 5, Doriot received a letter from Major C. A. Schimelfenig informing him that the War Department had finally figured out a plan to control its expenditures. Although the plan was modest in scope, the major told Doriot that it was a "happy solution quite in line with your recommendations that the Chiefs of Branches be given full responsibility for the expenditures made by them with a minimum of reports."

Whereas the Chief of Staff previously required monthly expenditure reports, now the military asked for them on a quarterly basis.

In late October, Doriot also helped host the Assistant Secretary of War, Colonel Charles B. Robbins, during his visit to Harvard Business School. As the Assistant Secretary, Colonel Robbins was responsible for overseeing the military's procurement system. Doriot introduced Colonel Robbins to a group of students from the Army that he had recently begun teaching and gave them a tour of the campus. The visit went very well, and a few days later Doriot received a letter of thanks from Major Schimelfenig. In December, on behalf of the War Department, Assistant Secretary Robbins sent Doriot a personal note of thanks for the "keen appreciation of the thought, advice, and material aid you have so generously given us throughout the year in the furtherance of our program of Industrial Preparedness."

In the spring semester, Doriot focused on the development of his eleven Army students. In March, he scored a win when the Ordnance Department told him that it would allow the students to focus on a few practical Army problems under Doriot's guidance—a long-time wish of Doriot. The Army's top priority was to give Doriot's student Colonel Edmund B. Gregory, a rising star and West Point graduate who had been recently ordered to the Quartermaster's Office, "some work to do in connection with purchasing methods as practiced by some of the larger corporations" because the colonel "will probably have supervision of considerable purchasing in the future." Doriot followed the order and also assigned his other Army students a variety of military problems. During World War II, Doriot's connection with Colonel Gregory would blossom into one of the most important relationships of his life.

Doriot finished out the semester and sailed for Europe on June 1 aboard the *S.S. Ile de France*. He left earlier than usual that year in order to tackle all the work left to do on the French business school. By this time, after gaining the support of the Paris Chamber of Commerce, he had finally received approval from Harvard to investigate and work on the project. From June 8 until July 9, Doriot spent practically every day at the Chamber of Commerce, mostly with Pierre Jolly, translating a number of Business School cases that would be relevant for the French or European economy. They also made the critical decision to skew the school toward seasoned managers and engineers rather than recent college graduates. "This may well have been the first middle management program anywhere as [Harvard] itself did not offer education to executives already in employment until 1943," wrote historian Jean-Louis Barsoux.

When Doriot returned from France in the fall of 1929, Dean Donham rewarded him with a second promotion for his hard work and initiative: Doriot was made a full Professor of Industrial Management. After just four years of teaching, with no previous experience, he had reached the top of the ivory tower. He was only thirty years old.

No doubt, Doriot had proved himself to be a trusty aide to Dean Donham, a reliable administrator, an increasingly popular teacher, and an effective marketer of the school. Perhaps most impressive, Doriot had shown an unusual ability to envision and build new enterprises. In rapidly promoting Doriot, the administrators of Harvard Business School implicitly recognized his talent for bringing various innovations to the new field of business education—techniques that are now considered standard in today's day and age.

Attaining the rank of professor was a major achievement for Doriot, the biggest of his life so far, and one that would set his mind at ease once and for all, at least as far his ability to teach was concerned. Just as appealing, the security of a full professorship, and the prestige and job security that came with it, would give him a wider berth to pursue his professional and personal interests with greater fervor.

Then the vagaries of the "real world" smashed into his cozy ivory tower. On October 24, 1929, in the middle of teaching his Business Policy course, the stock market crashed. By noon on "Black Thursday," eleven fairly prominent investors had committed suicide. On Monday, October 28, the slide continued with the Dow Jones recording a record one-day loss of 13 percent. The following day, "Black Tuesday," saw the market plummet even more as rumors spread that U.S. President Herbert Hoover would not veto an impending tariff bill. Fear and panic again ruled the day. The Dow nose-dived a further 12 percent. By the beginning of 1930, the stock market and the economy momentarily recovered. But late in that year, the market continued to lose ground and began a steady decline. The Great Depression, a global contagion that spread across North America and Europe, had begun.

Doriot, like many students of business and economics, studied the origins of the crash. For Doriot, one of Wall Street's biggest problems—and a major source of the crash—were the trusts organized by large investment banks. He poured all of his vitriol against these "great masters of frenzied finance" into a thirty-four-page white paper slamming the Goldman Sachs Trading Corporation and the famous investor and author Waddill Catchings. He titled the caustic paper, "The Investment Trust Racket." Joining a growing chorus of critics, Doriot's paper condemned Goldman Sachs and several interlocking investment trusts it created in the late 1920s as a scheme to defraud the public.

> *Mr. Catchings and his colleagues, by capitalizing on the stupidity and gullibility of the investing public, have made themselves tremendous profits within a short period of ten months . . . By his recent operations, Mr. Catchings has cast a stigma upon the entire banking field and has endangered the future legitimate use of investment trusts by banking firms which have adopted policies more sane and conservative than those apparently held by Goldman Sachs and Company.*

But Doriot's cautious nature prevented him from airing his concerns in public. In a November letter, Doriot asked Lewis Strauss for advice on the matter: "I'm afraid it can't be published but what I wish you will tell me is this, Should we rewrite it so that it can be published without any of us going to jail or should we try to get it as it is in the Congressional record? Dr. Nathan Isaacs believes that if published as it is, there would be a lawsuit, which probably we should win, but, of course, I am not anxious to get into that kind of thing. As far as I am concerned, business done along the lines outlined in this article is very bad and I must say that it rather makes me mad to see people getting away with it."

In his response, Strauss warned Doriot that the paper was too specifically directed at one man and one situation. The problem, as Strauss saw it, was that the paper would therefore leave the reader with the erroneous impression that Doriot had an axe to grind with Goldman Sachs and Catchings, or that they were the only perpetrators of these deeds. "I feel it would be best, if you intend to go forward with the article, to refer to several other situations of which you will have no difficulty in finding a wide selection," wrote Strauss. Doriot never published the paper due to the ongoing legal questions and his fears of the University's reaction.

Doriot may have been timid with a pen, but he was far more confident on the podium. By 1929, he had gained considerable confidence as a public speaker, and his lectures had begun to weave a hypnotic spell on his students.

No doubt, the content of Doriot's increasingly popular lectures were the main draw. But much of Doriot's effectiveness as a speaker stemmed from his tone and delivery, which one admirer described as his "easy flow from the platform." He spoke in a low, slow, and measured voice, with pregnant pauses, which made his students inch forward in their seats so they would not miss a word. His French accent, no doubt, added an exotic flavor and dose of mystique to the professor's performance.

Back at his Business Policy course, Doriot began to mix some philosophy into his pragmatic teaching method. Standing in front of the class, pacing back and forth from his quarterdeck, Doriot encouraged his students to ponder the purpose of life and business. It was a highly unusual technique but the students realized Doriot was giving them knowledge of much deeper value.

To Doriot, the objective of life was to better yourself and your family. And the most important part of management was the art of selection: matching the right person with the right job. Doriot peppered his lectures with a number of pithy aphorisms, which pupils studiously jotted down in their notebooks.

"One should not only be able to criticize but should always have a suggestion to make."

"Don't challenge others' statements; have them repeat them over again."

"Conditions which are best for workers will give best production!"

"Ask about prospects who didn't buy product."

"Always challenge the statement that nothing can be done about a certain condition."

In the second semester, Doriot used the Business Policy course as a forum to explore new subjects in business that were assuming greater significance in his view, such as entrepreneurship and leadership. Doriot devoted one class to the process of financing and building a new company. He asked the students to grapple with hard-nosed questions: How much of an advance is the company? How much money —don't underestimate—is needed? How reliable are the men presenting a new idea?

In another class on leadership, Doriot defined leadership as the ability to deliver results in a particular situation. Leadership, he believed, required large doses of both imagination and courage, tempered by caution. "Keep a fresh viewpoint that respects precedents but is not subservient to it," he told his class. For Doriot, it was paramount to take risks but never should one take blind chances. "It is more important to keep money than to lose it all trying to get all," he advised.

When Doriot spoke, people increasingly lined up to listen, including some of the most powerful people in the world. On December 3, before the semester came to a close, Doriot received a Western Union telegram from Joel T. Boone, the personal physician of President Herbert Hoover, who Doriot came to know through Lewis Strauss. Doriot also had one other important connection with the President: he had taught his son, Allan Hoover.

INFORMED YOU MAY BE IN WASHINGTON THE FOURTH IF SO THE PRESIDENT AND MRS HOOVER WOULD BE PLEASED TO HAVE YOU FOR LUNCHEON OR DINNER AS MOST CONVENIENT TO YOU

While Doriot wrapped up his fourth year of teching, he continued to finalize the last details of the French business school. By the beginning of 1930, the school's curriculum had been submitted for the approval of Harvard's executive council. At the same time, the Paris Chamber of Commerce asked Harvard to help prepare the school's case study-material. In response, Harvard agreed to send Edna Allen to France to organize the writing and collection of cases. On April 23, Edna set off on the S.S. *Degrasse*. Doriot arrived in Paris a few weeks later, and once again began spending nearly every day at the Chamber of Commerce.

In the midst of all of the work, though it was also a summer of love. As Georges and Edna hashed out cases for the school, their feelings for each other undoubtedly grew. One clear sign of his affection was that Georges introduced Edna to his family that summer. And we can only imagine that Paris, with its cobblestone alleyways, lush green gardens, and music-filled cafés, began to cast its romantic spell on the couple. Georges felt so strongly about Edna that he began to ponder asking her hand in marriage.

On September 4, Doriot returned to Boston, just several weeks before the Parisian school would open with a grand ceremony. On the verge of another major accomplishment, Doriot should have been bursting with joy. But in a letter he wrote to Lewis Strauss, Doriot expressed frustration and uncertainty about both his personal and professional life. Part of it was anger that he could not be in Paris for the opening of the school, but deeper resentments and anxieties stewed underneath his composed surface.

> I asked for not more than 150 students and I am endowed with 256. We are taking so many students that I begin to think that the School's training is getting useless.
>
> In not many hours from now, the French School will be dedicated. While I do not like formal functions, I should like to have been there. Newspapers have just stated that Harvard full professors were to receive a minimum of $8,000 next year. Another five years here and I ought to reach the minimum.
>
> Nothing else of importance to tell you. I have been trying to figure out whether I should get married or not. I would like to but my reason tells me not to and therefore am deciding against it. I shall regret it later but it will not be the first decision I take, knowing that I shall be sorry for it afterwards.
>
> Love to you and Alice,
>
> Georges

In the letter, Doriot's inner contradictions are revealed in full force. Like many men wrestling with the existential question of marriage, Doriot seems utterly confused about his life. Here we have a man who seems to not be driven by money complaining that he is not earning as much as other professors. Here we have a man who claims to adore the prospect of mentoring young men griping that he has too many students to teach. Here we have a man who admits to a dislike of formality then expresses displeasure that he is unable to attend a most formal event. And, most shockingly, here we have a man who wants to get married to a woman that he likes "very much" but is unable to commit to perhaps the most important decision of his life.

On October 11 in Paris, Dean Donham delivered a speech to dedicate the new business school before the President of France, the ministers of the government, the President of the Paris Chamber of Commerce, and a throng of news media. The school was called the Centre de Perfectionnement aux Affaires (CPA), or the Center for the Improvement of Businesses. The CPA marked another coup for Doriot, who more than any other individual made the dream turn into a reality.

When it came to the issue of love, though, Doriot's caution seems to have gotten the better of him. Based on the existing letters and notes, Doriot clearly had trouble proposing to Edna. Yes, he had discussed the subject of marriage with her and gotten some kind of positive response, but not a firm yes. Doriot's uncertainty may also have been due to fact that Edna was apparently considering two other suitors.

In one of the more remarkable stories from his life, Doriot's relationship with Edna came to a head at New York Harbor on November 6, when Edna returned to America. Doriot rushed down to Pier 57 to meet his sweetheart where she was arriving on the French Line. When Doriot approached the pier and noticed that two of his "competitor's for Edna's hand were there also," his heart began beating so rapidly that he could hear the blood thumping through his ears. Displaying his quick and clever mind, Doriot strode up to the marine superintendent, Tom Wood, a "great, big, tall, fine Irishman" whom he had befriended during all of his liner trips back and forth to Europe.

"Tom," he asked, "when the ship docks, who is allowed to go onboard?"

"The French Line personnel, the press, and people with passes, like you," replied Tom.

Doriot asked Tom for a big favor: would he mind changing the rules slightly and just let in French Line personnel and the press? Big Tom agreed, and when the ship docked, Doriot jumped aboard and left his two competitors waiting on the dock.

He found Edna and gave her a humorous if unromantic ultimatum: "Look, if you don't say that you are going to marry me—I know the French Line very well—you'll stay on that ship, and it will take you back to Paris." Edna relented and said she would marry Georges. "We decided to be married as soon as possible. Edna's mother was older and not well, living in California, and I didn't want my family to take a long, expensive trip to come," recalled Doriot.

To officiate his marriage, Doriot hired Dr. Minot Simons, the reverend of the All Souls Church on East 80th Street in New York. A Protestant minister of the Unitarian Church, Doriot had met Dr. Simons while on a trip in Cleveland. At first, Doriot proposed that the ceremony be held in Dr. Simons's study, but Lewis and Alice Strauss were kind enough to host the ceremony and a small reception in their home at 25 East 76th Street on the afternoon of December 20, 1930. One week before tying the knot, Doriot wrote a letter to Strauss alerting him to his travel plans. In the letter, Doriot expressed some last-minute jitters about the marriage. "I am very much in love with [Edna]; at least I think I am. I would like to be married without having to go through everything connected with it."

Doriot's wish for an unostentatious wedding was granted. Strauss sent a car for Dr. Simons and the ceremony began at four o'clock. Eighteen close friends attended, representing the span of Doriot's life. Edna was given away by Albert Spaulding Howe and was attended by Miss Edwina Herring. Lewis Strauss was Doriot's best man. Among those invited were Sir William Wiseman and his wife; Jerome Hanauer and his wife; Mr. and Mrs. Pierre Cartier; Jean Tillier, the U.S. manager of the French Line, and his wife; Allan Hoover; Dean Wallace Donham; Professor Nathan Isaacs; and a few other dear friends. It was a joyous yet simple occasion. The senior partners of Kuhn, Loeb gave Georges and Edna their silverware, glassware, and dinnerware, and the happy couple spent the evening at the Weylin, a quiet, dignified hotel on Madison and 54th Street.

FIVE

SLOUCHING THROUGH THE DEPRESSION

(1930–1940)

WHEN DORIOT RETURNED TO Harvard in the fall of 1931, he could look back on the past decade and smile with pride. In the relatively brief span of ten years, the young immigrant had conquered a new country. Not only had he found a profession that brought him satisfaction and security, he had earned a reputation as one of the leading lights of the most important business school in the country; he had spearheaded the creation of a successful new business school in Paris; and he had found the love of his life and convinced her to marry him. And yet there was still a fire that burned in Doriot, a passion that kept him searching for his next mission impossible.

Perhaps that is why the 1930s—a time of diminished expectations for the entire nation—were probably the most frustrating period of Doriot's life. He was always at his best when tackling an impossible job, but during the Great Depression, despite several attempts, Doriot never found a grandiose task to throw himself into as he had done so many times during the previous decade.

At times, a similar mood of discontent permeated the home of the Doriots. The 1930s would have been the ideal time for Georges and Edna to start their own family. But the Doriots never did have a child. No doubt, Doriot's lack of children profoundly shaped his character. Over the next forty years, he compensated for this absence by nurturing countless students and younger colleagues as if they were his own offspring. "He often said the only advantage of not having children is you choose them," says Claude Janssen, who studied under Doriot in the 1950s. "He chose three: Arnaud de Vitry, Robert McCabe and myself. We were really his three sons."

Nevertheless, the 1930s were hardly a lost decade. In retrospect, for the Doriots and the rest of the nation, it was a time for hunkering down, for planting seeds that could be harvested in the future. Indeed, the years of the Great Depression hold the answer to another great mystery of Doriot's life: How did a man with hardly any experience running a business come to be such a world-class businessman? The answer is that during those years, dozens of companies hired the professor to help guide them through the worst disaster that had ever hit the American economy. In that dark decade, Doriot gained a lifetime of experience as an officer, director, and consultant.

Between 1932 and 1941, when he was called up to join the military, Doriot served on the boards of twenty companies, while taking on executive-level positions in ten other firms. It was an astonishing volume of outside work that would never be allowed in today's age of vigilant corporate governance. In 1940, for example, Doriot was elected to take over the presidency of the struggling McKeesport Tin Plate Corporation, where he promptly put the company on firmer footing by negotiating the sale of its tin plate division to steelmaker Jones & Laughlin. Tending to all these companies, Doriot was like a circus artist juggling a dozen balls while walking a tightrope. Would he pull off the balancing act or would he lose his balance and come crashing back to earth?

In January 1931, after the Doriots returned to Cambridge from their unorthodox honeymoon, Georges needed to find a new place to live with his wife. They soon found an apartment in Cambridge. The first Sunday after they moved in, a throng of friends and colleagues called on them. Doriot, the self-described "most unsociable bachelor," never led much of a social life, devoting most of his evenings to work. Doriot's addiction to work made his colleagues and their wives even more curious about Doriot after he got married. Friends and coworkers continued to drop by their apartment to see the quirky professor and the woman who had agreed to marry him. So, after a few weeks, having realized that "all my evenings would be wasted and I could not do any work," the Doriots cancelled their lease and escaped to the Hotel Bellevue in Boston, where they stayed while Edna looked for a new apartment less central to the Cambridge social scene.

Even though Doriot was a professor, he and Edna led a spartan lifestyle. In the early 1930s, Doriot made about $4,000 or $5,000 a year, a comfortable middle-class income. But that security was compromised partly by the obligation he felt to regularly send money home to help take care of his parents and sister.

Still, the Doriots had it better than most Americans. In 1931, when the Great Depression kicked in, the U.S. unemployment rate surged to 16.1 percent, tripling from 3.1 percent in 1929. By 1930, breadlines broke out as desperate people lined up for free food doled out by states and cities. Hoovervilles—those shantytowns comprising hundreds of shotgun shacks cobbled together with cardboard boxes, egg crates, or corrugated tin—began sprouting across the American landscape. If Georges had strolled by Central Park's Great Lawn on a visit to New York, he would have gaped at a vast squatter's village with thousands of "utterly spiritless" people, in the words of writer Joseph Mitchell.

At least Georges and Edna had work, a roof over their heads, and money to pay for food and clothes. But they still pinched every penny. At the Hotel Bellevue, Georges and Edna studied the breakfast menu very carefully to see whether they could find a breakfast that would feed the both of them. Porridge, they learned, was the best choice. As for beverages, they concluded that tea was preferable to coffee. Coffee would usually yield one cup of drink, but a teapot provided enough water for two cups.

Luck, that mercurial commodity, was in short supply during those bleak times. One day, Edna splurged and bought a bigger heater for their living room, but when Georges placed the heater on top of a glass table, the glass broke.

A short while later, Edna found an attractive apartment at 5 Arlington Street in Boston. It was a second-floor unit with a balcony overlooking a garden and three high-ceilinged rooms. Most important, it was finally a place they both liked. "At the time there were few automobiles running on Arling-ton Street and we were not annoyed by their noise or smell," said Doriot.

Late in 1931, Doriot became transfixed with the idea of globalization, or as he called it, the "international mind." He believed the increasing inter-dependency of the globe would raise the chances of maintaining peace. In a series of articles and speeches, Doriot developed these ideas, and his remarks received significant coverage by the press. In one essay picked up by various U.S. newspapers, Doriot boldly called for the internationalization of all trans-portation systems in Europe—air, railroads, and steamships—as the most effective way to promote peace in that war-ravaged continent. By merging these transportation lines into a unified system owned by a group of interna-tional investors, Doriot argued that it would create a more efficient trans-portation network and, more importantly, "make national secrecy impossi-ble and tend strongly to minimize national jealousies." World peace could not be produced through political negotiations, he felt, but through indus-trial cooperation and coordination.

In November of 1931, Doriot expanded upon these ideas in an address he gave to the Two Hundred Fifty Associates of the Harvard Business School, a group of well-heeled donors. The address, titled "French and German Cri-sis," offered a comparative analysis of the strengths and weaknesses of the French and German economies. Doriot praised Germany as "clever, very clever," arguing that the nation's reindustrialization was "undoubtedly one of the outstanding feats of the century" and that "others should adapt them-selves to it rather than try to duplicate or compete." France, on the other hand, was following the "habit . . . of not talking very much about their trou-bles." In order to keep France and Germany from waging war against one another, Doriot proposed the formation of an international bank that would be given the power to "control and investigate all international loans." By this means, loans intended to finance military purposes would be hindered, thus preventing the suspicion that stokes a run-up to war, as had happened during the Great War.

Some of Doriot's high-minded ideas would eventually become realities, but once again he was too far ahead of his time. In just a few years, European nationalism would reemerge with a vengeance, making a mockery of his pleas for cooperation.

In the 1931–1932 school year, outside interests continued to draw Doriot's attention away from Harvard. In particular, Doriot was closely monitoring the progress of his Parisian business school, which was off to a strong start. The French Department of Education had awarded the school a first-class rating, applications were up, and almost all of the first-year students "were booked for important positions, sometimes as vice presidents of corporations."

On January 12, 1932, Doriot was invited by Major General Fox Connor to give a lecture to a large audience of regular Army, National Guard, and Reserve officers at Harvard's Baker Memorial Library. After several years of giving lectures, Doriot had established quite a reputation in the military. "There is one thing about Professor Doriot that has impressed me a great deal," said one colonel in his remarks introducing Doriot. "He is different from other professors in that he is intensely human and I think the affection that has been shown to him by the Harvard graduates, not only when he is here but when they are talking to me about him, is really very touching and he should be very proud of it."

On this January day, Doriot's subject was "Industrial Mobilization in a Major Emergency." Although Doriot envisioned various ways of promoting peace, this lecture and others he gave over the next few years showed Doriot believed war was always on the horizon. "We must formulate and perfect our preparedness plans in peace-time for war-time needs," urged Doriot. "In peace-time an order for supplies is delayed in delivery or fails of execution but no one suffers seriously or dies as a result. In war-time the delay in delivery of supplies for only a week may cause the loss of countless lives." Doriot ended the speech by calling for the creation of a "chief of natural resources as well as a chief of manufacturing" to help manage the coordination of wartime production needs. But, as with so many other visionary speeches he had delivered over the years, Doriot's warning and calls for action fell on deaf ears and empty government coffers.

Doriot had a more receptive audience in the business world. At the end of 1931, some of the country's leading companies began to court Doriot, including N. W. Ayer, the first U. S. advertising agency. In November, the firm offered Doriot a job. Founded in Philadelphia in 1869, N. W. Ayer coined some of the industry's most enduring jingles, including Morton Salt's "When it rains it pours." Doriot expressed hesitation about the offer to Lewis Strauss. "This does not mean I have decided to go with them," wrote Doriot, "but I have realized that they were in very close touch with many companies that might require good banking connections, and after all, since I am still free and 'my soul has not been sold'! it is normal that you should be the good banking connection." In early 1932, after careful consideration, Doriot declined to take the job, but he did accept his first consulting job.

For Doriot, the rest of 1932 did not bring much excitement. The real action was in Washington. All eyes were on the nation's capital as it was consumed with the presidential election of 1932, pitting the incumbent Herbert Hoover against the urbane democratic governor from New York, Franklin Delano Roosevelt. It was landmark election that realigned the political landscape of America, ushering in a new era of activist government. And Doriot was eager to jump into the fray.

After becoming a full professor at Harvard, Doriot began to take a greater interest in the nation's public life. In his speeches before the military, and in various articles he wrote or committees that he joined, we see a man becoming increasingly interested in using his power to shape public policy. One theme emerged as a leitmotif: like many businessmen of the day, Doriot was a critic of big federal government. "American businessmen are now handicapped as a consequence of the stupid regulation which now exists," said Doriot to one reporter in 1932. Doriot was particularly opposed to the government provision of direct economic relief to the unemployed. In January of 1933, Doriot weighed in on the issue in a four-page article he cowrote for *New Outlook* called "The Motorist Afoot." The story focused on the emergence of two Depression-era taxes: sales and gasoline. Mississippi was the first state to adopt a sales tax, and a dozen other states were contemplating similar measures "as a way out of the general depression and the distressed conditions of state finances." The tax on gasoline was the next step, to help Mississippi and other states refill their coffers. Doriot favored the sales tax but in his essay he criticized legislatures that adopted gas taxes to build and maintain roads, and then diverted the funds for direct unemployment relief. "The fallacy of taking revenue that is now providing worthwhile employment of public benefit and giving it to those who are unemployed is so obviously and utterly absurd that one marvels how legislators—supposedly representatives of the thinking citizens—can contemplate such measures and even carry them into effect."

In March, Doriot wrote Lewis Strauss and asked him to open a bank account for him. What seems like an unusual request today was actually a shrewd maneuver. In the early 1930s, the bank industry was imploding. With hundreds of banks declaring insolvency, Doriot tapped Strauss for his knowledge of this troubled industry. "Would you be willing to open an account for me in a bank which you think has a fair chance of remaining in existence for a period of months?" asked Doriot. "If the bank you pick should close two minutes after the account is opened, I shall not feel badly but shall merely come to the conclusion that it could not be helped." The amount that Doriot deposited in the account revealed the meagerness of his savings. It was only $3,500, less than a year of salary.

In June, at the height of the Depression, Doriot stepped up his attack on big government by slamming one of the key legislative proposals of the New Deal—the National Industrial Recovery Act. Passed on June 16, 1933, the law created the National Recovery Administration (NRA), an executive agency with the power to create "codes of fair competition"—codes which were intended to reduce destructive competition and to help workers by setting minimum wages and maximum weekly hours. The NRA, symbolized by the blue eagle, included a rash of regulations that imposed pricing and production standards for all sorts of goods and services. But the codes allowed cartels to be established in many industries. And as NRA-associated firms increased their prices, sales fell, employment fell, and the recovery stalled.

Most economic historians today consider the NRA to be a resounding failure but many respectable business groups praised its passage, including the U.S. Chamber of Commerce and leading labor organizations. Not Doriot. The professor believed in the collective wisdom of the market, not government bureaucrats. In a story published in the Boston Transcript titled "A Dissenting Voice on the Recovery Act," reporter W. P. Black devoted the whole piece to airing Doriot's views, who declared the act as nothing more than a bluff, a measure designed "to scare the manufacturers and make them behave." To carry out its provisions, Doriot said the United States would have to go "all the way to Bolshevism, which none but an insignificant minority wants in America." Doriot criticized many aspects of the act but the worst feature for him was that it gave the government the power to lend money to struggling businesses. "Bankers, and not the government, should determine what industries are worth saving," argued Doriot.

This time, Doriot hit the nail on the head. The professor correctly saw that the newly elected Roosevelt—and the government—had overstepped their bounds. But Doriot did not have to wait long to be vindicated. The law was so poorly conceived that on May 27, 1935, the Supreme Court over-turned the NRA in a unanimous decision, ruling that it infringed upon states' authority and gave powers to the executive branch in violation of the Constitution. The NRA quickly stopped operations. Doriot's campaign against the agency marked the first of many battles he would wage against the federal government, and what he felt were its misguided intrusions into the free market economy.

In July of 1933, when Doriot headed back France for the summer, the drums of war began beating again ever so softly. "There is no fear of war for the present," he told Strauss, "but many people even those of the war excited type seem to be convinced that Germany is getting ready for an eventual scrap." Earlier that year, in January, the German president Paul von Hinden-burg reluctantly agreed to appoint Adolph Hitler Chancellor of a coalition government. By that time, Hitler had already attracted considerable criticism, prompting the famous gossip columnist Walter Winchell to write: "Too bad that a man like Hitler can rise so high in politics, who hates so intensely."

Doriot ended 1933 by firing another salvo—this time at his homeland. Like many immigrants, Doriot maintained a love-hate relationship with his home country. But Doriot's feelings were more extreme than those of most immigrants. "Doriot in many ways was the most schizophrenic Frenchman I've ever met," says colleague and friend James F. Morgan. "He would go back and forth for this admiration for French wine and cuisine and the French language. But the French capacity to make very simple things com-plicated drove him nuts."

And now, for the first time, Doriot publicly expressed his disgust with France. Throughout the year, Doriot had been contributing a quarterly col-umn for a French magazine called *La Revue des Vivants*. In his December col-umn, Doriot attacked the French government when it refused to pay a $20 million interest payment on her wartime debt to America. Calling his country a "frivolous nation," Doriot was outraged that France would not pay this rel-atively small sum to a country that had come to its aid when it needed it most. "Without exaggeration," he thundered, "one can safely say that during the last four or five years France has done everything she could to have Amer-ica become disgusted with her."

In the beginning of 1934, Edna met a gentleman who owned a very nice duplex apartment for rent on the top two floors of 101 Chestnut Street in Boston. Although Edna declined at first, explaining that it was too expensive, the gentleman clearly wanted them to take the apartment, lowering the rent so that it was more affordable. The Doriots soon moved in, and Edna picked up a few new items to furnish their new home.

The couple liked the apartment but the new home did not brighten Doriot's spirits very much. For much of that year, he was in a "rather disin-terested mood," as he described it. "I have been in Boston trying to act as a nice teacher not burdened with any new ideas," Doriot confided in Strauss. "There has been no excitement up here, and I am looking for excitement." However, as the mid-term elections of 1934 heated up later that year, Doriot became entangled in an unusually public affair, giving him more excitement than he bargained for.

In a speech he gave in Philadelphia on October 18, Doriot denounced the very basis of the New Deal: "The New Deal will go down in history as one thing that has done more harm to the morals of the nation," said Doriot. "The idea that all men are born equal and that it is a desirable thing for every-body to be interested in government is wrong and fantastic, and sooner or later we must come to the conclusion that those who pay the taxes have more right to govern than those who don't."

These few sentences are probably the dumbest that Doriot ever uttered, and democratic politicians running for office picked up the remarks like they were a gift from the political gods. In a rare lapse of judgement, Doriot had crossed the line from iconoclastic to idiotic. In a speech in Boston on Novem-ber 2 before a throng of supporters, James M. Curley, the three-term mayor of Boston who was running for governor of Massachusetts, used Doriot's remarks on the New Deal to criticize Harvard University.

Looking over the crowd, Curley quoted Doriot's comments on the New Deal and then launched his attack.

"This is a most unusual statement for a supposedly educated man and coming from the assistant dean of Harvard University Graduate School does not reflect credibility upon this famous institution of learning. The dean overlooks the fact that the New Deal has been the most potent contributing factor for a higher moral order in America that has taken place in the past ten generations, in that it has taken children out of industry, permitting them to develop mentally and physically until such time as they are able in some measure to begin life's battle . . . If a knowledge of hygiene and a respect for lawfully constituted authority, which is the cornerstone of our form of government, is to be classified as immoral, then Professor Doriot is guilty of the most stupid statement that a supposedly intellectual man can make."

Curley won the election, as did many other Democrats. And Doriot learned his lesson. Never again would he attack such a prominent political figure as FDR in such a public way. Instead of lashing out, Doriot would apply his influence and charm behind the scenes.

The brawl between Doriot and Curley was part of larger battle brewing between the democratic New Dealers and the republican business establishment. Most of the business community initially supported Roosevelt's New Deal but after the government passed the Glass-Steagall Act of 1933, prohibiting commercial banks from owning brokerages, and then created the Securities and Exchange Commission in 1934, Roosevelt began to lose Wall Street. It didn't hurt him politically, though. The country wanted drastic action and Roosevelt gave it to them in spades.

Indeed, while most parties lose support in the first midterm elections, the Congressional elections of 1934 gave President Roosevelt large majorities in both houses, sparking a second wave of New Deal legislation. These measures included the Works Progress Administration, which set up a national relief agency that employed two million family heads; the National Labor Relations Act, which established the federal rights of workers to organize unions, to engage in collective bargaining, and to take part in strikes; and, most importantly, the Social Security Act, which created an economic safety net for the elderly, the poor, and the sick.

Contrary to Doriot's inane predictions, the New Deal helped revive the morale of the nation as well as the economy. After unemployment peaked in 1933 at 24.9 percent, it fell for three consecutive years until it bottomed out in 1937 at 14.3 percent. Although still a high level of unemployment, Roosevelt's policies clearly brought significant relief to a nation desperate for the chance to earn an honest day's work.

Doriot also began to benefit personally during these years as dozens of companies sought his guidance. On October 25, 1934, the Kansas City Southern Railway Company hired Doriot to become a director, his first board-level position since his days with Willy Wiseman at New York & Foreign Development Corporation. In December, railway car maker Budd Manufacturing also hired Doriot as a director, and he soon after was elected to the company's executive committee. In March of 1935, Doriot was made vice president of Budd Manufacturing, and in September, Budd subsidiary Budd Wheel offered him yet another director position. Lastly, in October, the Massachusetts Investors Trust, one of New England's largest investment managers, hired him as a consultant.

At the end of 1935, the head of Budd Manufacturing cabled Doriot, asking him to sail immediately for Europe. Budd had big plans for Europe and wanted Doriot's help. But the offer came at a bad time. At Dean Donham's request, Doriot had taken over the required first-year class in industrial management that year, though the Dean had asked him to teach it as a version of his Manufacturing class. With a staggering 450 students, it was the biggest class of his career, and Doriot knew Dean Donham would not release him for an extended period.

Even though Doriot was unable to accept the offer from Budd Manufacturing, it didn't stop him from accepting other outside assignments. In 1936, Doriot became a consultant to Ladenburg, Thalmann & Company, a New York–based investment bank. In 1937, Thornley & Jones, Incorporated elected Doriot to its board. Then in 1938 and early 1939, Doriot became director of more than ten other companies, including the utility, Standard Power & Light Corporation, and manufacturing concerns such as McKeesport Tin Plate.

Dean Donham allowed faculty to perform outside consulting as long as it did not interfere with the main work of the School. It was his best way of keeping low-paid professors on staff. Doriot's astonishing amount of outside work pushed the limits of the School's rules. But Doriot was one of the most popular professors, and he was tenured to boot. Since Doriot was a workaholic with no family responsibilities to divert his energies, he managed for the most part to pull off the balancing act.

Moreover, Doriot continued to develop innovative teaching methods that pleased Dean Donham. In 1937, Doriot adapted the approach of his Business Policy and Industrial Management courses to a new second-year course called simply "Manufacturing." Unlike his Manufacturing Industries course he taught as an assistant professor, the purpose of this new course was to "train the students in the thorough analysis of and in the administrative control of a manufacturing company." Emphasis was placed on " the study of new products, new ides, new developments and new questions of research," all under Professor Doriot's "imaginative and stimulating guidance." For the next forty years, Professor Doriot would use this course as his intellectual sandbox, training more than six thousand students in the arts of self-improvement and creative management.

Eventually, though, Doriot did make a few concessions. There were just too many balls to juggle. Between 1936 and 1938, he resigned from six, or about a quarter, of his outside positions, including those at N. W. Ayer & Son; Budd Manufacturing; Ladenburg, Thalmann; and Thornley & Jones, among others.

In his 1933 inauguration speech, Franklin Delano Roosevelt famously told the nation, "Let me assert my firm belief that the only thing we have to fear is fear itself—nameless, unreasoning, unjustified terror which paralyzes needed efforts to convert retreat into advance." Thanks to Roosevelt's bold and firm leadership, the United States was no longer in fear of dissolving into revolution or anarchy. But although unemployment declined and the economy advanced steadily throughout Roosevelt's first two terms, the New Deal failed to completely pull the United States out of the depression. The median joblessness rate during the New Deal was 17.2 percent, and until the United States entered the war, it never fell below 14 percent. The country was still in the grip of fear, but it was of a different sort. It was a profound fear to take economic risks.

The fact is, the crash of 1929 inflicted deep scars on the psyche of the nation—scars that would not heal until after the war. If Americans were afraid to deposit money in a bank, they were surely in no mood to invest in securities or any other venture that wasn't as solid as Manhattan bedrock.

Despite all the positives of the New Deal, and there were many, Depression-era tax policies had the unintended consequence of creating a "risk-less economy." A string of tax hikes and new taxes extinguished the nation's sparks of innovation. On top of the Revenue Act of 1932—one of the largest tax increases in American history, which doubled the estate tax, increased corporate taxes by almost 15 percent, and raised taxes on the highest incomes from 25 percent to 63 percent—the Revenue Act of 1935 raised new taxes on higher income levels, corporations, and estates. The Revenue Act of 1937 taxed short-term capital gains as ordinary income. And in 1936, Roosevelt added a higher top rate of 79 percent on individual income greater than $5 million—a rate that was increased again in 1939.

By 1937, the undistributed profits surtax severely restricted the ability of small companies to build up their capital out of earnings, and the large surtax on individual incomes discouraged wealthy individuals from investing in new companies. At the 1936 Investment Bankers Association (IBA) conference, MIT president Karl T. Compton warned that the new surtax illustrated "how government regulation has been directed almost entirely at the curbing of exploitation and has generally ignored and sometimes even penalized attempts toward technical progress."

The result was that more and more of the nation's funds flowed into superconservative investment trusts, and to insurance companies and pension funds. By the 1938 IBA convention, the financial community began to express deep concern about the nation's atrophied capital markets. "If investors throughout the land, large and small, refrain from purchasing unseasoned securities of a young industry and refuse to take a business man's risk, where will new industries obtain needed capital, and would not such a development slow down the economic progress of the country?" asked Dr. Marcus Nadler, a New York University finance professor.

In 1938 and 1939, various groups of New England industrialists and financiers became obsessed with fixing the nation's risk-less economy. One of the most prominent organizations was the New England Council, a group of politicians, businessmen, and educators, which formed in 1925 to "improve economic conditions for New England." Within this group, there was a growing awareness that New England's universities and industrial research labs were a valuable asset distinguishing the region from the rest of the nation. The most impressive asset in the region was MIT.

In 1930, Karl Compton, then the head of the physics department of Princeton University, accepted an invitation to become the president of MIT. Under Compton, MIT redefined the relationship between science and society. When

Compton took office during the Great Depression, science was attacked as a source of social ills. Over the next twenty-four years, Compton worked tirelessly to strengthen basic scientific research at MIT and to promote the importance of science to a skeptical and hostile public. Compton advocated a broad education for scientists, one that responded to the needs of the time.

In 1934, Compton proposed an ambitious program he called "Put Science to Work." The campaign called for the public financing of "scientific and engineering research looking toward better public works for the future." Instead of blaming labor-saving technology for society's ills, Compton proposed the bold idea that science gave birth to great new industries. "New industries are like babies: they need shelter and nourishment, which they take in the form of patent protection, financing, and the chance of reasonable profits," wrote Comptom in a long essay promoting his campaign. "But, before all, they need need to be born, and their parents are science and invention."

The egalitarian ethos of the New Deal stymied Compton's campaign to finance research at elite universities like MIT. So Compton turned his attention to the regional level. In 1939, responding to a suggestion by Compton, the New England Council formed a committee to examine how new products might help reverse the terminal decline of the region's textile and garment industries. The New Products Committee brought together eight of the most progressive minds in America, including Compton, Doriot, Ralph Flanders, a mechanical engineer who rose to become head of Vermont's Jones & Lamson Machine Company, and Merrill Griswold, president of Massachusetts Investors Trust. Doriot was charged with heading up one of several subcommittees; his was called "Development Procedures and Venture Capital." Was this his new impossible mission?

Over the course of his long career, Doriot participated in many committees. And he usually despised them. "A committee is an invitation to do nothing," was one of his famous maxims. But perhaps no committee was as important as the New Products Committee. It wasn't so much the work of the Committee that mattered, though they did undertake a series of important studies. More so it was the fact that it assembled the brain trust of individuals who would eventually pioneer the venture capital industry.

On November 8, 1940, the New Products Committee convened its first annual meeting to discuss the results of its research. One subcommittee concluded that although capital existed for new ventures, there was a need for an "organization and technique to appraise opportunities for specific enterprises." Doriot's subcommittee concurred that "the great need is for qualified technical analysis of situations, in order that venture capital investors may proceed with a reasonable degree of assurance." The outcome of the Committee was the creation of the New England Industrial Foundation. The Foundation's goal was not to invest in new enterprises but to create a sort of industrial research organization to "appraise opportunities for scientific enterprises in the New England area." After spotting those opportunities, the Foundation hoped existing New England businesses would prop them up with money and advice.

Around the same time, Doriot joined forces with another group of elite New Englanders working on the same problem: Enterprise Associates. Led by William Coolidge, an American physicist who in 1916 invented the prototype of modern X-ray technology, Enterprise Associates took a more direct approach than the Foundation, raising $300,000 from twenty stockholders to finance the final stages of promising research projects. Doriot joined the board of Enterprise, along with his Business School assistant William H. McLean, and a few others. Throughout 1938 and early 1939, the stockholders and officers of Enterprise met with various entrepreneurs, looking for ideas to finance. On May 7, 1940, they held a dinner where they learned about a young chemical company called National Research. They liked the idea and backed the firm.

Then history threw a wrench in their plans. On May 10, Germany invaded Luxembourg, Belgium, the Netherlands, and France, ending the so-called Phony War. Right after Germany unleashed its blitzkrieg on the rest of Europe, most of the people who attended the Enterprise dinner called up William Coolidge and told him they wished to withdraw from their participation in the financing of National Research. Coolidge refused to withdraw. Since he had made a commitment, he would follow through with it. Doriot, feeling bad, loaned them an assistant to help, and later joined National Research's board.

But it made little difference. The United States was facing a far graver risk—global fascism—and she needed to devote all of her energies and resources to fighting this dangerous and growing scourge. Enterprise Associates and pretty much everything else unrelated to the war were put on the back burner.

Still, the experience of Enterprise Associates taught the venture industry's pioneers an important lesson. "[The Enterprise] experience made Merrill Griswold and Karl Compton realize that it might not be a good idea to have a company with only enough money to find and study projects, then 'to pass the hat' for capital to start the new company," explained Doriot. A company should have its own capital, they concluded. That way, it would be insulated from events outside of its control.

For the time being, though, the war had snuffed out the formation of the nation's venture capital industry just as it was getting off the ground. Six years later, Compton, Doriot, and other members of the New England brain trust would revive their plans to create a regional venture movement. But first, they all had a war to fight.

SIX

WAR—THE
INFLECTION POINT

(1940–1946)

SMASH! BANG!! BOOOOOOOM!!! In the spring of 1940 fascism was on the march, and the Allies appeared unable to halt the goose steps of the Nazi storm troopers. The Allies had thought the thick forests of the Ardennes would be impenetrable by a modern, mechanized army, but during the first phase of the German invasion, the Wehrmacht's Panzer Division blitzed right through them. Then the Nazis broke through the French line at Sedan, and drove west across northern France, splitting the Allied forces in half. Meanwhile, Belgium, Luxembourg, and the Netherlands fell like dominoes against the attack of the German war machine. By June 10, German tanks rumbled across the Seine River. Four days later, Paris fell.

The fall of France shocked the U.S. military into a state of hurried preparedness. On May 15, President Roosevelt asked Congress for a supplemental defense appropriation of nearly $1.3 billion, calling for the production of at least fifty thousand planes a year—an astounding goal considering the paltry state of military aircraft production. And in September, Congress passed the Selective Training and Service Act, marking the first peacetime conscription act in the history of the United States.

Georges Doriot wanted to play his part in the war. So after the conflict began, he stopped by the French Embassy in Washington to see what he could do. Asked what his rank was at the end of World War I, Doriot answered, "Sergeant."

"Oh," replied the embassy official, "we could make you a Sergeant Major, and with some protection you can be the driver to the ambassador." Doriot, embarrassed more for France than for himself, walked out of the embassy.

By contrast, U.S. officials grasped that the organizational, financial, and technical skills of a man like Georges Doriot could play a vitally important role in the war. That was certainly the view of Edmund B. Gregory. An Iowa farm boy and graduate of West Point and the Harvard Business School, Gregory was a Colonel in the Office of the Quartermaster General when the war started, the division responsible for providing GIs with all of their food, gear, and equipment.

Colonel Gregory knew that his old professor was the kind of leader who would come in handy, the kind of man who could cut through red tape to get his troops what they needed. "I'm sure that's why General Gregory picked him," said Captain Robert D. Orr, who served under Doriot. "He knew he would be the kind of person that could accomplish miracles during wartime when rapidity was necessary."

In retrospect, Doriot learned how to become a venture capitalist during the war, for it was through World War II that he underwent the most significant metamorphosis of his life, transforming himself from a professor of business into a world-class builder of innovative new enterprises. When Doriot became head of the Military Planning Division in the Officer of the Quartermaster General, he began running, in a sense, his first venture capital operation. The purpose of his division was to identify the unmet needs of soldiers and oversee the development of new products to fill those needs. In order to pull off this engineering miracle, Doriot perfected the art of finding the right people for the right technical challenge, and then inspiring them to invent the future.

"Doriot started his venturing during the war," says Ray Hoagland, the wife of Harry Hoagland, one of Doriot's chief wartime assistants who later helped Doriot pioneer the venture capital industry. "He loved to come up with new ideas. He would hire people who were good inventors. He knew how to contact and find these little companies that had these bright inventions."

Doriot's assimilation by the U.S. Armed Forces began in 1939 when William J. Donovan, a distinguished World War I battalion commander who later founded the Office of Strategic Services, asked Doriot to meet with President Roosevelt. Donovan had become familiar with Doriot as one of the many military men who had taken advanced courses at Harvard Business School. A close friend of Roosevelt since their days at Columbia University's Law School, Donovan became Roosevelt's secret intelligence agent in the 1920s, taking covert trips for him after he became president. Despite their political differences, both men recognized that German and Japanese policies were driving the world toward another global conflict. As such, Donovan knew the commander in chief was eager to recruit men who could help his woefully ill-equipped country prepare for a fight with Nazi Germany. "This man will be able to make people work together, the military and the scientists and industry," Donovan told the President.

During their meeting, the President asked Doriot if he wanted to help the United States. Doriot jumped at the chance to participate not only in liberating his home country, but also to repay America for all the opportunity she had given him. But there was one problem: Doriot was a Frenchman. The President inquired if Doriot was willing to become a U.S. citizen. Doriot happily agreed, and was told he would be appointed a Lieutenant Colonel. On January 8, 1940, Doriot strolled into a federal court in Boston. When he walked out, he was a naturalized U.S. citizen.

On December 28, 1940, Doriot got the letter from Colonel Gregory he'd been waiting for. The previous April, Gregory was appointed Quartermaster General with the rank of Major General. "I believe the time has come to have you commissioned in the Quartermaster Corps as Lieutenant Colonel," wrote General Gregory. "Things have been developing pretty fast here lately and I believe it advisable to get you the commission as soon as possible so you can be called up to active duty at your convenience."

As it turned out, Doriot was a hot property. Besides the Quartermaster Corps, several generals in the Office of the Assistant Secretary of War were anxious to snap up the Harvard professor. But Doriot chose to work for his former student. He wanted to be an Army man. Thanks to his years of teaching at the Army Industrial College, he had made many friends in the Army, and the challenge of mobilization was something he'd been preparing for all of his professional life. But his admiration for General Gregory was the decisive factor.

"I had several offers from different parts of the Army and Air Force," Doriot explained the decision later in his life, "and the only reason I went to the Quartermaster Corps is that I considered General Gregory the most intelligent officer I knew. Working for him not only proved that I was right, but I developed for him an even greater admiration than I had before."

In spring of 1941, Doriot prepared to enter the Army. Beginning in March, after he consulted with an attorney on statutes governing possible conflicts of interest between the military and private sector, Doriot began to resign from a slew of directorships. On June 20, he passed his physical exam. A few weeks later he purchased $10,000 of life insurance for Edna, and $5,000 policies for his sister Madeleine and his niece Evelyn Poillot.

On July 18, after winning a fight to preserve his promised rank, Doriot was commissioned as a Lieutenant Colonel in the Quartermaster Corps Reserve, Serial # O-423479, and was assigned to its Motor Transportation Division. Many accounts of Doriot's life only mention his work for the Military Planning Division or the Research & Development Branch of the Quartermaster Corps, but Doriot actually occupied seven different positions within four divisions of the Quartermaster Corps, proof of his popularity as well as his versatility.

Before Georges left for the Army, he and Edna discovered they needed to find a new place to live. Although they liked the apartment at 101 Chestnut Street very much, the landlord was finally going to raise the rent. So Edna began house hunting. She found a gorgeous townhouse on 12 Lime Street in Boston's tony Beacon Hill district that was going to be auctioned off. Shortly after, on July 26, Georges was called to active duty. He told Edna to attend the auction without him, and days later Edna called Georges to tell him they had bought the house for $8,000. "That seemed to be a very extravagant price for us to pay for a house that was about my salary at Harvard," recalled Georges, "but Edna, who always had good, correct feelings about things and about the future, told me that she felt it was decidedly the thing for us to do." Since debt was a loathsome concept for Georges, the Doriots used their savings to buy the house.

When Georges Doriot arrived in Washington in July of 1941, President Roosevelt had already committed the United States to becoming the "great arsenal of democracy." But there was no guarantee the nation's superior economic strength could be quickly transformed into a military juggernaut. Indeed, stocking that arsenal appeared to be a seemingly impossible task after two decades of neglecting military preparedness. In fact, the Army was still relying on stockpiles of weapons, ammunition, and gear left over from World War I. Critical resources such as steel were dwindling, and since the military did not own the means of production, it had to convince the nation's industrialists to apply a substantial amount of their capacity to war production—just as they were rejoicing in the first prospect of profits in years. "They didn't want to invest a lot of their own funds in equipment to manufacture things they believed would not be in demand after the shooting ceased," said Reconstruction Finance Corporation head and Secretary of Commerce Jesse H. Jones.

Doriot encountered these vexing issues head on when he joined the Procurement Branch of the Motor Transport Division of the Quartermaster Corps. After moving into the Hotel Carlton, Doriot was told to shift motor transport production into higher gear. The ability to transport men and munitions and supplies was vital to winning the war. But in 1941, Detroit was anticipating strong consumer demand for cars. When United Auto Workers vice president Walter Reuther proposed the conversion of the remaining estimated 50 percent idle capacity in car factories to military aircraft production under government contract, Detroit carmakers simply said, "No thanks."

Doriot was an ideal candidate for this challenge. Thanks to his family legacy and his studies of the automobile industry at Harvard, Doriot was very familiar with the problems of Detroit automakers, and he knew the people that ran the industry, to boot. Immediately, Doriot undertook a survey to determine the Quartermaster's automobile needs and to size the automotive industry's capacity to produce finished vehicles, as well as component and replacement parts on a month-to-month basis.

To solve a broader array of contract delinquencies, the Army transferred Doriot in September 1941 to the Procurement Control Branch of the Planning and Control Division, then the most important part of the Quartermaster Corps, responsible for managing overall procurement. Still, his top priority remained the auto industry. On September 10, Doriot delivered a preliminary report stressing that military requirements were already "using a substantial part of the existing truck production capacity." He warned his superiors that the car industry was "mistakenly considered by many as a huge reservoir of production facilities . . . [that] can be tapped a few minutes before the flow of goods is required."

Sensing his leadership ability, one month later the Quartermaster Corps promoted Doriot. Now, as Chief of the Production Expediting Section in the Procurement Control Branch, Doriot was responsible for all supply planning programs just as pressure began building on the Quartermaster Corps to ramp up production. In late September, at the direction of President Roosevelt, the War Plans Division delivered the first systematic survey of wartime requirements. The so-called Victory Program concluded that the U.S. Army would eventually total some 8.7 million men, and that equipping the U.S. and Allied Forces would require at least a doubling of current production plans at the extraordinary cost of $150 billion. (The war's eventual cost was $304 billion.) In contrast, during the Great War, the United States had only mustered a two-million-man American Expeditionary Force.

By late fall, it became clear that some carmakers were failing to reach half of their production targets for important trucks. And without trucks, the Army would literally grind to a halt. To a certain extent, this was unavoidable. The necessity for all-wheel drive vehicles, such as the workhorse two-and-a-half ton Army truck, gave rise to heavy demands for new and complex components such as velocity joints and rear axles, which required the construction of a whole new motor plant. The concern over motor production became so severe that President Roosevelt dispatched John D. Hertz, a Czech immigrant who founded Yellow Cab Company and Hertz Rent-A-Car, to help fix the problem. Doriot carried out his study in conjunction with Hertz.

After the Japanese bombed Pearl Harbor, the time for dillydallying ended. On December 8, 1941, Undersecretary of War Robert P. Patterson issued a memo to the chiefs of the supply arms and services. "It is essential that our procurement be put into the highest gear at once," he wrote. "All steps must be taken to increase the speed with which contracts are let and to speed up maximum production of munitions."

How would Doriot meet the military's seemingly insatiable demand for trucks? The professor reckoned military vehicle production would require a careful balance of persuasion and precise forecasting. Having completed the survey of automobile requirements and capacity, Doriot and his counterparts understood what they needed from industry and what was humanly possible to produce. Now they just had to convince Detroit to shoot for the same ambitious targets.

Then another wrench was thrown into Doriot's plan: He discovered that he was competing for capacity with the U.S. Navy. On a phone call on the morning of December 27 with another Quartermaster Corps officer, Doriot laid out the problem. "The situation is a very bad one," he said. "Our facilities are melting away and disappearing very fast. On Wednesday I went to lunch at Chrysler, and there came a man from the Office of Production Management sent by the Navy, and they asked to turn over 2 plants for manufacturing of fighting planes for the Navy. I looked into the matter and found obviously that our truck facilities would be decreased."

During that same call, Doriot proposed a strategy: marrying the carrot of patriotism with the stick of shame. Acknowledging that the Army was in no position to run the auto business, his plan was to get high-ranking officers to charge car executives with personal responsibility for specific production goals. "Up to now they have been so fed up with our anxiety to operate them, they just sat back," Doriot explained. "The time has come when we have to do what other parts of government have done. I believe that we should send for Mr. Ford and Mr. Sorenson of the Ford Motor Co. and say, 'Gentlemen, from now on you are in full charge and responsible for the manufacturing of as many jeeps, quarter-ton trucks and one-and-a-half ton trucks as the Army needs.'" To make sure the carmakers met their production targets, Doriot ordered several Quartermaster officers to manage and monitor the relationships with Detroit. Later that day, Doriot led by example: he pestered a General Motors executive to make sure he was on target to deliver four thousand one-and-a-half-ton trucks per month. In the end, Doriot made dozens of phone calls like this during the winter of 1941.

Thanks to the clear production plan and tight links fostered by Doriot, the Quartermaster General was able to place orders for all of the Army's vehicles for 1942 during the last week of 1941. Delays were reduced to a minimum and the Army no longer encountered any major problems securing vehicle capacity. The conversion of the economy to wartime production also miraculously ended the Great Depression. As war orders poured into the factories, America's unemployment rate at the end of 1941 dipped below 10 percent for the first time in more than a decade. Although Doriot was beginning to make his mark, other larger challenges loomed in the near distance.

After Pearl Harbor, when it became clear that the war was going to last a while, Doriot told Edna to come down to Washington to live with him. At the end of 1941, the Quartermaster Corps went through one of its many wartime reorganizations. The Procurement Control Branch became the Production Branch and Lt. Colonel Doriot was placed at the new branch's helm. When Doriot started his new job, he encountered a small group of a dozen older women, occupying a room filled with ferns, cabinets, and mirrors. He quickly cleaned house. "After I removed the ferns, it had the atmosphere of a funeral parlor," joked Doriot. "I removed the old ladies because they were inefficient, and I gave the filing cabinets to the Director of Procurement."

Despite the sorry state of his group, the Production Branch was responsible for some of the most important work performed in the Quartermaster Corps. Specializing in the relationship between military supply and the national economy, the Production Branch handled such key tasks as studying critical and strategic raw material requirements, developing production programs, and bird-dogging contract delinquencies.

Conservation of scarce materials, in fact, was arguably the single most important factor shaping Quartermaster Corps research and development work. Enemy conquests of overseas production plants led to shortages of many raw materials, forcing the use of substitutes. By early 1941, shortages of aluminum, copper, nickel, brass, and stainless steel began jamming up the gears of the the Quartermaster's procurement program. But no material was more critical or in shorter supply than rubber. Cars, trucks, tanks, and planes all relied on rubber tires. If the government failed to increase its rubber supply, the war machine and domestic economy would "collapse," according to a government report. In December 1941, as the Japanese Army raced to the rubber-rich islands of Malaya and Indonesia, the U.S. government issued an order forbidding the sale of new tires.

Doriot set out to fix the rubber problem, conducting another survey of requirements for the precious resource. On February 25, 1942, Doriot delivered an extraordinarily prescient memo to the Chief of the Planning and Control Division. According to his calculations, the nation's stockpile of rubber would be "exhausted by the middle of 1943 if the projected rate of consumption is maintained, and if immediate steps are not taken to replenish it." To head off this catastrophe, Doriot proposed the formation of a "Rubber

Program." The program was based on three legs: conservation of Quartermaster Corps rubber, conservation of rubber by civilians and other military and government agencies, and, most important, increasing the rubber supply.

In his memo, Doriot argued that the rubber conservation program "must be a crusade, led by fearless and intelligent leaders" and proclaimed the failure to conserve rubber was as "damnable as abandoning or turning over war weapons to the enemy." He called for the substitution of rubber in shoes and clothes and even recommended "the rationing of gasoline as a tire conservation measure." Finally, he questioned whether moves were being made "to increase the supply of synthetic rubber," and requested the Quartermaster Corps take "active steps to investigate what is being done along these lines."

Over the next year, the President and U.S. government implemented virtually every recommendation in Doriot's memo. On May 15, 1942 the government announced a gas rationing program. Though gas was not in short supply, the program acknowledged Doriot's theory that gas rationing was the most effective way to conserve rubber. In mid-June, after rationing in seventeen Eastern states sparked outrage within the car-loving country, President Roosevelt initiated a nationwide rubber drive, and during a fireside chat he announced plans to jump-start a new synthetic rubber industry.

Once the rubber drive was successfully completed, Roosevelt appointed financier Bernard Baruch to head a committee that would eradicate the rubber shortage once and for all. The committee was composed of Baruch and Dr. Karl Compton of MIT and Dr. James Conant of Harvard, two of Doriot's closest colleagues. In September, 1942 Baruch released his report, which recommended a nationwide gas rationing program and the development of synthetic rubber plants. Over the next two years, the government invested about $700 million in fifty-one plants. By July 25, 1944, as the synthetic rubber industry churned out an ample supply of rubber, Bradley Dewey, the nation's rubber director, turned in his resignation. Doriot had played a key role in ensuring the supply of the nation's most essential raw material, but his most important job had yet to begin.

In March of 1942, as the mobilization lurched forward, the War Department underwent a major reorganization. The Department was carved up into three main parts: the Army Ground Forces, the Army Air Forces, and the Army Service Forces. Procurement and economic mobilization were taken away from the Office of the Undersecretary of War and given to the Army Service Forces under the command of a charismatic Lieutenant General named Brehon B. Somervell. "Good logistics alone can't win a war," Somervell famously quipped. "Bad logistics alone can lose."

As part of the restructuring, Doriot's responsibility grew. The Production Branch of the Planning and Control Division, which Doriot led, was combined with the Standardization Branch of the Supply Division to create the Resources Division. On April 14, 1942, Doriot was named Chief of the Resources Division. Now, the problems of production, materials conservation, and design specification were all combined in one place under Dariot's leadership.

As head of the Resources Division, the forerunner of the research and development organization of the Quartermaster Corps, Doriot began to foment nothing less than a revolution in military thinking and practice. The revolution was based on the idea that modern war "is in reality applied science." The problem, however, was that during the last two decades before World War II, the military and most of the private sector had essentially ignored peacetime research.

Doriot only served as the head of Resources for four months but he was able to jump-start his revolution with one bold stroke. In the spring, Doriot organized an advisory board composed of nearly one hundred leading American industrialists, scientists, and explorers. The board was a concrete recognition of Doriot's belief that the war could not be won without the help of industry and the scientific establishment. Researchers and executives from leading firms in the fields of chemicals, rubber, and textiles joined the board. Captain Edwin L. Hobson, who served under Doriot for four years, said this was a "brilliant" idea that "made it very easy for us to get things done."

Just as important, Doriot enlisted a number of university laboratories who assisted the military in the development and testing of a range of specialized equipment. The Fatigue Laboratory at Harvard University studied the effects of heat, cold, and altitude on human efficiency; leather problems were analyzed by the Tanners' Council at the University of Cincinnati; and the Textile Laboratory at MIT researched problems of fiber, yarn, and fabric properties.

The collaboration between the military and universities led to a number of ingenious advances. In one of the more creative examples, Doriot heard from General Joseph W. Stilwell, the commander of the China Burma India Theatre, that the locals in his region could easily spot his troops by the imprints of their combat boots. Doriot's team came up with a clever way to hide their tracks. They contacted the anthropologist Margaret Mead, who happened to manage the world's greatest collection of prints of indigenous feet and hands. After visiting Mead, they triumphantly returned with a bunch of molds made from the feet of those natives and took them to the U.S. Rubber Company for fabrication. "We made jungle boots with feet on the bottom," recalled Lt. Colonel William H. McLean, the Assistant Chief of Research and Development. "If you ran down a muddy road you'd swear that was not an American, it was a native." Later on, General Stilwell thanked Doriot and his team for helping to save the lives of his soldiers.

As the war machine revved up, it created yet another unforeseen challenge: staffing shortages. To the perfectionist ex-professor, lack of competent personnel was his most vexing problem. "Between the fact that there was nobody available and between the completely ridiculous personnel policies of the War Department there was no hope to do a good job unless the good Lord was with you," fumed Doriot.

Not surprisingly, Doriot found a way to tiptoe around this landmine. The Quartermaster Corps had three recruiting options: calling Reserve officers to extended duty, requesting transfers of officers from other branches, or commissioning civilians. Doriot took advantage of all three options, but he was particularly effective at recruiting civilians. How so? Over the past fifteen years, Doriot had taught thousands of superb young men at Harvard who felt an allegiance to their professor. So when Doriot was pressed for quality staff, he flipped open his extensive address book.

In that voluminous book, Doriot found the people who had done well in Business School, figured out what companies they worked for, and persuaded them to join the cause. A prime example was William H. McLean, one of Doriot's former assistants at Harvard who later became President of Merck Chemical Company. When Doriot was activated in 1941, he convinced McLean to become his chief assistant—a position he held throughout the entire war. The brilliance of this strategy was captured in a breezy newspaper profile of Doriot just after he had been promoted to the rank of Colonel in July of 1942.

"I don't do the work. I just pick the right, bright men to do it for me." Col. Georges Doriot says that is the reason for his success in the Quartermaster Corps. While teaching at Harvard Business School for the last 15 years, Colonel Doriot always had a sharp eye out for able young men. Today a lot of them are working for him, and never fail to deliver for their indefatigable chief . . . One word is omitted from Colonel Doriot's otherwise complete vocabulary. That word—"impossible." If a thing must be done, it can be done. When there's a need for a substitute Colonel Doriot will find it. But Brigadier General Edmund Gregory of the Quartermaster Corps knows one thing for which there is no substitute, and that is Colonel Doriot."

At the end of July 1942, the Quartermaster Corps underwent its second major reorganization after its vehicle manufacturing responsibilities were transferred to the Transportation Corps and Ordnance Department. As part of the new leaner Corps, General Gregory created a new Military Planning Division (MPD), which absorbed the Production Service of which Doriot was a part. Most importantly, the MPD was charged with developing "Quartermaster items to meet the changing needs and conditions" of global warfare. The Resources Division that Doriot ran was renamed the Research and Development Branch of the MPD, and Doriot was appointed its chief.

Doriot had found another mission: starting the world's largest research organization from scratch. As Doriot summed up the challenge, the military needed to be "prepared to fight in Maine in the summer and Florida in winter." This meant he had to develop a new combat gear system for millions of soldiers for all kinds of terrain and climate, amidst shortages of many raw materials—all while operating under the imperative to reduce the volume of equipment to lighten the soldier's load and conserve shipping space.

The R&D Branch was not perfect, and occasional mistakes were made. But under the leadership of Doriot, the Army developed and delivered hundreds of new items of clothing, food, and gear that contributed greatly to the safety and power of millions of soldiers. Although bombs, radar, and jet propulsion technologies garnered much of the limelight during the war, Doriot's compassion for soldiers coupled with his ability to bring together the best and brightest wrought a quiet revolution in engineering for Allied soldiers. "He is probably the best manager that I or probably anyone else in the Quartermaster ever encountered," said Major Edward L. Heller, who served under Doriot.

Doriot believed the military overlooked the human factor. "The Army has no interest in the soldier as a human being," Doriot told officers at the Army Industrial College. "I want to make a very strong point of that—that to this day there is a complete lack of understanding of the problems of human beings and the problem of making a human being a good fighting person."

Doriot sought to reverse that philosophy: He understood it is the soldiers that ultimately win a war, and without the proper food and equipment a soldier is not an effective fighting machine. The equipment developed under Doriot included dozens of innovative items used by both the military and civilians, including water-repellent fabrics and shoes, backpacks, insecticides, sunscreen, and plastic armor, among many other marvels of engineering. Before the war, no one thought to measure the foot space in a tank to see how the soldiers' shoes would fit in such cramped quarters. But Doriot did. In fact, Doriot once had a tank delivered to his parking lot in Washington, D.C.

Dozens of young men and women streamed into the Research Branch on the second floor of Temporary Building A near the Army War College. They were all smartly dressed in suits and ties and dresses, sat at long rows of desks, and couldn't be happier to be working for such a respected leader. "It was such a feeling of togetherness and wanting to do your best," says Isabelle Pounder, a secretary to Doriot's administrative officer. "We would work until 12 a.m. to get out a document. It was all for the boys and women. There was no profit motive and no glorification of yourself."

Doriot depended on two men to be his gatekeepers: Henry W. Hoagland, a former student and Colorado native who also earned a law degree from Stanford, and Henry R. Davis Jr. Both men were stationed in front of Doriot's office, filtering the flow of information and people. "Everybody had to get past Harry to see Doriot," said Ray Hoagland. "He would screen people but not ruffle their feathers. That's why Doriot liked him."

To understand the problems and needs of soldiers, Doriot developed a field observer group that spent extensive time in the battlefield gathering feedback on Quartermaster Corps gear. Whenever observer reports came back from the field, Doriot asked to see them immediately. "One of the wonderful peculiarities of General Doriot was that he didn't want word coming back from channels," recalled Captain Orr, one of his most trusted field observers, who later became the governor of Indiana. He continued:

He knew it would take forever. And they'd run into people that didn't agree and they'd get stifled. He wanted us to violate all kinds of rules and regulations and just write us a letter and put a stamp on it. It was a rare opportunity to express myself to someone who would read it with intense interest and start to do something about it. It would not be laid in a desk and forgotten about. It would not be stifled because of bureaucracy. It would be moved and action would be taken because that's the kind of person Georges Doriot was.

To perfect the creation of Quartermaster Corps gear, Doriot initiated an ambitious testing program run by the Special Forces section, an elite crew of explorers, mountaineers, and military globe-trotters who had spent years living in ice fields, deserts, and jungles. At any time, half of the Special Forces could be found in the field testing equipment. One significant mission given to the Special Forces was the testing of arctic, mountain, and emergency clothing and gear developed by the Quartermaster. Between late May and early August of 1942, in order to test this gear, a group of thirteen Special Forces soldiers and four men from the American Alpine Club achieved the first ascent of Mt. McKinley since 1932. Planes parachuted loads of garments, footwear, tents, and sleeping bags into the 18,000 foot basin of the mountain, where the Special Forces retrieved the supplies and tested them in bitter cold and heavy storms. It was dangerous work. One captain from the Royal Canadian Army, who fractured four vertebrae during the climb, nearly died before two of his comrades escorted him down through 15,000 feet of deep snow and narrow ridges to the base of the mountain. Captain Robert H. Bates, an officer with the Quartermaster Corps who participated in this ascent, wrote of their exploits in *The American Alpine Journal*. "At one point, two of us, to our great disgust, were unable to walk for five days, so energetically had we tested some special boots," he wrote. "But the skinned feet definitely served their purpose, for information we relayed to Washington by radio that day changed the design of the boots and saved many men this winter from equally painful feet."

On October 1, 1943, Doriot received another promotion. General Gregory appointed Doriot as Director of the entire Military Planning Division.

Doriot was the division's third director, and he held this position for the remainder of the war. Interestingly, even though Doriot was promoted, he held onto his job as Chief of the Division's Research & Development Branch, underscoring his belief that research was the keystone of the division's activities. Under Doriot, the division flourished. When it was first set up, it employed 542 people. By July 1945, when it peaked in personnel, more than two thousand men and women were working for Doriot. And it wasn't just the number of people that was so impressive; Doriot was also wielding a multibillion dollar budget.

Georges wasn't the only Doriot putting in twelve-hour days, seven days a week. Edna was doing her part to help win the war also, managing the Junior Army-Navy Guild organization, or JANGO, a volunteer group that took care of soldiers shuttling in and out of Washington. Mrs. Robert Patterson, wife of the Undersecretary of War, was JANGO's chairwoman. Edna helped to recruit personnel, mostly daughters of Army, Navy, and Air Force officers. Later on, Edna volunteered to head up the fund-raising committee for the Washington Symphony Orchestra.

Georges and Edna never went out socially during the entire war except for one memorable night. Lt. Colonel Charles MacArthur, the playwright who penned *Front Page*, had given Doriot two tickets to a play starring Oscar-winning actress Helen Hayes. Doriot invited MacArthur back to his apartment after the show, but being socially clueless he and Edna were not aware that MacArthur was actually married to Hayes. Afterward, Edna was astonished when the Colonel and his glamorous wife dropped by their apartment for a drink.

Edna simplified Georges's life in other ways. She eased his recruiting effort by arranging for more than a dozen men to live in their apartment building. Quite frequently, she was also pressed into improvisational hosting. "Often I would show up with one or two scientists or industrial people that Edna did not expect, so she had to do whatever she could to get food tickets and buy things in order to feed them," said Georges.

Food was on the mind of Georges Doriot quite a bit, actually. In December of 1942, the responsibility for developing food was transferred to the R&D branch of the Quartermaster Corps. The provision of nutritious, compact, and appetizing rations marked perhaps the most spectacular success of the Quartermaster Corps. "It is our opinion that the most critical and urgent problems are in the food field and it is there that the bulk of our attention will be focused," said Doriot in a 1944 address before the National Academy of Sciences. According to Doriot's calculations, the food industry spent less on research than any other industry, devoting only .02 percent of its income to this field. "It is because so little has been done in a scientific way on foods before the war, that we now find that so many unsolved problems confront us," said Doriot. "Food has more or less been taken for granted, not only by the consumers but by the processors and the scientists."

To solve the challenge of developing and distributing massive amounts of nutritious food on short notice, Doriot oversaw the world's largest set of nutrition experiments. The research was concentrated in the Subsistence Research Laboratory in the Chicago Quartermaster Depot, and also involved the coordination of a host of advisors, private companies, foundations, and universities. The Quartermaster learned much from these tests and quickly applied the findings to the improvement of rations. Researchers, for instance, determined that preflight and in-flight diets high in carbohydrates and low in fat and protein enabled flight crews to withstand the strain of high altitude far better than other diets. The finding resulted in a measurable decrease in the number of flying accidents that had heretofore been attributed to "causes unknown."

Like other aspects of procurement, there were a few failures. War food was not exactly haute cuisine, after all, but it wasn't supposed to be. Soldiers reserved a particular scorn for the powdered lemonade, which they found more useful as stove cleaner or hair rinse. And they despised the biscuits. "In the early days of the war, we made biscuits which were filled with so many things that are good for you that the men wouldn't eat them," admitted Doriot in a 1944 address to the Nutrition Foundation. "The biscuits now in the rations are less of a monument to Nutritional Science, but they are still nourishing, and the men find them more palatable monuments."

By and large, though, the food program was a remarkable success. Despite their complaints, soldiers ate millions of specially prepared rations, and it kept them going. All told, the Quartermaster Corps developed eleven special rations to meet the different requirements of global, mobile warfare. Fresh foods made up most of the "A" ration served in home training camps. The "B" ration, served in mess halls overseas, was comprised of canned foods, supplemented by local produce. Other rations were developed for the soldier in varying combat zones. The original "C" ration, for instance, was designed for men in combat. It contained six small cans, three with a protein, usually meat, and three with a carbohydrate, such as bread. The "K" ration, the most compact of the lot, was made up of three pocket-size packages labeled "Breakfast," "Dinner," and "Supper." Each of the packages contained meat or some other protein, two kinds of biscuits, a powder-made drink, a sweet, gum, and a few cigarettes of an unknown brand—a substitution that prompted the infamous war cry, "Wot! No Camels? No Luckies?" Still, military studies showed that the K ration more than doubled the fighting effectiveness of a combat brigade.

On February 1, 1943, the Quartermaster Corps drew heavy fire. Word got back to the Quartermaster Corps that Chief of Staff General George Marshall, following an inspection tour of the combat zone in North Africa, had come to the conclusion that the Army's present shoes "were unfit for field use." The shoe in the combat zone, wrote General W. D. Styer, "appears to be too light, and too much on the order of the garrison shoe, for field service. It is requested that the Quartermaster General look into this matter and be prepared to discuss it with the Chief of Staff when he so requests."

The shoe General Marshall criticized was the Type II shoe—a hastily revised version of a peacetime combat shoe—whose sole lasted only two to three weeks. In fairness to the Quartermaster Corps, the Type II shoe was compromised by various conservation directives. As shortages of leather, brass, and rubber increased in 1942, rubber taps and heels on initial versions of the shoe were replaced with lighter insoles, cork filler material, reclaimed rubber taps, wood-core heels and zinc-coated steel reinforcing nails.

Nevertheless, the Quartermaster Corps was prepared to deal with General Marshall's rebuke. During the fall of 1942, the Quartermaster had already initiated development of a boot to replace the much-despised shoe and canvas legging combination in use since the beginning of the war. Approximately fifteen new models had been built incorporating sturdier parts, including different boot uppers, closures, and sole materials.

Consequently, on February 5, 1943, when Colonel Doriot was invited with some top brass to a meeting to discuss the shoe problem, he was able to bring some new shoe samples with him. However, as a junior officer, he was ordered not to talk. Several officers and shoemakers told General Marshall the current shoes were fine. Then Marshall turned to Doriot.

"Your shoes only last 13 days in combat," said General Marshall, giving Colonel Doriot an opening. "Do you have anything to say?"

"Oh, yes, sir, a great deal," replied Doriot. "For four or five months we have been trying to get staff approval for this combat boot and we can't get it. We know that our present shoes are not good for combat; the shoe leather isn't good. I'm surprised they even get to the combat zone."

"What do you want?" asked General Marshall.

"I want approval for that combat boot," replied Doriot. "Industry does not want to make it but we must have it. The Army Services Forces Headquarters is completely opposed to it."

"This is a citizen's army," said General Marshall. "I want them well taken care of. I want to save their lives, and if you have to spoil them, do it, and from now any time you have trouble you come to me." General Marshall then gave Doriot his phone number on a piece of paper. "What do you wish from me today?" General Marshall asked.

Doriot asked for a large amount of shoes for a production test. A decision was made to shift production from the Type II shoe to a new Type III shoe, and to produce a new sturdier combat boot in limited quantities for testing purposes.

General Gregory and Colonel Doriot snapped into action. The Quartermaster Corps immediately changed the specification for the Service Shoe and delivery of seven hundred thousand pairs of Type III service shoes began in April 1943. Simultaneously, the Quartermaster Corps delivered one hundred thousand pairs of combat boots for testing. While tests took place in the field, Doriot enlisted the aid of the shoe and leather industries to study the specifications for the new combat boot. Consequently, it was recommended the boot include full rubber soles and heels, flesh-out leather, and reinforcement nailing of the sole. In November, the Quartermaster Corps Technical Committee approved the recommendations of Doriot's committee and standardized the boot's specs. By January 1944, the shoe industry began producing the combat boot for regular issue. In the relatively brief span of eleven months, Doriot had led the Quartermaster Corps to design and produce two entirely new shoes that vastly improved the fighting ability of Allied soldiers.

In the summer of 1943, as the mobilization kicked into high gear, the Quartermaster's R&D section once again almost ground to a halt due to personnel shortages. Between April and August, Doriot's branch lost sixty-three men, or about 20 percent of its staff, to the draft, to the Navy, or through resignation. Meanwhile, the Quartermaster's responsibilities continued to grow. On July 10, 160,000 American troops invaded Italy through Sicily in Operation Husky. A few weeks later, Benito Mussolini was removed from office by the King of Italy, Vittorio Emanuele III. In late November, at the Teheran Conference, meeting with Stalin and Churchill, President Roosevelt finally committed to a massive European attack. The Quartermaster Corps would have to supply almost three million troops for the final cross-Channel assault against Germany.

While the Quartermaster Corps geared up for Operation Overlord, Doriot was selected to take over the management of a confidential military project to develop a new type of plastic armor. This work was ultimately some of the most valuable service that Doriot performed during his military career, and its legacy continues today in the ongoing evolution of body armor. One of Doriot's staff officers recommended the name of "Doron" for the armor, as a way to honor him and provide camouflage for the project. The name stuck. Strict secrecy was maintained as Dow Chemical Company, Monsanto, and other manufacturers signed up on the project.

Indeed, the development of plastic armor, which required fast-paced and close collaboration between industry and the military, was a classic example of American wartime ingenuity. In order to achieve this engineering miracle, Doriot would have to overcome material shortages and the deeply felt skepticism of the Army and the steel industry towards this new material, while overseeing the development of new fabrics, resins, and complex manufacturing processes. Old-line Army ordnance experts were bitterly opposed to the theory that high-tensile-strength fabrics could offer superior ballistic protection to the conventional armor made of hardened manganese steel.

The story of Doron began in December 1940, when Rear Admiral Harold G. Bowen noticed a magazine advertisement showing Henry Ford hacking away with an axe at a plastic car fender. Bowen, who had been following the new plastics industry, called Dr. G. R. Irwin, head of the Naval Research Laboratory's ballistics section. Irwin immediately launched a research project on the ballistic potential of plastics. Following extensive preliminary work, the Navy Bureau of Aeronautics backed the program in order to produce antiflak suits for Navy and Marine Corps airmen, since a primary source of injury and death of Air Corps men was flak fragments. The Navy did provide aviators with steel flak suits at the time, but many flyboys refused to wear them because they were too hot and heavy.

Cut to 1942. In June of that year, Colonel Doriot ordered his Plastics Section to investigate the use of plastics for light armor after the Quartermaster Corps was unable to obtain Hadfield steel for the civilian defense helmets it was charged with making. The Quartermaster, which was also responsible for making the liners for combat helmets, thought that a plastic armor liner would prove a worthy substitute given steel shortages.

On September 29, 1943, the Commanding Generals of the Army Service Force and the Army Air Force approved the establishment of a "Joint Army-Navy Plastic Armor Technical Committee," dubbed JANPAC. The Quartermaster Corps would handle the development of the plastic materials, while the Naval Research Lab was responsible for overseeing the ballistic studies and test evaluations.

On November 13, at the second JANPAC meeting, Doriot was elected chairman of the group. Over the next few months, a variety of tests offered conflicting conclusions. Some tests found that the ballistic efficiency of plastic armor was superior to steel, while others proved the opposite. At one point, the Army ordered Doriot to drop the project. "But the Navy was kind enough to give me money on the side to continue the program," Doriot revealed at a conference of the Society of Plastics Engineers after the war.

In the spring of 1944, however, the Navy conducted a spectacular Doron demonstration, which helped the Army to overcome most of their opposition to plastic armor. In a shack near the Naval Medical Center in Maryland, two brave officers from the Navy Bureau of Medicine and Surgery staged a William Tell act. Lt. Commander Andrew Paul Webster aimed a .45 caliber automatic pistol at his friend, Lt. Commander Edward Lyman Corey, who wore a flak jacket stuffed with Doron plates. He fired away. The bullet smashed into the vest and fell harmlessly into the hands of Lt. Commander Corey.

"As a result of that, for one day I was a millionaire," recalled Captain Henry W. Clowe, who worked in the R&D Branch. Captain Clowe received a letter from the Bureau of Ships with a check for $5 million. "Will you please buy us 60,000 suits of body armor?" asked the Bureau. "I took it into Hobson, and we took it into Doriot, and we went ahead and procured those."

Doron was first used in the Pacific theatre. The Marine Corps equipped a whole battalion with plastic armor for landing operations. During the Korean War, the Army distributed eighty to ninety thousand flak jackets for protection. And the vests saved many lives. One soldier was on patrol when a mortar shell exploded ten feet away from him. "I picked five pieces of shell fragments out of my vest," said Marine Private First Class Lee Ward of Maplewood, Missouri. "Didn't bother me. Another guy on the same patrol stopped six burp-gun slugs with his jacket. All he got out of it was a couple of bruises."

In the beginning of 1945, with the United States on the verge of victory in Europe, a spate of reports appeared in top American newspapers that were highly critical of the U.S. military: "G.I.s Seen Poorly Clad and Freezing; Eisenhower Admits 'Isolated Cases'"; "Yanks Suffering From Cold, Lack of Proper Shoes"; "Trench Foot Scourge Ends, but Many Yanks Are Still Hospitalized." While troops always had plenty of food and medical supplies, the *Washington Post*, *New York Times*, and other papers reported that the military had let GI Joe down by failing to properly equip him to fight in harsh winter conditions.

The stories rocked the U.S. Army. In fact, the Chief Quartermaster of the European Theatre of Operations, Major General Robert M. Littlejohn, was so upset that in a letter to Lt. General Somervell he pointed the finger at the Office of the Quartermaster General, accusing it of spreading "deliberate lies" in a "malicious campaign" to protect its own hide. General Littlejohn even asked the Inspector General of the War Department to investigate the leaks. In March 1945, General Somervell responded by appointing Colonel Charles Garside to look into the matter. Six weeks later, Colonel Garside delivered a report mostly exonerating General Littlejohn, but the controversy continued to burn for nearly two decades after the war ended.

What had happened? Did the Quartermaster Corps or someone in Washington fall down on the job? Was it Doriot's fault? There is no simple answer. The failure of the U.S. military to adequately equip the American GIs during the winter of 1944 can be attributed to a spiderweb of wartime factors. The resistance of industry, imperfections in the procurement planning process, underestimating replacements rates, shockingly low requests for winter gear by U.S. commanders, prolonged periods of front-line service, limited shipping space, rubber shortages, and the virtual impossibility of eliminating cold and wet feet while operating in a brutal winter—they all played a part in the failure.

But the truth of the matter is that were it not for the brave actions of Colonel Doriot and a group of senior Quartermaster Corps officers, the problems would have been a whole lot worse. Spurred by the work of the Research Branch, Quartermaster Corps representatives took every opportunity to stress the importance of requisitioning shoepacs and overshoes that had been developed for winter operations. Doriot boldly exposed the heel-dragging of American shoe manufacturers, which helped to boost the quality and quantity of boot production. And when told to slash the production of winter jackets and sweaters by Commanding General Eisenhower, Doriot resisted the order at the risk of insubordination. By holding the line, the Corps was able to supply soldiers with hundreds of thousands of additional items of winter clothes, which kept them warm and dry. While only thousands of American GIs suffered from cases of frostbite and trenchfoot, the German Army in the East in 1941 alone endured one hundred thousand frostbite casualties, rendering the Ostheer virtually incapable of movement.

Doriot first stood up for GI Joe when he aired his concerns about the shoe program during a luncheon at the Boston Chamber of Commerce on May 26, 1944. His remarks were featured in a story in the *Boston Daily Globe* the next day. "Shoe Manufacturers Balk on Army Boots, Officer Tells Chamber," rang the headline. The story reported Doriot's remarks that "American soldiers are suffering needlessly from trench foot and jungle sores because New England shoe manufacturers are refusing or resisting the Army's requests that they manufacture in greater quantities a new type of combat boot with a leather collar." The story also reported Doriot's charges that manufacturers suggested the use of substitute materials or just refused to bid on contracts, shying away from making goods that would be outmoded after the war ended. "Altogether too many business men think that the war is over," Doriot was quoted.

A few days after the story came out, the shoe industry counterpunched. Major General Gregory received a letter from Colonel W. J. Calvert, the commanding officer of the Boston Quartermaster Depot. The *Boston Daily Globe* story, wrote Calvert, "has caused no end of unfavorable comment in the shoe industry, and has a tendency to neutralize the good will that had been built up by this Depot over a long period." Calvert ended the note by requesting that the Quartermaster General issue a press release "counter-acting the effects of this negative publicity."

Major General Gregory denied Calvert's request. To bolster his decision, General Gregory reiterated Doriot's point that many shoemakers went out of their way to slow down or stop the Combat Boot Program. "I believe [Doriot's] statements were correct and I believe that more shoes would have been delivered on time if you had made these same statements at an earlier date," wrote Gregory. "If you worked harder and did not collapse every time a manufacturer tells you he does not want to do something on time, there would have been no need for some of the statements made by Colonel Doriot!"

But it wasn't only the business community that thought the war was over. Some American military commanders also sensed a premature victory. On May 18, 1944, General Eisenhower, then Commanding General of European Theatre Operations, sent a secret radiogram requesting that neither the new popular field jacket nor the high-neck sweater—two key items of winter combat clothing—be shipped to the European theatre. And thus began a bureaucratic war in the military over the proper supply of clothing for the winter of 1944–1945.

General Gregory quickly wrote a memo to War Department General Staff and Lt. General Somervell warning that such action would leave troops "without any garment designed for efficiency of operations in wet cold climates." Gregory closed the letter by recommending the provision of the field jacket and high-neck sweater for European operations. Troops had begun clamoring for the three-quarter length, water-repellant field jacket, after proving its worth in the Italian theatre. General Gregory's initial entreaty failed. On June 9, the General Staff reissued the order to eliminate requirements for the two items, except for Parachute and Armored Force troops. A week later, after more Quartermaster Corps lobbying, European commanders reversed their decision on the sweaters. But they still held firm on the field jacket.

Then a series of directives threatened to turn the winter clothing problem into a fiasco. The success of D-day, and the breakout from Normandy at the end of August 1944, coupled with landings in southern France, saw the Allies advance toward Germany faster than anticipated. On August 31, Lt. General Somervell directed the Quartermaster Technical Services to reduce stock levels from ninety days to forty-five days. In September, the European theatre advised the Quartermaster Corps of its requirements for the fourth quarter. They were so low that mass cancellation of various clothing items seemed necessary at once. The stress of constantly defending GI Joe took a toll on Doriot. He was down to 138 pounds in November, 12 pounds below his normal weight.

Sensing disaster, Doriot sprung into action. Following his orders, the Military Planning Division limited its downward readjustments. As much as possible, Doriot delayed adjustments to lower stock levels into 1945. The Quartermaster Corps also refused the Army Service Forces' request to drop the shoepac, instead pushing through a huge requirement. In addition, Doriot's division wrote a memo to the headquarters of the Army Service Forces requesting that it put pressure on the War Production Board to ensure the delivery of fourth-quarter leather allocations for the shoe program. And on September 19, Doriot refused to approve the master production schedule that called for cutting in half the number of field jackets on the grounds that it "fails to meet the requirements for the European and North African Theatres of Operation."

At the end of the summer and through early fall, as it became clear the Germans were not going down without a big fight, European commanders began submitting requisitions for gear that were significantly larger than orders of the past few months—just as Doriot had predicted. Thanks to all of the steps taken by Gregory, Doriot, and other Quartermaster Corps officers, it was possible to fill a great number of those requisitions. Were it not for all of these measures, it is likely that hundreds of thousands of soldiers would have been unprepared to deal with the cold, wet winter during the Battle of the Bulge, the bloodiest and largest battle in U.S. military history.

As the war drew to a close, top officials in the military further recognized the technical and organizational genius of Doriot. On February 12, 1945, Doriot received a stunning promotion to the rank of Brigadier General. It was unusual for a Quartermaster Corps officer to receive such a high rank. But Doriot had proven not only his own value, but also the value of the Corps in fighting a modern global war. Commanding General Eisenhower sent Doriot a note of congratulations upon his appointment.

On May 7, one week after Hitler committed suicide in a concrete bunker underneath the chancellery, the German high command unconditionally surrendered all remaining German forces. The next day, as Western Allies declared V-E day, Doriot sent a humble memo of praise to the entire staff of the Military Planning Division. "We in the Military Planning Division can be proud of what we have done," he wrote. "Like everyone else we have made mistakes, but we have acknowledged them, and from them we have derived a lesson on how to do better."

On October 30, 1945, Doriot received the Distinguished Service Medal, the highest military award possible for a noncombatant. The citation succinctly captured Doriot's genius: "His professional knowledge, aggressive leadership, foresight, untiring devotion to duty, and executive ability contributed in high degree to the development of new and improved Quartermaster items. His energy, initiative, and outstanding supervision developed fundamental scientific facts concerning the clothing and feeding of the Army. General Doriot's outstanding accomplishments contributed greatly to the health and welfare of the military forces."

But it was the personal letters from top military officials that gave Doriot the most joy, for they were the people that he worked so hard to please. After the war, Doriot received dozens of letters of thanks from many military poohbahs, including the Secretary of War. He returned the favor: in early 1946, he sent hundreds of letters of thanks to companies, universities, and other institutions that had helped the Quartermaster Corps fulfill its mission. On May 6, 1946, Doriot was released from the Quartermaster Corps.

Doriot had been called to duty to accomplish his most impossible mission to date. But he had risen to the occasion on the world's biggest stage. Doriot and his men and women were not heroes in the traditional sense. They did not risk their lives fighting on the front lines. But to the extent that that they helped protect and save the lives of soldiers, they demonstrated a heroic effort. For while the United States lost approximately 400,000 people during World War II, 23 million people died in the Soviet Union, Germany lost 5.5 million, and Japan lost 2 million. "I want to congratulate you personally and officially on the very superior work that you have done in supplying the most durable and comfortable equipment that could be devised," wrote Major General R. B. McClure. "Without question, the U.S. forces in this war were the best fed, the best clothed and equipped troops in all military history."

Thanks to the war, Doriot had learned how to practice venture capital. Now it was time for him to put that experience to use for the good of the peacetime economy.

SEVEN

FOUNDING
FATHERS

(1946–1951)

FOR MANY MEN AND women who came of age in the mid-twentieth century, World War II was the defining experience of their lives. This was as true for Georges Doriot as anyone else. But Doriot's wartime experience was unique in one way: while Uncle Sam was eager to discharge millions of Americans and return them to private life after the war, the military brass were keen on securing the talents of the ascendant Brigadier General.

The recent conflict had proven beyond a doubt the value of bringing the nation's science and technology assets to bear on the art of war-making. Doriot was one of only a handful of military leaders who articulated that vision, and had the leadership skills required to transform it into reality. So after the war ended, Doriot received a call from the Secretary of War Robert Patterson, who asked him to head up a new office in the War Department General Staff dedicated to research and development. In case Doriot had any doubts, added Secretary Patterson, General Eisenhower himself believed Doriot was the right man for this job.

Along with Doriot, General Eisenhower was early to recognize the significance to the military of the nation's technical and industrial know-how. On April 30, 1946, Eisenhower, who had been recently appointed as the U.S.

Army's Chief of Staff, distributed a visionary four-page memo on this subject to senior military commanders. In the memo, he laid out a five-point policy designed to ensure the full use of the nation's resources under the leadership of a new Department of Research and Development. "The armed forces could not have won the war alone," wrote Eisenhower. "Scientists and businessmen contributed techniques and weapons which enabled us to outwit and overwhelm the enemy . . . This pattern of integration must be translated into a peacetime counterpart which will not merely familiarize the army with the progress made in science and industry, but draw into our planning for national security all the civilian resources which can contribute to the defense of the country."

It was a plum job, no doubt. But Doriot told Secretary Patterson that after devoting the last five years of his life to serving his country he needed to get back to Harvard and start making some money. Secretary Patterson didn't give up. He asked Doriot if he would serve as deputy for the incoming director while they set up the new research office. Doriot agreed. He stayed on the job for a few months but he did not like his boss, and the esprit de corps that had infused his wartime work had all but vanished. "There was no hope of doing anything very constructive and everybody was sort of bossed out and fed up with Army expenditures," recalled Doriot.

In the meantime, Doriot received another urgent call from a cabinet official, the Secretary of the Treasury John W. Snyder, who had recently been appointed by President Truman. Secretary Snyder told Doriot he had one very big problem: the disposal of Army, Navy, and Air Force surplus of all kinds. To get rid of $27 billion dollars of leftover equipment, gear, and supplies, Secretary Snyder said the government planned to merge all of the related surplus activities into one organization called the War Assets Administration, and that he believed Doriot should take over the new entity.

It was another extraordinary offer but Doriot politely declined. Secretary Snyder asked him to pick someone to head up the organization and Doriot recommended his old boss, Lieutenant General Edmund Gregory. Again, the military asked Doriot to serve as a deputy in the interim, but Doriot declined, informing the Secretary that he had already agreed to serve on the War Department's General Staff as deputy for research and development. But in response, Doriot recalled, Secretary Snyder barked, "The Army could wait but War Assets could not," and that he could arrange a peaceful transfer for

Doriot. Snyder followed through and Doriot became War Assets' deputy administrator for policy coordination. It was interesting and bewildering work, but Doriot knew he was not the right man for the job. "I had more friends than I could cope with," recalled Doriot. "Governors and presidents of companies would come looking for something to be purchased at low cost."

While it was true that Doriot did want to return to Harvard and resume his comfortable life as a professor, his thoughts were increasingly consumed by an entirely new enterprise that had little to do with teaching or the military, his two lifelong professional pursuits. Doriot was about to take on a new, seemingly impossible quest: the creation of a venture capital industry and entrepreneurial movement that would ensure the postwar prosperity of the American economy. Instead of fighting fascism, Doriot would battle for the next twenty-five years against an array of domestic forces that included clueless government regulators, shortsighted lawmakers, and ultraconservative investment managers.

The revival of the venture capital idea began quickly after World War II. Following the Japanese surrender, MIT President Karl Compton dusted off his plans to create a new type of financial firm that would finance the development of technical and engineering companies. It was time to put science back to work. So Compton gathered his old pals from the New Products Committee of the New England Council, including Ralph Flanders, Merrill Griswold, and Donald K. David, the dean of Harvard Business School, and persuaded them to form a venture capital firm.

On June 6, 1946, the American Research and Development Corporation (ARD) was incorporated under Massachusetts law by Flanders, Taft-Pierce Manufacturing Company President Frederick S. Blacksall Jr., former National Rubber Director Bradley Dewey, and MIT Treasurer Horace S. Ford. ARD was formed, wrote Doriot in the company's first annual report, "to aid in the development of new or existing businesses into companies of stature and importance."

ARD was one of a few venture capital firms created after the war. Early in 1946 two wealthy East coast families formed the venture capital organizations J. H Whitney & Company and Rockefeller Brothers Company. But

ARD was the first professional venture firm that sought to raise money from nonfamily sources—primarily institutional investors such as insurance companies, educational organizations, and investment trusts. This was a critical development since it greatly expanded the potential amount of money that could be devoted to venture capital. As the first public venture firm, ARD also distinguished itself by seeking to democratize entrepreneurship by focusing on technical ventures and by providing the intellectual leadership for this small, nascent community.

In hindsight, it's not surprising that Boston would serve as a springboard for the venture capital movement. Since its founding in the seventeenth century, Boston has always been fueled by an Enlightenment belief in scientific progress and human perfectibility. It is home to America's first public school, Boston Latin School (1635), and college, Harvard College (1636). After the American Revolution, Boston became a major shipping port and leader in manufacturing new mechanical or scientific instruments. And the city has always had a revolutionary streak, with movements for women's suffrage, antislavery, and the American Revolution itself all growing out of its cobblestone alleys and streets.

Georges Doriot embodied these same traits—innovation, risk-taking, and an unwavering belief in human potential—in human form. After the war, the stage was set for an explosion of innovation, and Doriot was in a perfect position to the light the fuse. As a professor of the leading business school and a director of dozens of companies, Doriot had become an expert in finance and technology manufacturing. And thanks to the war, Doriot had gained a lifetime of experience in organizing and managing new ventures in a pressure-cooker environment.

It is not surprising, then, that the former head of the New England Council's Venture Capital Subcommittee was ARD's first choice for president. But Doriot could not take the job, as he was still employed by the Army. So in the interim, the directors named him chairman of the board of directors. Flanders, in the midst of running for the U. S. Senate, was chosen as acting president until Doriot could shake free from the service. Joseph W. Powell Jr., a Harvard Business School graduate (class of 1926) and an energetic salesman and assistant director of advertising at Time, Incorporated, was appointed ARD's vice president. In addition, MIT provided much of the technical expertise through its three-member board of advisors, comprising MIT President Compton, chemical engineering professor Edwin R. Gilliland, and Jerome C. Hunsaker, the head of MIT's Department of Aeronautical Engineering.

The group of men who founded ARD believed it could crack the conundrum of the risk-less economy. And now that the war was over, they were in a position to do something about it. Money for new enterprises had been restricted, they believed, by the New Deal's onerous tax system, and by the increasing prominence of ultraconservative investment trusts. Investment trusts and life insurance companies accounted for an expanding portion of the U.S. savings market, but they were reluctant to invest in risky new ventures. Custom and prudence dictated that the trustees of these firms confined their investments to high-grade bonds or blue-chip securities. Flanders, who observed this problem during his presidency of the Federal Reserve Bank, succinctly explained the purpose of ARD in an address he gave in November 1945 before the National Association of Security Commissioners in Chicago.

"We have the [greatest] number of possibilities for new investments. We have various means for selecting the most attractive possibilities and for spreading the risk on those selected. Does this not furnish a sound business basis for trying new methods of applying development capital? We cannot depend safely for an indefinite time on the expansion of our old big industries alone. We need new strength, energy and ability from below. We need to marry some small part of our enormous fiduciary resources to the new ideas which are seeking support."

According to this theory, venture capitalists were like the matchmakers of the modern economy. They would marry money with people and their crazy, new ideas. And the result would be a stronger country with a growing supply of well-paying jobs.

In forming ARD, its founders were guided by an intuitive understanding of the dynamics of entrepreneurship. They realized that organizations with "enormous fiduciary resources" and the seasoned operators running them were not daredevils skilled in the art of invention, and that, conversely, inventors were struggling creative types with no money "trying desperately to become poor businessmen" in Doriot's witty description. ARD sought to bring together these two interdependent yet largely separate communities. Heeding the prewar lesson of Enterprise Associates, the founders agreed to raise $5 million in capital by selling two hundred thousand shares of ARD common stock at $25 a share.

The idea of venture capital was so new that ARD's founders were forced to reengineer aspects of various financial regulatory structures in order to make their idea viable. Before ARD could offer its stock, for instance, it had to obtain a number of exemptions under the Investment Company Act of 1940 from the Securities and Exchange Commission. ARD was aided by the fact that one of its board members, attorney Warren Motley, was also a counsel to the National Association of Investment Companies who helped write the 1940 Investment Company Act, a key piece of legislation that aimed to restore the public trust in capital markets after the 1929 stock market crash.

In writing the 1940 Act, Congress and the Securities and Exchange Commission sought to prevent investment companies from extending their control through investment pyramids, as was done frequently in the 1920s. Consequently, one section of the Act stated that an investment company could not own more than 3 percent of another investment company's voting stock. This would have precluded the Massachusetts Investors Trust from buying a large block of ARD stock.

Luckily, Motley used his connections and financial savvy to help ARD obtain exemptions from this section and others on the ground that it was "in the public interest and consistent with the protection of investors." The most important exemptions permitted ARD to hold more than 5 percent of the stock of a company, permitted any investment company to purchase up to 9.9 percent of ARD's shares, and allowed ARD to sell its shares to not only investment companies but also other fiduciary organizations. Final approval of the deal was based on ARD's receiving $3 million in subscriptions, with at least half of that coming from institutions.

ARD engineered other legal changes to boost its chance of success. The "blue sky" laws of some states prevented investment trusts from investing in common stocks that were less than three to five years old, or had not paid dividends for several years. Since ARD specified that half of its capital had to come from institutions, its founders felt it was necessary to lobby four states, including Ohio and New Hampshire, to modify their regulations. Dean Donald K. David of Harvard Business School, Merrill Griswold, the chairman of the Securities and Exchange Commission, and several other prominent industrialists and lawyers mounted a successful campaign to relax the laws of these states.

The formation of ARD was covered by many leading newspapers and magazines. All of the stories centered on its star-studded lineup and the firm's groundbreaking mission. A story in the *Boston Globe* started with the headline, "Venture Enterprise of Unusual Management," and concluded that "if this company does not pan out, it will not be because it has not plenty of the right kind of brains behind it." In explaining the purpose of the firm, its founders were unusually honest, admitting up front that failure was part of their financial calculus. "While all projects may not be successful," Flanders was quoted in a *New York Herald Tribune* story, "it is the consensus of those best acquainted with the mass of new developments coming out of the war activity that enough of the projects will turn out to be profitable so that the investment as a whole will be financially successful, as well as being an unquestioned social asset to the country."

Indeed, the war was a watershed for entrepreneurialism. While it was true that the war temporarily stunted the development of small business, it ultimately created a more fertile environment for the entrepreneurial economy to flourish. By its very nature, war encourages risk taking, and this particular war proved the value of taking risks on new technologies and methods of production beyond anyone's imagination. As just one example, the rapid development of the synthetic rubber industry demonstrated that pushing unproven technologies could produce a spectacular outcome. In addition, war transformed the capital markets. The extraordinary results of wartime technology "prepared many individual investors and institutional fund managers to take greater risks in war-time investing." Equally important, the Allied victory wiped out the last vestiges of Depression-era timidity, injecting the nation with a jolt of self-confidence that encouraged experimentation in all areas of life, including business.

The war produced other fundamental changes in U.S. society that bolstered entrepreneurialism: the GI Bill put millions of Americans through college, educating the next generation of technologists and entrepreneurs. And thanks to the war, the U.S. government was no longer a bit player in basic research. Expenditures for research in pure science in 1938 totaled less than $40 million, with the bulk of that money coming from industry. The war changed all that, with the U.S. government drafting universities and foundations into a vast network of military research. By 1943, the Office of Scientific Research and Development alone was placing $90 million a year in research contracts with universities. The Army and Navy placed contracts worth tens of millions more. And it was those defense contracts that constituted the seed corn of innovation.

⌒

After obtaining the necessary exemptions from the Securities and Exchange Commission, ARD set out to sell shares for its venture fund. But despite its roster of well-known backers, ample publicity, and a friendlier regulatory and investment environment, ARD's stock offering nearly failed. For starters, it was unable to persuade an investment bank to underwrite its offering. Instead, it hired two enterprising mid-tier banks, Estabrook & Company and Harriman, Ripley & Company, to pitch the deal on a best-efforts basis. Then, bad timing almost torpedoed the offering as the stock market swooned in the fall. ARD would have blown its November 1 deadline for raising $3 million were it not for a last-minute subscription by Lessing Rosenwald, the former chairman of Sears, Roebuck & Company.

By the end of December 1946, ARD officers and its partner banks were only able to sell 139,930 of the 200,000 shares, rustling up a total of $3.5 million. Of the sum, just over $1.8 million was purchased by nine financial institutions, two insurance companies, and four university endowments: MIT, Rice Institute, the University of Pennsylvania, and the University of Rochester. Individual stockholders, required to invest the considerable sum of $5,000, contributed the rest of the capital.

While the banks and directors raised money, ARD hit the ground in a full sprint. The company took office space at 79 Milk Street in Boston's financial district. Its small staff followed an open-door policy, and began to attract hundreds of business plans. "ARD does not invest in the ordinary sense," said Doriot. "Rather, it creates by taking calculated risks in selected companies in whose growth possibilities it believes." The firm set clear guidelines for making an investment: projects should have passed the "test-tube" stage, be protected "through patents or specialized knowledge and techniques," and afford an "attractive opportunity for eventual profits." From the very beginning, Senator Flanders stressed ARD should not be viewed as one company, but as a national social movement. "People ask me how we can do the work we do with the small staff I have," said Flanders. "My answer is that my staff is the United States of America."

From the get-go, ARD set a very high bar. ARD's staff rejected proposals to drill for oil beneath the polar ice cap, to develop a treadmill runway for airports, and to make a hot-water soap spray that replaced toilet paper. In November, after Flanders won election to the Senate, Doriot, as expected, took over the presidency of the firm on the condition that he could continue teaching.

By that time, Doriot had moved back to Boston with Edna, returning to their townhouse on 12 Lime Street. The Harvard Corporation reinstated him as a Professor of Industrial Management at an annual salary of $11,000. Most weeks, Doriot taught Monday and Tuesday, then spent the rest of the week, including Saturday, running ARD. Doriot's position at ARD gave his classroom lectures an extra degree of heft. "It made his notes and comments to us seem all the more appropriate and realistic," recalled Marvin S. Traub. "We all felt we were getting something special."

By the end of the year, ARD had done enough work to plow money into its first three investments. All three companies were developing new products. ARD invested $150,000 in Circo Products, a Cleveland-based company developing a handgun that melted car engine grease by vaporizing a solvent and injecting it into automobile transmissions. The other two companies it financed were developing cutting-edge technologies. A $200,000 investment enabled the formation of High Voltage Engineering Corporation, a company launched in a converted Cambridge parking garage by two MIT scientists who were developing a two-million-volt generator eight times more powerful than existing X-ray machines. And $150,000 went to Tracerlab, Incorporated, another outfit formed by MIT whiz kids that was the first commercial venture of the atomic age: Tracerlab, on the verge of bankruptcy when ARD came to its rescue, sold radioactive isotopes and made radiation detection machines.

Although ARD's policy was to take equity stakes with their investments, the company's hunger for cash led them to finance some of their companies through convertible debt or convertible preferred stock. In these cases, ARD financed a company with a loan, payable in installments, usually with options or warrants to buy stock at a later date. The Circo Products investment, for instance, was really a $150,000 loan with a 5 percent interest rate, convertible into 1,150 shares of preferred stock. The interest rate was more than double the return ARD was earning on its investments in government bonds. Even so, ARD ended its first year in the red. In 1946, the firm's income of $5,000 was dwarfed by $42,000 in operating expenses.

The first round of investments illustrated ARD's philosophy of going "beyond monetary investments" to "include managerial assistance and technical advice when necessary." Management expertise was just as important as money in Doriot's view. ARD provided such advice largely through placing its officers, directors, or advisors on the boards of its portfolio companies. So, for example, Doriot and Powell joined the board of High Voltage. "It wasn't a question of who has control but of getting the right kind of control," said High Voltage cofounder Denis M. Robinson. Compton and Griswold joined the board of Tracerlab, while Powell and a Cleveland businessman named Robert Hornung, who was Doriot's assistant at Harvard from 1931 to 1934, took board seats with Circo Products. Doriot best explained the formula in the 1949 annual report: "A team made up of the younger generation, with courage and inventiveness, together with older men of wisdom and experience, should bring success."

In 1947, ARD's first full year of operation, Doriot picked up the pace. More than four hundred nutty proposals streamed into the office. But ARD continued to remain as picky as the debutante of a Boston Brahmin. In any given year, ARD would never finance more than 4 percent of the projects it reviewed, and more often than not it would only finance 1 to 2 percent of its proposals. This year, ARD invested nearly $880,000 in five new companies. In February, it granted $225,000 to Baird Associates, an eleven-year-old Cambridge company that made instruments used in the chemical analysis of metals and gases. In April, it plunked down $201,000 in Jet-Heet, Incorporated, an Englewood, New Jersey, company formed after the war to develop a household furnace based on jet-engine technology. In July, Snyder Chemical Corporation received a $52,550 check to finance the development of new resins used in the paper and plywood industries. In October, on the recommendation of William L. Campbell, the head of MIT's Department of Food Technology, ARD branched out into another new industry, spending about $350,000 to buy the assets of the Colter Corporation from the Kroger Company. Colter, which caught and sold deveined shrimp and other fish products, was a profitable business under Kroger. ARD finished the year by pouring $45,000 into the Flexible Tubing Corporation, a company that ARD formed to acquire the Spiratube Division of the Warner Brothers Company of Bridgeport, Connecticut.

By the end of the year, however, the only thing that ARD had proven was that it was easy to spend a lot of money without having much to show much for it. Although its income had increased to $51,000, it ended the year with a $55,000 loss because its expenses had shot up after adding several new young employees: Davis R. Dewey II, Tom Cabot, and William Elfers. Moreover, it was not even close to proving it could help nurture a successful business. Only two of the eight companies in its portfolio were in the black. And most worrisome, with about 41 percent of its paid-in capital already deployed in illiquid investments, it would clearly need to raise more money soon in order to continue investing. The pressure was increasing on Doriot. If ARD failed or only turned in a middling performance, the venture capital experiment might never be repeated.

By the end of 1946, Doriot finished his work for the War Assets Administration and the Research and Development Division, but the military continued to seek him out for a variety of missions. In 1946 alone, after he had been released from the Office of the Quartermaster General in May, Doriot was called up for active duty on four separate occasions. In fact, the depth of Doriot's involvement with the military following the conclusion of the war is one of the most surprising and little-known aspects of his life.

From 1946 until 1959, when Doriot reached the age of sixty, the retirement age for Reserve officers of his status, he remained an active participant in the highest levels of U.S. military and government affairs. Dozens of times over that period, usually for a spell of three to seven days, Doriot was called down to Washington by the Office of the Quartermaster General, the Department of the Army, or various military schools. On several occasions in 1958 and 1959, President Eisenhower even asked Doriot to help him press his campaign to reorganize the Department of Defense.

During 1947, Doriot became involved in two high-level government projects, one of which was classified as top secret. On January 18, Doriot agreed to become an advisor to the newly formed Joint Research and Development Board (JRDB) under the direction of Vannevar Bush, the powerful adviser to President Roosevelt who oversaw the Manhattan Project. The overall aim of the JRDB was to coordinate the expanding research programs of the Army and Navy, making sure to eliminate any overlap or wasteful duplication of effort. In the short term, though, its priority was to build support among the sharply divided military services for a national guided missile program. Unfortunately, however, frozen by fruitless infighting, the Army and Navy never formed a satellite or guided missile program.

Reading the writing on the wall, Doriot resigned from the JRDB in June of 1947. Bush accepted Doriot's resignation but asked if he could still rely on his counsel. By that time, Doriot commanded even more respect; in February of that year he was appointed a Brigadier General in the U.S. Army Reserve Corps. "I request this because I feel that with your particular background, keenness for the national defense, and extraordinary analytical ability, you can reach to the heart of some of these matters in a way that will be of great benefit to the Armed Services," wrote Bush.

The next month, Doriot became entangled in the most bizarre and petty political battle of his life, stemming from his dream of establishing a peace-time military research organization. The highly public tussle, which turned on the question of where to locate the research facility, dragged on for four years, impugning Doriot's reputation and that of ARD, and threatened to derail the project altogether. Doriot, who called this hoped-for organization "The Institute of Man," proposed the vision as early as 1942, when the first Climatic Research Laboratory was established in Lawrence, Massachusetts, and he continued lobbying for it throughout the war. General Gregory liked the idea and in 1945 he recommended that the Quartermaster laboratories be consolidated in one location. The fight was over where that consolidated lab—and all of the money, resources, and attention it would receive—would be located. It came down to a bare-knuckled brawl between Boston and Philadelphia.

The project was seen as so important to the economic future of Boston that a group of leading businessmen from the area, including his ARD pals Merrill Griswold, Ralph Flanders, and Karl Compton, teamed up to lobby both Doriot and the government. "The last time we knew of anything comparable to this was when the SEC was moved away from Washington," wrote Griswold to Doriot on October 25, 1945. "The choice narrowed down to Philadelphia or Boston. Boston lost out. We simply cannot have Boston losing out every time."

Griswold and his fellow Brahmins approached Doriot because they heard through the grapevine that the Secretary of War was pondering the lab's location, and had indicated that great weight in reaching the decision "would be placed upon [Doriot's] personal recommendation." The lobbying proved successful. Doriot agreed with his colleagues that Boston was the ideal place because of its proximity to the largest concentration of universities and research laboratories engaged in similar research. On June 6, Secretary Patterson recommended Boston after a survey determined that it "possesses the greatest number of factors desirable in a site for the laboratory proposed."

The 80th Congress, led by republican Massachusetts Senator Leverett Saltonstall and democratic House Majority leader John W. McCormack, introduced a bill authorizing $6 million for the construction of the lab in Boston. With this announcement, the Pennsylvania pols began throwing punches. On July 2, 1947, before a hearing held by the House Committee on Military Affairs, a Common Pleas court judge from Philadelphia named Vincent Carroll attacked Doriot, implying that "Boston was selected due to your connection with the American Research and Development Company."

Several months later, the fight got nastier. On February 18, 1948, a Senate Armed Services subcommittee met to discuss the bill to create the Boston lab. During the hearing, Pennsylvania Congressman Hugh D. Scott said the Boston plan should be labeled the "Doriot Plan," because of its advocacy by Georges F. Doriot. Scott, who then noted Doriot's affiliation with ARD, alleged Doriot's choice of Boston was clouded by a conflict of interest. "Doriot," said Scott, "has strong personal reasons for wanting the laboratory moved to Boston. I admit it would be of extreme benefit to General Doriot's research corporation. This 'Operation Doriot' should be discontinued."

Senator Saltonstall interjected that ARD was formed to attract more tax dollars to Massachusetts and would not be associated with the Quartermaster lab. Doriot, who testified later, took exception to the suggestion that he might personally benefit. Infuriated, Doriot confronted Congressman Scott after the meeting ended, and told him he had never seen such despicable tactics. Congressman Scott listened politely, before giving Doriot a harsh lesson in the down-and-dirty business of Washington politics.

"Don't take it personally," Scott replied. "Your opinion on this question is so important that we have to destroy your character and wreck you, so that nobody pays attention to what you say. Do not worry about it—it is standard courtroom practice. You can check with any Philadelphia lawyer, and they will tell you that this is just standard procedure."

The mudslinging worked. The Senate and House bills were reported out of committee but the Rules Committee blocked its passage. For the time being, Doriot's dream was stuck in political limbo.

Although it was hard to gauge the impact of the Quartermaster controversy on ARD's reputation, the fight was clearly a distraction from the day-to-day operations of the firm. During the first six months of 1948, ARD made no new investments. It wasn't until July that the firm found a new venture it deemed worth backing. It was a coinvestment with Rockefeller Brothers in a tuna fishing outfit called Island Packers, Incorporated. ARD poured nearly $250,000 into Island Packers with the hope that by the summer of 1949 it would begin large shipments of canned tuna caught near the Fiji Islands.

In November, ARD purchased a $300,000 note from the Cleveland Pneumatic Tool Company, then the largest manufacturer of aircraft landing gear, in exchange for an interest in the company and a management fee for project evaluation. This was a new type of seed investment which funded a three-year program to investigate the development of a confidential project in the "field of physical chemistry and chemical engineering." Faced with a continuing need for fresh capital, ARD's tactic of charging management fees to its portfolio companies soon became a regular practice. If ARD could earn an operating profit while continuing to work toward its loftier goal of generating investment profits, the firm's backers felt it would reassure investors.

The last investment that ARD made in 1948 was in a potentially revolutionary company called Ionics, Incorporated. The Ionics deal illustrated the extreme ambition of ARD and the sophisticated techniques it used to lower the risk of its investments. In the fall of 1948, Walter Juda, a PhD candidate in chemistry at Harvard, struck up a conversation with a friend who worked for Tracerlab. During this chat, Juda told his friend that he was developing a new membrane with his colleague Wayne McRae that was designed to make brackish water viable for irrigation or drinking. The idea seemed interesting enough that the friend introduced Juda to ARD's technical assistant Davis R. Dewey II. Dewey was immediately intrigued by the results of the duo's plastic membrane, which showed an ability to sort metallic ions from nonmetallic ones. "The classic method is removing 96.5% of water away from 3.5% of salt," says Juda. "Our new method focused on removing the 3.5% of salt."

Dewey introduced Juda to Doriot. The technology also intrigued Doriot, but he wanted a reality check. So he called up a colleague at Dow Chemical Company, which was researching and developing ion exchange technology. After Doriot explained the concept, his colleague concluded the technology was impossible. Instead of arguing over the phone, Doriot asked Juda to send a membrane to Dow in the mail. Within days, Doriot's colleague wrote back: "That's the breakthrough." Doriot responded with a $50,000 investment, and Ionics was born. Doriot, Dewey, and Griswold joined the board, Gilliland was appointed president, and Juda was made vice president and technical director.

ARD ended 1948 with a feeling of cautious optimism, though its financial performance was hardly impressive. In his shareholder letter, Doriot wrote, "It is the opinion of the Board of Directors that the goals originally set can be met," that "it is expected that the company will have an operating profit in 1949," and that ARD could "become an increasingly important factor in furnishing venture capital to promising American businesses." In fact, ARD lost $44,000 that year, a modest improvement over 1947, thanks to $9,000 in consulting fees. And it was down to $1.2 million in capital.

A few positive developments, however, gave cause for hope. ARD showed an increase in its net asset value for the first time. Moreover, a sizable number of its portfolio companies began to gain traction. "When the company was organized, it was claimed by some people that if only one or two out of ten projects became successful, the American Research and Development Corp. would do well," wrote Doriot in the 1948 annual report. "The record to date is ahead of this average."

One start-up fulfilling its high hopes was Tracerlab. Its founder and president William E. Barbour Jr. credited Doriot with inspiring him to focus the company on its best opportunities. "The general provides the two things that a young scientific organization most needs: enthusiasm and appreciation," said Barbour. "Like all the others, I started out with a hatful of ideas and a lot of long-range plans. In a couple of years, I got bogged down in detail. Doriot stepped in just in time to pull me out of the rut. He stirs you out of your lethargy, keeps you looking five years ahead." In 1948, Tracerlab sales more than doubled to $700,000, helping it to turn a profit of $30,000. Consequently, ARD claimed its first capital gain of $37,000, when it sold 1,765 shares of Tracerlab for $29.93 per share. ARD pumped another $100,000 into the company.

Entering 1949, Doriot's chief concern was capital. As a rule of thumb, Doriot believed that ARD should raise funds whenever it was down to $1 million in cash and near-cash assets. After investing $100,000 in Mississippi car parts maker Berry Motors in February, and another $50,000 in New York metal parts maker Exmet Electrical Corporation in March, ARD was perilously close to that figure. So in early 1949, the ARD board authorized the sale of an additional 153,500 shares of stock to raise $4 million.

ARD's timing seemed right. Doriot, looking sharp in a pin-striped double-breasted suit, landed on the cover of the February 19 issue of *Business Week*. "In less than three years, Doriot's corporation has obtained guiding or controlling interest in 13 companies, with projects ranging from the conversion of isotopes for industrial uses to the canning of tuna on the island of Samoa," reported the brief but flattering story. What's more, in March, ARD enjoyed its first successful initial public offering of one of its portfolio companies when Tracerlab sold 104,000 shares of stock for $1.3 million through an investment bank. The offering enabled Tracerlab to triple its space by moving into a nearby six-story building.

Despite the successful offering and positive coverage in *Newsweek*, *Barron's*, and other outlets, revealing that about half of ARD's ventures were showing a profit, ARD could still not convince an investment bank to underwrite its second offering. Instead, ARD decided to pay a 5 percent commission to dealers through whom shares were sold. This time, ARD eliminated the requirement that investors purchase a minimum of $5,000 of stock.

Nevertheless, the offering was hardly a wild success. In April, May, and June, only 35,520 shares were purchased, and then it sold another 8,075 shares over the next six months. The net gain: barely more than $1 million, leaving the company's total paid-in capital at $4,465,365—more than $500,000 below its original 1946 target.

After turning down an offer to become a member of the Army-Navy Munitions Board and another committee of the Joint Research and Development Board, Doriot turned to Senator Flanders for help. He expressed frustration over the growing gap between the rhetoric and reality of the venture capital business, if it could be called a business. "I am afraid that, as usual, people believe in venture capital as long as somebody else's money does it," he wrote on May 11. "People will make long speeches explaining that they do not want the government to finance small businesses or new businesses, but still they do not want their own money to be used for either." Doriot was so downbeat that he floated the desperate, almost sacrilegious idea that ARD borrow $10 to $15 million dollars from the Reconstruction Finance Corporation, a U.S. government agency that loaned money to governments and businesses during the war.

On June 30, ARD moved out of its Milk Street office and into an office on the twenty-third floor of Boston's landmark John Hancock Building. Doriot imbued the office with the spartan aesthetic he cultivated in the military: a bunch of metal Navy desks and chairs were all that was necessary. For lunch, the staff often ate at the cafeteria in the building, where Doriot chatted up the waitresses and the busboys as if they were his colleagues. Doriot's office was small but finely furnished with a rug, tobacco box, telephone, and a writing table that held several bins of blank paper. From his window in the Hancock building, the city's tallest structure, Doriot could see the gold-domed State House, the emerald lawns of the Boston Commons, and the sparkling Charles River Basin. On his desk, Doriot kept a stopwatch. "Sometimes I use it to see how long it takes someone in a meeting to tell me the same thing three times," he said.

But all in all, despite the positive developments, 1949 was turning out to be a tough year for ARD. The firm seemed to be losing the momentum that it had been building since its inception. Or maybe that was just the nature of venture capital investing. Two steps forward, one step back. The large shipments of canned tuna that Island Packers had expected by the summer of 1949 did not materialize. Flexible Tubing had fallen on tough times. Colter reversed into red ink. And a national shortage of chlorine, the basic chemical for Circo Products' degreasing solvent, thwarted the company's growth plans.

Typically, ARD preferred to take a hands-off approach to its affiliate companies. They were there to coach, guide, and inspire. Running the business was the job of the entrepreneur. But quite often, as ARD's principals learned, circumstances called for more drastic action. In fact, every one of ARD's successes would face catastrophe at least once, sometimes twice. Doriot was learning that project selection was actually the easiest part of ARD's job. At least they had control over that decision. "The hardest task is to help a company through its growth pains," wrote Doriot. "That is particularly hard because we have to work with others." If companies survived those ordeals, it was "because of very hard work on our part and on their part."

Circo Products was one of those hardship cases. The chlorine crisis overwhelmed its management. In January of 1950, ARD acquired voting control of the company through a recapitalization and installed Joseph Powell as the firm's new president. It also brought in a young Harvard Business School graduate, Fenton Davison, as director and vice president, to identify a new product to sell. Davison canvassed purchasing agents in dozens of large companies, hunting for an easily produced gadget that was in high demand and short supply. His find: hose clamps. Hose clamps were not going to set the world on fire but it was cutting-your-losses time, time to preserve capital.

At the 1949 annual meeting, Doriot strained to put a bright face on a darkening picture. ARD ended its third full year of operations showing a $38,000 loss even though it had promised an operating profit the previous year. It could not afford to pay dividends unless it wanted to sell more Tracerlab shares, which would depress the company's stock price. And its shrinking bank account had become a handicap. ARD's small kitty limited its investment fees, and strained the company's ability to finance growth in its promising affiliates and hire more personnel to bring in new deals. "We are trying to construct a fairly big operation with too little capital," griped Doriot.

There were a few bright spots, though. Some of ARD's affiliates began to build momentum. Sales of Baird Associates leaped 165 percent between 1947 and 1949. Tracerlab's sales grew 30 percent, exceeding $1 million, and it took a one-third interest in a European affiliate—ARD's first overseas venture. After two years of struggling, the generators built by High Voltage were used increasingly for cancer therapy and nuclear physics research. "General Doriot understood that this would be a slow thing," said High Voltage CEO Robinson. "At early board meetings, I would try to give an accurate accounting of the profit and loss. He would look through me and ask what I really thought about when I was shaving." At the time, the grateful scientist scribbled in his journal: "Doriot's outlook inspires and transforms my own, lifting me above the worry plane."

Grappling with these myriad challenges led Doriot to believe that managing talent was the most important ingredient in the start-up equation. "The invention which American Research and Development Corporation would most like to receive is a device to evaluate men!" joked Doriot in the 1949 annual report. "An average idea in the hands of an able man is worth much more than an outstanding idea in the possession of a person with only average ability."

With just $1.5 million in government securities and corporate bonds, Doriot started 1950 facing the same nagging concern: ARD needed more money. The ARD board came up with a potential solution: Regional Committees. It was a page right out of the Doriot playbook. The idea was to create boards of advisors in several cities to help raise money, find and analyze new projects, and assist existing affiliates.

The first of these boards was formed in January of 1950 in Philadelphia under the guidance of Lewis M. Stevens, a partner in a local law firm. Besides Stevens, the board included business leaders from eight different companies, including the president of N. W. Ayer & Son, the executive vice president of the Fidelity-Philadelphia Trust, and the general manager of Sears, Roebuck. ARD set up another six-member board in Providence, Rhode Island in February of 1951.

Doriot proved his star power again by forming these boards of local industry titans, but they ended up being far less effective in practice than either the ARD board or the advisory boards Doriot created during the war. Consequently, ARD stopped composing regional committees after the experiments in Philadelphia and Providence. Although ARD prominently publicized the two boards in its annual reports from 1949 to 1951, after that evidence of their existence disappeared from its records.

Despite the money troubles, the mood of ARD's office was brightened by the emergence of two new leaders. One of them was a disciplined young man of high integrity named William Elfers, who joined the firm in early 1947 as its first nontechnical assistant. Elfers, a 1943 graduate of Harvard Business School who served as a lieutenant in the U.S. Naval Reserve from 1943 to 1946, was brought into the firm by Powell, who also served in the Naval Reserve during the war. "Most of the young men who came to ARD were former Doriot students," recalled Elfers.

Elfers had joined ARD after working as the first sales manager for a small company that published a magazine called *Modern Materials Handling*. Elfers quit because he did not like the publishing business, and wanted to gain more experience in sales, marketing, and finance. He was also intrigued by the idea of venture capital, of doing something that had never been done before, and he was impressed by ARD's board. "It looked to me like an adventure," recalled Elfers. "It was a fragile company. We didn't have a lot of money." Elfers ended up working at ARD for the next eighteen years.

From the start, Elfers demonstrated a talent for recognizing the human qualities that can make or break a business. This endeared him to Doriot, who threw Elfers into the fire rather quickly. After an ugly board meeting in 1948 for Flexible Tubing, Doriot and Powell gave Elfers a chance to save the troubled company. With only a year at ARD under his belt, Elfers found himself as Flexible Tubing's new director, treasurer, and manager. For part of 1948, Elfers moved to the company's headquarters in Branford, Connecticut, returning home to Boston over the weekends.

Immersing himself in the company, Elfers spotted the talents of a young manager named Eugene Swartz. Elfers took Swartz under his wing, helping him not only to smooth relations with the company's founder and the board, but also in focusing Flexible on meeting the needs of its big customers such as Jet-Heet. Under Swartz's steady hand, Flexible began to stabilize. After an unprofitable 1948, sales doubled in 1949, and the company turned a small profit. In 1950, as substantial deliveries were made to Jet-Heet, Flexible Tubing's sales jumped 400 percent, and profits increased. The company also began developing a special tubing product for the military, built a new manufacturing plant in Connecticut, and opened a new west coast sales office in Pasadena, California. As a result of his hard work, Elfers was promoted to assistant vice president at ARD.

By 1951, Flexible Tubing was doing well enough that Elfers vacated his position as treasurer and manager, remaining on the board only. The company reported its third consecutive year of profits, and made the first repayment of its loans. "The successful fulfillment of this assignment made my early reputation at ARD and was followed over the years by similar roles on troubled investments," wrote Elfers.

The other new leader to emerge at ARD was Henry W. Hoagland, Doriot's trusty aide in the Military Planning Division. After the war, Hoagland went into politics. Between 1946 and 1948 he served as the deputy director for the Joint Committee on Atomic Energy. Then he briefly managed the office of former Republican U.S. Senator John Danaher, who was executive director of the Senatorial Campaign Committee. Thanks to his stint on the Hill, Hoagland earned the friendship of important political figures and became an expert in the inner workings of Washington. "Doriot wanted the political connections that Harry had," says Harry's wife Ray Hoagland. But despite all of the "glamour of Washington, Harry said, 'I better get back to Doriot and make a living.'"

Hoagland joined ARD in 1949 as an assistant secretary. Doriot, who appreciated his reliability, strength, and judgment, quickly assigned him to the boards of Control Engineering Corporation and Ultrasonic Corporation, two investments ARD made in January of 1950. Although Hoagland did not broker these investments, his legal expertise and congenial self-effacing personality allowed him soon enough to cultivate a number of important deals. When Hoagland joined ARD, it had made a few investments outside of the New England area. But Harry's love of travel and his familiarity with the West pushed ARD to expand its geographical horizons. "Doriot didn't think a thing of California," recalls Ray Hoagland. "He used to say, 'I'm glad where California is. I hope an earthquake happens and it floats off and becomes an island.'"

As 1950 drew to a close, ARD underwent a flurry of activity. Staffers pored through hundreds more proposals from aspiring entrepreneurs. No. 251 envisioned a "rocket auto." No. 307 proposed a "whistling lollipop." And No. 458, well, that was for an "Xmas-tree turner with music box." More whimsical ideas thrown into the waste basket. In the last three months of the year, though, ARD picked five companies to back. Two of the deals—Airborne Instruments Laboratory, Incorporated and Reaction Motors, Incorporated— were coinvestments in military technology firms along with Rockefeller Brothers.

It was a somewhat surprising move given that ARD's first investment with the Rockefeller family had just imploded. After two years of intensive work near the Fiji Islands, the backers of Island Packers concluded that, while tuna could be caught in the area, the schools were so small that they could not yield a big enough catch to support a profitable operation. In December of 1950, the major stockholders of the company put Island Packers into bankruptcy.

Island Packers was ARD's first loss and it cost the company dearly. The tuna fishing fiasco led to a $239,000 write-off, pushing ARD's accumulated deficit to $432,000. On an operating basis, ARD ended the year close to breakeven, with a $19,000 loss. More importantly, the two thousand employees of its twenty-two affiliates charged ahead, claiming impressive combined sales of $20 million. Thanks to gains in Tracerlab shares, the massive deficit was offset on paper by an unrealized gain of $521,000. Maybe ARD could generate some capital gains after all. Through all the ups and downs, Doriot maintained his sense of dark humor. "Never go into venture capital if you want a peaceful life!" he warned a group of businessmen in 1950. "Keep on financing concrete that doesn't move, that doesn't call you at two o'clock in the morning to tell you about a new human accident."

The spring of 1951 brightened Doriot's mood. In fact, March 1951 was one of the happiest periods in Doriot's life. Years of indefatigable labor were beginning to bear fruit. The first harvest came for ARD when Harriman, Ripley and Estabrook led a successful underwriting for the balance of its authorized but unissued stock. The two firms, which stood with ARD from the start, sold 81,615 shares of stock for $25 a share to more than five hundred new shareholders, netting the firm just north of $2 million.

Later that month, Doriot was informed that the Department of Defense, after four years of endless deliberations and studies, finally approved Natick, Massachusetts as the location for the Quartermaster laboratory. Amazingly, critics continued to hurl invective against Doriot and the lab. But the Secretary of Defense stuck to his guns and made sure there were no more postponements or delays. On April 19, 1952, the military held a groundbreaking ceremony for the Natick Labs, as it was called. Doriot, however, chose not to attend.

Major General George A. Horkan, then Quartermaster General, wrote Doriot, expressing regret that he would miss the event. "I realize that you were the subject of much personal criticism among those of selfish interest and those that were misinformed," he wrote. "Your absence, although you will be missed, will not detract from those of us who know of the great contributions you have made in this realization."

A week after the groundbreaking, Doriot wrote a letter to Assistant Secretary of the Army Karl R. Bendetsen explaining his absence. "This laboratory can be very outstanding and render a great service," wrote Doriot. "There is no time to lose in selecting the top staff and getting them going . . . [A]ll I did was my duty and I did not think I should go and look like the man who got his way." The letter was vintage Doriot: humble and modest but urging constructive action.

Clearly, 1951 was shaping up as a banner year. Five consecutive years of nurturing High Voltage, Tracerlab, Baird Associates, Flexible Tubing, and many other children of the ARD family had finally begun to pay off. By the end of 1951, combined sales for ARD's portfolio doubled to $40 million and total employment rose to three thousand workers. Of ARD's twenty-six investments, twenty-one, or an impressive 81 percent, reported profitable operations. ARD even managed to salvage $75,000 from the canning plants and boats of Island Packers when it sold the assets to Wilbur, Ellis & Company of San Francisco.

ARD wrapped up 1951 in the strongest position of its five-year history. The company had raised enough money to continue its existing rate of investment for another four years. It showed $651,000 in paper profits, up 25 percent over the previous year. And its business model had matured to the point that income from consulting fees and short-term investments covered all of its operating costs. In fact, the firm showed its first operating profit ever, ending the year $46,000 in the black. "Although the goals of dividends and higher earnings per share still remain ahead," Doriot wrote in his 1951 letter to stockholders, "your management believes that the profitable operation of the Corporation indicates at least one important milestone has been passed."

But investors remained stubbornly unimpressed with ARD's performance. The banks that underwrote ARD's offering in March were unable to stem the slide in the company's shares. While the Dow Jones average increased 14 percent in 1951, the bid prices for ARD shares drifted downward to $19 by year-end. Investors who bought in at $25 a share in 1946 were down 25 percent after holding the shares for more than five years.

Doriot defended the firm's poor stock returns in his letter, taking issue with the way that ARD was being compared to investment trusts. His answer was that investors needed to be more patient. And in exchange for patience, ARD held out the promise of bigger returns. "The Corporation does not invest in the ordinary sense," wrote Doriot. "It creates. It risks. Results take more time and the expenses of its operation must be higher, but the potential for ultimate profits is much greater." But after five years, how much more patience could investors be expected to show? And now that Doriot had raised the stakes, would ARD be able to generate returns that beat the market?

EIGHT

THE BIRTH OF VENTURE CAPITAL

(1951–1956)

A FEW MINUTES BEFORE 1 p.m. on a Monday afternoon in September 1949, Georges Doriot marched into a classroom in Baker Hall on the Harvard Business School campus. It was the first day of his Manufacturing class. The professor, showing everyone who was boss, shut the door precisely as the clock struck the top of the hour. No one would be allowed to enter his class after it began. Doriot viewed his class as a business meeting. That meant strict enforcement of punctuality and a dress code of coats and ties.

"Gentleman," said General Doriot to a room of 150 students, "what I have to say, I shall say only once." The students, all turned out in dark suits, crisp white shirts, and somber ties, shifted toward Doriot, hanging on to his every word. "I shall do all the talking, you listen, think and make notes, about what surprises you, what interests you, what further thinking it suggests to you. And what you think you disagree with."

Before the war, Doriot was already a Harvard legend. Now, having helped save the free world from the Nazis, General Doriot was practically a god in the eyes of these impressionable young men. Many students began to affectionately address him as "The General." "If you ask most any Harvard Business

School graduate between 1946 and 1966 who was their favorite professor, the answer was invariably Georges Doriot," said Marvin S. Traub, class of 1949, who rose to become the chairman and CEO of Bloomingdale's, Inc.

At the same time, Doriot's soaring profile aroused a fair amount of jealousy within the petty, competitive environs of the university. Not everyone liked him. Some of Doriot's colleagues derisively referred to him behind his back as "Le Grand General."

Back in class, Doriot demanded that his students not ask questions because he felt it wasted the time of other students. If they wanted to question him, Professor Doriot welcomed students to visit him after class during office hours.

Doriot's course was not for everyone. The heavy workload scared many Harvard men from taking his class. Other students perceived Doriot to be a didactic, irascible lecturer who refused to adopt the school's then-dominant case method pedagogy. Still others were turned off by what they felt was a cold, aloof personality.

Doriot's students did not love his course because it was a breeze. They loved it because he pushed them to work harder and think more creatively than any other professor. "It was a true energy sink," says John A. Shane, who took the Manufacturing course in 1959. "There was no end to what you might do in the course."

After the war, Doriot rethought his course. He now believed so strongly in the value of real-world experience, he transformed his Manufacturing course into the simulation of a real business. Doriot's aim was to give his students a sense of "operation" rather than "administration." Indeed, Doriot loathed the word "Administration" in his school's name. "The word 'administration' to me indicates something static," snarled Doriot. "You administer, push buttons. The word I very much like better is the word 'operation.' Operation to me means movement."

Through his lectures, Doriot framed the objectives of the course and inculcated his philosophy about the proper way to run a business. Regular visits by VIPs in industry and government enhanced the real-world flavor. Doriot invited dozens of prominent leaders to his class who inspired his students to think in new and different ways, including Leslie Groves, the leader of the Manhattan Project, Henry Dreyfuss, the noted industrial designer, General James Gavin, an expert in military research, and Margaret Rudkin, the founder of Pepperidge Farms.

Doriot always respected the outside speakers but he often questioned their views. In 1947, for instance, Doriot invited the president of U.S. Steel to address his students. "U.S. Steel does not know what business they are in," Doriot told his class after the company's president had left the classroom. "They are in the materials, not the steel business. They are completely ignorant of aluminum and plastics." Zalman Bernstein, founder and chairman of Sanford Bernstein & Company, said Doriot was the first person to think in such a broad and creative way. "He had more influence on what has happened in American business than the rest of the Harvard faculty put together," said Bernstein.

In addition, Doriot preached the value of pragmatism through the introduction of two new and innovative assignments: the company report and the topic report. The topic report was an exercise in creative business thinking. The assignment required students to "write a report on a subject of your own choosing which will be a contribution to the future of American business." Over the summer, Doriot's students split up into smaller groups of seven to eight people and identified a worthy topic. "These things allowed you to see the importance of organizing people," says Ralph P. Hoagland, class of 1962, who credits Doriot with inspiring him to found the CVS drugstore chain.

After researching the topic, Doriot asked the students to produce a report, but with a twist: instead of discussing the current state of an issue, students had to imagine the impact of the problem, product, or technology ten years into the future.

Some of the topic reports tackled cutting-edge subjects and made quite a splash. In 1951, a member of the Atomic Energy Commission requested one hundred copies of a topic report on nuclear power, "Swords into Plowshares: A Study of Current and Future Developments in Commercial Atomic Power." In 1965, Prentice Hall published a book based on a topic report about creative collective bargaining. Perhaps the most famous topic report was written by John Diebold, class of 1951. A midshipman in the Merchant Marine during World War II, Diebold became fascinated by the concept of automated machines while observing his ships' automatic antiaircraft fire control mechanisms. Diebold and his team wrote a report titled "Making the Automatic Factory a Reality." The following year, he published a book based on the report called *Automation*. It was a very influential work that predicted the integration of computers and business, and is today considered to be a management classic.

If the topic report was about letting your mind soar, the company report was all about learning the nuts-and-bolts of a business. After picking a group leader, the teams identified two local manufacturing companies to work with. "In the first half of the year, they study these companies," said Doriot, explaining his technique. "What's the advantage of that? Up until that time when the students read that the price of copper went up, to them it was just statistical information which they might feed back to the teacher. In this case, I want them to say, 'What does it mean?' And also very important, 'What do I do about it?' I want them to learn to have pains in the stomach, you see what I mean?"

In the second semester, the group performed a consulting project for the company. It was a novel, effective technique that gave the students an insider's view of the operations of a business—and helped local industry to boot. "At the time, Doriot was the only one who brought students outside the school," says Arnaud de Vitry, a close friend of Doriot who graduated in the class of 1953. "When you hear the same things taught in a course it may not register. When you see a man discussing his problems it leaves an impression."

In the class of 1949, Marvin Traub teamed up with two of his best buddies, Sumner Feldberg and Wilbur A. Cowett, to tackle the company report. The three men became close friends while attending Harvard as undergraduates. After serving in World War II, they reunited at Harvard Business School. For the report, Marvin, Sumner, and Wilbur chose the Croft Brewing Company of Boston, a local brewery run by Winslow Sears, class of 1921. "Great," said Sears, "I have a tap room that will be your office, and the beer and ale has not been taxed, so you are entitled to all the ale you want."

They split up the company: Marvin took sales and packaging, Wilbur grabbed finance, and Sumner analyzed operations. Every night in the taproom, they cracked open a can of Croft Cream Ale ("The only brewery in the United States producing a Cream Ale exclusively!" blared its advertisements) and a can from the competition. Inevitably, one would come in clear with a nice head, and the other would be cloudy with no head. "Very quickly I discovered the cloudy one without a head was Croft Ale," recalled Traub.

The numbers of Croft Brewing told a similarly murky tale. Sales were down 25 percent in the last three years, profits were tumbling, and the company was losing market share. Realizing they did not have a winner on their hands, the trio felt the stomach pains of Croft Brewing. "We ended up saying as nicely as we could in a report that you should sell out or merge," says

Traub. "We not only delivered the report, we also delivered two cases of ale to the General marked Exhibit A."

Eighteen months later, they were proven correct. After Croft Brewing failed to raise money to save the company, Narragansett Brewing Company bought their rival brewer in 1952. It was a great learning experience for the three young men. In retrospect, though, Doriot's true influence was more profound and lasting. "He motivated and heightened in me the drive always to be the best in every situation," Traub said. "Even today, 14 years after I left Bloomingdale's, I derive great pleasure from the sales associates stopping me to reminisce about how 'we were the best.' That urgency to be the best and understand every situation is what I felt Manufacturing was all about."

On February 20, 1952, ARD held its annual meeting in a suite in the John Hancock building. Over the years, the meeting had blossomed into a star-studded yet collegial event attended by stockholders, portfolio companies, investment bankers, friends, and the press. Entrepreneurs flew in from all over the country to spend a few days with Doriot and his entourage. Arnold Kroll, an investment banker with Lehman Brothers who attended many of the meetings, said the annual affairs helped build a venture capital community by giving a "dignity or a substance to the process."

In the morning, Doriot invited the presidents and other executives of ARD's affiliates to gather in private, providing an opportunity for executives to network, trade ideas, and get to know one another. Then Doriot typically picked a speaker to address the executives. This year, MIT president Karl Compton spoke, followed by ex-ARD director Bradley Dewey Sr., former National Rubber Director and Quartermaster Corps advisor who was president of the Dewey and Almy Chemical Company.

"We all loved going to these meetings," says Parker G. Montgomery, chief executive of Cooper Laboratories, a pharmaceutical company that became one of ARD's most successful investments. "Your company was on display. There was nothing like that. The networking that was created and the introductions that were possible, all of that was very important. Anything that helps you keep your confidence, when you have no reason to have confidence is valuable."

In the afternoon, Doriot threw open the annual meeting to the public. It attracted 150 people. Scanning the faces in the crowd, Doriot spied a *New York Times* reporter and two of ARD's new employees. The first was William H. Congleton, a quiet yet effective former Doriot student who left the research department of Standard Oil Company to join ARD in 1952 as its technical director. "It was a thrashing around," said Congleton of his early years with ARD. "Nobody had ever done that kind of work they were doing. In the postwar hustle and bustle, there were so many men and women who had felt bottled up for the past 5, 6, 7 years. We had been in military oriented jobs and been given duties and responsibilities that in truth were beyond our normal capacities. There was a great pent up demand to . . . get going."

The other staffer was Dorothy E. Rowe, a petite, green-eyed administrative assistant to Doriot who was recently promoted to assistant secretary. Rowe's pedestrian title belied her considerable power. A home economics major from Syracuse University and former Lieutenant in the U.S. Navy's Bureau of Ordnance, Rowe was a trailblazer who eventually became one of the most powerful women in American business by earning the respect and trust of Doriot. "The only aspect of Women's Lib with which I can agree is equal pay for equal work and I've never had any discrimination on that score myself," she told a *Boston Globe* reporter near the end of her career.

A quiet and charming woman, Rowe had an uncanny ability to cut to the heart of a matter. "Business was her whole thing," said Brian Brooks, an auditor with Lybrand, Ross Brothers & Montgomery, ARD's accounting firm for its entire existence. "Everyone got along well with Dorothy. She could deal with any of these business people. She never was out blowing her own horn. She always made everyone feel great."

Doriot often reminded the ARD affiliates that the annual meeting was an ideal place to deliver an announcement, and Ionics took full advantage of the opportunity. At the end of the meeting, MIT Chemical Engineering Professor Gilliland stood up behind a podium and announced a startling new development. Gilliland, who doubled as the president of Ionics, demonstrated the company's new membrane that desalinated seawater more cheaply than any other existing technology. The demo and related testimony by Dr. Compton and Harvard chemistry professor and Ionics director Arthur B. Lamb was so compelling that the *New York Times* published a page one story about the development: "New Process Desalts Seawater; Promises to Help Arid Areas."

The story written by William L. Laurence hailed a "revolutionary new process for desalting seawater" that promised to "open up vast new reservoirs of fresh water for use in agriculture, industry and the home wherever water is now scarce."

The page one scoop was a coup for both ARD and Ionics, generating publicity and contracts for the new company. After the story came out, Senator Flanders received a visit from Sheridan Downey, a former U.S. Senator from California. Downey, who was representing the city of Long Beach, said he was "tremendously interested in the announcement" and expressed a desire to jump-start the first field trials of the technology for the city. Senator Flanders arranged for Downey to speak with Ionics cofounder and vice president Walter Juda. The meetings eventually led to one of Ionics's first commercial contracts. In the mid-1950s, the town of Coalinga, California purchased a system from Ionics, replacing the water supply it formerly brought in by railway.

The growing success of Ionics and High Voltage Engineering convinced ARD's directors that early-stage investments in technology companies represented its best opportunities. The riskiest investments, they were learning, held the potential to generate the greatest financial returns and the highest personal satisfaction. It was quite a turnabout in ARD's thinking. After ARD invested in High Voltage and Tracerlab, Merrill Griswold told a *Fortune* reporter that "some of our friends began to say, 'Oh, Lord, not another longhair project. Why doesn't ARD back something commercial and make some money. We learned our lesson. Now we realize that our best things are longhair."

ARD ended 1952 reporting a 50 percent jump in net income to $61,000 and $1 million in unrealized capital gains, another 50 percent leap over the previous year. More impressive, many of its affiliates, such as High Voltage and Reaction Motors, were taking on giant corporations such as General Electric and DuPont and beating them at their own game. ARD was not only helping to create new industries, it was also increasing the competitiveness and efficiency of existing industries by financing new entrants.

ARD was clearly making progress but investors still weren't buying the story. By December, ARD's bid price dropped to about $20. Much of Wall Street still viewed ARD as a freak philanthropic enterprise dreamed up by a strange mélange of Harvard professors and State Street financiers. A 1952 feature in *Fortune* magazine captured the ambivalence. While largely positive, the *Fortune* article noted that skeptics, particularly stockbrokers, believed this "mighty aggregation of brains has brought forth a financial mouse," and that the "market is uneasy about the lack of a dividend after six years of operation."

In fact, the ARD board was conflicted over the topic of dividends. In early December, Doriot spent an evening with the three gentlemen who ran the investment bank Harriman, Ripley & Company, seeking their advice about raising more money, and inquiring about the divident issue. The bankers told Doriot in no uncertain terms that ARD should not pay a dividend because ARD stock was sold on the "basis of capital gains," and that a dividend "would have a bad effect on the stock of ARD."

A week later at the ARD board meeting, Merrill Griswold told his fellow directors that he believed that ARD should pay a dividend that year. Doriot sided with Griswold. "As far as I am concerned, your opinion as a founder and director of American Research is far more important and valuable than the opinion of our investment bankers," Doriot wrote Griswold. As a result, ARD began to make plans to offer a dividend.

To help stimulate even more investor interest in ARD, Doriot came up with a brilliant idea. Instead of the typical annual meeting, in February of 1953 Doriot created a companion exhibition with the cheery name "Products with a Future." It was a stroke of genius, a three-ring circus designed to showcase the impressive span of products cranked out by ARD's expanding portfolio of twenty-five companies. In addition to gathering ARD's entrepreneurs in one room, Doriot was now a ringmaster who let them show off their latest products in booths that encircled the walls of the hotel suite where they were meeting—in effect, it was the world's first technology tradeshow. The exhibit was a wild success, attracting more than four thousand visitors and the lavish attention of many leading publications.

"Onlookers sampled shrimp, vein-removed with special patented equipment, washed down with a drink of fresh water drawn from an automatic desalter that turns out 200 gallons an hour from salt water," gushed a three-page feature in *BusinessWeek*. "They donned earphones to listen to the roar of a freight train produced by a two-dimensional sound recording unit, gaped at such items as rocket engines and a "Chillow" to keep your face cool on summer nights."

Still, *BusinessWeek* detected another agenda behind the dazzling exhibition: "Company heads hoped it would make it easier for the stockholders to swallow its progress report that, though the company is in the black for the second consecutive year, the day of dividends is still distant." Stockholders showed faith in Doriot, though. Before the meeting adjourned, they approved a doubling of ARD's authorized common shares.

In the middle of 1953, Harry Hoagland set off for a trip to Texas. Hoagland hated to fly; he preferred to cross the country by train. Often on these trips Hoagland would be invited to dinner by the president of a bank or local industrial firm. Many of the men Hoagland met had reached an age where they were inclined to cut back or cash out on their business dealings. One of those executives was Paul R. Mills, the founder and chairman of Camco, Inc, a Houston company that specialized in the manufacture of oil drilling equipment. During his meeting with Mills, Hoagland learned that Mills was looking to raise some money for his drilling venture.

ARD investigated the company and learned that it was a pioneer in deep oil well drilling gear, the only maker of a retrievable valve that allowed an oil operator to install and remove gas-lift valves without disturbing the other valves. The technology saved oil operators a lot of money and headaches. So ARD purchased a 6 percent ten-year note for $150,000—its first investment in the oil industry. Hoagland joined the board of the company, and he recruited Grover Ellis, the vice president of the First National Bank of Houston, to join the board as well. Camco became one of ARD's most successful investments, increasing 800 percent in just three years.

As 1953 drew to a close, however, Doriot became increasingly gloomy about the state of venture capital. Besides Camco, ARD that year had only invested in two other new situations: a $200,000 investment negotiated by Hoagland in the Diamond Oil Well Drilling and the Diamond Oil Company, and in July the purchase, for $25,000, of all the outstanding common stock of the American Research Management Corporation, a related firm ARD set up to provide management consulting to its affiliates.

More importantly, ARD was down to $1.5 million in capital, its net asset value declined for the first time in four years, and its first employee flew the coop. Joseph W. Powell Jr. accepted a position as vice president and director at Harris Intertype Corporation in Cleveland, where he received an attractive package of stock options and other benefits. Elfers was now ARD's number two man, and Hoagland was promoted to treasurer. On top its internal problems, ARD also found itself tangling for the first time with the Securities and Exchange Commission, which began to question the propriety of some of its investments.

In November, Doriot set down his thoughts on the state of the industry for the 1953 annual meeting. His conclusion: "venture capital is not fashionable anymore." In public, Doriot blamed the declining prospects of small companies on the Korean War, excessive profits taxes to pay for the war, shortages of raw materials, and the "search for security instead of hard work and daring opportunities." While these factors fueled the expansion of large companies, they sapped the strength of start-ups. Doriot and ARD were learning an important lesson. Just as there was a general business cycle, the climate for entrepreneurialism was governed by its own rhythms and forces.

Innovation was not like a river, flowing constantly over time. It was more like heavy surf, with waves of technology seeming to come out of nowhere and crashing onshore every twenty or thirty years. The trick for a venture capitalist was to catch the wave several years before it crested and to bail out before it crashed. In the early- to mid-1950s, ARD was flailing around in the white water, waiting for the next wave to come. "It is interesting to see how the great interest that existed seven or eight years ago in venture capital has disappeared and how the daring and courage which were prevalent at that time have now waned," wrote Doriot. Confirming his dark assessment, ARD's stock price hit an all-time low in December of 1953 when its bid price plummeted to $16.

Even though the outside world was losing faith in venture capital, Doriot looked for ways to regain the public's confidence. On January 13, 1954, the directors of ARD declared a dividend of twenty-five cents per share—the corporation's first dividend, a $75,000 payment distributed from capital gains of $92,000. Another milestone had been achieved, but it also raised the pressure on ARD to sustain future payouts.

In retrospect, the eighteen months spanning the end of 1953 through 1954 were probably the nadir of ARD's existence, although Doriot would never admit as much in public. It was not just the humiliation of seeing its stock price free-fall to $16, though that was the most public sign of its troubles. It was also the growing chasm between investors' perceptions of ARD and the value of the firm's assets. In the first half of 1954 ARD's bid price hovered between $17 and $18, trading at a massive 37 percent discount to its net asset value of $28, the largest discount of its history. During this period, ARD also reported the second biggest write-off of its history: a $206,000 investment in Brunswick Enterprises, the company it formed in 1952 to acquire the assets of the shrimp distributor Colter Corporation.

More disturbing, Doriot and his men were running out of juice. In 1954, for the first time in its history, ARD did not invest in one single new company. Its deal flow was slowing to a trickle, compared to the previous seven years. "We do not know of any interesting new projects," confessed Doriot in a May note he wrote to himself (he often wrote notes or memos like this to clarify his thoughts). "We do not know where to go to find interesting projects." From 1947 to 1951, ARD received an average of 382 projects per year for review. In 1952, the number dropped to 133 projects, and the next year it dipped again to an all-time low of 117 projects reviewed. 1954 wasn't much better: ARD received 127 projects, about half of the projects it received three years before.

Adding to ARD's troubles were growing battles with government regulators. When ARD was formed in 1946, the SEC bent over backward to accommodate this new type of investment vehicle. But in the beginning of 1954, Doriot mused in an anguished letter to the SEC Chairman Ralph H. Demmler "whether perhaps there is not a misunderstanding on the part of the SEC of the kind of work that American Research is involved in." The letter was a follow-up to a meeting that Doriot and Griswold held with Demmler in the fall of 1953. In the four-page letter, Doriot detailed a number of cases in which SEC regulators questioned the fairness of several ARD investments.

The crux of the conflict was the valuation of ARD's investments. When ARD wanted to invest more in one of its portfolio companies, it had to submit an application to the SEC to receive an exemption from certain legal restrictions. Specifically, the 1940 Investment Company Act prohibited investment companies such as ARD from purchasing the securities "from any company controlled by such registered company" unless the terms of the transaction are "reasonable and fair and do not involve overreaching on the part of any person concerned." It was a well-intentioned law designed to prevent shady deals between affiliated companies but it could also function as thick red tape in the hands of a cautious, overburdened agency.

In fact, during the early years of the Eisenhower administration the SEC's enforcement and policy-making powers were less effective than at any other time in its history. In 1941, the SEC boasted a staff of more than seventeen hundred persons. During the Truman administration, the SEC still employed an average of twelve hundred people, but the Korean War and President

Eisenhower's zeal to cut the federal budget gutted the agency. By the end of the 1953 fiscal year, its staff was down to 773 people, draining "much of the Commission's vitality," said one SEC commissioner. Case backlogs grew, and by June 30, 1955 the SEC hit an all-time postwar low of 666 people.

Every time ARD wanted to change the capitalization of one of its companies, it essentially needed to prove to the government that the transaction was on fair terms. It was not exactly the most efficient way to do business, and Doriot was becoming increasingly frustrated with regulators who were denying or delaying ARD's financial moves. "I wonder if our personnel and directors are not more qualified to decide on that valuation than even the most distinguished person at the SEC," wrote Doriot. "I wish to state that with the present system we are greatly hampered. It is expensive, and in some cases dangerous . . . In other words, while the SEC believes it is protecting our stockholders, they are actually suffering."

The SEC was not the only government organization giving Doriot headaches. In the spring of 1954, Doriot grew worried over proposed changes to the Internal Revenue Code that would tax formerly tax-free mergers. Doriot knew that if the proposed changes were carried out, it would make it extremely difficult if not impossible for ARD to merge one of its affiliates with another company. Mergers had become a crucial tool in ARD's financial toolbox: it had engineered three mergers and acquisitions in the past four years.

The reason? Mergers were at times a quicker way to stabilize its affiliates than growing through retained earnings. Doriot knew that most entrepreneurs would not approve a merger if it meant being hit with an immediate tax. So he wrote to Senator Flanders to see what he could do about it. "When I first started teaching at the Business School, taxation was an important item in the life of the businessman, but one considered operating decisions first and taxation later," he wrote. "However, in recent years, taxation itself has become the dominating factor in the making of operating decisions."

The middle of 1954, fittingly, brought a dose of sad news. On June 22, Karl Compton passed away. He was sixty-six years old. Doriot recognized the death of this giant in ARD's semiannual letter to its stockholders. "In the passing of Dr. Karl T. Compton, the Corporation has lost a most valued friend and advisor," wrote Doriot. "Dr. Compton's foresight and vision were responsible in great part for the formation of American Research and Development Corp., the affiliated companies, and particularly Tracerlab, Inc., and

High Voltage Engineering Corp., on whose boards he served, will miss his wisdom and counsel."

Buy low, sell high. It was Wall Street's hoariest truism. And in 1954 a few savvy investment brokerages realized that ARD shares were so beaten down that it just might be a smart time to jump on the Doriot bandwagon. ARD was no longer seen as a growth investment; it was a value play!

In March, Belmont Towbin of C. E. Unterberg, Towbin Company, a forerunner to today's boutique investment banks, published a note recommending ARD shares because "the original investments are somewhat more seasoned and a few of them appear to be on the threshold of substantial expansion." Towbin had skin in the game, too: his firm had recently "taken a position in the shares." On April 15, brokerage H. Hentz & Company published a positive research report: "Although continued growth is likely, the shares are available at a large discount from net asset value and well below the 1952–1953 high of $29." On October 21, Towbin touted ARD in another column for the *Commercial and Financial Chronicle* titled "The Security I Like Best." Towbin's theory was now based on the idea that some of ARD's maturing affiliates would offer their shares to the public in early 1955.

The reports raised Doriot's spirits but not nearly as much as a radical new idea consuming the professor's thoughts. And so in the summer of 1954, Doriot seized another potential opportunity—this time in France. When Doriot was approached in 1953 to participate in the twenty-fifth anniversary of the Centre de Perfectionnement aux Affaires, the school he brought to life in the 1930s, he told the Paris Chamber of Commerce that he wanted to talk about the future rather than past. To Doriot, the anniversary would be an ideal time to announce the next logical step in the school's development: the creation of a European graduate business school. It was a radical idea in that it proposed an alternative vision of Europe, a vision unbound by tradition, social class, or geography.

Doriot was early to recognize the importance of globalization in business, and his experience running ARD only reinforced his belief that business demanded a global viewpoint. As early as 1949, ARD companies had begun doing business in Europe. And so a school that saw Europe as a holistic region operating within a global economy could serve as the ideal training ground for the business leaders of the future.

The notion of a pan-European business school also struck a personal chord with Doriot. When Doriot graduated from a lycée in Paris there was no place in Europe where he could seek advanced studies in business administration. He believed there should be such an opportunity, so that the Georges Doriots of the future would not have to leave Europe to pursue a world-class business education.

In late July, representatives from the Chamber of Commerce set up a meeting with Doriot to discuss his proposal. Doriot told them the school should last one year and be based on a residential campus, that students should come from all over Europe, and the teaching should be multilingual and based on the case method. Harvard would provide technical support, and Doriot held out the hope that the Ford Foundation would pony up some funds. The Chamber would be responsible for financing the set-up costs, providing teaching facilities, residences, and necessary improvements. The representatives said they liked the idea but needed time to think about it. Doriot returned to the United States, hopeful that his enhanced stature would ensure the realization of this new dream.

When Doriot returned to Boston, his top priority was fixing ARD's staff problem. ARD needed to hire more people to find and investigate new projects. In part, ARD did not make any new investments in 1954 because one of its top deal-makers was out of commission. In the late summer and fall, Doriot granted a temporary leave of absence to Henry Hoagland so he could help the Republican National Committee during the midterm elections of 1954. Committee chairman Leonard W. Hall, a former Long Island Congressman who ran Eisenhower's presidential campaign, dispatched Hoagland to four states where republican candidates were in trouble. Even though Hoagland was on leave, Doriot promoted him to vice president—an affirmation of his value to the firm.

In the second half of 1954, ARD hired two new employees. One was staff associate David B. Arnold Jr. The other was Grover Ellis Jr., Hoagland's banking buddy from Houston. Both men took Doriot's Manufacturing class and graduated in the class of 1947. With Hoagland's recommendation, ARD created a new position for Ellis, Southwestern Representative. The idea of a representative was to put someone in a region to prospect for investment opportunities. It was not a full-time job, however. The First National Bank of

Houston, where Ellis still worked as vice president, allowed him to work part time for ARD.

Building on that momentum, ARD ended 1954 on a positive note. Thanks to $80,000 in net income, ARD reported its first accumulated operating profit, exclusive of capital gains and losses. The corporation declared its second consecutive dividend of twenty-five cents per share, distributing another $75,000. It claimed a 200 percent jump in its net asset value to $2.8 million, mostly due to a tripling in the value of High Voltage Engineering shares. And ARD's stock finally showed signs of life, ending the year with a bid price of $28. After such a difficult eighteen months, the year's strong finish inspired Doriot to claim in his annual letter that ARD was in its best position ever. "Its affiliates," he wrote, "in spite of their youth when measured in years of existence, are displaying the characteristics of industrial maturity."

Doriot seized the moment, sending out a number of ARD's annual reports to powerful people such as General Leslie R. Groves and even President Eisenhower himself. "I believe that the support which you have given to new developments is of tremendous value to the country as a whole, and I am glad to note you have reached a point where you can safely declare dividends," wrote General Groves to Doriot on February 16, 1955. That same day Doriot received a letter from the White House. "It was nice to hear from you," wrote President Eisenhower, "and I am, as you suspected, enormously interested in the report of the American Research and Development Corp."

One week later, the ARD report again paid dividends. President Eisenhower wrote Doriot asking if "it would be convenient for you to come to an informal stag dinner on the evening of Tuesday, March fifteenth. I hope to gather together a small group, and I should like very much for you to attend if it is possible for you to do so." It was only the second time Doriot had ever been invited to the White House.

The invitation was just the latest sign of the Doriots' ascendant social status. Indeed, since returning to civilian life, Doriot and Edna had become a prominent couple on the Boston society circuit. Their prominence was mostly due to Georges, but Edna had become quite a force in her own right. In 1947, Edna became a secretary of the French Library in Boston, which had been established in 1945 to promote cultural relations between the United States and France. The library's founders got their start by rescuing books that were put in storage after the Germans occupied France. In 1949, Edna was elected a trustee of the library. For the next few decades, the Doriots played a central role in the library's development. "I was always very fond of Georges and Edna," says Janet Testa, a library trustee and friend of the Doriots, whose husband Richard became their personal lawyer. "Edna had great charisma. She was just the sweetest person. She would inspire people to come out and help out. She really helped the organization."

But Edna didn't stop there. Without children to tend to, the caring and thoughtful Edna poured herself into a variety of other nonprofit or philanthropic organizations. Starting in 1947, Edna also became a director and treasurer of the Girls Club of Boston, working on many committees. She joined the executive committee of the Florence Crittenton Association of Greater Boston, a nonprofit set up to help unwed mothers. And she also served as a director for the Massachusetts Society for the University Education of Women. As recognition for serving as a trustee and on various administrative committees of Emerson College, in 1955 Edna received the Isaacher Hoopes Eldridge Citation for Character and Service, given each year to the "one person chosen by the Executive Committee of the Alumni Association for outstanding devotion to the College."

It is early January 1955. Even though Doriot was a workaholic, he always looked forward to coming home to 12 Lime Street and having dinner with his beautiful wife. After questioning Edna's decision to buy the townhouse, Doriot had come to realize it was one of the smartest things she ever did. The building was simply a stunning piece of architecture. A former blacksmith's shop, it looked and felt like a castle, with arched doorways shaped like knight hoods and a huge ground floor dining room whose ceiling soared fifty feet to the roof of the house. There were two bedrooms upstairs, but the centerpiece of the second floor was a capacious living room with twenty-foot floor-to-ceiling windows overlooking the leafy, residential street. Doriot spent most of his time, though, in his study, a cozy room on the left front side of the ground floor. Arriving home, he would stroll into the study and mix up a martini. "This is where he came to sit, and work or read or smoke his pipe and think," says James M. Stone, a close friend who later purchased the house from Doriot. "This is also where he entertained people."

After dinner, Doriot and Edna retired to their bedroom. They always went to bed at 11 p.m. At 2 a.m. Doriot woke up, his sleep roiled by worries about

ARD. He turned to his night table, grabbed a little notepad of blue paper, and scribbled down some thoughts without turning on the light so as not to disturb Edna. In the morning, Doriot took the squares of blue paper, stuffed them into his suit jacket pocket, kissed Edna, and set off for work.

The John Hancock Building was so close to Lime Street that Doriot was spared a painful commute. Doriot simply ambled across the Boston Common on his way to the building, a dapper figure decked out in a dark suit with a Legion of Honor rosette pinned on his lapel, a white shirt, black homburg, and a handkerchief popping out of his breast pocket. It was a cold day so Doriot threw on his trusty trench coat. Arriving at the office, Doriot handed the blue notes to Dorothy Rowe, who expertly deciphered his scribbling. One of the notes mentioned a major concern: selling stock of ARD affiliates.

The chasm between ARD's stock price and net asset value made a public offering of ARD stock highly unattractive to both ARD and any potential investment bankers. That meant Doriot and his directors would have to come up with a way to generate cash without raising more money from investors. The only solution was to sell the shares of portfolio companies. The trick was figuring out which ones to sell.

Doriot's formula? Sell when "hope seems gone" or when "all is right but not outstanding" or when the "best growth period is behind." In 1955, ARD received nearly $1.4 million from debt repayments and sale of the shares in eight companies. The sales produced a capital gain of $369,000. The sales did not increase ARD's capital, though, because that year it invested $1.5 million into four existing affiliates and four new ones. But ARD's growing stock holdings gave the firm a decent degree of financial flexibility. By that time, eight of ARD's twenty-six affiliates were trading either over-the-counter or on the New York Stock Exchange. The market quotations allowed ARD to record a 37 percent increase in its unrealized capital gains to nearly $5 million, up from $3.6 million.

By the middle of 1955, ARD stock had jumped to $30, an all-time high. It is perhaps not surprising then that some early investors bailed out of ARD. In 1955, after nine long years, MIT, one of ARD's founding investors, sold all of its holdings. Other factors pushed toward a sale. ARD's main champion at MIT, University President Karl Compton, was no longer around to defend the company. Horace Ford, treasurer of ARD and MIT, also recommended a sale. (Later on, Doriot wrote that Ford was a "weak and uninteresting man" who "never believed in ARD.") And the university was under intense pressure to increase its investment returns. By the end of 1955, ARD shares had pulled back slightly to about $28. But the year brought another milestone: in 1955, for the first time, ARD filed a federal tax return as a regulated investment company.

In the first half of 1956, ARD continued to sell some of the stock of its affiliates. It cashed out its holdings of the Flexible Tubing Corporation, netting $100,997. It also sold one of its few wholly-owned subsidiaries, the Natural Gas Odorizing Company, to the Cue Fastener Corporation for a profit of $83,774. In the second half of the year, Doriot hired a new staff associate, Wayne P. Brobeck, a former officer with the Quartermaster Corps who recently worked on the staff of the Joint Committee on Atomic Energy.

By year-end, ARD's sales of eight of its affiliates cleared $196,000 in capital gains. But it reported a net loss on operations of $18,000, its first loss in five years. Meanwhile, it invested about $450,000 in two new companies and two existing affiliates, leaving it with just under $1 million in capital—below Doriot's safety margin.

If ARD continued its policy of distributing dividends out of realized capital gains, it would mean slicing its dividend in half. Doriot wouldn't stand for that. In order to increase last year's dividend, ARD came up with the ingenious idea of distributing one share of High Voltage Engineering stock for each ten shares of ARD, amounting to a dividend of $1.90 per share.

A decade after its founding, Doriot had led ARD to a fairly successful record. Thanks to ten years of trial and error, ARD had begun to codify the principles of venture investing. It had nurtured several innovative and successful businesses, most notably High Voltage Engineering, Tracerlab, Camco, and Ionics. And it had found a way to deliver operating profit and modest capital gains. But ARD had yet to fulfill its grander ambition of creating a venture capital community, nor had it produced a blockbuster company of "stature and importance." But that was all about to change.

NINE

A STAR IS BORN

(1957–1961)

I N THE EARLY 1950s, the postwar euphoria of the previous decade that had infused Americans with a sense of infinite possibilities morphed into a Cold War miasma of fear and paranoia. Yet underneath the surface of fear, a subculture of experimentation and rebellion flourished. In the early- to mid-1950s, Allen Ginsberg, Jack Kerouac, and William Burroughs developed a radical new form of literature that emphasized "stream of consciousness" writing. Modern abstract painting by Jackson Pollock, Willem de Kooning, and Mark Rothko overthrew European conventions of beauty and form. And in laboratories and universities across the northeastern seaboard, a bunch of scientists and engineers tinkered away on strange but powerful new electronics and computer devices that promised to completely change the way people communicated and conducted business.

"We felt electronics was going to revolutionize industry," said Kenneth H. Olsen, a U.S. Navy veteran who entered MIT after the war to study electrical engineering and ended up working at the school's Lincoln Laboratory. The university established the Lincoln Lab in 1951 with money from the Department of Defense in order to concentrate on building new computer technology for the Cold War. The whiz kids at MIT had already proven their chops by building the Whirlwind, the fastest computer during the 1950s, which was made out of clunky vacuum-tube circuits. Lincoln's new mission was to build a better computer for the Air Force that would anchor the nation's defense system. And in early 1952, Olsen, a cocky twenty-six-year-old, was asked to participate.

Whirlwind formed the basis of SAGE, the Semi-Automatic Ground Environment Defense System. Olsen, then pursuing his masters in engineering, was picked out of sixty engineers to lead a team to build a smaller test computer to make sure SAGE was viable. Olsen was not a superb student or intellectual wizard. But facing intense deadlines, MIT needed someone like Olsen, a child of strict, industrious Scandinavian immigrants known as "a guy who gets things done."

The head of SAGE, a dynamic engineer named Jay Forrester, believed a test computer could not be built in less than a year. After all, Whirlwind had taken more than four years to create. Olsen chose fifteen engineers to work on the project, including a feisty young man, Harlan Anderson, the only student from the University of Illinois who responded to Forrester's recruiting efforts for SAGE. Olsen flourished in the freewheeling atmosphere. "There was a lot of trust, a lot of freedom, a lot of competition between very bright people," recalled Olsen, who was given $1 million to build the machine. Miraculously, Olsen and his team finished the Memory Test Computer in nine months. In October 1952, the U.S. Air Force selected IBM and Lincoln Lab as the two main contractors to build its main air-defense computer: a jackpot for the SAGE project.

Olsen had established his reputation as a pragmatic leader. But the engineer also had a more spiritual side. At heart, Olsen was a thoughtful, religious man who saw profound connections between religion and science. "The books written before those years often were about the conflict of Christianity and science," said Olsen. "But it's obvious that the main theme of both is the same, which is searching for truth, which implies a certain humility."

After successfully overseeing the test computer, Olsen was picked to become MIT's liaison with IBM on the air-defense computer project. Olsen was immediately put off by the hierarchy, secrecy, and bureaucracy of the IBM culture. The people that frustrated Olsen were the same business types that scholar William H. Whyte wrote about in his 1956 classic, *The Organization Man*. Olsen despised the "organization man," with his perfectly trimmed hair and immaculate grey suit and his neat suburban tract house. He believed in the individual engineer and in collaboration with small teams of colleagues that quickly developed products that changed the world. Slogging away with Big Blue convinced Olsen that he could beat these suits at their own game.

As a favor to Olsen, MIT allowed him to work outside of the defense project on the exciting new field of transistors. One of the greatest inventions of modern history, transistors were first developed in December 1947 by three engineers at Bell Labs, William Shockley, John Bardeen, and Walter Brattain. Transistors were smaller, cheaper, faster, and more reliable conductors than vacuum tubes. In 1955, Olsen began working on a transistor-based computer called the TX-O. "The reason for building the TX-O was to demonstrate how efficient in power, how fast in speed, and how easy it would be to build a computer for defense," recalled Olsen.

Olsen developed the computer, unequivocally demonstrating the superiority of transistors. For this accomplishment, he expected businessmen to shower him with praise. But that was hardly the response of the organization men running corporate America. Instead, their silence implied a belief that Olsen and his team were irrelevant academics. In the end, "nobody cared," said Olsen. If Olsen was going to get the commercial world to respect and value his ideas, he realized he needed to start a company, he needed "to do something in business that people would care about." In the spring of 1957, he teamed up with his buddy Harlan Anderson. During lunch one afternoon, they threw together a crude business plan to launch a computer company that would make machines that were cheaper and easier to build and use than the hulking, expensive IBM mainframes.

Olsen and Anderson had an idea and a plan. Now they needed some money. Unfortunately, the business climate at this point was not very hospitable to new ideas. According to Olsen, "A number of companies had started in the Korean War. A number were no longer in existence . . . A recession was starting." They approached General Dynamics for financing first. "They turned us down flat because we didn't have any business experience," says Anderson. "We were pretty naive." Without connections or capital, the two engineers visited the Small Business Administration office in Boston. "They mentioned ARD to us." So the duo penned a letter to the head of ARD—literally the only venture capital firm in town.

Doriot was intrigued by the proposal, and ARD was hungry for some brilliant new ideas. The General turned over the proposal to Congleton, Rowe, and Brobeck. Congleton told Olsen and Anderson to submit a more formal business plan. After studying the history and finances of other companies, they put together a four-page proposal typewritten with white letters on a black background. They sent it over to ARD. But Congleton wanted more details. So on April 22, they wrote Congleton a letter explaining why their company had a high chance of success, and included their résumés as requested. Olsen and Anderson vowed their computer would contain features that "are unmatched in the development laboratories of the leading computer companies." The price of "our computer would be significantly less than the large scale computers commercially available today even though the capacity and speed would be higher." The computer could be produced in a "comparatively short delivery time" and, as a cherry on top, they claimed that "in the general purpose digital computer field today, it is a seller's market. The large backlog of orders bears this out."

ARD invited Olsen and Anderson to present their proposal before the ARD board. Congleton and others were nervous about the presentation, so they offered the duo three last bits of advice. "One was, don't use the word, 'computer,' said Olsen, "because *Fortune* magazine said no one was making money in computers and no one was about to. So we took that out of our proposal. We were going to make modules first, anyway. And they said, 'don't promise five percent profit.' You see we looked in the library. All good companies seemed to make about five percent on sales. The staff said that if you're asking someone to give you money, you've got to promise better results than that. So we promised ten percent. The third thing they said was, 'most of the board is over 80, so promise fast results.' So we promised to make a profit in a year."

The presentation went well but the ARD board did not make them an offer on the spot. Doriot told Olsen and Anderson they'd get back to them. "They clearly wanted to discuss it without us," said Anderson. "They said, 'Nothing is final. Don't quit your job.'" A few weeks passed. "It felt like an eternity," says Anderson.

After Olsen and Anderson submitted their proposal, General Doriot called up his former student and family friend Arnaud de Vitry and asked him to review it. At the time, de Vitry had formed an operations research unit for Mobil Oil, using computers and complex mathematical models to improve the production and distribution of oil refining. He examined the proposal and also had some engineers who worked for his father-in-law take a look. De Vitry saw the value of the idea to develop a more practical computer that was

10 percent of the cost of an IBM machine. "I told the General it was a worthwhile project," says de Vitry. "He said fine but go on the board."

After conferring with de Vitry and the ARD board, Doriot concluded that the business case for Olsen and Anderson's company was fairly impressive. More than that, when Doriot and his fellow directors saw Olsen and Anderson speak in person, they realized that these were two fine young men who had the passion and dedication required to create a successful business from scratch. In this special case, Doriot saw that ARD had the perfect formula in its hands: two Grade A men paired with an outstanding idea.

The duo sought $100,000. ARD offered them $70,000 in equity financing for a 70 percent stake in the company, and a $30,000 loan to be given later in the year. It was a take-it-or-leave-it-deal. With no other offers and no clue how to negotiate a better offer, Olsen and Anderson took it. It was the only new investment ARD made in 1957. "We thought we could succeed with that amount of money and we wanted to do the computer company so badly that we were willing to accept the terms," recalls Anderson. "The excitement of creating a company was more important than the terms of the deal."

Seven hundred of the one thousand founding shares of ARD stock went to ARD, Olsen and Anderson got two hundred, and one hundred were reserved for a seasoned manager who could help run the business. As the unquestioned leader, Olsen took 12 percent of the shares, leaving Anderson with 8 percent. Olsen never liked any of ARD's suggestions for a manager and one candidate turned down the job so the spot went unfilled. Since the 100 shares for the manager were never issued, that meant ARD owned 77 percent of the venture. To provide some degree of financial assistance, General Doriot assigned Dorothy Rowe to serve as the company's first treasurer. Since ARD did not want the company to build computers initially, Olsen and Anderson changed the name of Digital Computer Corporation to Digital Equipment Corporation.

But before Doriot signed the final deal, he had one last request: he insisted on meeting privately with the wives of Olsen and Anderson. "He wanted total devotion of everyone to the business," says Anderson. The wives impressed General Doriot, and at last he blessed the deal. As a final hedge, Doriot stocked the Digital board with five trusted advisors: Brobeck, Congleton, de Vitry, Hoagland, and Horace Ford.

In August of 1957, Olsen and Anderson incorporated Digital and embarked on an adventure, fired up with capital and confidence. "You never had much in the Depression and you didn't worry about very much," recalled Olsen. "You never really worried about failure because, you know, it didn't make any difference."

On October 4, 1957, the Soviet Union shocked the United States and the rest of the world when it launched the *Sputnik I* satellite. Until that humiliating moment, the United States believed it was the world's leader in missile development and space technology. The success of *Sputnik* and subsequent failure of the first two U.S. satellite launch tests proved the nation was a second banana, while raising larger fears about U.S. competitiveness and national security. "The vital problem facing the nation, and the free world as a whole," wrote one author in a 1957 *New York Times* article, "is the fact that Russia is training scientists and technological personnel at a pace four times that of our own, and that unless something is done about it as a large-scale national effort, Russia will surpass us in the future, with consequences too tragic too contemplate."

Like World War II, the *Sputnik* crisis marked a profound turning point in the history of American innovation. Over the next year, the U.S. government inaugurated a host of federally sponsored programs that became the bedrock of the high-technology, entrepreneurial economy. In February of 1958, the Department of Defense created the Advanced Research Projects Agency, a high-level organization to execute long-term research and development projects, which later became the Defense Advanced Research Projects Agency, or DARPA. (DARPA was responsible for funding development of many groundbreaking technologies, including the ARPANET computer network, which eventually grew into the Internet). In July 1958, President Eisenhower signed a bill creating the National Aeronautics and Space Administration, and Congress dramatically increased funding for scientific research. "Sputnik was a wake-up call for science and engineering," says Harlan Anderson.

Sputnik also galvanized public support for venture capital. Bills to create publicly sponsored venture capital organizations had been introduced in Congress over the last two decades but they had always been too controversial to pass. The Sputnik crisis silenced the critics of the languishing bills, mostly Federal Reserve officials who believed the modest growth potential of many new ventures justified the small pool of venture capital. And so on August 21, 1958, President Eisenhower, once unenthusiastic about proposals for federally sponsored investment companies, signed the Small Business Investment Act of 1958. Congress appropriated $250 million to start the Small Business Investment Company (SBIC) program, which offered tax breaks and subsidized loans to aspiring entrepreneurs.

Gauging the impact of the SBIC program is a complex and contentious issue. Many of today's most successful venture capitalists rightly point out that the SBIC program never created a company of considerable or lasting success. But if the SBIC program did little to advance the art and practice of successful venture investing, it did help propel the venture industry by attracting talented young men who later became pioneers of the field. Moreover, SBICs helped to transform an atomized community into a national phenomenon. Before the SBIC legislation, the entire venture capital market consisted of a handful of firms investing less than $100 million. By 1967, 791 licensed SBICs had invested more than $1 billion. Franklin P. "Pitch" Johnson, a Doriot student who graduated from Harvard Business School in 1952 and formed the venture capital firm Asset Management Company in 1965, credits the SBIC program as an important force in building the venture capital industry. The law made the nation "see that there was a problem and that this was a way to do something," said Johnson. "It formed the seed of the idea and a cadre of people like us."

Money, money, money. It seemed as if Doriot never stopped worrying about it. Despite the rise of the SBICs, 1958 was no different. With only $1.1 million in capital available to invest, ARD continued to operate with its hands tied behind its back. At ARD's annual meeting held in January 1958, Doriot told his directors that they needed more capital. "We miss projects because of lack of capital," he said. Some of the missed projects presented opportunities with larger, older, and safer companies. "If we could go into some of those larger ones," said Doriot, "we could then feel more courageous about going into a restricted number of small ones appearing dangerous but challenging."

To raise more money, Doriot proposed two ideas. One, hold an offering for the three hundred thousand ARD shares that had been authorized but not issued. The sticking point was that ARD wanted $35 per share but its stock was only trading around $20. The other idea: appeal to the nation's growing fear of "bigness" by selling ARD stock to dozens of the nation's largest corporations. In truth, it was a half-baked idea that smacked of frustration and would have reinforced the falsehood that ARD was a social or philanthropic experiment. Doriot shunned SBICs because he thought that debt—and its attendant interest payments—was a burdensome financial mechanism for a young firm.

Back at Harvard, with thirty years of experience to fall back on, Doriot was more successful at solving problems. The professor was particularly effective at finding jobs for his students. Occasionally, Doriot would even help a student who dared to avoid his class. Robert McCabe was one of those lucky ones. McCabe applied for a job at Lehman Brothers, where Doriot happened to be friends with the bank's head, Robert "Bobbie" Lehman, a financier and world-class art collector who became a legend by transforming his namesake into one of the most powerful investment banks on Wall Street. But that's not why Doriot liked him. "The General said he liked Robert Lehman because he was the only investment banker with compassion," says Robert's wife Dina McCabe. "He also liked Robert Lehman because he felt he was a statesman compared to heads of other big firms who were out for the last penny."

Lehman called Doriot for a recommendation. The General told Bobbie that he was very distressed about the fact that McCabe had not taken his course. But he agreed to meet him, inviting the young man to his house for a Christmas party. "We got along well," says McCabe. "The fact that I spoke a little French helped." Doriot gave McCabe the thumbs up to Lehman. "I am glad to hear what you say about Robert McCabe," Lehman wrote to Doriot, "as I told his father that I would like him to come down to see me in order to talk about his future and the possibility of working here at Lehman Brothers." After graduating in the spring of 1958, McCabe got a job in the New Business Department of Lehman Brothers.

Doriot's growing reputation and popularity with the student body continued to induce envy within some quarters of the hypercompetitive Harvard faculty. While Doriot was very active in faculty affairs before the war, since returning from Washington he devoted less and less time to the school's social life. Some colleagues perceived that as arrogance. "It was all kind of subtle," says Vernon Alden, a 1950 graduate of the school who became associate dean in 1957. "You would hear wisecracks about the amount of time Doriot spent on campus. He thought faculty meetings were a waste of time. He came and taught his courses. There would be committees and he was never part of that."

Some of the ill will stemmed from misguided impressions that ARD was making Doriot a rich man. Doriot's income had indeed received a nice boost from his extra salary, but he had not yet attained any great wealth from his extracurricular activities. As associate dean, Alden reviewed the salaries of professors with the school's new dean, Stanley F. Teele, who took over in 1955 from Dean Donald K. David. "I was astonished to discover that Doriot was making about half of what other professors were making," says Alden. Most professors made $60,000 to $70,000. Doriot made about $30,000. Dean Teele, says Alden, justified the low salary on the grounds that Doriot was pulling in so much money from ARD he should not receive a full salary. But Alden pointed out to Dean Teele that ARD paid modest salaries, and that in any event, several professors were doubling or tripling their income from outside consulting. "This was all news to Stanley Teele," says Alden. "He immediately boosted his salary."

Doriot had grown to despise committees, but the larger truth was that he was an insanely busy, creative, and ambitious man. Most people would be satisfied managing one career, let alone two. Not Doriot. While many Harvard professors took off the summer to relax, Doriot traveled to France on his annual working vacation. He did not tend to business for Harvard or ARD, though. For the last few summers, he pressed on with his latest idea to form a European graduate business school. Two leading French businessmen had joined his cause: Raoul de Vitry d'Avaucourt, Arnaud's father, who was the president of Pechiney, France's largest aluminum producer, and I Iely d'Oissel, president of Saint Gobain, a French glass giant. "They gave their time, their support, their reputation," wrote Doriot. "I made several speeches. They were always there."

Doriot also recruited several former students who were from France, including Claude Janssen and Olivier Giscard d'Estaing, the brother of the future President of France, who was teaching at the Institut d'Études Politiques. "Doriot considered me his man on the scene," says Janssen. "I helped devise the project. Since I was living in Paris, several times he asked me to go and see people to push the thing. I knew a lot of people and was not very shy." One key contact: Janssen was a good friend of the son of the treasurer of the Paris Chamber of Commerce, Jean Marcou. "I had easy access to him," he says. "So I went to see him a few times on Doriot's behalf to push the idea."

All of their hard work paid off in July of 1957. After three years of coaxing, the Paris Chamber of Commerce at its general meeting agreed to establish the school. The school's sponsors were buoyed by the recent signing of the Treaty of Rome, which established the European Economic Community, the first important step toward the creation of a common market with free movement of goods, service, labor, and capital. A few days after the meeting, on July 9, the chamber and the French General Association of Free Enterprise announced the school's creation. The chamber supported all of Doriot's main suggestions, and said first classes would begin in the autumn of 1958.

In the spring of 1958, Doriot received confirmation that the European business school had finally persuaded two people to take the school's top jobs. It was a difficult sell. Claude Janssen and Arnaud de Vitry did not jump at the opportunity. "I had just started my business career," says Janssen, then just twenty-seven years old. "Although I was interested in creating INSEAD, I was not interested in being a professor." The Paris Chamber of Commerce convinced Willem Posthumus Meyjes, the retiring Dutch ambassador to Greece, to become Director General, with Olivier Giscard d'Estaing as his second in command. Janssen thought Olivier was a better choice anyway. "Olivier's brother was just arriving in government," says Janssen. "So his connections were better than mine for a project like that. Doriot also thought he was a better choice."

Owing to the hiring delays, the school's opening date was pushed back to September 1959. The postponement was a blessing in disguise. "The school was a virtual entity, without premises or even a firm location, without professors, without fixed legal status, without a selection process for students or a course outline to propose to them, and with only a portion of its funding guaranteed," according to Jean-Louis Barsoux. In late July, Doriot toured the Paris region with Giscard d'Estaing and Janssen looking for "any worthwhile available building."

General Georges Doriot was a twentieth-century maverick and Renaissance man. After emigrating to the United States from France in 1921, Doriot went on to become a world-class professor, soldier, and financier. Scaling each of these peaks, Doriot bucked the prevailing system. Instead of following Harvard Business School's famous case study method, Doriot lectured students with his philosophy of business and life and gave them practical experience by sending them on consulting assignments with companies. In the military, he led a revolution by applying science to the art of war, spearheading research and development that led to dozens of innovative items such as bulletproof armor; cold-weather uniforms; and portable, nutritious K-rations. And in the financial world, as president of American Research & Development, the first successful venture capital firm, he proved that there was big money to be made from patient investing in and nurturing of small, unproven companies. (Photo courtesy of Archives Photo Collection, Knowledge and Library Services, Harvard Business School. © Baker Library, Harvard Business School. Used with permission.)

Monsieur et Madame Auguste DORIOT sont heureux de vous faire part de la naissance de leur fils GEORGES.

83, Boulevard Gouvion-Saint-Cyr.

Top: Armand Peugeot entered one of his machines in the world's first automobile race, the Paris-Rouen Trial of 1894. Auguste, who won the race driving a Peugeot, sits in the winning car besides Pierre Giffard, the editor of *Le Petit Journal*, a well-known French newspaper. (Photo courtesy of Poillot family. © Doriot family. Used with permission.)

Above: A reproduction of the birth announcement sent out by Auguste and Camille Doriot illustrates the significance of the automobile to the Doriot family. (Photo courtesy of Poillot family. © Doriot family. Used with permission.)

Left: Georges Doriot when he was about ten months old. (Photo courtesy of Poillot family. © Doriot family. Used with permission.)

Above: Georges Doriot enlisted in the French Army in 1917 and joined the R.A.L.T., a motorized heavy artillery regiment. (Photo courtesy of Poillot family. © Doriot family. Used with permission.)

Left: A photo of the Doriot family taken in 1908 shows father Auguste, mother Camille, Georges, and his younger sister Madeleine. (Photo courtesy of Poillot family. © Doriot family. Used with permission.)

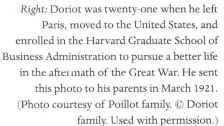

Right: Doriot was twenty-one when he left Paris, moved to the United States, and enrolled in the Harvard Graduate School of Business Administration to pursue a better life in the aftermath of the Great War. He sent this photo to his parents in March 1921. (Photo courtesy of Poillot family. © Doriot family. Used with permission.)

Above: By 1929, Doriot had become a full professor at Harvard Business School. The doctor of "sick businesses" is shown aboard the *Ile de France*, a famous ship of the French Line, in 1931. (Photo © CORBIS Corporation. Used with permission.)

Inset: Doriot met his wife-to-be, Edna Allen, after she was hired as his research assistant at Harvard in 1927. Photo courtesy of The French Library and Cultural Center, Boston. © The French Library and Cultural Center. Used with permission.)

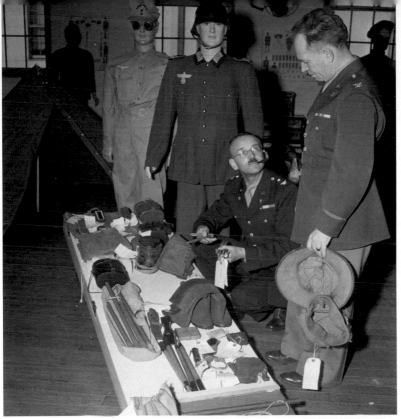

Above: Pipe-smoking Colonel Doriot and Colonel D. H. Cowles inspect equipment taken from captured German soldiers in 1943. Always looking for an edge to help American GIs, Doriot was surprised by the quality of German gear and the amount of aluminum the Germans used, for example, in the tent stakes he holds. (Photo © CORBIS Corporation. Used with permission.)

Right: In 1946, Doriot was recruited to run American Research & Development, the first public venture capital firm. The famous inventor Charles F. Kettering predicted ARD would go bust in five years. Doriot proved him wrong over the next quarter century. (Photo courtesy of *BusinessWeek.* © *BusinessWeek.* Used with permission.)

BUSINESS WEEK

FEB. 19, 1949

WEEK AGO

YEAR AGO

Georges F. Doriot: Funneling venture capital into new fields opened by research (page 6)

Right: Doriot, Edna, and his "surrogate son" Arnaud de Vitry at the 1951 coming-out party for a family friend. (Photo courtesy of The French Library and Cultural Center, Boston. © The French Library and Cultural Center. Used with permission.)

Below: Doriot was one of the most accomplished and influential professors at Harvard Business School, teaching more than six thousand students over a forty-year career. Many of those students went on to become leaders of corporate America. (Photo courtesy of Archives Photo Collection, Knowledge and Library Services, Harvard Business School. © Baker Library, Harvard Business School. Used with permission.)

Bottom: An innovative force in education, Doriot was early to recognize the importance of globalization and creativity in the business world. Decades before economists appreciated the value of technology, Doriot realized that innovation was the key to economic progress. (Photo courtesy of Archives Photo Collection, Knowledge and Library Services, Harvard Business School. © Baker Library, Harvard Business School. Used with permission.)

Top: American Research & Development financed and nurtured the venture capital industry's first spectacular success—Digital Equipment Corporation—inspiring legions of entrepreneurs and financiers to create the next big thing. (left to right) Henry W. Hoagland VP, ARD; John Barnard Jr., general counsel, Massachusetts Investors Trust; Jay W. Forrester, professor, MIT; William H. Congleton, VP, ARD; Harlan E. Anderson, VP, cofounder, DEC; Kenneth H. Olsen, President, cofounder, DEC; Dorothy E. Rowe, treasurer, ARD; Vernon R. Alden, president, Ohio University; Arnaud de Vitry, European Enterprise Development; Wayne P. Brobeck, director of consumer relations, Vitro Corporation of America.(Photo courtesy of *Fortune.* © Gordon College. Used with permission.)

Above: American Research & Development's first successful investment was in High Voltage Engineering, a Massachusetts company started by two prominent MIT physicists in a converted garage. (Photo courtesy of *Fortune.* © Ivan Massar. Used with permission.)

Above: General Doriot sitting in the study of his beautiful townhouse in Boston's Beacon Hill, flanked by awards and personally inscribed photos from Presidents Herbert Hoover and Dwight Eisenhower. (Photo courtesy of *Fortune.* © Ivan Massar. Used with permission.)

Right: Doriot posing beside a portrait of Edna. After a forty-eight-year storybook marriage, Edna passed away in 1978. Photo courtesy of The French Library and Cultural Center, Boston. © The French Library and Cultural Center. Used with permission.)

In August 1958, after Doriot returned to the United States, Olivier and a friend of his struck up the idea of establishing the school in conjunction with the American Art School in the Chateaux of Fontainebleau, Napoleon Bonaparte's favorite haunt thirty miles southeast of Paris. The art school occupied the Louis XV wing of the Fountainebleau palace for two months every summer. The facilities were vacant the rest of the year, and the area offered many local residences. By October, Giscard d'Estaing wrote Doriot telling him that talks with the American Art School were coming along well. There was one catch, however. The Minister of Culture, the great writer and political activist Andre Malraux, held the power to approve the use of the school. A formal request was made and summarily rejected on the grounds that the palace was reserved for "artistic activities." Doriot gamely replied that business was an art, but his argument bombed like a bad joke.

Back in Maynard, Massachusetts, in a Civil War–era woolen mill, events were unfolding at a much quicker pace. In the first half of 1958, ARD invested another $30,000 in Digital with a ten-year promissory note. For the last year, Olsen and Anderson had been setting up shop in an 8,680 square foot space in the mill of the American Woolen Company, a massive building twenty minutes from MIT's Lincoln Lab. After the World War II textile boom, the mill struggled, before closing in 1950. Since then, it had been occupied by Raytheon, American Can, and more than a dozen smaller businesses. It was hard to miss the symbolism: new industries sprouting from the ashes of dying trades.

Olsen and Anderson ran a shoestring operation, mimicking Doriot's frugal ethic. Olsen appropriated an old rolltop desk left behind by the previous tenants, while Anderson recycled a desk he had built in junior high school. ARD loaned them a couple of steel desks for their secretaries. Olsen and Anderson were so miserly they didn't install doors, even in bathrooms. They cost too much, said Olsen. Digital did not skimp on everything though. ARD advised them to hire a Boston lawyer and bank, as well as their accounting firm, Lybrand, Ross Brothers & Montgomery. Olsen and Anderson would not normally hire such high-priced help but they deferred to their major stockholder.

For its organizational culture, Olsen and Anderson looked no further than MIT. They wanted to capture the competitive, yet creative environment of a top-tier research university. "We had so much confidence in MIT that we even followed the MIT operations manual," said Olsen. "We took the same hours, we took the same vacations, we paid the same holidays."

By early 1958, Digital shipped its first products: modules used in the testing of computer memory devices. The modules were in great demand by Lincoln Lab, Bell Labs, the California Institute of Technology, and other research facilities. "The potential customers were readily easy to define because they were the people who wanted high speed circuits," recalled Olsen. "And so we went to trade shows and we'd call on people we knew." Digital also hired its first salesman, Ted Johnson, a former Doriot student who graduated in the class of 1958. "I was one of his best students," says Johnson, who majored in electrical engineering at the prestigious California Institute of Technology, or Caltech as it was known.

Johnson had made an immediate impression on Doriot back in his Harvard days. After forming his work group at the business school, Johnson and his team invited Doriot out to dinner. "As soon as he came into the room he shook the hands of everybody," says Johnson. Doriot, who highly valued titles and academic credentials, grabbed Johnson's hand and said, "You are the man from Caltech. Good school. Good school." Doriot was so impressed Johnson went to Caltech that during dinner he wouldn't stop talking about it. And when Doriot left, he looked at Johnson one last time and said, "Good school. Good school."

Johnson did not aim to be an organization man either. Although most graduating students preferred to seek jobs in banking or finance, Johnson wanted to work for a small manufacturing company. "People would not work for small companies and they would not work in sales," says Johnson. "It was kind of an oddity to do that unless they had a family business. It was in my second year that *Sputnik* flew over. That started the whole high tech race. It led to the Kennedy moon-shot. It certainly gave a big impetus to high technology. It was coming along anyway. The government started taking a much stronger role. The timing was perfect."

Johnson knew about Digital because during his second year he took a job working sixteen hours a week at Lincoln Lab. At Lincoln, many of the staffers were buzzing about two researchers who left the lab and started a company named Digital Equipment. In the spring of 1958, Johnson finagled a meeting with the company. He told Anderson that if Digital hired a sales force, it could make a million dollars a year. "Harlan Anderson turned around and made me an offer for $6,000 a year," says Johnson. Johnson had two other offers, both for more money, so he visited Doriot to see what he thought about the job.

"You are Scandinavian aren't you?" asked Doriot.

"Yes," replied Johnson.

"Scandinavians work very hard," replied Doriot. "I could use another hard working Scandinavian. You do that, you work for DEC and make them work hard as hell."

Johnson then met Olsen for the first time. Impressed with the founder's confidence, Johnson took the job. He was Digital's tenth employee.

At the end of Digital's first year, the company actually turned a profit. It was a small profit, a rounding error in the neighborhood of $3,000, but a profit nonetheless. Olsen took Digital's financial statements over to Boston and proudly dropped them on Doriot's desk, expecting his congratulations. "I'm sorry to see this," said Doriot, looking up from his desk. "No one has succeeded this soon and ever survived." It was almost as if Doriot was channeling his father and asking Olsen: "And why not first?"

In the beginning of 1959, something miraculous happened: ARD's stock price started to climb. Sure, the stock market was booming again after the 1957 recession, and a rising tide typically lifts all boats. But ARD's stock did not boom during the last bull market of 1950–1955. Something else was at play. Portfolio companies such as Camco, Cutler-Hammer, Digital Equipment, High Voltage, Ionics, Machlett Laboratories, and Tracerlab were all reaching escape velocity. At the end of 1958, ARD's stock price hit an all-time high of around $38, nearly twice the previous year's value.

The market's revival, the impressive growth of many ARD affiliates, and ARD's increasing stock price led Doriot to propose an offering of one hundred thousand shares of ARD stock at its annual meeting in March. Doriot spent most of the meeting, however, discussing the peculiar nature of ARD's problems. "Our troubles have been principally human ones," Doriot told the audience. "People who seemingly showed good potential and who even proved excellent in being able to start something [but] do not make the grade later on. But, like a child in school, you don't—you can't—let him down just because he flunks in one grade or class. You continue to hope."

Doriot realized that ARD needed to act quickly because it could not match the financial benefits offered by the SBIC program. Various officials asked ARD if it wanted to participate in the program but Doriot was adamantly against debt financing—especially with government money. ARD would have to push through the stock sale. On April 21, Lee Higginson Corporation, C. E. Unterberg, Towbin Company, and Merrill Turben & Company offered one hundred thousand shares of ARD stock on a best efforts basis for $40 a share. After discounts and expenses, the offering generated nearly $4 million, more than tripling ARD's capital.

Doriot was right to fear SBICs. One of them, Electronics Capital Corporation, received its license in June of 1959. That same month, investment bankers led by Hayden, Stone & Company raised a stunning $18 million in a public offering of Electronics Capital stock. In one transaction, without hardly any track record, Electronics Capital had raised nearly twice as much capital as ARD had raised over its thirteen-year history. Even if SBICs did not represent a competitive threat, they were siphoning capital away from ARD.

When it came to creating new business and capital gains, though, ARD was unrivalled. Indeed, many ARD affiliates were attracting increasing interest from various suitors. ARD received 2,200 shares of Cessna Aircraft Company after its affiliate Aircraft Radio Corporation was sold to a Cessna subsidiary. And after affiliate Machlett Laboratories merged with the Raytheon Company, ARD received about $1.6 million in Raytheon common and preferred stock for its initial $660,000 investment. In addition, ARD continued to plow money in its growing companies. Digital got another $25,000.

With ARD on firmer financial footing, Doriot began to ponder steps that he thought would further solidify its future. In August he sent a letter to the president of the New York Stock Exchange, inquiring if it was possible that ARD could meet the listing requirements of the Big Board. The Exchange's executive vice president Edward C. Gray wrote back to Doriot, notifying him that "we will make an informal and confidential review of the eligibility of the Company and advise you of our opinion shortly." Gray also gave Doriot a heads up that it might not work. "It would appear that the Company does not meet our standards for established earning power of $1,000,000 per year," he wrote. "However, we are aware of the fact that the objective of the

Company is capital gains rather than current income and will take this fact into consideration."

Doriot headed back to France in the summer of 1959 to complete his mission there. In early July, the school finally received approval from Andre Malraux to use the Fountainebleau palace to house its lecture room and four offices. It had taken several months of lobbying important civil servants and the intervention of one of Doriot's friends to convince the minister. A small group of volunteers, including Claude Janssen and Olivier Giscard d'Estaing, plugged away on the school's operating policies and course outlines. Doriot provided unlimited access to Harvard case studies and donated several hundred books to the school. Professors were recruited and brochures were distributed to big companies and top U.S. schools. Willem Posthumus Meyjes and Olivier Giscard d'Estaing had started pitching the school in the fall of 1958 on a tour of elite European universities. By July 20, 1959, when the school's supervisory committee met, it had received 130 applications.

But the French government almost killed the project three weeks before its opening when it passed legislation eliminating deferments of military service. France was bogged down in the Algerian War and needed to muster all the young men it could to crush a growing insurgency. "We had a problem," says Janssen, who was allowed to work on the school part time by his employer, Worms & Cie. "The people we were looking for would eventually be drafted in the army." In late August the French Minister of the Interior assured the President of the Paris Chamber of Commerce the school would be added to the list of institutes eligible for service deferments.

And then in May, the Ford Foundation announced it would not finance the school. The school had enough money to start but without the Ford grant it did not have enough money to last the entire year. So the founders got by on tuition fees until new funds could be raised later on. "We had professors for the first year without being sure we had the money to pay them," says Janssen. "But . . .they came and we finally paid them." Satisfied that the school was finally launched, Doriot returned to the United States to start teaching his class. "Now you have left again, we feel how much we need you," wrote Posthumus Meyjes to Doriot.

On Saturday September 12, the school's founders gathered at Fountainebleau for registration day, expecting sixty-two students. "It was terrible," says Janssen. "We were working like mad here in the summer. We were all waiting for the students. At lunchtime, 10 or 15 students showed. We had a very difficult lunch." But thankfully, most of the other students arrived that afternoon, and the rest came on Monday.

Janssen and his two associates cabled Doriot: "The ship is launched. 57 registered today. Opening ceremonies completed." In a longer note sent several days later, Janssen personally thanked Doriot: "It remains for us to thank you for starting up the whole idea and giving us the opportunity to contribute to an endeavor with so much future."

The official dedication ceremony of the Institut Européen d'Administration des Affaires (European Institute of Business Administration), called INSEAD for short, took place on October 9, 1959 in the Salle des Colonnes at Fountainebleau. Although Doriot had missed the dedication ceremonies for the CPA and Natick Lab, this time he was present. Scanning the Mannerist sculpture, metalwork, and paintings lining the gilded room of columns, Doriot proudly observed an audience of three hundred distinguished guests, including the general secretary of NATO.

When it came time for Doriot to address the crowd, he gave credit to INSEAD's first American donation. It was not from a corporation but from a former Manufacturing student, Thomas E. Congdon, class of 1952, who donated a few hundred dollars. The Business School had done so much for Congdon that he wanted to help Europeans in any way so they could get the same opportunity.

All told, Doriot raised $122,650, or 18 percent, of the school's initial donations from U.S. donors. The money came from students, colleagues, and friends of Doriot, including Robert Lehman, Morgan Guaranty, and Pepperidge Farms founder Margaret Rudkin. An even more impressive demonstration of Doriot's influence came later that day when Posthumus Meyjes read a letter. "The President extends his congratulations to all those who have taken part in the establishment of this Institute which is destined to play a creative role in the economic affairs of Europe and the world." The note, signed by U.S. President Dwight D. Eisenhower, topped off a perfect day for Doriot.

"One of the ideas of INSEAD, in addition to creating a business school, was that creating a European business school, at the time when the Treaty of

Rome was signed, was another way of avoiding in the future that people of Europe would fight against each other," says Janssen. "So having a letter from Eisenhower saying he thought it would be a good idea for peace in Europe, was a very good sponsorship."

The ceremony went off without a hitch, and was covered extensively by both the European and U.S. press. "He was moved and very happy," says Janssen, who spent the day with Doriot. "After all, he had been struggling a lot for this day, and he saw the first fruit of the struggle. He always wanted the things he was involved with in the States to find some development in Europe. He didn't know if it was going to survive. But at least it was formed."

Energized by millions of dollars in fresh capital, ARD set off on an investment spree in the second half of 1959. Doriot and his team poured more than $1.5 million into six new companies and three existing affiliates. Textron Electronics, a subsidiary created in 1959 by the conglomerate Textron, Incorporated, received the lion's share of the year's proceeds, with a $750,000 investment. Doriot took a seat on its board.

ARD also poured another $100,000 into Digital Equipment. Since the investigation phase of a project was often very short, especially if the process was accelerated by competition for the deal, ARD frequently financed companies in "steps" as a way to reduce its risk. Digital Equipment exemplified this strategy.

Olsen and company continued to crank out modules. But in the summer of 1959 Olsen decided it was time for Digital to develop its first computer. ARD's $100,000 infusion would help fund the creation of the PDP-1, an interactive computer that would be easy to install and use, and be sold at a fraction of the cost of an IBM mainframe, the dominant machine made by the dominant computer manufacturer. Olsen wanted to liberate computing from the tyranny of the elite. "The concept of an interactive computer was strange," recalled Olsen. "Some people thought it was wrong. Computers are serious, you shouldn't treat them lightly. You shouldn't have fun with them. They shouldn't be exciting. They should be formal and distant with red tape involved."

The second biggest bet of the year was a $190,000 investment in a Texas oil rig manufacturer Zapata Off-Shore Company. In the middle of 1959, the oil exploration company Zapata Petroleum spun off its subsidiary Zapata Off-Shore and tapped a young World War II hero named George H. W. Bush to be its president. Henry Hoagland, who came to know Bush during his frequent trips to Texas, brought the deal to ARD.

Zapata Off-Shore specialized in the business of building and leasing off-shore rigs to oil production companies. The company accepted an offer to design and build a new oil drilling machine from R. G. LeTourneau, a prolific inventor of construction equipment who made his name supplying the U.S. Army during World War II with earthmoving scrapers. LeTourneau completed the first rigs in late 1957, and Zapata began leasing them in the Caribbean, the Gulf of Mexico, and the Central American coast.

"The majority of the Zapata Petroleum board feels that it will be some time before Petroleum can realize anything tangible from its offshore holdings," wrote Bush in a confidential memo to one of his investors, explaining the spin-off. "They feel it would be better to dispose of the stock for cash and then put the cash to work in Zapata primarily by buying oil producing properties . . . I have overall confidence in the Gulf Coast area, and although I am not happy with our emphasis on oil drilling equipment, I feel we have in Zapata Off-Shore Company a vehicle through which with some diversification [we] can grow and prosper."

The contemporary image of George H. W. Bush is of an aloof, yet charming man, a foreign policy expert whose presidency was brought down by failures in managing the economy. But Bush's experience running Zapata Off-Shore shows he was a fairly clever and successful businessman, skilled in the arcane ways of tax shelters and finance. Zapata Off-Shore lost money in its first two years but turned profitable in the early- to mid-1960s. The company's profits stemmed not just from running a well-managed operation but also from "shrewd utilization of offshore subsidiaries—in Bush's case, a half dozen with names like Zapata de Mexico, Zapata International, and Zapata Overseas." By the time Bush was elected to Congress in 1966, seven years after ARD patiently supported the company, financial filings showed the forty-two-year-old's holdings in Zapata Off-Shore were worth $1.1 million. Later on, Bush continued to cash in on his many oil connections to help finance his political ambitions.

Bush, like Doriot, was a prolific letter writer, constantly churning out correspondence to business associates and friends. "I have heard a good deal about you from Harry Hoagland and Grover Ellis and I would like very much to have a good visit with you some day," Bush wrote to Doriot on November 16, 1959. "Our company is progressing satisfactorily although we have had some problems in the last couple of months," continued Bush. "More and more of our contract work is being done in foreign waters. Right now we have one rig working in Venezuela and one in Mexico, with another scheduled to move to Trinidad shortly."

ARD's investment windfall came at a propitious time for Doriot. On September 11, 1959, he received a letter from the Headquarters of the U.S. Army Reserve Corps. On September 24, his sixtieth birthday, the military informed him that he would reach the "maximum age prescribed for your grade for retention in an active status." Doriot had to choose between being transferred to the Retired Reserve or being discharged from his Reserve commission. He chose Retired Reserve. After nearly two decades of distinguished service, Doriot's military career was over.

One of Doriot's maxims was you should always raise money when you don't need it, having learned through hard experience that when you do need money, chances are, you are unlikely to get it. So even though ARD raised nearly $4 million in 1959, Doriot and many ARD directors wanted to raise more money in 1960. At one point, ARD had considered forming a second investment company in partnership with brokerage Smith Barney, a project that was code-named Ardsbury. Smith Barney suggested Elfers could serve as president of the new fund on a part-time basis. But Doriot rejected the idea in the spring of 1959, and in early 1960 he again dismissed Ardsbury.

That left the investment banking route. Surprisingly, Robert Lehman told Doriot he would sponsor an offering. It would be ARD's first underwritten deal, a sign of growing confidence in the firm's future. In the meantime, Doriot prepared for the 1960 annual meeting. He invited many executives from his affiliates, including George H. W. Bush, asking him to display the work of Zapata at the product exhibition. "I think the best way to get across the story of Zapata to your stockholders and other interested people is through pictures, since we are dealing with such unusual equipment," wrote Bush to Doriot. "We are having four 3 ft. x 2 ft. enlargements of our main pieces of equipment made . . . I am looking forward to seeing you on March 2. At that time I shall have just returned from a trip to Venezuela and Trinidad so I will be able to let you know first hand how things look down there for Zapata."

Back at Harvard, Doriot was more popular than ever. On Monday and Tuesday mornings, Doriot hopped on the subway, took it to Harvard Square, and walked over the Charles River to campus. At noon, his new teaching assistant, Charles P. Waite, always met him at his office. The two would then amble over to Kresge Hall, a new dining facility. Doriot ate the same lunch every day: sliced bananas on corn flakes. It was not the most appetizing fare but it kept him nourished and trim as a pencil. "He was very nervous before teaching," says Waite. "He always had butterflies. He felt that [cereal] was a settling sort of luncheon."

Typically, 150 to 175 students applied for Manufacturing, but Doriot only took about 125 of them. "It used to make a lot of people mad," says Waite. "They paid all this money and they could not take Doriot's class. I had to go through all the people and cut 40 or 50 people. You figured out who would contribute and benefit from the class." Most assistants at the Business School wrote cases, but Doriot's men focused on assembling study groups, grading exams, and occasionally teaching a lecture. "It was a remarkable experience," says Waite. "He was a man of enormous experience and power in the world. He was one of the grand professors."

At the end of the school year, Doriot asked Waite to join ARD. It was the first time Doriot had asked one of his assistants to work at the firm, and Waite couldn't have been more proud to be chosen. He took the job. A graduate of the University of Connecticut who sold candles to help finance his way through school, Waite was not your typical Harvard MBA. He was short and stocky, a scrappy fighter who would top the competition by working harder than everyone. "That's how I got started in the venture capital business," says Waite. "I didn't take the teaching assistant job thinking it would lead to a job at ARD. We used to call each other father and son."

Joining the firm as a staff associate, Waite saw an industry that was stuck in a prolonged adolescence. "When I came to ARD in 1960 venture capital had been around for fourteen years or so but it was still an academic experiment in some ways, because Doriot was head of it, and he was more than anything else a teacher," said Waite. "He was in the business to test a thesis. Making money wasn't really a very high objective. He wasn't opposed to it but the salaries were modest. There was no ownership in the company for anybody. There was a missionary zeal about it—that's how Doriot got away with underpaying us all, because we believed we were doing something for the greater good, making America a better place." Waite's starting salary was $10,000.

Waite's primary role at ARD was to find deals, which was a perfect fit for his go-getter personality. He was on the road all the time, working sixty hours a week, hunting for a promising small company. As a first test, Doriot threw him on the board of a struggling affiliate, Synco Resins, Inc. "It was a fourth rate company," says Waite. "Whoever had invested in it made a mistake. When I was there it got sold two or three years later. I got credit I didn't deserve."

Waite spent a lot of time in New York getting to know the new breed of bankers catering to the small companies that rose to prominence after the war. The top boutique players at the time were C. E. Unterberg, Towbin and Alex Brown & Sons. Any small firm with ambition or promise would eventually find its way to an investment bank, so they were a good source for deals. Waite also relied on "finders," brokers who would identify promising companies for a fee. "They played a pretty important role 25 years ago," says Waite. Besides bankers and finders, Waite pestered ARD's entrepreneurs, and he often wandered around the hallways of elite universities. Doriot gave Waite subway tokens to go to MIT, the old ARD stomping ground. "The U.S. government was providing research grants to scientists at great universities," says Waite. "The game was to turn those professors with research grants into commercial enterprises."

In June of 1960, one of those MIT scientists was drawn by the magnetic pull of Olsen and Digital Equipment, a brilliant engineer named Gordon Bell. With a master's in electrical engineering and a Fulbright scholarship in Australia under his belt, Bell was now working on his doctorate in MIT's speech lab when Digital Equipment emerged. Bell had not heard of Digital but he was familiar with the work of Ken Olsen. He was one of the many MIT students who lined up, sometimes at two in the morning, to use Olsen's TX-O computer. It was the dawn of the age of computer hackers. "These computers were so captivating that a number of times the administration thought of getting rid of them because people stopped washing, stopped eating, stopped their social life, and, of course, stopped studying," said Olsen. "But out of that group of bright students came so many things which we take for granted today, including time sharing and video games."

When Bell visited Digital to buy some of their modules, they started wooing him. "Fundamentally, I was sold," says Bell. "I had looked at a bunch of other companies and I didn't like the idea of going to work." As a co-op student at General Electric, Bell had developed an aversion to large companies. Here was a firm where he could make a difference. Digital made good circuits and they were starting to put them into computers. "There was something really nice about having a chance to do some real engineering," says Bell. "From my point of view it was not risky at all. Maybe I could go back to MIT if it didn't work. I had no idea about that massive upside."

In June, Bell accepted the job at Digital and withdrew from his PhD program. As the company's second computer engineer, he began working on the PDP-1 under Ben Gurley, another MIT colleague who had worked with Olsen on the SAGE project. It would prove to be the most important hire Digital made in its history. For most of the next two decades, Bell, called the Frank Lloyd Wright of computers by *Datamation* magazine, forged the computing vision that led Digital to become IBM's strongest competitor.

In August, Lehman Brothers fulfilled Bobbie's promise and led an underwriting of ARD stock for 350,000 shares at $24.70 per share. It was the financial coup Doriot had been dreaming of for the last fifteen years. The deal generated a whopping $8,003,165 for ARD, relieving Doriot for the foreseeable future from worries about ARD's money problems.

Another record was set in 1960. The company invested about $3.6 million in eighteen companies, fourteen of which were new affiliates—its most active year ever. Some of the investments led ARD into new industries, including publishing, musical instruments, and medical devices. Indeed, one of the most promising deals was an $112,500 investment in Cordis Corporation, a Miami-based maker of medical devices, which was started by William P. Murphy Jr., a brilliant medical entrepreneur whose father won the Nobel Prize in medicine in 1934 for developing anemia treatments.

Since he was a boy, the younger Murphy demonstrated a flair for invention. He built a snowblower in high school and sold it to a local lawnmower company for $1,500. After medical school, Murphy developed his first medical invention, a projector that displayed full-size X rays. In 1957, he founded his first company, Medical Development Corporation, which became Cordis.

With money from ARD, Cordis developed some of the profession's most innovative devices, including angiography injectors, catheters, and pacemakers. "I came to admire Doriot enormously," says Murphy, who appreciated ARD's ability to help but not interfere with a company's operations. Later on, Murphy credited ARD with helping Cordis to balance its excitement for research with the need to meet the bottom line. "Charlie Waite pointed out you had to modify your enthusiasm for R&D," he says. "We did need some of that."

In 1960, Doriot also announced that it was applying for listing of its shares on the New York Stock Exchange. His expectation was that the "shares will be accepted for trading within a short period of time." At year-end, ARD's net asset value soared to nearly $39 million, up from $23 million. And its stock hit an all-time split-adjusted high of $66.

The financial press couldn't help but recognize ARD's impressive results. "Scientific Risk-Taking Keeps Paying Off for American Research & Development" declared the deck of a long feature in *Barron's*. The story of this "Back Bay parvenu" noted that while many early investors "grew discouraged and sold out, for those who kept the faith the venture has paid off handsomely." The story reported that ARD's net asset value stood at nearly ten times the value when it was launched, thanks to investments in Tracerlab, Ionics, High Voltage, and Technical Studies, a venture set up to evaluate plans for a tunnel under the English Channel. The story credited "much of this achievement" to Doriot, a "gentle, soft-spoken man" who "seems ill-suited to the title 'General,' except that he goes about investing American Research money with a sort of idealistic fervor, as though directing a crusade."

ARD's good fortune allowed Doriot to take some bigger risks. In the fall of that year, Doriot got a call from two young men who had just started their own company. Alex d'Arbeloff and Nick DeWolf met at MIT in the late 1940s, reunited in 1960, and then started Teradyne above Joe and Nemo's hot dog stand in downtown Boston. Both thirty-two, the two made quite a pair. DeWolf was the company's technologist, a skinny geek with a shock of wild red hair who made model airplanes and home radios as child and had just cut his teeth as the chief technology officer of semiconductor maker Transitron Electronic Corporation. Transitron was one of the first successful companies to set up shop along Boston's Route 128, the burgeoning hotbed for young technology companies that Digital Equipment put on the map. D'Arbeloff was Teradyne's business man, a Russian immigrant with a management degree and a penchant for speaking his mind. Since leaving school ten years ago, d'Arbeloff had been canned from three jobs. "I always thought I was pretty wild because I was fired three times," he says. "Nick was actually wilder than I was."

DeWolf hatched a plan while at Transitron: he saw that testing would become a bottleneck in the manufacturing of electronic components unless the tasks performed by technicians and laboratory instruments could be automated. His idea was to develop a new breed of "industrial grade" electronic test equipment to be used by semiconductor makers. D'Arbeloff called Doriot with confidence because ARD had recently invested $10,000 in United Research, a company started by his brother.

The pair needed $150,000 to get the company off the ground but they couldn't even get past the front door of a bank. "I went to Europe on a junket, helping the world understand what was cooking on Route 128" recalled DeWolf. I remember in France saying, how many of you could raise two years of your salary to experiment. I never met a single person in Europe or Japan. There was no such thing as raising a capital for a business."

Despite their lack of options, the duo scrounged up $140,000. D'Arbeloff and his brother threw in $35,000 of their own money after selling some United Research stock. The rest came from friends and family. "That was the only way to raise money," says DeWolf. "We were judged for ability or our brains. Most of us were very young. We didn't have such things as entrepreneurial celebrities."

They needed another $10,000 from Doriot to reach their target. Doriot invited them over to the ARD office. He greeted them, they gave a short presentation, and then Doriot asked a flurry of probing questions. The discussion lasted a few hours.

"What do you want me to do?" asked Doriot at the end of the meeting.

"We have $140,000," said Alex. "Give us the other $10,000."

"Alex," said Doriot, "you don't understand. The people are saying Doriot is playing games. If you want us to invest, we'll invest more."

They took the ten grand, and an offer from Doriot to invest another $200,000 down the road if they needed it.

That time came fairly soon. Although they bootstrapped the development of Teradyne's prototype with the $150,000 seed investment, one year later the company was running out of money. DeWolf felt confident in his product, but customers had not yet bought into the premise. "Our balance sheet looked awful," says DeWolf. "We had a few months to go before we pitched in the sponge."

They went back to Doriot. At that point, ARD's staff was not too thrilled with Teradyne. It had fifty employees on the payroll and hadn't sold a thing. Teradyne was one of ARD's sick young children. DeWolf took comfort in the fact that he and Doriot had formed a strong connection. "We had an amazingly warm faith in each other," says DeWolf.

Doriot and DeWolf went out to lunch. Doriot looked at DeWolf with his piercing blue eyes.

"Nick," said Doriot, "I think you are in trouble."

"You are correct General," replied DeWolf. "But we are on the verge of a big breakthrough."

"Nick, I like you," said Doriot. "Are you really sure you can pull this thing off?

"Yes," said DeWolf, expressing faith in his machine. "General, we will do it."

"OK," said the General. "I will go along with you."

ARD invested another $100,000 in Teradyne. It saved the company, giving the dynamic duo enough time to explain the value of their technology to customers. In 1962, companies started buying DeWolf's testers. "It was an agreement based on animal faith," says DeWolf. But Doriot also knew that the technology was taking off. "He could sniff that semiconductors were coming along," says DeWolf. By the fourth quarter of 1962, Teradyne turned profitable, and DeWolf and d'Arbeloff never looked back.

Doriot kept up a torrid pace in 1961. In the first half of the year, ARD invested $2 million in nine companies, five of which were new ventures. It also realized about $750,000 from the sale of stock in Raytheon and two other companies. On March 8, ARD's stock was admitted for trading on the New York Stock Exchange with the ticker symbol "ARD"—the first venture capital company to list shares on the Big Board. The listing reflected the General's belief that you should always associate yourself with the best institutions. "It was a good housekeeping seal of approval," says John A. Shane, one of Doriot's former teaching assistants.

The flurry of activity at ARD created the need for a new associate, and in the spring of 1961, Doriot asked Shane if he'd like to come down to the ARD office. Doriot thought that Shane, a tall, bright Princeton graduate with a wry sense of humor who had just finished four years of service in the U.S. Navy, was up to the job. "I started to parade down to ARD on Saturdays," said Shane. Shane passed the test and Doriot offered him a position, which he accepted. "I liked the people," he said. "I liked the variety of work."

By that time, ARD had developed a top-notch team with a clear division of labor. Elfers was in charge of managing the portfolio—primarily worrying about ARD's affiliates and figuring out ways to help them. "Bill was very good at those issues," says Shane. "Bill was sort of the number two guy without being anointed." Congleton was in charge of new projects, and Shane worked primarily with him. Hoagland and Waite canvassed the land looking for new deals. And Rowe focused on running the financial side of ARD. "She was very good at judging people," says Shane. "She was the general's closest confidant."

On March 9, Doriot traveled to Illinois where he delivered an extraordinary address before the Chicago Society of Security Analysts titled "Creative Capital." In the beginning of the talk, he provided a brief overview of ARD's performance. To date, ARD had invested in sixty-six ventures, including a current interest in thirty-seven companies in which it had invested approximately $11 million. As of December 31, 1960, "these securities had a value of approximately $30,250,000 or two-and-a-half times their original cost." Sales of twenty-nine other ventures had yielded capital gains of $3 million, offset by a capital loss of $850,000 from only nine failures. Thirty of the sixty-six affiliates were in New England, with the others spread across the United States, including six in Texas and one each in California, Florida, and Indiana.

The more insightful part of the talk focused on Doriot's explanation of ARD's investment philosophy. Doriot was like a prophet delivering a sermon, and the congregation listened closely. The first tenet was that "the riskiest part of the spectrum has to date proved the most rewarding, and the greatest capital gains have been earned in companies which were started from scratch." Second, most venture investing has not been "built on achievement of dramatic overnight successes, but on the steady growth of soundly based, well-managed affiliates." Third, "technology has proved a rewarding field for American Research and is particularly well suited for creative capital investment." The reason? "In specialized technical areas with products protected by patents and know-how, it is easier for small companies to compete with large organizations," explained Doriot.

ARD's biggest hurdle was usually convincing these small, yet proud companies that they needed outside help. But Doriot didn't hold that against them. He knew that if entrepreneurs weren't self-driven and a bit egotistical they'd be punching the clock for IBM or General Electric. The General closed his lecture by stressing the importance of management assistance in the venture business. "There is always a critical job to be done," said Doriot. "There is a sales door to be opened, a credit line to be established, a new important employee to be found, or a business technique to be learned. The venture investor must always be on call to advise, to persuade, to dissuade, to encourage, but always to help build. Then venture capital becomes true creative capital—creating growth for the company and financial success for the investing organization."

In April, at an ARD board meeting, Doriot and his fellow directors spent much of the afternoon grappling with the consequences of Wall Street's latest bull market. From the late 1950s until 1962, the United States experienced its first boom in high-technology stocks. The Dow Jones rocketed from a low of 388 in 1955 to a high of 734 in late 1961. But the real action was in "hot issues" or "new issues" trading in the over-the-counter market, the mid-century equivalent of the NASDAQ. Stocks with names like California Microwave, Chromatronics, or almost any new issue with a Buck Rogerish tinge to its name was bound to soar into the stratosphere. The exuberance over new issues was captured in a 1960 cover story in *Time* magazine called "The Yankee Tinkerers." To tell the story of the "spectacular rise" of "growth and glamour stocks," the writer profiled Sherman M. Fairchild, the sixty-four-year-old founder of Fairchild Camera and Instrument, describing him as the "epitome of the new scientist-businessman-inventor."

ARD's portfolio was dominated by new issues trading over-the-counter and Doriot was prescient in recognizing the problems brought on by such speculation and overhyped expectations. A few months back, when a visitor looked at a chart of ARD's booming net asset value, Doriot said he did not place it on a wall to please the firm; rather, it was posted there to "scare"

ARD's employees. ARD's holdings are "valued very high and some of the price earnings ratios remind one of 1929 when the relationships to earnings were staggering," Doriot told the ARD board. "Sometimes there will be no bid and then a collapse. Many years of continuous so-called growth cannot possibly bring up the earnings of many small companies to a level which would warrant most of the present-day prices. Many companies going public never had good earnings. Some have never had real earnings."

The boom in hot issues led some of ARD's stockholders to pressure ARD to increase the valuation of Digital Equipment, but Doriot opposed the move. Digital was still a young company, and while it was doing very well, Doriot was not sure it could "cope with the problems of increased size, increased competition," and the need to develop new technologies. Doriot's preference was to build up a "cushion" made up of "reputation, cash and unlisted securities" kept "close to real value."

The truth was that the stock market was the least of Doriot's problems. For financial regulators were on the move. The momentum began to build in 1961, when Columbia University law professor William L. Cary took over the SEC, signaling President Kennedy's resolve to revitalize anemic federal regulatory agencies. During the Administration's first year, Congress added 250 new employees to the SEC's staff, and appropriated $750,000 to fund a "Special Study of the Securities Markets." The blandly named report was the single most influential document ever published in the history of the SEC, providing a blueprint for the next fifteen years of security industry reforms.

The report examined all aspects of the securities markets but focused much concern on the explosion of activity in highly unregulated over-the-counter shares. In a 1961 *New York Times* article discussing the Special Study, an assistant of Cary named Philip A. Loomis Jr. issued a thinly veiled criticism of ARD when he described hot issues as "these glamorous sounding companies with 'ionics' in their name somewhere." Ionics was not a fraudulent company peddled in boiler rooms by con men or carnival barkers. It was an innovative company with real earnings. But Loomis's message was loud and clear: ARD was back on the SEC's radar, and that probably meant more trouble for Doriot.

TEN

THE FIRST HOME RUN

(1962–1967)

"I AM THE ONE they talk about," proclaimed General Doriot, striding dramatically into a classroom full of women in the beginning of 1962. After the war, the General inaugurated a new lecture in his Manufacturing class, one that he asked only the fiancées and wives of his students to attend—perhaps the most striking example of his unorthodox teaching style. To Doriot, the point of the lecture was to explain the purpose of his course and to instruct the spouses in the proper habits and manners that a businessman and his wife should follow. "Everybody was sort of a bit petrified of him," says Molly Hoagland, Ralph Hoagland's wife, who attended the lecture in 1962. "He commanded their attention in a way nobody else did."

In today's society, lecturing the wives of students would be castigated as the height of male chauvinism, and probably constitute grounds for termination. But in the postwar period, the lecture partially reflected the conservative social climate. After all, Harvard Business School did not allow women to enroll until 1960.

Even so, most of the spouses arrived at Harvard prepared to dislike Doriot. This was the taskmaster who had taken their husbands away from them. But the surprising thing is that many of the women left Doriot's classroom bowled over by his charm and thoughtfulness. The women appreciated that Doriot not only viewed a husband and wife as a team, but believed that wives played a crucial role in the success of their husband's careers. They also relished the tips that he gave them, such as stressing the importance of punctuality, volunteerism, and philanthropy. "It was all these mannerly things, things that nobody else would ever say to a group of people," says Molly. "I thought I would find him chauvinistic, but I didn't. He was letting us in on the secret that he wasn't this ogre. I was surprised he was so personable. That was how most of the other women felt."

Still, the lecture gave heartburn to some of his male students. James F. Morgan was already in trouble because he had mistakenly told his wife that year two at Harvard Business School would be easier. And then came the evening lecture with the wives. Morgan, who had a very outspoken wife, was fearful about her reaction, or what she would say to Doriot. While she went off to the lecture, Morgan stayed home with the kids.

"How was it?" he asked his wife rather sheepishly when she returned home.

"He's wonderful, just wonderful," she said. "He said we should tell you to work harder."

Morgan thought to himself: "The son of a bitch has charmed them all."

Since the creation of ARD, Doriot had always believed the global economy would eventually require the firm to do business in Europe. During ARD's early years, he advanced the idea by pushing some of its affiliates to enter into various business deals in Europe, such as setting up factories or marketing and sales agreements.

Then in 1961, Doriot's belief in globalization became an obsession of sorts. Pioneering a financial movement in the United States wasn't enough of a challenge. Doriot's new quixotic quest was to spearhead an international community of venture capitalists. His first milestone on this path was laid in January of 1962, when a group of British investors under the advisement of Doriot formed Technical Development Capital, Limited, a British venture firm with $2 million pounds of capital.

Doriot was just warming up, though. The General did not want ARD to set up its own firm overseas, but he was interested in spurring a community of other like-minded investors. The idea was to provide money and support to a firm established by a consortium of distinguished financial and industrial interests. It just so happened that some other financiers were thinking along the same lines. One of them was an adventurous young Canadian named Gerald D. Sutton, a former pilot with the Royal Canadian Air Force who headed the research department at the Canadian investment bank Nesbitt, Thomson and Company. Sutton was keen on the idea of financing small young companies, and when he heard about ARD in 1961, he arranged to pay them a visit while on a trip to his company's Boston office. That spring, Sutton invited Dorothy Rowe to lunch at Locke Obers restaurant to talk about how ARD worked. "We chatted about things," says Sutton. "Doriot could not join us. I think he was using Dorothy as a bit of a screen."

Sutton passed the test and Rowe invited him back to the office to meet the General. After explaining to Doriot his interest in venture capital, the General opened up and showed him ARD's records and explained to him why they approved or rejected a project. "He would put an accent on a word and it was quite dramatic," says Sutton. At the end of their interview, Sutton told Doriot he wanted to set up a similar company in Canada, and that he would like to form a close relationship with ARD in order to tap into their gold-plated Rolodex. Eager to encourage the growth of the venture capital community, Doriot was happy to help. Energized with confidence, Sutton then asked the General if he would invest in the company. To his surprise, Doriot told him ARD would put up 10 percent of the money they needed to launch.

When Sutton returned to Canada, he asked the president of his firm, Deane Nesbitt, for permission to form a Canadian venture capital company. His boss readily agreed. Now all Sutton had to do was raise the remainder of the start-up funds. He approached several wealthy industrial firms, but one after the other turned him down. As a last resort, Sutton asked for an introduction to the vice president of Sun Life, a conservative insurance giant. This time, Sutton got lucky. It turned out that Sun Life had been exploring a similar proposal in England and it was interested in the concept.

In the summer of 1961, Doriot flew up to Montreal to give a talk before Sun Life's chief economist and assistant treasurer. Doriot spoke for an hour, proposing the idea of a venture company backed by a host of financial institutions, a sort of Canadian ARD. "We went back with some enthusiasm for what Doriot was proposing," says Derek Mather, Sun Life's assistant treasurer.

Sun Life formed a steering committee with Doriot, Sutton, and a few others, and the insurance giant led the fund-raising and recruiting effort. They all made the rounds. When the prospective investors heard that Sun was on board, people suddenly changed their tune. The old boy network still worked after all. In the summer and fall, Doriot visited Canada several more times, using his charisma to wow the Canadians.

By October, it was a done deal. Twenty-two of Canada's leading financial institutions ponied up $5 million to launch the Canadian Enterprise Development Corporation—one of the first Canadian venture firms. Over time, Doriot had come to dislike the word "research" in his firm's name because it led people to believe that ARD was a quasi-academic organization, rather than a commercial enterprise. So he used the birth of Canadian Enterprise Development to rethink the branding of the venture capital movement. Research was out; enterprise was in.

Canadian Enterprise Development put together a board of directors and opened a headquarters in Montreal. Doriot recruited Derek Mather to become the company's treasurer. Doriot's vision of an international community of venture capital was coming to life.

⌒

Doriot spent much of his time tending to the problems of his affiliate companies. But like a parent with a favorite child, one company began to attract an increasing amount of Doriot's attention: Digital Equipment Corporation. In part, the intensifying of his focus was driven by financial reality: by the end of 1962, after just five years in business, Digital had become ARD's most valuable affiliate, surpassing High Voltage Engineering.

But Doriot also clicked with Ken Olsen in a profound way. On the outside, Olsen and Doriot couldn't appear more different: Olsen was a strapping thirty-six-year-old Scandinavian who liked to wear clumsy, thick-soled black shoes and flannel shirts; Doriot was a refined sixty-three-year-old professor never seen without a suit and tie. But beneath the surface, the two men were strikingly similar: both were hugely ambitious yet humble men who were driven not by money, but by an insatiable desire to create a better world through building great products and companies. The General feared success led entrepreneurs to buy "twenty-cylinder Cadillacs" and "fifty-room man-sions." That was never a problem with Olsen, a rock-ribbed neo-Puritan and churchman who drove a Ford and mowed his own lawn. After Olsen became wealthy he did not buy a Cadillac; he splurged on a second canoe.

Doriot would never claim credit for Digital's growing success. But it is also true that Digital would never have become as successful as it did without the constant and close support of Doriot and ARD during its difficult early years. ARD never influenced Digital's technical direction but it played a criti-cal role in virtually every other part of the business. Sometimes, it was the lit-tle things that made a difference. "Doriot said don't just lay a circuit board on a desk," said Harlan Anderson. "He said put it on a sheet of purple velvet, kind of like a jeweler. He was quite a showman."

Doriot exerted much of his influence through the Digital board, which was stocked with the General's acolytes. As a sign of the cozy relationship, Digital held its board meetings at ARD's office in Boston. "The General had more influence on Ken than Ken would candidly admit," says Jack Shields, a Digital senior executive who ran sales, service, and marketing.

Doriot was Olsen's professional lifeline. He would frequently reach out to Doriot, asking for his advice on any number of issues. Olsen, for example, never hired a senior person without the General's input. "He was always there as a mentor and a help," said Olsen. "Most of his ideas he didn't present in a way you had to accept. He presented them in a way which, after it was done, you thought you had thought of them yourself."

Sometimes, the teacher was so effective that when Olsen spoke he uttered phrases that sounded as if they came straight out of Doriot's mouth. When Olsen said things like "growing gets you in trouble" or "a good manager never had to make any decisions," that was Doriot talking. Olsen followed to a T Doriot's philosophy of running a business on simple and sound practices—paying modest salaries, aiming for aggressive but reachable goals, and seeking satisfaction not from growth and gobs of money but from the joy of constructive building. "I think the General had a very profound values-oriented role," says Ted Johnson, who often heard Olsen talking over the phone to Doriot.

In Digital's early years, ARD received numerous offers to buy its preco-cious child. As the company's majority owner, ARD could have easily sold out Digital for a quick, easy profit. In 1958, engineering research outfit Itek Corporation offered $1 million of its stock for all of Digital. In 1962, Beckman

Instruments was interested in discussing a merger. In subsequent years, Xerox, Hewlett-Packard, and other firms also courted Digital. But Doriot and the board rejected every single offer, betting the company could prosper on its own, even though its long-term success was far from certain.

Olsen appreciated the wisdom of Doriot's philosophy of patience. "[ARD] wouldn't buy and sell companies at the first opportunity," said Olsen. "This sounds obvious but it's very hard for someone who owns a major part of the stock to be patient. The General really preached this and really practiced it. It was his contribution. Any other company would have attempted to sell when somebody was doing well and clean up on the profit."

The support started to pay off in 1962 when Digital moved beyond circuit boards and modules and released its PDP-1 computer. "Production shipments of our new computer, the Programmed Data Processor, were a major highlight of the year," wrote Olsen in a letter to Doriot that February. "We now have delivered ten of these units and have a significant backlog of unfilled orders for it." Olsen told Doriot that the company opened sales offices in Washington and New York and increased its head count to 337 people, up from 194 the year before. Later that year, Digital received its breakthrough order when International Telephone and Telegraph bought 15 PDP-1s to control its message switching system. The PDP-1 made Digital's reputation, providing a reliable stream of business for the next seven years. On June 30, 1962, the end of Digital's fifth fiscal year, it reported $807,000 in profit on $6.5 million in sales.

The rise of Digital and the formation of the Canadian Enterprise Development Corporation were coups for Doriot. But the General was stirring up another revolution at the same time. In August of 1961, Doriot had begun sounding out the idea of a European venture capital firm with various bankers and financiers, and he had found some interest. In October of that year, he presented his ideas to the ARD board. The recent emergence of the European Common Market, thought Doriot, was one reason justifying the formation of a pan-European investment firm.

It was also part of a grander scheme. With the Canadian venture outfit coming together, Doriot began to envision ARD as the catalyst and hub of an international community devoted to the development of enterprises around the world. "He felt that venture capital was not a uniquely American phenomenon," says staffer John A. Shane, who became the firm's liaison with Canadian Enterprise Development. "He felt the same kind of stimulus could work in other places."

And yet, Doriot was acutely aware of the unique challenges presented by the hidebound Continent. "One talks about 'Europe as such,'" wrote Doriot in a 1961 memo to the ARD board, "but one must remember that 'Europe as such' is still a nebulous entity made up of different and divergent parts, which may not come or stay together unless private and governmental relationships are created and developed in a constructive and desirable way to the point where disengagement becomes undesirable and difficult."

That the idea was riskier made it all the more attractive to the General. Doriot applied his ample powers of persuasion to convince Banque Worms and the Morgan Guaranty Trust Company of New York to back the idea. With these two distinguished banks on board, Doriot was sure he could raise the rest of the money.

But would government regulators approve such a radical venture? In March of 1962, ARD's law firm, Gaston, Snow, Motley & Holt, wrote a letter to the SEC asking if the agency agreed with its opinion that the firm would not be prohibited by the Investment Company Act from making such an investment. In August, the SEC's chief counsel told ARD, much to Doriot's surprise, that an investment in a European investment vehicle, referred to as ERD, would not be prohibited, with one caveat. As long as the "underwriting activities of ERD are *de minimis* in nature, this Division will not recommend any action to the Commission."

The coast was clear. In late 1962 and early 1963, Doriot pitched the deal to a few more banks. He was aided by a banker from Morgan Guaranty and by his former student and INSEAD co-conspirator, Claude Janssen, now an executive with Banque Worms. Their goal was to raise $8 million. They found more interest, but no company was ultimately willing to fork over a big chunk of money. The number of founding investors would thus have to be enlarged. At ARD's annual meeting on March 6, 1963, Doriot coyly concluded his address to stockholders with a nod to the possibilities lying beyond U.S. shores.

"Creative ability knows no boundaries," he told the shareholders. "Who knows whether the next interesting project for us here may not come from Europe or Canada . . . What better ways are there for us who are proud of what has been done here than to sell abroad the idea of what free men can create with their faith in free enterprise. New Englanders developed America—ARD, a New England company, can show the way to the future in a small but definite way."

By the end of 1963, Doriot and Janssen had raised about $2.5 million from an impressive array of eighteen shareholders hailing from eight European countries and the United States. The investors comprised fourteen large European banks and financial institutions, including Credit Lyonnais, Amsterdam-Rotterdam Bank, and Credit Suisse. Affirming Doriot's vision of a global venture community, both ARD and CED pitched in a few hundred thousand dollars. They named the firm European Enterprise Development Company (EED).

On the twelfth of December, EED was incorporated in Luxembourg. Doriot attended the conclave before heading to Brussels the next day to participate in EED's first meeting. At this meeting, Doriot was named president and Arnaud de Vitry was appointed vice president. The number three man of EED, its general manager, was Jean Gueroult, a French banker with the Banque de Paris. Robert Lehman turned down Doriot's offer to become a director of EED but senior-level employees of many of EED's shareholder banks joined the board. Some participants, including de Vitry, observed the peculiarity of this situation. "EED was surrounded by a board of bankers who selected a man named Jean Gueroult who was also a banker," said de Vitry. "Doriot was always saying do not put a banker on your board."

As Doriot ended 1963, his blue eyes sparkled a little more than usual. His vision of a global investment community was coming to fruition. ARD's portfolio had recovered much of the value it lost after the 1962 stock market crash. Thirty-one out of its forty current portfolio companies were profitable, with nearly half of them reporting record sales and profits. Even the mainstream press began to recognize Doriot's accomplishments. Earlier that year, *Time* magazine ran a story, "The Profit-Minded Professor," describing Doriot as "the dean of the businessmen-professors." The story concluded that, by helping to father seventy-eight companies, Doriot's venture firm "has profited handsomely, losing money on only 10 investments."

Then the SEC lowered its hammer. On November 7, 1963, Georges Doriot received a chilling letter from Allan F. Conwill, the director of the SEC's Division of Corporate Regulation. Conwill's letter marked the beginning of a torturous ten-year battle with the SEC and IRS over a mind-numbing rash of issues. Yet despite several investigations and surprise audits, ARD was never found to be in violation of any accounting or tax rules. "The SEC was the General's bête noire," says Patricia A. Clark, who was Doriot's personal secretary from 1957 until he retired in 1974.

Government regulators challenged numerous ARD practices but none struck at the firm's heart more than the issues surrounding stock options. Indeed, that was the matter in question in the winter of 1963 when the SEC contacted Doriot. SEC director Conwill was responding to Doriot's letter of August 9 in which the General requested an opportunity to discuss the SEC's views on the issuance of stock options in ARD affiliates to ARD's officers or directors. The SEC had expressed concerns to ARD that such a practice could pose a conflict of interest. Conwill said he'd be glad to meet with Doriot at a mutually agreeable date to discuss the matter but reiterated his concerns to Doriot.

"It appears that there would be conflicts between the responsibilities of such officer or director to the investment company and his personal pecuniary interest in the portfolio company," wrote Conwill. "The decisions which such officer or director may make for the portfolio company in determining what risks it should assume in developing its business, how it should raise additional capital, and similar matters may well be influenced by his desire to foster his own interest rather than that of the investment company." Conwill ended the letter by welcoming Doriot to consider and comment on these concerns.

On November 29, Doriot wrote Conwill a rambling, impassioned, yet humble letter explaining his predicament. "I often wish that options had never been invented, but I supposed that had they not been, then something else would have been developed which would give you and me a different but probably equal or similar problem," wrote Doriot.

The problem, as Doriot saw it, was that the emerging culture of wealth and instant gratification brought on by the booming market for new issues had created a new "generation of people, young and old, engineers, scientists, businessmen, etc., who have convinced themselves that the best way to accumulate capital is through the option route." An experienced man had little reason to come work for ARD "since he can get a position carrying option privileges with any number of other companies, including our own portfolio companies." If ARD was prohibited from granting staff members options in its affiliate companies, that would be a problem not only in running ARD now, but in "building it up for the future."

As an olive branch, Doriot proposed to Conwill several restrictive conditions under which the SEC might allow the issuance of options. If ARD could not grant options on affiliates, Doriot asked Conwill if the SEC would allow ARD to issue options on ARD stock to its personnel. Doriot pointed out the strict rules that ARD put in place to prevent insider trading. It would be unfair to deny the great majority of ethical investment professionals the opportunity to benefit from options, noted Doriot, because of the "few that may abuse the privilege." Doriot sent off the letter and awaited a response.

Before he heard back, ARD got slammed with another proposed SEC amendment. This rule, 14a-3, raised the possibility that ARD would have to include proprietary financial data of its subsidiaries in its reports to stockholders. Subsidiaries, according to the SEC definition, were companies in which an owner held 25 percent or more of its voting stock. SEC rule 17d-1 governing stock options already hampered the ability of ARD to recruit and attract talent. Now this rule jeopardized ARD's attractiveness as an investor in some of its affiliates. "Companies come to ARD for financing because they prefer private ownership to premature public ownership," explained Dorothy Rowe to Joel Harvey, a partner with Lybrand, Ross Brothers & Montgomery, ARD's auditing firm. "If we are forced to publish company figures prematurely, ARD will be at a distinct disadvantage in getting good projects which have available to them other sources of venture capital." That ARD owned less than 25 percent of many companies, some of whom were not on a calendar year, made it likely that such disclosure would "present a distorted picture of ARD's operations and would be impractical to obtain." Rowe ended the note by asking Harvey to draft a more polished letter that General Doriot could review when he returned from a business trip in late December.

In May 1964, Doriot became so fed up with the government's interference in ARD's affairs that he typed up a blistering three-page memo. He attacked the SEC's lack of understanding of ARD methods of operation, its frequent shifts in personnel, and the agency's confrontational stance. "ARD has more knowledge of what is right and wrong than the average person at the SEC," wrote Doriot. His frustration had reached such a peak he suggested the absurd idea that for a period of three years "ARD should be allowed to operate without consultation with the SEC with reference to Section 17 of the Act." If that wasn't possible, Doriot proposed ARD be allowed to deduct from its taxes SEC-related legal expenses, which had exploded to hundreds of thousands of dollars. The memo was never sent.

Instead, Doriot took the more prudent path of getting ARD's lawyers to approach the SEC. In June, ARD's counsel John W. Belash wrote a letter to the SEC urging the commission to consider issuing an order that would permit ARD to issue stock options to its own employees. ARD was encouraged by SEC director Conwill, who after reviewing ARD's situation, actually recommended to the SEC that ARD should be allowed to issue the options. But in 1964, Conwill, after a three-year term at the SEC, left the agency and returned to private practice.

This was the second time that ARD's hopes had been dashed by a high-level departure in the SEC. In the 1950s, Lawrence Greene, an attorney who joined the SEC in 1938 and helped implement the Investment Company Act of 1940, became an ally of ARD. "He took the time to study our problems and allowed the granting of options on affiliates to ARD personnel," wrote Doriot in a note to himself. Thanks to Greene, ARD granted options to employees in several companies. Four ARD staffers, for instance, received options in Digital Equipment: Henry Hoagland, William Congleton, Dorothy Rowe, and Wayne Brobeck. But Greene left the agency and "later on some of his decisions were nullified by successors who again made no effort whatsoever to become acquainted with our work."

Any remaining hopes that ARD held for reaching a rapprochement with the SEC were crushed when two investigators from the SEC's regional office showed up at the John Hancock Building on the afternoon of July 20, unannounced and uninvited. It was a humiliating moment for the high-minded Doriot. The SEC inspectors ambushed Doriot because the Investment Act authorized the agency to conduct periodic inspections of registered investment companies. Section 31b of the Act required investment companies to keep highly detailed records of all of their investments and reams of related information. The inspectors dug into ARD's files. "They fully expected that we were here with nothing else to do but receive them and spend the next two days with them," fumed Doriot.

The inspectors requested confidential documents on ARD affiliates. Doriot handed them over; in his mind he had nothing to hide. Doriot, unfailingly polite in the most trying of circumstances, tried to be helpful. He asked the inspectors if they needed any more information, or if they had any more questions to ask. Each time they answered that they were satisfied, that they had received everything they wanted, and that there was no information they had asked for and had not obtained. But the inspectors were not there simply to gather information. They were there, picking through Doriot's files, trying to determine whether ARD was in compliance with the Investment Act. Doriot welcomed constructive suggestions but the inspectors held their cards close to their chest.

Brian Brooks, the day-to-day auditor of ARD and dozens of its portfolio companies from 1964 until 1972, recalled how Doriot always wanted to make sure ARD took the high road when it came to accounting and compliance issues. Nevertheless, it was clear that Doriot's high standards were failing to placate government regulators, and that their lack of appreciation for the importance of venture capital was driving the General mad. "He was always meowing about the SEC," says Brooks. The tragic irony of this bitter struggle with regulators was that they were lowering the boom on ARD just as investors and economists were beginning to recognize the significance of Doriot's achievement. "Some of the SEC examiners did not know what they were doing," says Brooks. "They did not want to be intellectually challenged."

In the spring of 1965, the gap between Doriot's private thoughts and public comments began to trouble his closest allies. Pressure was growing on ARD to divulge its growing mess of regulatory problems, and to take Digital public. ARD's investors and Wall Street believed that an offering of Digital would unleash untapped value in ARD's shares.

But Doriot did not think Digital was ready to deal with the unforgiving spotlight of public ownership. At ARD's 1965 annual meeting, Doriot told shareholders that it would take its affiliates public "whenever the proper time has come." It was more of a duck than an explanation of company policy. In his 1965 letter to stockholders, Doriot addressed the pressures with his biting humor. "A rather unrealistic situation was created by which investors expected too much, and many young companies tended to come to the conclusion that words such as 'earnings' and 'dividends' had been erased from the vocabulary," he wrote. "Price/earnings ratios were abandoned as an unnecessary drag and weight in the ascension towards greater profitless technical heights and were replaced by price/hope ratios."

More significantly, Doriot knew that Digital was not ready for prime time. It was fighting through another wave of growing pains, in fact. The company's lack of seasoned managers and loosey-goosey manufacturing operations had recently triggered an outbreak of bottlenecks. Orders were delayed or went unfilled. Its engineering office was becoming like a bumper car ride, with small teams of technologists flying off in their own directions or crashing into each other. The disorganization was reflected in Digital's bottom line. In fiscal year 1964, Digital's sales only grew 9 percent to $10,860,000; worse, its profits actually fell 24 percent to $917,000. Ken Olsen began to chew out his underlings in staff meetings. And while sales resumed their growth in 1965, profits were on track to fall again. This was no time to take Digital public. This much Doriot knew.

On March 22, Doriot received another letter that he had been dreading. "You are right in your assumption that the reason I wished to come to see you was to talk about your retirement," wrote Harvard University's President Nathan M. Pusey. "It is my usual practice to call on professors one year in advance of their reaching retirement age so that I may inform them of their status and try to express to them appreciation for the contributions they have made to the University. Since George Baker has already spoken to you about the Corporations' decision that you should expect retirement as of August 31, 1966, perhaps this letter can serve as formal notification."

The letter hit Doriot like a punch in the solar plexus. He had already been forced to retire from his first love, the Army. Now his second love was being taken away from him, and there was nothing he could do about it.

The sadness that Doriot felt was momentarily lifted by a flattering four-page *BusinessWeek* profile, which appeared later that week. Titled "Idealist—With a Realistic Touch," the profile declared that the Harvard professor "proves that theories can be converted into profits." A pleasant pattern had emerged over the last few years. ARD's unique annual meetings often sparked a round of positive press coverage after reporters came back to their newsrooms jazzed up from seeing Doriot's three-ring circus. "His ideas on doing business are credited largely with keeping ARD not only alive, but prospering," wrote the reporter. The story highlighted the creation of ARD's latest corporate children, CED and EED, but cautioned that Digital's valuation of $14 million now accounted for a third of ARD's total asset value. "Critics ask: Isn't it too big? Don't you have too many of your assets in one place? Shouldn't it go public?"

Doriot replied with a clever analogy. "When a man has a stable of horses, and one wins the Grand Prix, do people say 'what a good stable this man has?' Or do they say 'you should get rid of your winner and develop the others?'"

Doriot's cleverness, however, could not forestall the encroaching hand of government regulation. On March 26, ARD got the letter it had been waiting for, and the news was horrible. The letter, addressed to ARD's counsel, was from the SEC's Director of Corporate Regulation, Solomon Freedman: "The Commission has instructed me to advise you that its unwillingness to grant exemptions for the issuance of stock options by investment companies had been publicly stated a number of times before Congress and otherwise and that the Commission is not inclined to change its position with respect to the request made on behalf of the above corporation."

In the summer of 1965, Doriot took out his growing frustrations on ARD's staff. He began complaining about ARD's lack of new investments. In 1964, ARD only financed one new company, a $100,000 investment in Synergy Chemicals, Incorporated of Linden, New Jersey. And increasingly it was losing projects at the last minute just before it was ready to finance them.

To help bring in new ideas, Henry Hoagland had hired a new representative in Southern California named Robert E. Rhodes. But both Rhodes and ARD's southern rep Grover Ellis had yet to discover any worthwhile investment candidates. ARD's field rep system, according to John A. Shane, "never did work out very well." Rhodes was an interesting fellow who came from a lot of money. He lived a good life and traveled in an elite social circle. But it turned out he wasn't driven to help ARD. "His personality and the General's were diametrically opposed," says Shane. About the only thing you could count on Rhodes for was that if you visited him "you knew you were going to have a wonderful time."

In 1965, ARD also hired a new staff member, Samuel W. Bodman III. After completing his doctorate of science in MIT's chemical engineering department, Bodman was invited to interview for a job as ARD's technical advisor. He trotted out to Doriot's office on a Monday morning, and was greeted by the General's current teaching assistant James A. Henderson. "Jim and I stood there waiting for the General's arrival," recalls Bodman.

"The General was behind his hour. He came racing up, declaring that he had left the Business School to come out here for lunch but he didn't have any money." By running ARD, Doriot had made at least fifty millionaires, but he didn't have enough money to pick up the tab for lunch. Doriot then looked to Henderson, and asked if he had money for their lunch. But Henderson's pockets were empty. The General and Henderson turned to Bodman. When Bodman raced out of the house that morning to meet Doriot, he stuffed in his pocket the only $5 he had, which he and his wife kept in the sugar bowl. "I handed them the money," said Bodman. "I got the money back in a week with a nickel interest. Even then he was providing leadership." Despite his amusement—and mild alarm—that these supposedly wealthy venture capitalists couldn't even pick up the tab for lunch, Bodman took the job.

On October 1, the SEC lined up ARD in its crosshairs. The agency had finally digested the work of its inspectors from last summer. The result was a tart two-page letter written by the SEC's assistant chief enforcement attorney Robert J. Routier challenging ARD's valuation of Digital Equipment, and its failure to disclose the investments of ARD directors and officers in certain portfolio companies. "The examination of the books and records of the subject investment company . . . disclosed the need for certain revisions in the practices and procedures of the investment company," wrote Routier.

Specifically, the SEC claimed that ARD had a "pronounced" need to revalue its Digital investment. The SEC also requested that ARD expand its written disclosure policy to "include personal investments by directors of the company" and warned the firm that such "dual relationships present the possibility that future investments by the [ARD] and its officers and directors in these portfolio companies might violate" section 17d of the Investment Company Act. The SEC had not charged ARD with violating the law but it felt like the government was fingering the trigger of a gun pointed at Doriot's head.

One week later, the depth of ARD's problems became clear. On October 8, 1965, William Elfers, Doriot's right-hand man for the last fifteen years, submitted his resignation. Even though Doriot was sixty-six years old and had been forced to retire from the Army and Harvard, Elfers had reached the sad and unfortunate conclusion that Doriot was far from relinquishing ARD's helm. The year before, Elfers learned that Doriot had negotiated a six-year employment contract with the firm's board. But it was more than that. Elfers knew that Doriot dominated the board—whose prominent members he had handpicked. And even without a contract, Elfers was sure the directors "would undoubtedly let him decide his own retirement date."

With his Harvard workload, Doriot had come to rely heavily on Elfers to run the firm's day-to-day operations. "Doriot did not like to make decisions," says Charles P. Waite, then an assistant vice president of the firm. "He always played the devil's advocate. Bill was the one more often than not who made a decision." But now, after working in Doriot's shadow all these years, Elfers wanted a chance to prove himself, to see if he could succeed at the venture game on his own. "He felt he had earned it," says Waite. "He was very disappointed at not getting a chance."

Everyone who worked for ARD believed Elfers was more than up to the task, and that knowledge made his subservience to Doriot all the more grating. "There was nobody more qualified than Bill Elfers to run the company, but the General never offered him the job," says John A. Shane. "That was the General's fatal flaw in his make-up. I just don't think his heart was in trying to find a successor." Charles P. Waite also believed Elfers understood the venture business better than anyone. "The perfect one to have run ARD was Bill Elfers," says Waite. "It should have been done in 1965. Everybody in the company looked to him as the leader, and I think Doriot was jealous of that."

There was one more reason Elfers left. He realized, along with an increasing number of investors in new companies, that venture capital and the stock markets mixed as well as oil and water. Elfers could see the government's increasing interference with ARD's affairs was not going to end any time soon. The SEC letter challenging ARD's practices, which ARD received a week before Elfers resigned, was proof enough of that.

For Elfers, the solution to many of ARD's problems was to take advantage of a new organizational form: the limited partnership. Although it might be too complicated to convert ARD into a partnership, it was not too late for Elfers to form his own. He wouldn't be the first person to realize the advantages of such a structure. In 1959, the first limited partnership for venture capital was organized in Palo Alto, California when Army officer, banker, and diplomat William H. Draper Jr. formed Draper, Gaither & Anderson. In 1961, Arthur Rock, an investment banker who was a student of Doriot at

Harvard, and Thomas J. Davis, a real estate investor, formed Davis & Rock, the industry's second significant partnership.

Adapted from the oil wildcatting business, the limited partnership offered several distinct advantages over the publicly traded investment company registered under securities laws. General partners who ran the firm received not only a management fee that covered salaries and expenses, they also received a share of the capital gains. That feature eliminated ARD's compensation problems, as well as wiping out the pressure to generate investment income to fund operations. The firm's limited partners also maintained a long-term horizon that allowed them to forgo dividends or interest payments. And as a private entity, a limited partnership would avoid the glare of public disclosure and the requirements to release proprietary financial data.

Elfers left ARD to form his own venture capital partnership, Greylock Capital. Greylock was one of the first venture firms to raise money from several families, rather than a single limited partner such as J. H. Whitney & Company. In 1965 Elfers raised $5 million from five wealthy families, including the Watsons of IBM, Warren Corning of Corning Glass, and Sherman Fairchild, the founder of Fairchild Semiconductor. "I knew Doriot wasn't perfect," says Elfers. Still, Elfers acknowledged "it was not easy to leave ARD."

Doriot did not have much time to fret about Elfers's departure. The SEC was breathing down his neck; he had to prepare for his retirement from Harvard; and, most important, the General had decided that it was time to take several ARD companies public, including its star child Digital Equipment. After stumbling in 1964 and early 1965, Digital had steadied its ship, organizationally and financially, and was ready to embark on a new adventure.

Indeed, the SEC's decision to officially question several of his firm's practices pushed Doriot over the edge. In October of 1965, instead of writing a note that got filed in his "Unsent" folder, Doriot mailed a withering five-page letter to the SEC's Assistant Chief Enforcement Attorney Robert J. Routier and the agency's Boston Regional Office. In the letter, Doriot challenged the SEC's unsubstantiated insinuations and its sloppy language.

On the issue of Digital Equipment, Doriot inquired: "Why is there need for revaluation? Is the valuation too high? Is it too low? Just what is wrong with it?" Doriot then explained the highly detailed and rigorous process that ARD had developed to value its investments. "I rather resent, after twenty years of experience, to have two men come here, spend two days, and tell us that we do not know what we are doing," wrote Doriot. "We know what we are doing and we know why we are doing it." On the issue of disclosing personal investments of ARD directors, Doriot asked for specific cases to address. "We conduct this company on the highest ethical standards," wrote Doriot. "I do not enjoy your very wide and general remarks."

After this outburst, Doriot took a plane down to New York City to test the waters for an offering of Digital Equipment. On the trip, he adhered to the company's frugal philosophy. Walking out of LaGuardia Airport, Doriot took a bus to Manhattan. Then he hopped on a train that took him from midtown to Wall Street. "Young people at our firm who were junior associates would have a stretch limo pick them up at Kennedy Airport," says banker Robert McCabe, who would often meet with Doriot on his trips to New York. "The General did not operate that way. When he was older I would insist we take a taxi."

Doriot came to New York specifically to visit Longstreet Hinton, a new ARD director who was an executive vice president of the giant Morgan Guaranty Trust Company of New York. Hinton also headed Morgan Guaranty's investment committee, which had the power to approve large deals. James F. Morgan, who joined ARD in early 1967, said Doriot told him that Hinton offered to buy 20 percent of Digital's offering. "That basically made the deal," says Morgan.

With a promise to snap up 20 percent of the IPO from one of Wall Street's most prestigious investment houses, Doriot rung up Robert Lehman. Doriot invited Lehman Brothers to lead an offering for Digital Equipment and Lehman signed on. "I am delighted to know that you are anxious to have American Research be even closer to Lehman Brothers than they have in the past," wrote Lehman in October of 1965. "You know that our feeling for you is a very warm one and nothing would make us happier than to work even closer with you and your company than in the past."

ARD could have taken Digital public years ago during the stock market boom in the mid-1960s. But it was not the right time for Digital. Now Doriot knew the time was ripe. After a tumultuous sprint, in the fall of 1965, Digital unveiled the PDP-8, a new machine priced at the breakthrough level of

$18,000—a remarkably low price for a high-performance computer. The PDP-8 redefined the minicomputer industry and sent Digital's sales through the roof. In 1966, Digital's revenues more than doubled to $38 million, and profits multiplied six-fold to $4.5 million.

Digital was able to reap this harvest thanks to a new organizational structure put in place by Olsen. The structure, dubbed the matrix, gave one senior executive profit and loss responsibility for managing a single product line. The matrix provided a much-needed degree of accountability to Digital while also providing an incentive structure for success. Olsen, in effect, made each product manager an entrepreneur. The other key was the hiring of Peter Kaufman, a manufacturing whiz recruited from Beckman Instruments in California. Kaufman, a young, irreverent, yet seasoned manager with an MBA, initially rejected Digital's offer. But after General Doriot pressed him for four hours, discussing the job and his manufacturing philosophy, Kaufman signed on. He quickly became Olsen's right-hand man and the staff rallied around him.

In the spring of 1966, Doriot prepared for ARD's annual meeting. Always eventful, this year's gathering was an unusually raucous affair. Many of ARD's new friends from EED and CED had traveled long distances to attend the meeting, including Arnaud de Vitry, Gerald Sutton, and Robert Rhodes. During this meeting, Doriot took up the SEC's challenge to explain to investors how ARD valued its privately held investments. His main point was that it was not advisable to provide detailed financial figures for young affiliates. "In the early years figures are meaningless to anyone not very close to the company," said Doriot. "It is easier to pass judgment on a 24-year-old man than a 3- or 4-year-old child." In making his case for the difficulties in valuing young, unproven companies, Doriot highlighted the thoughtful process by which ARD sought to offset those challenges. Valuation entailed the consideration of many factors, including the company's product evolution, financial results, management experience, problems facing the company, plans for the future, and the company's willingness to accept advice. As the General once explained, "Our biggest hurdle usually is convincing them they need our help." After evaluating these factors, ARD's staff would determine a valuation target, which was submitted to the Executive Committee and the board, who reviewed the numbers. ARD repeated this process four times a year during quarterly valuation meetings.

It was a convincing argument but one investor did not buy it. Otto Hirschman of New York City, who owned 14,600 shares of ARD stock, stood up and criticized the company's management—the first time it had been publicly faulted in its twenty-year history. Hirschman argued that management treated its stockholders unfairly by undervaluing the company and not paying out enough in dividends. Hirschman's lament underscored the impossible situation that Doriot and his directors faced: While the SEC had privately criticized ARD for placing what it felt was an excessively high valuation on Digital (one hundred times its acquisition cost, noted the SEC's chief enforcement attorney in a response to Doriot's attack letter), shareholders like Hirschman demanded an even higher valuation.

"A new board of directors should be elected to better represent the interest of all stockholders," declared Hirschman. "The stock is worth $45 to $50 a share in liquidation and $150 a share if we had another board." Hirschman voted against the reelection of the present directors. But the board was overwhelmingly reelected.

Had Doriot confided his future plans in Hirschman, the activist investor probably would have never attacked the ARD board. For Doriot was laying the groundwork for an offering that would delight Hirschman and other shareholders like no other IPO had ever done before—the IPO of Digital Equipment.

Although Lehman Brothers banker Robert McCabe had become Digital's primary banker, since he was an investor in a competing computer firm it was decided he would not lead Digital's offering. McCabe chose two other bankers to lead the deal, Steve Fenster and Bill Osborne. But before they could pitch the deal, the task for building the investment case for Digital fell to a thirty-one-year-old junior banker named Arnold Kroll. Even though Robert Lehman agreed to take Digital public, there was a lot of skepticism within the firm about underwriting the IPO. "I was a young associate and no one at Lehman had the slightest interest in doing an offering for a minicomputer," says Kroll. "No one knew what a minicomputer was. There was a prejudice that IBM was the only company that would ever do good. It was a throwaway and it was thrown at me."

ARD had helped Digital in innumerable ways since its inception but Doriot's orchestration of the public offering for Digital—and dozens of other affiliates—was one issue in which his influence was unquestioned and unquestionably crucial. "It was incredibly important to the shareholders of ARD for the General to be involved," says Jack Shields, then a rising star within Digital. "There was not any expertise in the Digital management team for IPOs."

Kroll grabbed the ball that no one wanted and ran up to Maynard. Burrowing into the company, he analyzed Digital's management, its products, and its market. He dealt mostly with Doriot and Digital's treasurer Harry Mann. Ken Olsen stood in the background. Doriot guided the process the whole way, articulating the value and uniqueness of the company to Kroll and the staff of Lehman Brothers. "Clearly, General Doriot was a visionary," says Andrew G. C. Sage II, a former Lehman Brothers president who was then a managing partner running its syndicate desk. "Everybody liked him. Everybody knew him. He generated excitement about new ideas and new companies."

Kroll wrote a report strongly recommending the Digital offering. The biggest concern was potential competition from IBM. But Digital and Doriot convinced Kroll that minicomputers would grow and IBM wouldn't eat its lunch. "I came away with the feeling that the company would be able to make its internal projections, which were very high," says Kroll. "With that kind of a bullish memo [Kroll's internal report] and the relationship between Doriot and [Robert] Lehman it would have been very unlikely to turn it down. There was no magic. I am not claiming to be smart." The firm green-lighted the offering.

Over the summer, Lehman bankers pitched the deal. Back in the mid-1960s, there were no "road shows." The sales process consisted primarily of meetings between Lehman associates and potential investors in New York and Boston. Ken Olsen made a number of talks. And Doriot played a major role, infusing the pitch with his charm and gravitas. "People got very intrigued by it," says Robert Shapiro, who as part of Lehman's syndicate desk was responsible for identifying a nucleus of long-term investors. "It was because of Doriot and the reputation that he enjoyed." Ultimately, the deal was oversubscribed, attracting far more demand than supply. Then there was a tussle over the price. Lehman Brothers wanted to price the shares at $17 but Digital's board held out for $22 a share.

All in all, the stars seemed to be aligning for ARD. On May 5, Clark Dodge & Company led an offering for ARD affiliate Optical Scanning, a document scanning gear manufacturer that Charles P. Waite had brought back from oblivion. "It was near death because the original development process to get it from startup to having product took much longer and took much more money than projected," says Waite. ARD had either to put up more money or shut down the company. Waite struck up a friendly relationship with Optical's embattled CEO, visited some of its potential customers and determined that several schools would buy the machine. "I helped to convince Doriot that it was a meritorious company and we should keep putting money into it," says Waite. Then on June 16, W. E. Hutton led an offering for Tridair Industries, a California maker of airplane cargo equipment that ARD financed in 1963. Both offerings were successful.

As the summer drew to a close, it was Digital's time to come out, time for ARD's Cinderella to put on her glass slipper. On August 19, Lehman led an $8 million offering to sell 375,000 shares of stock in Digital Equipment under the ticker "DEC." The offering easily sold out. At $22 a share, Ken Olsen's 13 percent stake of 350,000 shares was worth $7 million on paper. ARD's 65 percent stake of 1,750,000 shares was valued at $38.5 million. In nine years, ARD's $70,000 investment had skyrocketed in value by a factor of five hundred, validating Doriot's model and proving the shortsightedness of SEC inspectors.

But there was no celebration inside Digital's woolen mill. "It didn't seem like it was that big a deal," says Digital executive Winston Hindle, one of about thirty employees who owned shares in the company at the time of the offering. "I don't think anyone viewed it as a way to get rich quick." Other employees echoed those humble sentiments. "It was a quiet sense of enthusiasm and pride," says Jack Shields. "It reflected the board and Ken's and the General's style."

After the initial public offering, Digital offered options to a wider group of employees. Many of them seized the opportunity. But four weeks after the offering, the stock market swooned, and Digital's shares slipped along with the market. By early October the shares fell in over-the-counter trading to about $17. "Some of the people tried to give the options back," says Ted Johnson. "People felt that they had been had."

Robert McCabe discussed the predicament with the General. Around the same time of Digital's IPO, Lehman underwrote another offering for the Greyhound Computer Company, with the stock symbol GEC. "The General joked with me that your salesmen must be saying GEC instead of DEC," says McCabe.

But the stock market quickly recovered. And as shares in Digital and ARD began to rise, more and more people grew intrigued by this fairy-tale story. In February of 1967, James F. Morgan, a former Doriot student who had gone on to become a consultant with Booz Allen, joined ARD as an assistant vice president. One of his first tasks was to pick up Arnold Kroll and drive out to Maynard where Digital was holding its first-ever meeting with financial analysts. Kroll and Morgan sat in Digital's dingy cafeteria and listened as Ken Olsen scared the heck out of Wall Street. "The first meeting with security analysts was a disaster," says Morgan. "The banks sent their junior person. You had this monosyllabic CEO who didn't want to speak with them. They were grunting at each other. Half of the people that were there went home and sold their stock. It wasn't until the bottom line starting coming in that it was seen as a money machine."

The shrewder analysts realized that Digital was sitting on a gold mine. The company's PDP-8, a cheap but potent machine, quickly caught fire and achieved a production run as large as the IBM computers. Thanks to the new device, Digital's sales and profits grew in the mid–double digits for years.

By March of 1967 Digital shares topped $50. Over the summer, they hit $80, and in September they crossed $100. Shares of Digital had become a proxy for ARD stock since Digital represented almost 60 percent of ARD's total asset value. With Digital trading close to $110, ARD's stake was now worth nearly $200 million. In October, just as Otto Hirschman had hoped, ARD's stock reached a record high of $152. Digital Equipment was the venture capital industry's first home run, single-handedly proving that venture capitalists could generate enormous wealth by backing the leader of a hot new business. "There's no question that the public offering of Digital was the most important event in ARD's history," says Charles P. Waite. "It created this huge win for ARD."

James F. Morgan believes the Digital IPO amounted to a financial revolution, signaling the power of start-ups in the American economy. "I'd say it was a sea change in the attitudes toward venture capital investing," says Morgan. "There really had never been a phenomenal, enduring success. The blood started pumping. If a klutz like Ken Olsen can do that, why can't I? Digital blew open the restrictions that anyone had ever applied to entrepreneurial ventures. It was really mind-blowing, that you could take such a small amount of seed capital and get ownership of a company that was worth more than IBM in a fairly short period of time."

During the course of its existence, ARD financed 120 companies. But it was the development of Digital Equipment that allowed Doriot to accomplish his ultimate goal. "Doriot was very important because he was the first one to believe there was a future in financing entrepreneurs in an organized way," says Arnold Kroll. "[ARD] really created and he created the venture capital community."

ELEVEN

THE TAKEOVER

(1967–1972)

AFTER FINISHING AN ILLUSTRIOUS forty-year career at Harvard Business School, Georges Doriot sat back and watched as the accolades began pouring in. The President and Fellows of Harvard University appointed Doriot Professor of Industrial Management, Emeritus. His students also paid tribute to the school's most influential and popular professor. In May 1966, the Harvard Business School Club of New York named Doriot the Business Statesman of the Year and feted him with a dinner party at the Waldorf Astoria hotel. More than four hundred former students showed up in black tie. "Remember that our happiness is in direct proportion to the contributions we make," Doriot told the crowd, ending his speech with one of his favorite stories.

On a road somewhere, three men were breaking stones. They were asked what they were doing.

One said, "I earn a living."

One said, "I break stones."

One said, "I help build cathedrals."

Let us build cathedrals together.

Doriot's final cathedral was American Research and Development. The French immigrant had made his indelible mark on the military and the university. And now, through ARD, Doriot was the evangelist of a new financial age, an age driven by young, small companies that performed miraculous feats of invention, an age that generated enormous amounts of wealth for the players who understood the rules of the game.

By the end of 1967, the remarkable results of Doriot's last mission had become apparent. Thanks to Digital Equipment's blockbuster IPO, ARD met Doriot's goal of generating superior performance by producing a 17 percent rate of return during its twenty-one-year history, a significantly better return than the 13 percent average of the Dow Jones index during the same period. But ARD's success transcended the bottom line. Digital Equipment had also become the paragon of entrepreneurial success, inspiring a whole generation of technologists to drop out of Corporate America and tune in to the possibilities of start-ups. By the late 1960s, Route 128, the sixty-five-mile highway surrounding the Boston-Cambridge heartland, had come to be seen as the nation's most innovative plot of land, the "Golden Semicircle" claiming headquarters or branches of 690 technology-oriented companies.

In August of 1967, *Fortune* editor Gene Bylinsky enshrined Doriot's achievement by writing a ten-page story titled "General Doriot's Dream Factory." It was the longest and best article ever written about Doriot, explaining the General's peculiar genius and the spectacular success of his venture capital firm. "It is a very special, sensitive kind of assistance these companies need, and it is not surprising that only a few backers of new ideas do well in bringing up such baby firms," wrote Bylinsky. "Among the most successful ones, probably the most astute, is Georges F. Doriot, president of American Research & Development Corp., the Boston-based, publicly held risk-capital company."

But despite his considerable insight and intelligence, Bylinsky missed the real story. The real story was that ARD faced fundamental problems that threatened its very existence. Not once in the whole feature did Bylinsky mention the Securities and Exchange Commission or the Internal Revenue Service. That was an understandable omission. ARD's battles with the SEC and IRS were a tightly guarded secret. But Bylinsky overlooked one obvious sign of trouble: the departures of William Elfers, and more recently, Charles P. Waite. If Bylinsky had dug into the reasons behind those departures, he might have understood ARD's conundrum: because ARD could not offer stock options to its staff, it was difficult for the firm to attract and retain top talent.

The gravity of ARD's compensation problems became clear to Charles P. Waite soon after he helped take Optical Scanning public. "I had made a very substantial contribution to that company," says Waite. "The CEO's net worth went from 0 to $10 million and I got a $2,000 raise. I agonized a lot over that. I remember thinking at the time I should have gotten a bigger raise. I loved what I was doing but I thought I should be somewhere where I was compensated adequately. And so, that was what eventually led to my leaving the firm."

Waite originally planned to take a job with an industrial company but when William Elfers heard about his move he asked Doriot for permission to talk to Waite. Both Doriot and Elfers thought it was a mistake for Waite to leave the venture capital industry. After a few interviews with the limited partners of Greylock Capital, Waite was offered and accepted a job with the new firm.

Other staff members began to grumble about compensation issues. The elephant in the room was the explosive success of Digital Equipment and the fact that only four ARD employees had received options in the company. Dorothy Rowe, William Congleton, and Henry Hoagland, who had all received twenty thousand founders' shares of Digital stock according to ARD auditor Brian Brooks, were sitting on paper gains worth many millions of dollars. Wayne Brobeck, who had also received Digital shares, had left the company.

Digital's success created a deep division in the ARD office: there were those who had Digital shares and those who didn't, and the reason for the difference seemed all too arbitrary. "It didn't matter when it was dimes and nickels, but when it was $20 million per person we were somewhat disappointed," said John A. Shane. "The General was quite arbitrary in that aspect of management. If the thing were managed in a little better fashion where we split up the options, it would not have been an issue."

In January of 1967, compensation problems were not at the top of Doriot's mind however. The taxman was. ARD's auditors had just learned that a bizarre legal quirk jeopardized the firm's status as a regulated investment company. To qualify as a regulated investment company, firms like ARD had to satisfy all sorts of tests. One of them—known as a diversification test—

was that an investment company could not own securities in one company amounting to more than 5 percent of the market value of the investor's total assets, and not more than 10 percent of the outstanding voting securities of the company it invested in. Congress, however, wrote an exception into the law years earlier, specifically for ARD, exempting venture capital companies from the diversification test. The exception permitted ARD to exceed the diversification restrictions for a period of ten years from the date of investment in a security.

The problem for ARD, of course, was its stake in Digital Equipment. After Digital's IPO, ARD held 60 percent of the voting stock of Digital, and its investment in the company exceeded 50 percent of the value of ARD's total assets. For ARD, this was a blessing. But the government saw it as a curse. On August 27, 1967 ARD's investment in Digital would be ten years old, and the exception would no longer apply. "It presently is unclear but quite possible that ARD will then cease to be a regulated investment company," wrote ARD's auditor William Barnes.

ARD's options were limited. Feeling bullish about the company's future, Doriot was loath to sell its investment in Digital. And it would be a folly to try to invest nearly $200 million in new companies that such a sale would generate. ARD could distribute its shares of Digital to ARD shareholders but that would not benefit ARD that much either. "It is strange to believe that ARD stockholders should suffer because ARD has been successful," confided Doriot in a personal memo. "If Digital had been a failure, or only mediocre, ARD could retain its regulated status, and its stockholders would not be penalized."

Doriot was in a bind. He asked his auditing firm for their opinion. In August, Lybrand, Ross Brothers & Montgomery recommended to Doriot that ARD could make new investments as long as the transaction did not exceed 10 percent of the outstanding voting securities of the new company. For ARD's existing investments, the firm recommended that ARD not exercise any warrants or make additional investments that would exceed the 10 percent limitation. It was a huge handicap for the firm but it seemed it had no choice.

Or did it? In March, Doriot was one of thirty people invited to testify before the U.S. Senate's Select Committee on Small Business. The Committee, under Chairman George A. Smathers, decided to hold hearings to ensure that "in an era of breathtaking change" Congress brought its "thinking up-to-date . . . to assure that every program of the Federal Government is brought forward into the space age." In his testimony before Congress, Doriot explained his philosophy of venture capital and the record of ARD. Only once at the end of his remarks did Doriot address the issue of government regulation. "We do have some problems there, and have some slight problems with the Internal Revenue Service," said Doriot in perhaps the greatest understatement of his life. "The SEC and the IRS have been very understanding and very kind to us. But I think a little bit of flexibility would make our work a lot easier."

It wasn't until the congressmen reviewed Doriot's prepared statement that they grasped the true depth of his "slight problems." Doriot devoted the bulk of his statement to suggesting a host of changes to federal tax legisla tion and the Investment Company Act. The changes proposed fixes to every single one of ARD's regulatory problems, from its questionable status as an investment company, to its inability to issue stock options, to its restrictions on transactions with affiliated persons.

As a last resort, Doriot turned to ARD's new junior lawyer Richard J. Testa. A young attorney at the Boston law firm Gaston, Snow, Motley & Holt, Testa had recently begun working on some of ARD's business. When ARD's lead lawyer left Gaston, Snow to become an investment advisor with Massachusetts Investors Trust, Doriot searched for a replacement. "The General interviewed all of the partners and he did not like anybody," says Janet Testa, Richard's wife. "He complained to several people including Ken Olsen at Digital." Olsen suggested Testa, who also worked at Gaston, Snow, and whose legal work for Digital impressed Olsen. Doriot went back to the firm and asked why they had not introduced him to Testa. "You only asked to interview partners," they replied. Doriot met with Testa and they struck up an easy rapport.

A young, hungry associate with a keen mind for business, Testa was also blessed with an unusual sensitivity for the difficulties faced by young companies. Testa proved himself on the IRS diversification conundrum by coming up with an ingenious legal contortion. On September 29, 1967 ARD formed American Enterprise Development Corporation (AEDC) as a wholly owned venture capital subsidiary. On the same day, ARD acquired from AEDC all of its outstanding stock, which did not violate the 5 percent value test. In exchange for the stock, AEDC received most of the liquid assets of ARD— except its shares in Digital—with the idea that all new investment situations would be handled by AEDC. Testa got the SEC and IRS to certify AEDC as a regulated investment company. In effect, Testa escaped from the diversification trap by creating another investment firm that was not hampered by the Digital investment.

On December 31, Doriot invited a few dozen friends and colleagues to 12 Lime Street for his annual New Year's Eve party. The guests walked past two seven-foot high iron gates, the kind usually seen marking the entrance to a city park, and gathered in the living room courtyard. They drank champagne, admiring the fifty-foot ceiling and massive stone fireplace. Normally, Doriot preferred martinis but tonight he drank champagne. Edna, radiant as ever, flitted around the room, talking to guests, whispering sweet nothings in Georges's ear. One hour before midnight, Doriot issued red vests with fake medals to all of the men. He ascended to the top of the staircase overlooking the atrium and gave a speech, an annual ritual that marked the highlight of the evening.

He spoke in a soft voice so people had to listen closely. Doriot said he was quite unhappy that he could not become President of the United States since he was born overseas. But he had another idea to usurp control: he would create and oversee a union of computer programmers, which would allow him to take over the U.S. government and all of the nation's banks. "It was very funny," says Robert McCabe. But few people glimpsed the darkness underlying the joke's irony. At that point in his life, Doriot would have done practically anything to get the government off his back. At the end of the party, Edna turned on the stereo and played "La Marseillaise," the French national anthem. The whole house full of people chimed in and sang the night away.

At ARD's board meeting in January of 1968, Doriot took action to stem his staff's rising tide of discontent. At his firm request, the directors approved the promotions of five ARD staffers. Hoagland and Congleton were promoted to senior vice president, and Rowe, Shane, and Morgan were bumped to vice president. The directors also elected two new board members: Kenneth H. Olsen and William H. Wendel, the president of the Carborundum Company, a chemical maker based in Niagara Falls, New York, whose largest shareholder was the Mellon family of Pittsburgh.

As a director, Olsen's main goal was to compel ARD to reduce its holdings in Digital Equipment. Olsen, rightfully so, was afraid a hostile takeover of ARD would leave his company in the control of someone he did not trust.

At ARD's 1968 annual meeting, Doriot presided over the affair like a grandparent proud of his growing clan. Looking around the Dorothy Quincy Suite, Doriot watched as more than five hundred friends, entrepreneurs, bankers, analysts, and others filled up the room. During the meeting, Doriot reviewed ARD's six new investments, including $250,000 in Seattle Cablevision, Incorporated, a new cable television operator, and $400,000 in Western Video Industries, Incorporated, a Los Angeles–based provider of television production facilities.

Doriot also touted the progress of its foreign venture partners. To date, CED had invested in twenty companies, including one joint investment with ARD, and EED had bought stakes in fifteen companies. Both ventures were off to a promising start, producing capital gains on a few early investments. "Those two companies and ARD do have what I would call a material value," explained Doriot. "[B]ut way beyond that, they have a spiritual value, and that spiritual value I rate far above the material value one may place on them. Based on creativity, on hard work, on cooperation, on faith in the future, we have created our own common market. It is the common market for creative people. We believe in it. Please help us carry it out."

Over the summer, Doriot realized that promotions and the modest raises that came with them would not mollify his staff. So at ARD's July board meeting, he proposed the creation of a stock purchase plan for ARD personnel, to be given in lieu of options. The board, at Doriot's request, formed a committee to recommend a solution.

In August, Lybrand, Ross Brothers & Montgomery wrote Doriot with some good news on the regulatory front. Although the bill it had been working on to extend ARD's status as a regulated investment company had stalled in the spring, it was reported favorably to the Senate on August 1. In addition to Senator Smathers, ARD was now getting help from an old friend, George H. W. Bush, who was now a junior Congressman. Bush introduced an identical bill in the House that was approved by the House Ways and Means Committee. Lybrand's William Barnes now told Doriot that "the climate is favorable for passage" of its bill "during September or early October."

As often happens in Washington, though, the bills languished in committee. Congress adjourned in early October without passing either of them.

This meant ARD would have to start its legislative project from scratch in January. Another drawback of the delay was that Senator Smathers, their chief ally, would no longer be in the Senate to shepherd the bill along.

To make matters worse, the SEC turned up the heat on Doriot once more. The agency requested by letter that ARD withdraw from its proxy material any mention of its proposed stock purchase plan. Richard Testa called the SEC to find out what happened and was told that the SEC staff would submit ARD's stock plan to the Commission with a recommendation against it. Adding insult to injury, the SEC informed Ken Olsen he could not exercise his options in Digital stock since he was now a director of ARD.

In November of 1968, Doriot read the handwriting in Washington and penned an astonishingly candid memo. The opening line of the memo was this zinger: "ARD is not competitive any more." The unrelenting stream of bad news from Washington had forced Doriot to take a brutally honest assessment of his beloved venture firm. Doriot was like a world-class boxer pummeled into submission. He had not thrown in the towel but his legs were getting wobbly. "The SEC never understood, and I believe never made an effort to understand the problems of compensation of ARD personnel," wrote Doriot in his ten-page salvo. "There has been no effort on the part of the SEC to ask for legislation. In 100 years from now it will be the same! In the meantime, even the Constitution seems to be submitted to different interpretations."

ARD, he wrote, was no longer competitive with partnerships or large companies practicing venture capital that operated free from SEC restrictions. What constructive action could Doriot take given these trying circumstances? He offered four possible answers. The first was to start another venture fund, most likely a private one. The second idea was to marry ARD with its favorite son, Digital Equipment. The remaining options were to merge ARD with another financial company or with an industrial firm. Doriot believed a merger with an industrial firm probably constituted the best option because industrial firms build businesses, as opposed to the financial engineering practiced by investment firms. But whatever course Doriot took, one thing was clear: business as usual was no longer an option.

In the spring of 1969, ARD's merger discussions began to percolate. ARD's new director, William H. Wendel, proposed a union with the Carborundum Company. Doriot liked the fact that Carborundum was a respected industrial firm. Dan Lufkin, the president of Donaldson, Lufkin &

Jenrette, proposed ARD merge with Digital Equipment and Mohawk Data Sciences. Doriot was uninterested in this proposal because he didn't have a high opinion of Mohawk. G. William Miller then submitted to Doriot a confidential plan to a merge ARD with Textron, Incorporated. In less than ten years, Miller, a short, hard-driving Oklahoma native, had transformed Textron from a moderate-size textile manufacturer into one of the world's first conglomerates, a giant aerospace concern that sold everything from consumer goods to Bell UH-1 helicopters, or Hueys, the workhorses of the Vietnam War. Of the three, this idea held the most promise for Doriot, who had been a director of Textron since 1962. ARD also held shares of Textron in its portfolio.

Two more proposals came in later that year. Doriot rejected the first, an offer to merge with Boston Capital, an SBIC run by former ARD exec Joseph W. Powell. "Powell close to [Doriot's] age—personnel good but nothing special," scribbled Doriot in the margins of a personal note. Then Don Christensen, the head of Greater Washington Industrial Investments, another successful SBIC, proposed a merger. "ARD might be interested," Doriot told the board in July. "They have a good location. Christensen is good. Is he outstanding? He is certainly a very good No. 2 man." Lastly, Lehman Brothers approached ARD later that month with a proposal from Sutter Hill, an SBIC based in San Francisco, to acquire a large swath of its holdings. "The personnel seem to have done well but we do not know them so well," wrote Doriot. "We do like the location and are studying the company."

At the same time Doriot was considering merger candidates, he also finally began approaching possible successors who could lead the firm into the future. He reached out to three men: Dennis Stanfill, a Rhodes Scholar who was vice president for finance at the Times Mirror Company; Alex Daignault, his former Quartermaster charge who was now executive vice president of chemical company W. R. Grace; and Thomas J. Perkins, a former Manufacturing student who was a rising star at the West Coast electronics firm Hewlett-Packard.

Stanfill wanted to stay on the West Coast. Daignault preferred to become the number two man with hopes of becoming the top guy. And Perkins, while somewhat interested and flattered by the entreaty from his former professor, told Doriot he could not accept the offer. "I had a tremendous respect for him," says Perkins. "He was the second most important mentor in my life, after Dave Packard."

Of all the prominent and successful men that ARD considered as Doriot's successors, Perkins stood out as the most impressive candidate. In Perkins, Doriot saw an ideal leader, a seasoned corporate manager who displayed a flair for entrepreneurship and a deep understanding of technology. In the mid-1960s, while a manager at Hewlett-Packard, Perkins convinced Dave Packard to let him launch and run a start-up called University Laboratories, a maker of laser technology that shared a glass-blowing studio in Berkeley with the LSD maker Augustus Owsley. "Packard was an entrepreneur and he loved entrepreneurs," says Perkins, who majored in electrical engineering at MIT. "He liked me. He trusted me that [University Laboratories] wouldn't interfere with HP. It was very, very unusual. I was the chairman and I hired people to run the company." A few years later, following the advice of investment banker George Quist, Perkins sold the company to laser-maker Spectra-Physics, and he became a multimillionaire. "I had in effect become a venture capitalist," says Perkins.

Perkins told Doriot that several personal reasons prevented him from accepting his offer, but he hid the real explanation. After his experience building and selling University Laboratories, Perkins wanted to set up his own venture capital firm. He would have loved to take over ARD but the compensation issue was a deal-breaker. "There was no way to make significant money because of the structure of ARD," says Perkins. "It would have to be restructured." Perkins admired Doriot's accomplishments, but if he was going to get in the venture game, it would have to be in the form of a private partnership. There was just no other way to do it.

By the middle of 1969, compensation problems had become the kryptonite of ARD. Elfers and Waite had already left ARD because of them, and candidates to take over ARD were repelled by them. And now, it was Henry W. Hoagland's turn to leave Doriot's nest. But ironically, Hoagland left because ARD had made him rich: he felt his big cut of Digital gave him and his wife enough money to retire. "We felt wealthy enough that we didn't have to punch that clock for Doriot anymore," says Ray Hoagland. "Harry was getting restless. I think Doriot was surprised." It was another heavy blow to ARD. The company had lost its most senior employee, a twenty-year veteran who reeled in many successful deals.

Henry and Ray took off for a three-month trip to Europe. "When we got back Harry's phone was ringing off the wall," says Ray. The President of

Fidelity Management and Research Company was one of the people calling. He wanted Henry to take over the firm's fledgling venture capital firm. "They had a little VC fund that was going absolutely broke," says Ray. "It sounded so charming and they made it sound so easy." Henry took the job, ending his retirement after just a few months. ARD was now competing against one of its most prominent alumni.

To replace Henry, Doriot offered a job to Daniel J. Holland, an officer at the First National Bank of Chicago. As another Harvard Business School alumnus, Doriot was familiar with Holland and his skills. In 1968, he got to know Holland even better when he accepted a part-time job as ARD's unpaid Midwestern correspondent. "It is quite an honor, General," said Holland of the new offer. "Let me think about it."

"Don't think about it too long," Doriot replied.

After discussing the offer with his wife, Holland packed up his four kids and spouse and moved to Boston to take the job. Since Holland had avoided Doriot's course at Harvard—a major lapse in Doriot's eyes—he gave Holland a suitable alternative. "He said early on that I could rectify that deficiency in my background by getting together every Saturday morning and taking a lecture on manufacturing," recalls Holland. "By the time I joined we were down to one Saturday a month."

Although the modest salary had not scared Holland away—he was still young and did not expect to get rich from the job—the compensation issue continued to be ARD's biggest quandary. In October, ARD's compensation committee held its first meeting. The committee decided to hire the consulting firm Arthur D. Little to design an executive compensation program that it could review at ARD's December board meeting.

At the end of November, Arthur D. Little submitted its report. The consultant concluded that ARD's present compensation was "inadequate" and would not "meet the needs of ARD in the years ahead." It recommended that "steps be taken now to substantially increase the level of compensation of management and staff members and to introduce new forms and modes of payment." Specifically, Little recommended that compensation include an annual incentive bonus of 15 to 50 percent of an employee's salary. It also recommended the creation of a profit-sharing trust funded by ARD payments, and an enhanced package of pension, medical, and life insurance benefits. After reading the report, Doriot said he did not want to pay a bonus for

1969 because "we have done poorly on new projects and on some of our affil-iates." But he ultimately voted for a 15 percent bonus, acknowledging that "we must be competitive" on personnel issues.

The bonus did not satisfy everyone. At the end of 1969, Samuel Bodman submitted his resignation. After six years at ARD, Bodman decided it was time for him to make some big money. The General encouraged Bodman to get an MBA instead. But Henry Hoagland had already offered him a well-paid job at Fidelity's venture arm. "I was the father of three children," says Bodman. "I was broke. I was offered a job for $35,000—twice what I was making then." So the two agreed to disagree on Bodman's future course, and Bodman took the job. Eight years after joining Fidelity, the Johnson family asked Bodman to serve as president of the entire company, a position he readily accepted. A few weeks later, he received a card from Doriot.

Dear Sammy,

You were right. Congratulations.

Best regards,

Georges Doriot

In 1970, the United States invaded Cambodia, National Guardsman gunned down four students at Kent State University in Ohio, and Simon and Garfunkel's "Bridge Over Troubled Water" topped the charts.

Like the county at large, ARD was engulfed in turmoil. For the last two years, the ARD proxy had reported that Doriot would step down in June of 1970. But the board was no closer to selecting a successor than they were in 1968. During an ARD annual board meeting in March of 1970, ARD's direc-tors tried to accelerate the succession process by creating the "Committee on 70"—a search committee chaired by Doriot that included directors Gene K. Beare, Byron K. Elliott, M. C. Kaplan, John A. Lunn, and Kenneth H. Olsen. The ARD board chose Doriot to be chairman in order to show that he approved of his successor. Doriot asked the committee to outline its specifi-cations for a new leader and suggested a new candidate named William Bentley, an executive at Cincinnati Milling.

In June, despite the chaos in the company, Doriot tried be constructive by inviting a handsome, athletic man named Charles J. Coulter over to his office to discuss another dire staffing need. He had come to know of Coulter through his work at Boston Capital. The two clicked and Doriot hired him on the spot as a vice president. Coulter knew about the compensation problems at ARD but it did not matter that much to him since Boston Capital could not offer him stock options either. "To go to work for ARD was considered more than the top of the line," said Coulter. "We all looked at ARD as the mecca of venture capital."

Coulter was the second graduate of Harvard Business School Doriot hired who had not taken his Manufacturing class. No one told Coulter, however, about the Saturday morning meetings. This commitment posed a problem for Coulter, who had a wife and children. Although no one had ever questioned the Saturday workday before, in his first week, Coulter raised the issue with the General.

"General, I've got a family," said Coulter. "I owe them something."

"Ah, Charlie, you have a good point," replied Doriot. "We shall no longer have our Saturday meetings."

"Everyone else was amazed that he did that," says Coulter. "I really had to bite the bullet there. Before that, ARD was an entire way of life."

The move was a necessary concession to reality. In all likelihood, say associates, Doriot gave up the Saturday meetings because his fight was all but gone and because he couldn't afford to be so stubborn at this stage in ARD's life. He desperately needed a replacement for Hoagland and Bodman.

In September, Doriot wrote a memo to ARD director Byron Elliott, the retired chairman of the John Hancock Mutual Life Insurance Company who had been appointed chairman of the Committee on 70. Doriot told Elliott that he had renewed his flirtation with Thomas J. Perkins. Since Perkins turned down Doriot more than a year ago, he had been having trouble raising money for his venture capital firm, and his two proposed partners bailed on the project and took other jobs. In fact, a few months ago Perkins asked ARD if it would help finance his firm but the board turned him down. "[Perkins] came to see me last week while he was in New England and told me he would very much like to be ARD's man on the West Coast," wrote

Doriot. But secretly Perkins still preferred to start his own venture partnership. "He probably thought I was more interested than I was," says Perkins. "I suppose I was trying to keep all my options open. I was being nice to the General. And in the back of my head I was thinking we could do deals together."

One year after it was founded, the Committee finally proposed a succession plan. Doriot would stay on as chairman of ARD, Olsen would be vice chairman, and Curtis W. Tarr was identified as the leading contender for president. A Harvard MBA with a PhD in American history from Stanford University, Tarr served for six years as president of Wisconsin's Lawrence University. Then in 1969 he left the school and became Assistant Secretary of the Air Force. Tarr had met several directors but he still needed to meet a few more before the board could decide if it wanted make him an offer. For the number two job running the affiliates, the board now considered William Bentley and Thomas Perkins as the top candidates.

In addition to the issue of succession, the board also pondered various merger options. Doriot and his fourteen directors had turned down the Sutter Hill idea. In its place, Textron had risen to the top of the list. Earlier in the year, the ARD board welcomed G. William Miller, Textron's CEO, as a new director. Now, Miller was in a perfect, if conflicted, position to influence the merger contest. He seized the opportunity. In November, one of Miller's associates prepared a detailed memo laying out the structure, risks, and requirements of the merger. "I feel fairly confident that the transaction described would not be blocked by the SEC," wrote Miller's associate. But Doriot knew nothing was guaranteed when it came to the SEC.

***

At ARD's affiliate dinner in March of 1971, Doriot remained in a dark, yet feisty frame of mind. For the first time ever, Doriot did not invite anyone to address his band of entrepreneurs. "We are alone, very alone," said Doriot. "That is the way to gain strength, and now we all need strength to have a very good 1971."

At the annual meeting the following day, despite the SEC's recommendation, ARD directors approved the stock option plan before its shareholders. "Before any options are granted under this plan we must receive the approval of the Securities and Exchange Commission," said Doriot. "Government agencies being what they are, I hesitate to tell you when this plan will become effective."

During the company's board meeting on March 7, the directors continued to drag their feet on succession. The Committee on 70 had turned into the Committee on 71. Over the last few months, the board rejected many of Doriot's possible successors, including Curtis Tarr. Since the board was seeking unanimity, a negative vote from one or two directors was enough to snuff out a candidate.

The board then discussed merger options, which seemed to be gaining momentum as the easiest and most popular exit strategy. Textron's Miller trumpeted the benefits of a merger with his conglomerate, while the directors also considered a merger with the International Basic Economy Corporation, a successful international investment and operating conglomerate started by the Rockefeller Brothers. Doriot was still hopeful for a merger between ARD and Digital, even though Olsen was against the idea from the start.

By July of 1971, Textron emerged as ARD's leading suitor. Doriot stepped up his talks with Miller. Later that month, Miller sent Doriot a letter outlining the tax implications of such a merger. The least expensive way to join the two firms, according to Miller's counsel, was for ARD to distribute its Digital stock to ARD shareholders as a dividend, and then merge the remaining ARD with Textron. "As we continue to seek consensus on an ARD-Textron combination, I agree that we should not delay further in selecting a good man for ARD," wrote Miller. "Of course, 'good' by definition means someone who sees the world as you and I do. I will give this more priority, still hoping that Plan X or Y or Z or AA will finally prevail!"

As summer gave way to fall, Doriot's interest in Textron—and Miller—continued to grow. In September, Doriot wrote in his personal notes that G. William Miller "has what it takes to be trusted with the future of ARD." He liked Miller's idea that ARD would operate under Textron with unusual autonomy, including its own president and board of directors. Precedent existed for such an arrangement: Textron-Atlantic, a wholly owned subsidiary of Textron, also had its own board. "ARD directors have to choose between the future of the company being in the hands of a new president and a relatively new board of directors or being part of a well managed industrial company under the leadership of an able man," wrote Doriot. "While some of the staff of ARD might be upset by such an idea, ARD could obtain and reward personnel far more easily than it can do now."

On September 8, the Committee on 71 met again. It recommended that Doriot make a last-ditch effort to find a successor. The Committee agreed upon two names: Henry Schacht, the president of Cummins Engine, and John P. Horgan, the recently retired partner at the private venture capital firm J. H. Whitney. In truth, it was a Hail Mary pass. Schacht told Doriot he was "very surprised, very pleased and very flattered" but begged off since "it would be quite wrong for [Schacht] to give up his job at this time." The conversation with Horgan went just as poorly. During a dinner with Horgan, he told Doriot that he was "1% interested." But in a phone call afterward, Doriot reported that he seemed "much more interested." As he had done with Perkins, however, Doriot was guilty of wishful thinking. While working for J. H. Whitney, Horgan let it be known that he had accumulated more than $2 million, a sign that compensation was going to be a problem.

As the Textron merger discussions progressed, tension developed between Doriot and Olsen. For the first time the two were at loggerheads. The crux of the difference was over what to do with ARD's substantial holdings of Digital. Over the last few years, ARD had sold several hundred thousand shares of the company but it still held a large stake. Doriot wanted to hold on to its remaining Digital shares, while Olsen wanted ARD to sell everything at once. At an ARD Executive Committee meeting on October 8, Olsen forcefully argued that ARD should distribute its 45 percent stake of Digital as soon as possible to ARD shareholders. But Doriot wanted ARD to retain its Digital stock to ensure that it would have a sizeable kitty to invest in the future. Still fearful of a hostile takeover of ARD despite the fact that the company had sold some of its holdings in Digital, Olsen refused to discuss ARD's future unless its directors agreed with his point. ARD's stake had also created an overhang on Digital's shares; a takeover discount was built into its stock.

Doriot held firm. He wanted to keep its shares in Digital as a hedge in case the Textron deal was not consummated. "I do not believe we should make the single decision to distribute all of ARD's DEC holdings unless a firm decision has been made as to ARD's future—unless we know that the Textron idea can and will be carried out," Doriot told the Committee. "If the Textron idea is not possible, then ARD should sell some DEC stock before giving any away to stockholders."

In response, Olsen cut off the ARD employees serving on Digital's board. Starting in August, ARD-appointed directors no longer received monthly financial figures, nor did they receive a capital expenditures budget or a general budget. Consequently, outside directors did not learn of a $2.5 million plant expansion until Digital's annual meeting on October 26. "Outside directors know nothing—are told nothing," wrote Doriot.

In November, Doriot began to withdraw from the world of venture capital. Later that month, he traveled to Brussels to attend an EED board meeting. There, he told the directors that he wished to resign as EED chairman and director before the firm's annual meeting the following May. After asking each director to give him suggestions for a new chairman and new directors, he returned to Boston to attend to more pressing matters.

On the last day in November, the ARD board gathered in a special meeting to discuss the firm's future. There, an extraordinary discussion was held in which some of the most powerful men in American business ultimately decided the fate of ARD after years of fruitless discussion and foot dragging. The directors immediately tackled the Textron merger option.

"Bill Miller has to understand my feelings are very negative," said H. D. Doan, former president of the Dow Chemical Company. "I am not opposed to Textron, but this venture business is important to the U.S. ARD is the leader in free enterprise and I would like to see it remain as an independent entity. There are 500 venture capital operations, probably 1,000 in all, but they don't represent what people need."

"I would like to see ARD remain independent," said Longstreet Hinton, chairman of Morgan Guaranty Trust Company of New York, one of ARD's largest shareholders. "The Textron merger might do more financially, but sentimentally, no."

The pro-merger camp weighed in:

"I end up favoring the Textron merger," said George P. Baker, retired dean of the Harvard Business School. "I don't want to see ARD start a different kind of business. What you have done is superb. I want it to end with a superb record. I bet 8 to 2 we won't find anyone like Georges. I would distribute Digital and fold the rest into Textron. We won't find anyone like you."

"Sentimentally, I say stay as is," replied Doriot. "My reasoning says give it to Miller."

"On reason grounds alone, ARD will do better with ARD alone than in Textron," argued Doan. "The idea that Georges has to be replaced as Georges is wrong. Others can do the job but will do it differently."

"No matter whether it is Textron, General Motors or any other company, I hate to see ARD merged," said Gene K. Beare, executive vice president and director of General Telephone & Electronics Corporation. "ARD is No. 1 and can remain so."

"I don't think Miller would pay a very high premium over asset value," said M. C. Kaplan, chairman and director of United Brands Company.

"I don't know," said Hinton. "They have in the past. There is skepticism these days with so many in the venture capital business. We started a fund at the bank with $10 million and have $2 million left. We don't understand how Georges did it."

After a long pause, Kaplan looked at Miller and asked, "Wouldn't you pay a premium for the name and staff?"

"No," barked Miller, playing hardball. "There is a substantial risk. If the board wants to spin off Digital and go alone—that is alright."

"You would be buying a tremendous amount of goodwill," said Kaplan.

"We would pay a reasonable amount after accounting for unpaid taxes and bearing in mind the risk," Miller shot back. "I have answered your question and you keep grilling me. Don't give me the third degree. Or forget the whole deal."

At that point, the board took a vote on whether or not to advance merger discussions with Textron. Seven directors voted yes, and three directors voted no. The directors then agreed to gauge shareholders' interest in such a sale. They also set an Executive Committee meeting in December to offer a definitive recommendation on the merger. But Doan had a hard time swallowing the fact that ARD was going headlong down the merger path, and he piped up one more time.

"If William Miller does his job, ARD will not be the same kind of company," warned Doan. "I started a venture group in Dow and unless

Textron is different from Dow, ARD will disappear. Turning it over to Textron is just paying the stockholders and bailing out."

"Who makes the decision?" asked Hinton, getting in the last word. "The stockholders."

On January 11, 1972, ARD's fate was sealed when Textron submitted a merger proposal to the company's board. The confidential document described the potential benefits of the merger and contained the coup de grace that had been missing from all other previous discussions: an offer price. The offer of $66.16 a share represented a 20 percent premium over the recent closing price of ARD's stock, although it was 4 percent below ARD's estimated net asset value of $68.60. Still, the price seemed fair. Investment companies typically traded at a discount to their net asset value since a buyer has to assume the firm's unpaid tax liabilities, which must be paid off after its assets are sold. Also, the risk of venture investments, coupled with the fact that many of ARD's affiliates required ongoing capital, bolstered the case for a discount.

Now it was up to the ARD board to vote on the proposal. By that point, though, ARD's merger with Textron was a fait accompli. During the three years that Doriot and the ARD board spent trying to create a succession plan, they were unable to develop a viable structure or agree upon a candidate to take over the firm. Their window of opportunity was closed. Moreover, if ARD walked away from the deal it could have opened itself up to shareholder lawsuits. "It would have been hard to turn down that deal," says Thomas J. Perkins. "They probably took the only option they had."

It's hard to call ARD's sale a failure. After all, this was a company that started with $3.5 million, pioneered an entire industry, and fetched an offer of more than $400 million. But given the special heritage of ARD, it is hard not to consider it a profound disappointment that the firm was unable to remain an independent entity continuing to lead the venture industry for another twenty-five years.

Virtually everyone who worked with Doriot laid much of the blame for ARD's failure to remain independent at his feet. In the same way that Doriot ended his Manufacturing course at Harvard because he thought no one else was up to the task, critics say Doriot did not believe anyone could fill his shoes at ARD. "The reason ARD folded is the same reason why there is no Doriot professorship at Harvard," says John A. Shane. "He was not good at picking successors. I don't think he tried very hard. I'm convinced that was the reason."

Frances J. Hughes, a venture investor who was friends with Richard Testa, says ARD's lawyer also believed this theory. "Dick observed this whole process and concluded that it was Doriot's refusal to deal with succession that sent them on their path to being bought out," says Hughes. In his defense, though, Doriot wrote often of the need for him to be replaced, and some friends take him at his word. "He was not a man who thought he could not be replaced," says Claude Janssen. "That he didn't find a man who could is another thing. It was not a philosophy of his."

Whatever one believes about Doriot, the ARD board clearly deserves some of the blame as well. The last best chance for ARD to remain strong and independent was in the early 1960s, when the board could have forced Doriot to turn over the reins to William Elfers, giving him the freedom and authority to solve the firm's structural problems. "It should have been done in 1965," says Charles P. Waite. "I believe everyone in ARD would have stayed." Certainly, the subsequent success of Greylock Capital provided unquestionable proof that Elfers was more than up to the task. But the majority of the board stood by Doriot all the way to the end. "The General was such an extraordinary person and had so high a standing in the investment community and with entrepreneurs that the board may have thought he was a hard act to follow," says Robert McCabe.

Perhaps the board's biggest mistake was that other than the easy path of a merger, for three years it neglected to investigate a solution to the firm's structural problems—even though it was that very issue that led many possible successors to reject the firm's entreaties. While the board pondered successors, notes from ARD's board meetings contain virtually no discussion of the idea of taking ARD private.

That absence, more than any factor, is the strongest evidence supporting the theory that ARD was never serious about remaining independent. Granted, taking private the assets of a public venture capital firm had never been done before. But that was precisely the kind of innovative deal Doriot aspired to—unless of course he didn't want ARD to continue independently. "It would have been a very, very complicated thing," says Robert McCabe.

Still, McCabe, who believes the merger was the best solution at the time, admits "there would have been some way to work it out."

On January 12, the day after receiving the Textron proposal, ARD released a statement announcing that its board of directors "endorsed in principal" a plan to merge the two companies. An article in the January 22 edition of *BusinessWeek* entitled "A Risk Capitalist Bids a Golden Adieu" quoted Miller on the deal's rationale. "ARD gives us a hedge against change and a chance to participate in technologies, such as computers, that we should know about," he said. "There's always the possibility of another DEC for our shareholders. Just one DEC, or half a DEC, in 10 years would be very nice."

On the fourteenth of March, Doriot presided over ARD's last annual meeting as an independent firm. At the affiliate dinner, Doriot struck an optimistic yet defensive tone. "The association between ARD-Textron should have great strength, and if carried out, I look forward to the next 25 years of ARD as extremely constructive ones," said Doriot. "Once in a while I have been told that ARD did not do enough for its affiliates. Today I am suggesting that we marry one of them. What more can I do?"

The next day, at the ARD annual meeting, Doriot told the stockholders that the ARD board had approved the merger plan. The board acted on the proposal after the IRS gave the merger a favorable tax treatment and Lehman Brothers advised ARD's directors that the deal terms were fair to shareholders. Then Doriot stumped for the deal one last time, casting it as a historic opportunity. "If the ARD stockholders approve the suggested relationship between ARD and Textron, the president of Textron, its board of directors and executives, will be given an opportunity to do something which perhaps had never been done before," he said. "That is: to run a successful venture capital operation in relationship with a large manufacturing operation."

One brave man spoke up against the deal, however. Parker G. Montgomery, the president of Cooper Laboratories, a drug maker that had become one of ARD's most successful investments, stood up and spoke from his heart. The room was so quiet you could hear the paper shuffling. "I feel as though I am watching a loved one making a fatal mistake," said Montgomery. "I feel even worse because I am powerless to stop it." Montgomery believed it made no sense to "sell to a conglomerate with a wheeler dealer who didn't know how to run anything."

On May 18, at Textron's headquarters in Providence, Rhode Island, a handful of picketers protested against the company's role in the Vietnam

War. Inside, Textron shareholders approved the ARD merger in a landslide, with nearly 27 million shares for the merger and 736,000 against it. In Boston, ARD shareholders gathered for a special meeting to vote on the deal. It was also a clear-cut victory: 4.7 million ARD shareholders approved the merger and slightly more than 200,000 voted against it.

Under the agreement, ARD shareholders received three-quarters of a share of Digital Equipment stock, and three-tenths of a share of Textron stock for each share of ARD stock. At the meeting, Doriot announced he was giving up the presidency of ARD to become its chairman. The new leader of ARD was now Robert S. Ames, a Textron senior vice president. ARD, the company that Doriot had envisioned, nurtured, and led to prosperity for the last twenty-five years was gone.

TWELVE

HOW THE
WEST WON

(1972–1980)

A RD'S MERGER WITH TEXTRON "was a mess from day one," says
James F. Morgan, then a vice president of the firm. "A total mess."

Even before the two companies sealed the deal, Textron's management reckoned their acquisition of ARD was not going to be a harmonious affair. A short time before the merger vote, a dinner was arranged at 12 Lime Street at which G. William Miller and his top lieutenants tried to "make love to the ARD staff," according to Morgan. But instead of a love-fest, the dinner devolved into a food fight.

ARD staffers were already unhappy that their beloved baby had been sold out from underneath them. Now, as they watched Miller blow smoke about the merger, their anger only intensified. He promised that they would be part of one big family, with unprecedented access to capital and contacts. He also assured them that they would gain experience with a range of industries. But the staffers saw through his act. "It was the standard big company snow job," says Morgan. The spinning was so egregious that William Congleton, a quiet and gentle soul who never uttered a bad word about anybody, exploded during the dinner and walked out.

After the dinner, John A. Shane told General Doriot he was going to resign from ARD to start his own venture capital partnership. Now that the Textron board would hold the authority to approve its investments, Shane believed strongly that the best start-ups would no longer come to ARD for financing. "I was convinced they would not get the companies I like," says Shane. He promised Doriot, however, that he would remain with the firm until the merger was approved.

Compensation issues continued to divide the staff as well. Although Textron boosted the salaries of ARD's employees and offered them options in Textron stock, the company required that option holders stay with the company for two years. More distressing, Textron refused to pay staffers a percentage of the division's profits. "It was obvious that in the new partnership structures, partners were getting carried interest of 25% to 30% of the gains," says Shane. "We had many discussions with Textron but they said we can't do anything for you because it would throw our compensation out of whack."

Even Doriot understood that the likelihood of ARD thriving under a corporate umbrella was about as great as George McGovern's chances of taking the White House. While Doriot trumpeted the benefits of the union in public, in private he emphasized the many reasons why large companies just didn't get venture capital.

Indeed, the day of the merger's shareholder vote, Doriot stood before the Textron board and rattled off a list of reasons explaining why the deal was destined to fail. "It was classic Doriot," says McCabe, who attended the meeting. "It was disarmingly frank."

"Yardsticks, measurements to be used in judging the work of a venture capital organization are very different from those of a normal industrial company," said Doriot. "The fact that the venture capital subsidiary would still have its own board of directors is of no help. The board would still have no way of getting money unless the board of the large company would vote for it." In addition, he added, "[m]ethods of remuneration used by large manufacturing companies may be quite ineffective in attracting, keeping, and rewarding personnel."

And on and on and on he went. But the Textron directors were not as surprised as you would expect. After many months of deliberating the merger, the Textron board was "used to the General doing those things," says McCabe.

Despite Doriot's pessimism, he remained committed to making the deal a success. Doriot could be critical but the General was no quitter. To smooth the integration, he turned to Dorothy Rowe, his most trusted confidante. In May, he wrote a confidential nine-page memo to Rowe, providing her with detailed instructions on how to handle the move to Textron. "You know ARD better than anyone else," he wrote. "Go all out to help Robert Ames."

A respected fifty-three-year-old leader of the aerospace industry with a master's degree in engineering from Columbia University and a master's in management from MIT, Ames was the Textron senior vice president hand-picked by Doriot to become ARD's new chief executive officer and president. But Ames also kept his job at Textron.

From the start, Ames gave ARD his best shot. To get up to speed on the company, he traveled across the United States to visit many ARD affiliates. But he knew that in order to succeed he would have to carve out an autonomous space free from Doriot's dominating personality. So he asked Doriot to not attend ARD staff meetings. Doriot obliged, but as chairman he still attended the company's board meetings.

After Textron bought ARD, Jean Gueroult, EED's executive vice president and second in command, invited James F. Morgan to come work for him in Paris. On the surface, EED seemed to be doing fairly well. A February 1972 article in *BusinessWeek* hailed EED as a firm in the vanguard of Europe's budding venture capital industry. "The irony is that the most ambitious and successful of the European venture firms has a distinctly American flavor," the reporter noted.

Morgan agreed to fly out and meet with the staff. If nothing else, he thought it would be a wonderful opportunity to take his wife on a trip for their tenth wedding anniversary. They arrived in Paris and met Gueroult at the EED office.

The contrast with ARD was stunning. EED had set up shop in a magnificent brownstone in a tony arrondissement. People ran around interrupting each other's meetings. And the office was overstaffed even though the firm was burning through cash. When Morgan went to lunch with his wife, Gueroult, a few EED staffers, and some of their entrepreneurs, he almost lost his cool. "It was the standard half hour to pick what wine to choose," says Morgan. "They showed off how much they knew about wine."

Gueroult asked Morgan's wife what she did during the morning.

"I went to the Tuileries Garden," she replied.

"What?" said Gueroult.

"The Tuileries Garden," repeated Morgan's wife, doing her best to simulate a real French accent. The two went back and forth three times before Gueroult's wife interjected and told him in perfect French where Morgan's wife had visited. "He's giving her a French lesson and I wanted to slug him," says Morgan. "I had seen this chaos and one-upmanship and arrogance. These are very intelligent people and they love to flaunt their IQs and their cultural depth. This thing was out of control. They were spending too much money."

The most troubling part of the trip was that Morgan learned EED had been flouting ARD's operating style in an attempt to outdo their parent firm. Instead of showing a light touch with its affiliates, Morgan learned that EED was meddling in the affairs of its portfolio companies. "They'd go in when they thought the company was not growing fast enough and muck it up," he says. "EED was determined they would do better. The implication was we're so much smarter than you guys we're going to have a better record than you." Morgan happily returned to the United States with his wife. "I felt I dodged a bullet there," he says.

Looking back on those days, Gueroult says he never recalled hearing criticism that EED spent too much money. And he denies the notion that EED thought it was superior to ARD. "ARD was a large success," says Gueroult.

However, confidential memos between Georges Doriot and Claude Janssen support Morgan's contention that Gueroult was an arrogant, ineffectual manager. In one memo from July 1970 in which he suggested replacing Gueroult, Doriot wrote, "It seems that Jean Gueroult is very able in managing a small group of men but is not able to handle a large organization . . . Jean Gueroult cannot stand supervision even of the friendliest most helpful type . . . and has an absolute desire or call it a necessity to completely master people."

When Morgan rejoined ARD over the summer, though, it was no picnic. Another senior staffer checked out. William H. Congleton, a twenty-year veteran of ARD in charge of finding and assessing the firm's investments, left ARD to join John A. Shane. After walking out on Textron at the Lime Street dinner, Congleton stayed a while to see how things shook out. But it didn't take him long to figure out it wasn't working.

In July, Shane and Congleton formed the Palmer Service Corporation, an investment management firm that ran three limited venture capital partnerships. The firm's name was an homage to a Shane ancestor and Edgar Palmer, an alumnus of their alma mater, Princeton University. To help them set up the firm, Shane and Congleton enlisted the aid of another Doriot man, Richard J. Testa, who they hired to serve as their counsel.

In putting out their own shingle, Shane and Congleton drew inspiration from ARD's first offspring, Greylock Capital, which had matured over the last seven years into one of the early leaders of the venture capital industry. Building on the philosophy of Doriot, Elfers led Greylock into a number of successful investments, including clinical laboratory network Biomedical Resources, kidney dialysis manufacturer Cobe Laboratories, and its biggest winner, Continental Cablevision. By 1993, Greylock's $10 million pool of capital would quadruple in value to $40 million.

Along the way, Greylock helped drag the rest of the venture industry into the future. In 1972, the year ARD was sold, Greylock made the decision to grow its business by forming a new partnership, rather than by bringing fresh money into its existing fund. This was an important innovation for several reasons. First, it allowed the firm to increase the ownership stakes of the younger general partners, who were taking on more responsibility in the firm. Second, a new fund made it easier to add limited partners because it eliminated the problem of valuation. And third, by completing the partnership at a fixed date, calculating the performance of the partnership was greatly simplified. Nowadays, most venture capital firms copy this technique, creating funds with a limited ten-year lifespan.

Back at ARD, management turmoil continued to distract the firm's operations. On October 12, 1972 ARD associate Daniel J. Holland got a call from a *Wall Street Journal* reporter. The journalist told Holland that he was in possession of a Textron press release announcing that Robert S. Ames was stepping down from ARD to return full-time to Textron. But the real shocker was the second half of the release: Doriot was being brought back to run the firm! Holland told the reporter that he would discuss the situation, but only if he was granted anonymity. The reporter agreed. One hour later, the ARD staff was told not to speak to the press about Ames's departure. But it was too late.

When the story came out the next day, ARD's management was enraged by the quotation from an anonymous source who was clearly in the know.

"After a layoff of less than five months," the story began, "73-year-old Georges F. Doriot has apparently resumed his post of chief executive of American Research and Development Corp., a Textron subsidiary." The article reported that Ames "has been succeeded as president by Charles J. Coulter" and that Ames will "resume his full-time duties as a Textron senior vice president." Then came the disconcerting part of the story. It went on to quote "one source close to American Research," who said that the "basic reason for the change was that Mr. Doriot wanted to run the company again, and Textron is allowing him to."

That morning, Morgan walked into Holland's office holding a tie around his neck like a noose. "Doriot and others were poring over a list to find out" the identity of the anonymous source," says Holland. Thinking he had probably already committed career suicide, Holland admitted to Doriot and the ARD board that he was the source of the leak. But surprisingly, they did not fire him. "They were relieved to know," says Holland.

Like many strong-willed company founders, Doriot was reluctant to relinquish control of ARD. But no one could fault his timing of the merger. In hindsight, the spring of 1972 was a near-perfect moment to fold ARD's hand, strictly from a financial point of view. For in 1973, the bottom fell out of the venture capital market and the economy at large. The twin economic evils of inflation and recession joined hands to create a new type of monetary demon, stagflation. Then OPEC's oil embargo sent the sputtering economy into a tailspin. Between 1973 and 1975, the Dow Jones index was nearly sliced in half.

As they surveyed the wreckage around them, the remaining staff members of ARD suddenly seemed happy to have a new roof over their heads. "Fortunately we had this big corporation that kept paying the checks," says Morgan. Morgan and his colleagues also knew a downturn was one of the best times to invest in new companies. With fewer dollars fighting for the same amount of deals, it was a buyer's market. ARD invested about $400,000 in three new companies, including Fusion Systems Corporation, a long-hair deal in a maker of ultraviolet lamps used in industrial manufacturing. "We were 50 percent of the entire venture capital industry in the country in

1973," says Charles Coulter. "Then the Californians really picked it up and venture capital moved west."

But the newfound optimism could not defuse tensions that were growing between Textron's chairman and Doriot. "I think Doriot was disappointed in G. William Miller," says Coulter. "Miller was a little fellow. He never really measured up. Doriot realized that after his placement." Miller also came to some realizations of his own. By acquiring ARD and reinstalling Doriot as chief executive, Miller had created an unusual problem. As Textron chairman, Miller was Doriot's boss. But since Doriot had been a director of Textron since 1962, the General was technically Miller's boss at the same time.

It was an untenable situation for Miller, a man whom some associates say was a control freak who surrounded himself with sycophants. Miller knew he could not control Doriot and let him spout his candid comments in board meetings. "The consequence was Miller told Doriot he could never set foot in the office again," says one former staffer. In early 1973, Doriot left the Textron board.

The General knew the jig was up. After twenty-eight years of running ARD, it was finally time to let go of his beloved baby once and for all. On June 30, 1974, almost two years after rejoining the company, Doriot officially retired as chairman of American Research and Development Corporation. "It was time for him to quit," says Coulter. "He already overstayed it to a fair degree." The General still kept his seat on the ARD board of directors, though. It was an extremely quiet exit in an abnormally quiet year. In 1974, ARD made no new investments.

Today many financiers and entrepreneurs assume the west coast always dominated the VC business. They simply don't realize the industry was pioneered by ARD and a few other Northeastern firms in the three decades following World War II. But the rise of the West was far from predestined, and was not even obvious to the industry's movers and shakers more than thirty years ago.

So why did Silicon Valley take over leadership of the venture capital industry in the 1970s? Part of the answer is in its geography and history. In pre–World War II America, the Northeast enjoyed a regional advantage based primarily on its technological and financial superiority. MIT was the nation's top university for science and technology. Harvard Business School was the undisputed leader in business education. And New York was the financial capital of the world. Combine all of those ingredients and it goes a long way toward explaining why ARD was able to grab an early lead in the venture game.

After the Allies won World War II, the Northeast's entrepreneurial advantage grew as Boston became the nation's epicenter of military research and development. Other than the Manhattan Project, MIT ran arguably the two most important government research labs of the mid-twentieth century: the Radiation Laboratory, a division of the National Defense Research Committee founded in 1940, which invented much of the radar technology deployed during World War II; and the Lincoln Laboratory, founded in 1951 with funding by the Department of Defense, which developed some of the first computers and later gave birth to the first minicomputer company, Digital Equipment Corporation.

But in the 1960s, the West Coast began to take over the tech industry. A hospitable climate and a greater acceptance of ethnic diversity certainly gave the west an edge in attracting creative talent. But higher education was the key. The University of California and California Institute of Technology by then had gained a reputation for cutting edge research in science and engineering. Much of the credit for the creation of Silicon Valley, though, belongs to a visionary professor and provost of Stanford University, Frederick Terman. In a move equal parts genius and chutzpah, Terman stole the MIT playbook and used it to establish the west coast as a center of technological and entrepreneurial excellence. The crux of his vision was forming a nexus between academia and business—the key to rapidly transferring technology from the research lab to the marketplace.

The son of Lewis Terman, a professor of psychology at Stanford who invented the IQ test, Terman studied engineering under Vannevar Bush at MIT. In 1924, he earned a Doctorate of Science in electrical engineering, and in 1925 landed a part-time job teaching electrical engineering at Stanford. The following year he began teaching full-time. He specialized in electronics and started a research laboratory. While teaching, Terman wrote a landmark book in his field, *Radio Engineering*. Although funds for an electronics lab were limited, Terman built an impressive program. By 1937, he was named head of the department.

Even as Stanford University's engineering program flowered under Terman's watch, he was disturbed to find most of his top students fleeing to the east coast to find jobs. In 1934, two of his best students, Dave Packard and William Hewlett, followed this same path after earning their undergraduate degrees: Packard enrolled in a management training position at General Electric in New York, and Hewlett began graduate work at MIT. But a few years later, Terman wooed them back to Stanford with fellowships and part-time jobs. One of Terman's favorite things to do was take students on field trips to local electronics companies. These trips left a deep impression on Packard and many other students. "Here for the first time I saw young entrepreneurs working on new devices in firms which they themselves had established," he recalled. "One day Professor Terman remarked to me that many of the firms we had visited, and many other firms throughout the country, had been founded by men who had little formal education. He suggested that perhaps someone with a formal engineering education and a little business training might be even more successful."

In January 1939, with encouragement from Terman and $539 in working capital, Hewlett and Packard set up a company, working out of a garage behind Packard's house. When the founders were unable to settle on their first product idea, Terman found them odd jobs and suggested they build a working model of an audio oscillator, the focus of Hewlett's graduate research. Terman also introduced them to Harold Buttner, a former student who became HP's first customer. After taking the oscillator for a test drive in the garage, Buttner, then the vice president of research and development at International Telephone and Telegraph, purchased the foreign patent rights for $500. Soon after, the duo made their first big sale—eight oscillators that Walt Disney used to fine-tune the soundtrack of *Fantasia*.

During the war, Terman found a new outlet for his talents when Vannevar Bush, then a top science adviser to President Roosevelt, asked him to head up Harvard's Radio Research Laboratory, a counterpart of MIT's Radiation Lab, which developed radar-jamming technologies. When he returned to Stanford after the war as Dean of the Engineering School, Terman turned the school into a world-class program by recruiting top talent and landing U.S. government contracts, which funded research into new technologies such as semiconductors. As dean, Terman continued to mentor scientists and ease their transition from the ivory tower to high-paying industrial jobs. In

1956, for instance, Terman helped Nobel Prize winner William Shockley recruit some of the bright young men for the Shockley Semiconductor Laboratory, a division Shockley set up under Beckman Instruments in Mountain View, California.

While Terman helped transform Stanford into the MIT of the west coast, northern California's private sector began to churn out a string of groundbreaking commercial enterprises. Hewlett-Packard, Varian Associates, and Ampex led the way in the 1940s. Then, in 1958, eight talented engineers from Shockley Semiconductor left the notoriously difficult founder that they worked for and created the world's first tech spin-off, Fairchild Semiconductor. The engineers didn't even conceive of starting their own company; they merely tried to sell their collective talents to an existing company.

"There was no such thing in those days as forming a company, what with the amount of capital that they needed to enter the semiconductor business," says Arthur Rock, an investment banker at the New York firm Hayden, Stone & Company. Rock found out about these young men when Shockley engineer Eugene Kleiner, whose father had a brokerage account with Hayden & Stone, contacted his father's rep at the bank. Rock was intrigued by the opportunity and flew to California with a partner from the firm to meet the renegade engineers. "I thought it was fairly interesting and came out to California with one of the partners of the firm," recalls Rock. "We thought maybe we could form a company."

Rock asked thirty-five companies to finance the chipmaker. But all of them passed at the opportunity because they felt it would upset their organizations. Rock and the "traitorous eight," as they became known, were ready to give up when Rock convinced the maverick inventor Sherman Fairchild to back the young upstarts. The talented engineers set up shop in Santa Clara, California, and Fairchild Semiconductor was born.

These companies put California on the map. And they laid the foundation for greater prosperity in the future by serving as an entrepreneurial finishing school. In California, "young people are able to step up into serious management roles at an early age," says Donald T. Valentine, who by the tender age of thirty was heading up sales and marketing at Fairchild Semiconductor. "It is much more of a meritocracy than the highly structured East Coast."

All of a sudden, semiconductor makers started popping up all over northern California as fruit trees had when Santa Clara County was an agricultural paradise known as the "Valley of Heart's Delight." Of the thirty-one semiconductor manufacturers established in the United States during the 1960s, only five existed outside the fertile strip of land in northern California. Many of the companies spun out of Fairchild. A Fairchild advertisement of the time showed a collage of all of the different companies' logos with the annotation *"We started it all."* Among the last of the original eight founders to leave were Robert Noyce and Gordon Moore, who struck out in 1968 to found Intel, Fairchild's most prominent offspring. By 1971, a computer journalist named Don Hoefler rechristened the area as "Silicon Valley" to describe the concentration of the region's computer-related industries.

With world-class universities, a budding commercial track record, and a seasoned pack of entrepreneurs, the region was poised to take over the technology industry. All it needed was a steady supply of venture capital to fuel the fires. In 1958, General William H. Draper Jr. cofounded Draper, Gaither & Anderson, considered the first west coast venture firm of prominence. But Draper retired only eight years later. In 1961, Arthur Rock and Thomas "Tommy" J. Davis Jr. became the leading west coast venture capitalists when they set up the San Francisco venture capital firm Davis & Rock with a $5 million kitty. A Cincinnati blue blood who could charm the pants off a preacher, Davis left the Kern County Land Company when its directors balked at investing beyond cattle and real estate. In their first year, Davis & Rock put up $280,000 to help start Scientific Data Systems, a computer maker that Xerox bought in 1969 for $950 million. In 1968, Rock, then working for his own firm, cemented his reputation as the leading VC on the west coast when he put together the deal to found Intel.

"I got a call from Noyce one day in 1968," recalls Rock, "and he said, 'Gee, I think maybe Gordon and I do want to leave Fairchild Semiconductor and go into business for ourselves.' And so we talked about it for a while and I asked him how much money they needed and he said two and a half million dollars." Given the sterling reputations of Robert Noyce and Gordon Moore, Rock was able to easily raise $2.5 million. He also wrote their business plan. "It was a page and a half, and I had raised all the money before I even sent the plan out," says Rock. "People knew me and knew Noyce and Moore, and they were anxious to invest."

Despite's Davis & Rock's unarguable success, they ran a tiny shop and could only investigate, finance, and nurture a very small number of companies. What's more, in 1968 Davis & Rock dissolved their partnership after a striking seven-year run. If the west coast was going to take over the VC industry, it needed a bigger pool of capital and venture firms. Gib Myers, a partner at the Mayfield Fund, a venture capital firm cofounded in 1969 by Tommy Davis, said the entire venture capital community in California "would meet at the Mark Hopkins Hotel for lunch. It was 20 people. This was a very small industry." Thanks to ARD, Rockefeller Brothers, Greylock Capital, and Fidelity Ventures, the east coast was still king of the venture hill.

But in the early 1970s, the West Coast's venture movement reached critical mass when a slew of partnerships sprouted in northern California. Besides the Mayfield Fund, they included Sutter Hill Ventures, an SBIC reorganized as a partnership in 1970; and Institutional Venture Associates, a fund started in 1970 by Reid Dennis, an analyst at the Fireman's Fund, who formed one of the first angel investing networks in the 1950s.

Among the bumper crop of creative capitalists, two other venture firms distinguished themselves from the pack, firms that solidified the west coast as the dominant force in venture capital. The first was Kleiner, Perkins, which raised $8 million for its first fund, then the world's largest private venture capital partnership. The creation of Kleiner, Perkins represented the culmination of twenty years of Silicon Valley evolution, illustrating the importance of the region's deep-rooted networks. Kleiner was an alumnus of Fairchild Semiconductor, the mother of all Silicon Valley spin-offs, and Perkins was a product of Hewlett-Packard, arguably the first tech start-up. "The structure of Kleiner, Perkins was influenced by ARD," says Perkins. "We never wanted to become a public company."

The second firm was Sequoia Capital, founded in 1972 by Donald Valentine, a Yonkers native and graduate of Fordham University who caught the California bug and ended up working for a number of successful technology firms, including Fairchild. "It was very clear to me I was living in the right part of the world," he says. "I never had to cross the Mississippi because of the microprocessor revolution."

West coast venture firms will happily take credit for inventing many of the key attributes of the venture business. But that's not the entire story. Kleiner, Perkins, for example, is often credited with being the first venture firm to practice hands-on management, first to organize portfolio companies to create a sort of keiretsu (a set of companies with interlocking business relationships), and also first to implement corporate governance measures such as distributing audited quarterly and annual reports. In truth, ARD had pioneered and been using these practices for more than two decades before any other west coast firm. Still, it's clear that Kleiner, Perkins and other Valley firms brought other important innovations to the VC business.

To begin with, Kleiner, Perkins was the first venture firm to successfully incubate businesses from within a firm. The two financiers invented this concept out of sheer necessity after their first few investments blew up. One deal with a semiconductor maker went belly up a month after they invested. Another deal for a tennis shoe resoling company went awry after the entrepreneur decided to make his own tennis shoe to compete against Adidas. "They were very embarrassing," says Perkins. But the most humiliating failure was an investment in the aptly named company, Snow-Job, which created a kit to convert a snowmobile into a motorcycle. But just as they were preparing to sell the kit, the federal government prohibited the sale of gasoline to recreational vehicles. "Gene Kleiner and I said, 'Look, this isn't working.' We decided to do our own deals."

Kleiner and Perkins fell back on what they knew best: the computer industry. Perkins knew computers because in the late 1960s Dave Packard asked him to serve as the marketing manager for HP's new computer division. Perkins revamped the division's marketing, and later became its general manager. It soon became HP's largest and most profitable business. To incubate a computer company, Kleiner, Perkins turned to one of its new employees, James "Jimmy" Treybig, a talented Texan who Perkins had hired out of Stanford Business School in 1968 to run marketing for HP's computer group. "I wanted to start a company," said Treybig, who joined the firm in 1973.

Treybig and Perkins cooked up the idea for a company that would manufacture fault-tolerant computer systems, computers that would continue to operate at a reduced level when another part of the system fails, rather than failing completely. The idea was to market the machines to banks and other financial services firms, which would use the technology to power ATMs and stock trading systems. In 1974, the two founded Tandem Computers, with Perkins as chairman and Treybig as CEO. "I had the product idea and marketing," said Treybig. "He helped me write the business plan and raise money."

Tandem was Kleiner, Perkins's first home run. Perkins helped Treybig recruit Tandem's first key engineers, hone its strategy, and organize three rounds of venture financing over the next few years. In 1977, Tandem went public with $7 million in sales from Citibank and other financial firms. By 1980, it was ranked by *Inc.* magazine as the fastest growing public company in America, with annual revenues exceeding $100 million. When Treybig retired in 1996, Tandem was a $2.3 billion company employing approximately eight thousand people worldwide.

While Doriot and ARD showed the world how to build innovative companies, Silicon Valley's venture firms were the first to create entirely new markets or industries from scratch. Kleiner, Perkins and Sequoia Capital showed the way.

Like Perkins, Donald Valentine soaked up the art of venture capital while working for a successful startup in the Valley. Valentine had learned how to evaluate technologies and markets while heading up sales and marketing at Fairchild Semiconductor and National Semiconductor. "In both of those companies we had a very limited and highly desirable resource: We had engineers who could do things electronically," says Valentine. "We had to develop a selection program to decide where to invest our engineering. I devised a system of determining which customers we did business with based on a small number of criteria." Valentine gained even more experience by putting his own money in a few of these companies.

While at Fairchild, Valentine was approached by the Capital Group, an asset management company. In 1972, the firm hired Valentine to work within a small division called the "special situations group," which raised about $5 million from institutions such as the Ford Foundation to invest in small, private companies. While working within the Capital Group, which had financed Walt Disney's *Fantasia*, Valentine organized two venture capital funds called Sequoia I and Sequoia II.

At the Capital Group managing Sequoia funds, Valentine did some research, which showed that the microprocessor was giving birth to new forms of entertainment and computing. As one example, Valentine reckoned the tiny chips of silicon that produced massive computing power would zap gaming out of the archaic era of pinball machines and penny arcades into the future of electronic games.

If that new era had a start date, it would be 1972, when two engineers from Ampex, Nolan Bushnell and Ted Dabney, founded the computer game maker Atari. After designing a clunky game called Computer Space, Bushnell realized he had to develop a computer game "so simple that any drunk in a bar could play it." The result was Pong, a simple tennis-like game whose first version consisted of a black and white television, special game hardware, and a mechanism that swallowed the quarters of millions of teenagers.

The game was a smash, attracting legions of copycat machines. To stay ahead of the leeches, Atari released a version of Pong for the home. Sears sold out 150,000 units before the game even hit store shelves. By fiscal year 1975, Atari earned about $3 million on $40 million in sales. Not bad for a three-year-old company run by a bunch of "amateurs." But like many fast-growing companies that finance their operations from earnings, Atari often skirted the edge of bankruptcy. To grow, Atari need more capital.

In 1976, Bushnell turned to Valentine, who by then had become one of the more well-known VCs in the Valley. Valentine jumped at the offer, organizing an investment round that included Time Inc. and the Mayfield Fund, who matched the $600,000 Sequoia put into Atari, plus $30,000 from Fidelity Venture Associates of Boston, the firm that Henry Hoagland took over after leaving ARD. The money enabled Atari to finance the development of several successful games, including Breakout and two driving titles, Le Mans and Night Driver.

But by the summer of 1976, Bushnell and his advisers realized they needed to raise a whole lot more money. Tens of millions of dollars would be needed quickly to finance the development and marketing of a new invention they had on the drawing board, a video computer game system that used the latest chip technology. VCs couldn't afford that tab, and the stock market was sinking. So Bushnell and his colleagues decided to sell the company. By September, Atari was acquired for $28 million by Warner Communications, netting Bushnell $15 million, while his investors made a quick and sweet return. At great risk, Warner poured $100 million into developing the video computer system. The kids loved it. By the end of 1979, Atari had sold a record-breaking 350,000 units of the Atari 2600, a microprocessor-based console with separate game cartridges that created the template of modern gaming.

Valentine's investment in Atari led to his most famous and successful deal—one that sparked the creation of yet another industry based on the microprocessor. One of Atari's young employees was an unwashed but bright young man who, in the eyes of Valentine, looked like Ho Chi Minh: Steve Jobs. In 1977, Jobs, the designer of Breakout, asked Bushnell to invest in a minicomputer company he and his friend, Steve Wozniak, had launched in a garage in Jobs's parent's house. Bushnell said he was too busy but he told him to call Valentine, with one wise proviso: "The longer you can go without having to go to those guys, the better off you are." Yet unlike Bushnell, who had nine years of experience when he started Atari, Jobs was a twenty-year-old college dropout. That meant Jobs and Wozniak would have to give up more control and equity of their seemingly quixotic venture.

When Jobs called on Valentine, Sequoia Capital was an independent firm. Valentine had taken it out of the Capital Group in 1975 and set up a private partnership structure. Valentine, the microprocessor guru, agreed to back Jobs on one condition: he had to hire a sales and marketing executive. "Neither one knew anything about marketing," said Valentine. "Neither one had any sense of the size of the potential market. They weren't thinking anywhere near big enough." Jobs agreed and asked Valentine to send him three candidates. Jobs didn't like the first guy, and the second guy didn't like Jobs. The third was A. C. "Mike" Markulla, a sharp young marketing manager Valentine hired at Fairchild who had just retired from Intel after four years, one of the Valley's new breed of multimillionaires. Luckily, they all got along. Markulla, thirty years old, joined the company as chairman, investing $250,000 of his own money for a one-third stake in the new firm. In January 1977, the trio launched Apple Computer.

Although Valentine did not invest in Apple at the time, he eagerly put skin in the game a year later. By then, Markulla had hired a president to run the company's day-to-day operations: Mike Scott, Markulla's former boss at Fairchild, who was running a manufacturing line at National Semiconductor before he joined Apple. The company had also released its first complete working computer, the Apple II. But when problems with the computer's casing threatened to exhaust the company's credit line, Markulla approached some VCs. In January of 1978, Markulla raised $517,500, giving the company a $3 million valuation. Venrock, the venture arm of the Rockefeller family, invested $288,000, Sequoia kicked in $150,000 and Arthur Rock was good for another $57,000.

Markulla and Scott asked the investors to keep their shares for five years. But in the summer of 1979, Valentine unloaded his stock when Apple raised another $7.2 million in late-stage financing. Valentine told Jobs and Markulla, who also sold $1 million of stock, he needed to sell because one of his partnerships was expiring, and for tax reasons, he needed to distribute the fund's proceeds to investors. If Valentine had held on longer, though, Sequoia would have made an even bigger killing. When Apple went public in December of 1980, Arthur Rock's $57,000 stake was worth nearly $22 million.

Sequoia Capital's investment in Apple led Valentine to develop another new technique in the venture game that has often been copied. Valentine calls it the "aircraft carrier" method of investing. As with an aircraft carrier, which only sails with a fleet of other ships for servicing and defensive purposes, Valentine would build a cadre of other smaller companies around a critical venture. "It's a simple concept that reinforces the idea of using a core investment and building new investments to make the core stronger," says Valentine. "We try to make clusters of investments around the aircraft carrier."

In this case, Apple Computer was the aircraft carrier, a powerful ship that unleashed the personal computer revolution. After the company introduced the Apple II, Valentine realized that Apple needed related technologies to reach its full potential. The Apple II was a beautiful machine that became the market leader thanks to its low price, sharp design, and colorful graphics. But the first version used an audio cassette as a memory device to download programs onto the computer—clearly not an optimal solution since even the simplest programs took an hour to download. "It became very obvious we needed a memory product company," says Valentine. So in 1978 Sequoia Capital started a company to make disk drives, Tandon Corporation. All told, Sequoia Capital made investments in thirteen other companies to serve Apple Computer, many of which followed the company down the road to success.

Around the same time that Seqouia helped give birth to the personal computer market, Kleiner, Perkins was on the verge of creating another spectacular industry, one that would prove the value and importance of venture capital to the American mainstream. As a replacement for Jimmy Treybig, in late 1974, Kleiner, Perkins hired Robert Swanson, a twenty-seven-year-old MIT grad with a bachelor's degree in chemistry and an MBA from the Sloan School of Management. Kleiner met Swanson while Swanson was working as an investment officer with Citicorp Venture Capital Limited. "Eugene had been impressed with Bob's ability to think straight and get things done," says Perkins. "So when Bob was looking for a new position, we hired him."

In his first year with Kleiner, Perkins, Swanson handled various deals, but none of them worked out well. One deal in particular with a company called Cetus strained relations among the firm's small staff. In 1975, Kleiner, Perkins bought a stake in Cetus, a California company developing a system that automated the screening of microorganisms. Perkins, Kleiner and Swanson all tried to convince the scientists and management of Cetus to tackle the more ambitious challenge of splicing genes, a new frontier of medical technology hailed for its potential in the diagnosis and treatment of disease. But Cetus rejected the idea, feeling it would take too long before the technology could be perfected. So Kleiner, Perkins advised Swanson to look for a new job.

"Their names were on the door, Kleiner & Perkins, and clearly I was very much the junior partner," says Swanson. "They said, "You can continue to have a desk and a telephone until you find what you're going to do." There is nothing like that to give you motivation."

But Swanson refused to leave. He wanted to dive headfirst into the emerging field of biotechnology. If Swanson could get something going in this area, Perkins told him, he'd be interested in backing him. "I said to myself, 'This is really an important event, and wouldn't it be wonderful if you could really use microorganisms to make [genetically modified] products? And why is it that it can't be done today?'" recalls Swanson. So he started cold-calling people to learn all he could about the field. One name stuck in his craw: Herbert Boyer, a forty-year-old biochemistry and biophysics professor at the University of California at San Francisco who had codeveloped an ingenious technique to engineer drugs by splicing DNA from one organism into the genes of another.

In January of 1976, Swanson dropped by Boyer's lab and the two retreated to a nearby bar to hash out their ideas. Boyer told Swanson that the commercialization of the technique would take ten years of basic research but Swanson kept pressing him to think of ways to speed up the process.

His persistence paid off. On April 7, Swanson and Boyer each put in $500 and incorporated Genentech. It was a lot of money for Swanson, who was still jobless and surviving on a monthly $410 check from the unemployment office. "My half of an apartment in Pacific Heights was $250," says Swanson. "My lease payment on the Datsun 240Z was $110, and the rest was peanut butter sandwiches and an occasional movie."

One month later, after Swanson had raised some additional money for the company, Kleiner, Perkins invited him and Boyer to make a presentation. "I was very impressed with Boyer," says Perkins. "He had thought through the whole thing." But Perkins was unnerved by the tremendous risk. He would go along but only if they found a way to remove some risk from the venture—a classic ARD technique. Perkins came up with the answer: Genentech would subcontract the initial research so the company would not have to foot a multimillion dollar bill to set up its own laboratory.

Kleiner, Perkins bought a 25 percent stake in Genentech for $100,000. The investment paid for the proof-of-concept experiment to synthesize their first gene. Genentech's ultimate goal was to synthesize human insulin but Boyer and the researchers he hired convinced Swanson that it would be smarter to start with somatostatin, a simpler hormone. By the fall of 1977, Genentech and the three institutions it hired to conduct the research—the University of California at San Francisco, the City of Hope medical research foundation, and the California Institute of Technology—had cloned and expressed the somatostatin gene. This accomplishment enabled Swanson to raise more money to make insulin. "The day we announced [the gene], it was the headline in the *San Francisco Examiner*," says Perkins. "That woke up the world to what we now call genetic engineering." In 1978, Genentech scientists cloned human insulin. The following year, the company manufactured human growth hormone. In 1980, Genentech held the first IPO of a biotechnology company and raised $35 million. The stock shot up from $35 to $88 on its first day of trading—one of the biggest first-day pops ever.

"Biotechnology jumpstarted the public's fascination with VC," says Frederick Frank, a former banker at Lehman Brothers and director of the Salk Institute, who took public many biotechnology companies. "You had cover articles on this new world of molecular biology. It became an investment of passion. People realized they could not only help but also do well. That's when the public really became involved in VC."

The Genentech IPO was important for one other reason: it cemented Silicon Valley as the dominant force in venture capital and entrepreneurial capitalism. Over a spectacular ten-year run, west coast venture capitalists had nurtured no less than four technological revolutions: the development of the semiconductor, electronic video game, the personal computer, and biotechnology. Ever since, the Valley has ruled the venture capital industry with unquestioned dominance.

THIRTEEN

A LOVE STORY

(1974–1987)

$\mathbb{A}$RD, SADLY, FAILED TO capitalize on the birth of the microprocessor and biotechnology. And as the firm entered the mid-1970s, Doriot's fears about practicing venture capital in a large corporation were realized. Although the venture market was anemic at the time, ARD's inability to find the next Digital couldn't be blamed on external forces alone. ARD's management, which had been eviscerated over the years, could no longer sniff out the best opportunities, nor could it provide the best guidance to struggling affiliates. And as Shane and others predicted, the smartest entrepreneurs avoided ARD and chose instead to work with private venture firms. "[ARD] had to go back to the parent to invest," says Morgan. "Any entrepreneur didn't want to work for a flunky who had to go back to the parent."

In a confidential memo written in March of 1974, Doriot admitted as much: "We do not have the freedom to provide funds for portfolio companies that we used to have," he wrote, and "we can never be certain that funds will be available if we need and want them."

Even though ARD never became Textron's engine of innovation, the division remained a cash cow for the conglomerate, with substantial yet unrealized capital gains amassed over the last twenty-five years. Whenever Textron needed a boost in income, Charles Coulter would dutifully milk ARD's portfolio.

But Coulter struggled with Textron's emphasis on the bottom line. He knew, as Doriot had predicted, that the short-term emphasis of a corporation and the long-term nature of a venture firm did not mesh well. "The corporate world has a thing called the bottom line," says Coulter. "Everything is driven by profits. But that is something you don't look at in venture capital. Value does not show on the bottom line until, god knows, maybe 10 years. The two don't fit. You don't sell things in venture capital until the right moment. And that's not December 31."

In 1975, Dorothy Rowe and Patricia Clark both left ARD. Besides Morgan, who joined the firm in 1967, the two women were the last vestiges of the old ARD. Even the ARD board was unsure of its own role. Kenneth Olsen expressed these concerns in a letter to G. William Miller written in April 1975: "Some thought there was no need for the Board and that we just kept on for sentimental reasons. In the old days the staff had the advantages and disadvantages of a family operation. There was little room for personal accomplishment but at least there was a team spirit and the feeling of team accomplishment. I dreamed that with the Textron takeover, there would be goals, measures and budgets . . . but I am afraid that we have the disadvantages of the family operation but none of the advantages, and I am afraid that the morale of the staff is very low."

At the end of the year, ARD moved out of the John Hancock Building and moved into a new office near Beacon Square. The following April, the ARD board voted to disband itself, confirming Olsen's concerns that it was more of a symbolic entity than a source of real influence. With the board's dissolution, Doriot's nearly thirty-year affiliation with American Research and Development had finally ended.

❦

Doriot's ARD was gone but the General had one last battle to fight. European Enterprise Development, one of his grandest dreams, was in deep trouble. The firm's management and directors had little experience with venture capital, and despite the formation of the Common Market, Europe was still a Balkanized region retarded by economic nationalism. "The financial world was still very compartmentalized," says Claude Janssen, an EED director since 1970. "We [sold] a company in Italy at a profit and we couldn't move the money out of Italy to France for a French company. The markets were not fluid at the time. That's something that all of us did not realize."

But there was one more immediate problem threatening the firm's survival. When EED needed capital, Jean Gueroult, the executive vice president of EED who ran the firm's day-to-day operations, pushed the firm into borrowing money from a consortium of banks. "Unfortunately the market was not the same as the States," says Gueroult. "If you don't have sufficient equity you have to borrow money."

The loans saddled EED with high interest payments. Arnaud de Vitry disagreed with the decision but Gueroult had more influence over the board than he did. "I tried to get rid of him," says de Vitry. "I think he should have been fired. We should have fired the whole board also." Doriot wrote the board members in an attempt to remove Gueroult but he was not successful either. "Doriot was a bit distant from the picture," says Janssen. "He didn't have the feeling he could [fire Gueroult]."

When business was strong EED met its debt obligations. But with the global economy and stock markets in a funk, EED was on the verge of defaulting on its loans. To help save the firm, Doriot visited the directors of several large European banks in a valiant attempt to raise equity capital for EED. "[Doriot] didn't let the thing go," says Janssen. "He fought, which was in his character."

But Doriot's fight was in vain. The bankers wanted ARD to guarantee the loans or they would withdraw their money. In 1975 and 1976, EED's board held several more meetings with various banks to try to raise more capital, through either debt or equity, but the talks went nowhere. "The board assessed the situation and said there was no hope," says Janssen. "Nobody was ready to put up enough money to go on." In July of 1976, EED filed for bankruptcy under the direction of EED director Lord Shawcross, chairman of the International Council of the Morgan Guaranty Trust Company of New York. "Doriot was really a forward-looking person," says Frederick Frank, a vice chairman of Lehman Brothers who knew the General. "In this case he was too ahead of his time."

"Never did a more brilliant guy have such a spectacular failure," says former ARD executive Morgan. But later on, according to Morgan, when Doriot was in a lighter mood, he liked to joke that EED had "the most elegant bankruptcy in the history of investing."

Not too long after EED's demise, though, the seeds of entrepreneurialism that the General had planted in Europe sprung back to life. B. W. M. Twaalfhoven, president of Indivers N.V., a Dutch manufacturing firm in which EED invested in 1972, believed that the development of European venture capital companies stemmed directly from the efforts of Doriot and

EED. He would know. In 1982, Twaalfhoven set up Gilde Venture Fund, Holland's first venture capital firm. "Many deals which I have been able to accomplish today both in the United States and Europe come as a direct result of what he has taught us and the networks he built up," wrote Twaalfhoven, who was a Doriot student in 1954.

Europe's entrepreneurial culture owed Doriot one other huge debt. INSEAD, his beloved school, fulfilled Doriot's dream of becoming a training ground for the future entrepreneurs of Europe. Today, INSEAD is considered the leading business school of Europe, and is regularly ranked among the best in the world—more proof of Doriot's remarkable vision. "With regard to the INSEAD Business School," wrote Twaalfhoven, "we are today the beneficiaries of many of their fine students."

As Doriot withdrew from the world of venture capital, he embraced the warm and comforting cocoon of his family and friends. He spent a lot of time visiting with McCabe, Janssen, and de Vitry, his three surrogate sons.

In her infinite wisdom, Edna had planned for her husband's retirement many decades earlier. In addition to purchasing the Lime Street townhouse, after World War II Edna had also bought two plots of land in Manchester, Massachusetts, a sleepy village fifty miles north of Boston on the North Shore. The Doriot's property was a bit more than a mile outside of the village in a place called Smith's Point. It was a beautiful three-acre parcel, dotted with pine trees and scrub brush, with a crag overlooking the rocky coastline. The Doriots never wanted to live in the suburbs but Georges and Edna very much liked the idea of buying a country house and building their own garden, like the one Georges's family enjoyed in the south of France.

The Doriot's property did not actually come with a home, though. After the previous owner's death, his wife bulldozed the massive six-story stone structure on the land—known as Kragstad to the locals—because the taxes were so high. "What we were doing was buying a large plot of land with much rubble," explained Georges. So Georges bought a little Walpole tool shed to live in. The shack shoehorned a bedroom, sitting room, tin shower, and a kitchen with a pot-bellied stove all in about one-hundred square feet. Georges described it as his "very happy little love nest."

The Doriots made up for their spartan accomodations with a luxuriant garden, cultivated over the years by Edna and the Doriot's trusty housekeeper Ida Aellig. They removed the remaining rubble from the mansion, lifting piles of boulders and stones from a big hole with pulleys and ropes, carting out the rocks with a wheelbarrow. They built a fence and a set of steps in the garden with leftover railroad ties. When the General was still working, Edna often headed out to Smith's Point during the week. But Doriot didn't want Edna to drive up to Manchester in traffic. So Edna would call up Patricia Clark, the General's secretary, and whisper in the phone, "Don't tell Georges. I'm going out to Manchester. I just want you to know what is going on."

Even in his twilight, Doriot still exuded a magnetic aura. In 1973, Charles Dyer, a pilot with Eastern Airlines who graduated from Harvard Business School, surveyed the house next door to the Doriot's property. It was the carriage house of the mansion. "It was more than I could afford," says Dyer. But when the broker told Dyer that General Doriot was building a house next door, Dyer was resolved. "I've got to get this house," he said to himself. Dyer was eager to rub elbows with the legendary professor because he was never able to take Doriot's class at Harvard. Doriot's final year of teaching was Dyer's first year at school. The Dyers moved into the house next door in 1974.

During his retirement, Doriot devoted some of his free time to a favorite new hobby: painting. Georges leaned toward an impressionistic style, painting vivid still lifes of flowers on small 7" by 10" canvases. He gave away many of the works and occasionally auctioned them off with a maximum price of 39 cents. Once in a while, Doriot, flashing a Cheshire cat smile, mentioned that two of his works resided in the Metropolitan Museum of Art, one in the office of a former student and the other in storage as part of the collection of Robert Lehman. "When he painted he used to hold a roll of toilet paper to wipe his knives," says Dina McCabe. "He didn't paint with brushes because you had to wash them with turpentine and that was messy."

Georges's retirement freed up Edna to fulfill a longtime dream of her own. After twenty years of vacationing in a cold, dusty tool shed, Edna yearned to build a new home out of the ruins of Kragstad. Over the years, she had drawn up a set of plans. After Georges stopped working, she found an architect who understood her design sensibility, and a contractor to handle the job. Georges also had the money to pay for the house now as well. When ARD merged with Textron, Doriot and his wife owned 13,192 shares of stock in Digital Equipment. Even though it was less than one-tenth of one percent of the company's outstanding stock, the shares were worth more than a million dollars.

A stone and glass house that cantilevered over the cliff, the Doriot's dream home was a spectacular piece of architecture. By blending into the rocks and surrounding area, it conjured Frank Lloyd Wright's Fallingwater masterpiece. And the sheets of glass that encased the dwelling called to mind Philip Johnson's infamous glass house. The home had an absolutely perfect south-facing view. On the left, Georges and Edna could see the lighthouse in Gloucester, and on the right they relished a field of pine trees from Smith's Point.

"You had said once that you would like to have a little land somewhere to plant a garden," Edna told Georges after the house was done. Then she laughed and said, "We now have it." On August 8, 1974, the day that President Nixon resigned from office, the Doriots moved into their new home. Throughout 1975, Georges and Edna savored their dream house, cooking dinners for friends, and taking leisurely walks along the coastline.

"Is it not *just wonderful* to know that we have so much to look forward to together?" Edna wrote to Georges in November of 1975. "We will both be very careful in every way—not to allow sickness—accidents and such to mar this happiness. You will be home in just a few days and we will get all our things in order and relax comfortably and joyfully together."

But in a cruel twist of fate, Georges and Edna never had much time to savor the fruits of their lifelong labor. In 1976, Edna contracted lymphoma. For a short while it seemed like she might recover. But the cancer metastasized.

When word spread about Edna's sickness, she began to reap the rewards of a lifetime of showing kindness to strangers as well as friends. In December of 1976, the French government nominated Edna to the National Order of the Legion of Honor, making the Doriots one of the few couples to have both received the honor. The following October, Edna received the Pride Citation from Simmons College. And then in March of 1978 Emerson College awarded Edna the honorary degree of Doctor of Humane Letters.

To help treat her lymphoma, Georges checked Edna into the Sidney Farber Cancer Center in Boston. Edna lost weight, her hair began to fall out, and she began to wear a wig. Pondering her mortality, Edna's weakening body was flooded with emotions. In the last page of her diary in 1977, Edna jotted down some private thoughts for Georges. "The art of communication is lacking in me. I cannot appreciably transmit to you the width and depth of my feelings—nothing shallow about that. I want to transmit to you the fullness of feelings Georges I feel for you, for all you are doing, how much it means to us, the spirit in which you are doing it."

In the summer of 1978, Edna's days were numbered. On June 3, Georges and Edna drove out to Manchester for one last trip to their love nest. Edna did not feel very well, and the next day, they returned to Boston. "She was very sad; so was I," wrote Georges. "She felt badly saying goodbye to Manchester." On June 5, Edna checked back into the Farber Center. She would not return home. During the month, her condition deteriorated, the cancer continuing to eat away at her withering body.

To salve her considerable pain, at times Edna would jot down various bits of scripture. "Be not afraid, for I am with you. Be not dismayed for I will strengthen you, I will help you. I will uphold you with my victorious hand." She also continued to write little love notes to Georges. In July, Edna wrote a poem to her husband.

> *Georges Dear*
> *Think of me*
> *Love me*
> *As I always did*
> *For you.*
> *Let us love each other*
> *Very much.*
> *As we always did*
> *One day*
> *We shall be together*
> *Again*
> *For ever*
> *Be courageous my love*
> *I am near you*
> *Your Edna dear*

On July 6, Georges spent the night in Edna's bedroom at 12 Lime Street. The next morning, at 10:55 a.m., Edna passed away.

Edna's remains were cremated, as she wished. On July 12 at 4 p.m., Richard Testa, Arnaud de Vitry, Dorothy Rowe, and Ida Aellig joined Georges at the

Doriot's house in Manchester. As Georges sobbed, standing alone, without his devoted wife of the last forty-eight years, Arnaud spread Edna's ashes on the ocean from a rock below her bedroom window. On September 14 at 12:30 p.m., a memorial service was held for Edna at the Park Street Church in Boston. The ceremony was performed partly by Pastor Roland Poillot, Doriot's brother-in-law. In his pocket diary, Georges inscribed a single, simple note: "Edna went to heaven."

Edna's death devastated Georges. "When you have only your wife you are more alone than if you have a family," says Janssen. Doriot mourned for two straight years. Like many people who have lost a soul mate after a long and happy marriage, Doriot found it enormously difficult to go on, refusing at times to believe Edna had really left him. Although he could no longer touch Edna, he still heard her voice. He wrote her love poems and visualized her with him. At night, he sat in her bedroom and spoke to her. "I tell her what I did during the day," said Doriot. "I tell her what I will be doing tomorrow."

He also cherished Edna's belongings. "I still keep her handbag with her money, her cab receipts, her comb, a little clock in a leather case," said Doriot. He was truly lost without Edna. "When she passed away Doriot did not know how to fill out a check to pay a bill," says Arnaud de Vitry. In fact, for his whole life, Doriot, the Business School professor, put Edna in charge of all of their money. She kept a monthly ledger, with one side for income and the other for expenditures. "I never looked at those sheets, ever," said Doriot. "I trusted her."

Dorothy Rowe, Doriot's longtime friend, emerged as the main balm for his loneliness. She accompanied him on business trips, helped plan his social calendar, and was a constant dinner companion.

The darkness of 12 Lime Street was invariably lightened by a constant stream of friends and well-wishers. "It was a Doriot salon," says Morgan. "I went to see him all the time. A lot of former students would bring their sons by to meet a great man."

As Doriot faded in the background, the outside world began to acknowledge his seminal contributions. In the spring of 1979, the editors of *Fortune* elected Doriot to the Hall of Fame for Business Leadership, along with Cornelius Vanderbilt, Levi Strauss & Company founder Walter Haas, and a few other business titans. At a ceremony held to honor the inductees, Doriot read one of his love poems to the audience.

You wish to write about my life
There was no such thing as "my life."
There was "our life."
In many ways, perhaps, now,
Even deeper than ever,
It is still "our life."
The story of my life
Is not a business story.
It is a love story
So deep and profound
That, it cannot be separated.
No love story ever is.
God separated us, for a while.
But still, we are together.
Please do not separate some more
What must remain as one.
I am too weak to survive it.
Please spare me for her sake.
Do I need to suffer more
To be worthy of her?

The poem touched the hearts of many of the illustrious people in the audience. Lucille Ball, the first woman in television to run her own production company, thought the poem was so poignant that she framed a copy of it, and sent it to Doriot with a letter.

My Dear General Doriot,

I haven't for a moment forgotten you. You made such a wonderful impression on all of us that evening.

Took the liberty of preserving this beautiful poem of yours for you and myself in this manner.

Hope you are in good health and remember me with love . . .

Always,

Lucy

Doriot's award came at a propitious time for the venture capital community. While the west coast VCs followed Doriot's lead and pushed the venture industry to new heights, policy makers, the bane of Doriot's existence, boosted the market with two bold strokes. First, in 1978, Congress cut capital gains taxes to 28 percent, from 49.5 percent. And then in June of 1979, after lobbying by pension fund managers, venture capitalists, and entrepreneurs, the U.S. Labor Department clarified the "prudent man" rule of the 1974 Employment Retirement Income Security Act. The old rule held that pension fund managers could only make investments that a "prudent man" would make. Consequently, many pension fund managers avoided venture capital. The new rule, however, allowed fund managers to take into account the diversification of their entire portfolio when determining the prudence of an investment.

The ruling opened the floodgates to venture capital. Pension funds in particular poured rivers of money into the industry. In 1978, 23 venture funds managed about $500 million of capital. By 1983, there were 230 firms overseeing $11 billion. Almost one-third of that new money came from pension funds, up from 15 percent in 1978. Many of the firms dreamed of finding the next Digital Equipment Corporation and repeating the success of American Research and Development.

In the fall of 1979, as Doriot approached his eightieth birthday, Robert McCabe and Sanford C. Bernstein decided to organize one last hurrah for the General. As the party's showcase, the two men convinced Doriot to give a final refresher course. He agreed on one condition: that the event double as a fundraiser for the French Library. Since Edna's death, Georges had replaced Edna as president of the library, and in honor of his wife he wanted to perform one more good deed for their beloved institution.

On September 24 at 4 p.m., five hundred former students, spouses, friends, and business colleagues of Doriot began arriving at Burden Hall on the Business School campus. The organizers had reserved a small classroom for the refresher course. But so many more people showed up that they took over a larger auditorium. "I remember the stairs coming down to the room were filled with people," says McCabe. "I was standing near the door at the top of the stairs and could find no place on the ground to sit down. It was really wonderful and an indication of how much people felt for the General. They all had strong feelings and memories."

The General—lean, trim and well-dressed as ever—enthralled the auditorium for more than an hour. As he spoke, slipping in his favorite maxims, the audience laughed and nodded appreciatively as they remembered the old Manufacturing class. "Anyone who thinks AT&T should be broken up should be sent to France and told to try to use the telephone system there," said Doriot to the chuckles of the crowd.

Afterward, the General was besieged by dozens of his admirers, including American Express chairman James D. Robinson and Goldman Sachs partner Sidney J. Weinberg. He called each of them by their name, referred to a shared experience, offered a compliment, shook hands, and greeted the next old friend. By night's end, Doriot had raised nearly $200,000 from the most distinguished captains of industry. "They only made one mold when they made him," remarked Raytheon executive Charles Francis Adams to a *Boston Globe* reporter. "I can't imagine anyone else pulling that many people."

Speaking to a reporter for the *Harvard Business School Bulletin*, Kenneth H. Olsen said that despite the General's age, "he's in greater demand by more people than ever before. He's even more pertinent with his comments than in the past. When he speaks about retiring from our board I tell him to come back in ten years and we'll talk about it."

In fact, since Doriot's retirement and ARD's sale to Textron, the special bond shared by Olsen and Doriot grew even stronger. More than ever, Doriot acted like the proud parent of his precocious child. And after all these years, Olsen remained a devoted pupil. Since becoming a director at Digital, which had blossomed into a multibillion dollar enterprise, Doriot often wandered around its factories and spoke to groups of managers, imparting his special brand of wisdom. "He always talked about love," says Ted Johnson. "Ken himself would never talk like that. Ken was not one to praise. Doriot was good at that. He provided a voice that was missing."

Entering his eighth decade, Doriot continued to be constructive, to give himself to others. To help Olsen deal with Digital's explosive growth, Doriot arranged a luncheon at his home in the fall of 1979. The purpose of the lunch was to introduce Olsen to his former student, Philip Caldwell, now the president of Ford Motor Company. The meeting went off well and Olsen was elected a director of Ford that October. The following September, Olsen reciprocated and Caldwell was elected to become a director of Digital Equipment.

Other disciples of Doriot continued to make their mark. In 1982, James F. Morgan and Daniel J. Holland, two ARD refugees, founded a new venture capital firm, Morgan, Holland Ventures. The year before, Morgan finally left ARD after Textron management considered his proposal to spin off ARD as an act of disloyalty. "The software opportunities were starting to become obvious," says Morgan. It was the fourth venture firm to be founded by alumni of ARD.

The long and fitful development of Doriot's start-up nation, the movement that the General had patiently nurtured for four decades, crystallized in January of 1984 when *Time* magazine put a venture capitalist on its cover— an indubitable sign that venture capital had entered the American mainstream. The January 23 cover story, "Cashing in Big: The Men Who Make the Killings," featured an illustration of Arthur Rock wearing a suit and tie composed of stock certificates and dollar bills. "A new crop of exceptionally rich people is springing up in America, almost from nowhere," reported Alexander Taylor III. "They have a gambler's nerve, a fortuneteller's insight and a prospector's nose for gold. They have prospered first by starting or investing in small, unknown companies, and then capitalizing on the 17-month old bull market that has sent the Dow Jones industrial average to one new high after another."

Venture capital was here to stay. In 1983, as the stock market boomed, nearly nine hundred companies made initial public offerings of stock, raising $12.8 billion, nine times more capital than was raised in 1982, and "even more than the amount for all the years since 1971 put together," according to *Time*. After highlighting some of the most successful VCs and start-ups, including software maker Lotus Development, Genentech, and Apple Computer, the story concluded, "while the new multimillionaires are making a bundle for themselves, they are also making the U.S. economy stronger."

In 1985, Doriot was getting so old he even began to pull away from Olsen. At Digital board meetings, Olsen always sat beside the General and chatted with him. Olsen would lean over and ask the General a question, and Doriot would whisper a response in his ear. But in 1985, the General stopped sitting beside Olsen. He gave up his seat to Philip Caldwell. "The General sat between Dorothy and I," says Eileen Jacobs, a rising star at Digital who began attending board meetings in 1984 after she was promoted to treasurer. "He was making a conscious decision to have Phil Caldwell be Ken's new ear."

Meanwhile, at a different board meeting, the story of ARD took an absurd twist. Charles J. Coulter, still the president of ARD, was attending a board meeting for one of its portfolio companies when one of the company's other directors turned to him and said, "Charlie, I understand Textron is trying to sell ARD."

"That's right," replied Coulter.

"What about coming to me?" asked the director, signaling his interest in buying the firm.

"Certainly," said Coulter.

In the early to mid-1980s, the height of the takeover era, Textron became the object of several hostile buyout offers. Textron executives felt that the ARD portfolio had become a bull's-eye because it was a lucrative unit with many investments recorded below market value. "By the 80s it got to the point that Textron would call up ARD to make up the year," says Francis J. Hughes, who joined ARD's staff in 1981. "We always had something in the portfolio that was worth ten times book value. That could only work so long." So when the Textron told the ARD team that it should spin out the firm, Coulter pounced on the offer. "Having been told to go find a home for ourselves, when the second takeover came along [in 1984] we found a buyer," says Hughes.

In July 1985, Textron spun off ARD to a limited partnership led by Coulter. Textron retained the eight public companies in ARD's portfolio worth an estimated $35 million. The remaining stakes in twenty-eight private firms were purchased by Coulter's group for about $25 million. An item in *Venture* magazine reported that Textron "shed a highly profitable unit—one scoring annual returns of 40% for six out of the last seven years." After all these years, ARD was finally taken private, but the deal was twenty years too late.

The identity of the purchaser who led the ARD buyout was not disclosed in public, and has never been divulged since. But according to Charles J. Coulter and James F. Morgan, the buyer was an heir of the Mellon family based in Vermont. The Mellon heir kept five ARD staffers to continue running the firm: Coulter, Hughes, Wade Blackman, George McKinney, and Courtney Whitin. The team started a new fund called ARD II with about $80 million in assets. In 1988, it created ARD III with around $25 million. "ARD was one of the first five venture firms to raise a $100 million portfolio," says

Hughes. The most successful investment in the portfolio, however, was Fusion Systems, a deal made in 1972 when Doriot was still running the show.

Around the same time, Doriot received a letter reminding him of the remarkable influence he had on so many successful and important people. "I simply wanted to send along to you my respectful good wishes," wrote Vice President George Bush to Doriot. Bush was inspired to connect with Doriot after Indiana Governor Robert Orr, his old Quartermaster charge, brought up Doriot's name over a lunch. "I think back to those early days when American Research and Development really took an interest and helped Zapata, our struggling new company. Though politics has been good to me, and in a sense fully rewarding, I will never forget the confidence that a handful of people placed in me many years ago."

It was a very thoughtful gesture. But Doriot's thoughts remained mostly with Edna as he entered the final stage of his life. Doriot did not fear his mortality, for he believed his death would only bring him closer to his love. "I believe that I shall be reunited with my Edna and my friends and family," he wrote in his journal. "How and in what form I do not know, and it does not matter as long as we are reunited."

Doriot's dreams became particularly vivid. In one dream that came to him at two o'clock in the morning in summer of 1985, he saw Edna sitting down on a low chair.

> She was dressed in black with a black hat. She seemed sad. Georges went to her and said, "Edna dear, do not be sad, come back with me, to me. I am waiting for you." She said sweetly, "Yes Georges dear, I want to be with you and I am coming back to you. I was so happy . . . so very happy . . . she expected a baby . . . then it seems that she got up and left with several ladies. Georges followed her but could not find her.

Then he woke up, crying yet joyous at the thought that Edna wanted to be together with him again.

At the end of 1985, sickness struck Doriot. It was lung cancer. All those decades of smoking Peretti tobacco in his pipe had finally caught up with him. The General dropped down to 140 pounds and developed a horrible, constant cough. To boost his immune system, Doriot gobbled a handful of vitamins every day—a legacy of his wartime food research program. His passel of doctors at Massachusetts General Hospital prescribed him a medical cocktail. Pyridoxine helped fight off the cancer by promoting red blood cell production; nitroglycerin relieved his chest pains; Triaminic soothed his sore throat; and flurazepam hydrochloride helped pacify his bouts of insomnia. Georges moved out of his small sleeping quarters and into Edna's bedroom.

Doriot relied on three people to help him through his final days: Ida Aellig, Kenneth H. Olsen, and James M. Stone. An economics PhD from Harvard who became friendly with Doriot in the early 1970s, Stone became one of Doriot's last surrogate sons. "I went to see him at his office about a business idea," says Stone. "He wasn't interested in my idea. But he had a counterproposal. He would pay me $1 a year to come have lunch with him once a month. He would write out contracts. 'This year I am giving you a cost of living increase,' he would say. 'It will be a $1.07.' I used to go have lunch with him once a month and earn my dollar."

In the beginning of 1986, Doriot also started radiation treatments. "I used to walk him over sometimes when he had treatments," says Stone. But it was Ida who really took care of the General. "She was there every second," says Stone. "If he said, 'my throat is dry,' she went and got him a glass of water."

Out of respect for the General, Olsen held the General's last five Digital board meetings at 12 Lime Street. The directors convened upstairs in the grand living room of the house. Olsen had one last bit of good news to share with his mentor. In October of 1986, *Fortune* magazine named Olsen "America's Most Successful Entrepreneur." Over the last twenty-nine years, Pete Petre wrote, Olsen "has taken Digital from nothing to $7.6 billion in revenues. DEC is bigger, even adjusting for inflation, than Ford Motor Co. when death claimed Henry Ford, than U.S. Steel when Andrew Carnegie sold out, than Standard Oil when John D. Rockefeller stepped aside." The little start-up that Doriot financed and nurtured for three decades had come to dominate the minicomputer market and was deemed the greatest entrepreneurial success of all time. The news must have brought a twinkle to Doriot's eye, even though he knew that someone somewhere was trying to make Digital obsolete.

Then, during one Digital board meeting in 1987, Doriot felt ill. "The General tried to whisper something and I could not hear him," said Jacobs, who got Doriot's nurse to wheel him out of the living room. The cancer could not be stopped.

In May, Claude Janssen, like many of Doriot's closest friends and colleagues, paid his last respects to the old man. He too had good news for the General. A few months back, INSEAD had decided to build a library. Claude

Janssen, INSEAD's chairman since 1982, called Ken Olsen for some help. "There are two outstanding success stories in Doriot's life: Digital and INSEAD," Janssen told Olsen. "You make the money. We need the money." Digital donated $2 million for the library.

Janssen informed Doriot about Digital's generous donation. And he was especially proud to let him know that the library would be named in his honor. The General, not surprisingly, abhorred the idea. "He told me it should be: Georges and Edna Doriot Library. Then we said goodbye."

On the morning of June 2, 1987, Ida called Olsen and Stone. The cancer took Doriot's life, she told them. Georges Frederic Doriot died peacefully in his sleep at 5:45 a.m. He was 87 years old. Then Ida called the police. "We got there just after the body was removed," says Stone. "Ida knew what she was supposed to do. She had instructions. It was on a sheet of paper that she carried around with her." Dorothy Rowe and Arnaud de Vitry also came by to help.

Doriot never set out to be a rich man but he ended his life with an enormous amount of wealth. In his will, Doriot bequeathed all of his property, excluding cash and securities, to a trust whose terms were kept private. The trust's main asset was 31,298 shares of Digital Equipment Corporation, worth $52 million.

Separate funerals were held in Boston at the Park Street Church and another service was held in Paris. The hundreds of people who came to pay their last tribute did not view Doriot's body. For Ida's instructions carried one very important request. After Edna died, Georges told the executor of his estate, Richard Testa, that he did not want to be buried underneath a headstone. He wanted to be cremated like his wife.

And so, on a sunny day in June, about 150 of Doriot's friends and family gathered at Smith's Point in Manchester. Arnaud de Vitry gave a eulogy in front of Edna's rock. Then Testa took Doriot's ashes and spread them exactly where Edna's remains had been dispersed nine years earlier, reuniting Georges and Edna in the cold blue waters of the Atlantic Ocean.

EPILOGUE

Even though it had been nearly twenty years since Georges Doriot passed away, the General could still draw a large and distinguished crowd. It was October 8, 2005, and the French Library, the cultural center that he and Edna had dedicated their lives to building, was holding a tribute to Doriot on the occasion of its sixtieth anniversary. More than a hundred friends, colleagues, and admirers showed up at the Library on this unusually warm, humid evening to pay homage to the man who had played such a significant role in their personal histories—and in the history of America's twentieth century.

It was also an especially important event for me. I had recently received a contract to write this book, and realized that attending this event was my top research priority—the catapult that would launch me out of the starting gate. Thanks to Roanne Edwards, the library's director of development, I knew that many of Doriot's surviving colleagues would be in attendance at the affair, enabling me in one fell swoop to establish face-to-face connections with the very people who could open the doors to Doriot's life.

I arrived early at a beautiful townhouse on Beacon Hill. But when I got there, the lower floor of the library was already buzzing with dozens of dignitaries. I found Roanne, who had organized the guest list, and she kindly began pointing out the people I needed to meet. There was Charles P. Waite of Greylock Partners, which had grown into one of the nation's most successful venture capital firms. There was Daniel J. Holland, an ARD alumnus who had served as the president of the New England Venture Capital Association, and is today still going strong as an advisor to the Cambridge VC firm Flagship Ventures. There was Alexander D'Arbeloff, the former founder, chairman, and CEO of ARD affiliate Teradyne, who is today a professor at MIT's Sloan School of Management, and the honorary Chairman of the MIT Corporation, the university's governing body. And there was Samuel W. Bodman, another ARD alumnus who had recently been appointed by President Bush to become the eleventh U.S. Secretary of Energy.

It was an undeniably impressive group that testified to the continuing power and legacy of Georges Doriot. And it fired me up with even more passion that sustained me throughout the project.

As part of the tribute, the library had converted one entire room on the lower floor into a sort miniexhibition of Doriot's life. The room was filled with photos, paintings, and little bits of memorabilia that brought Doriot to life, such as his smoking pipe and his monogrammed leather briefcase. Walking around the room, I spotted black and white photos of Doriot at the opening of INSEAD, and of General Dwight D. Eisenhower and President Herbert Hoover, both signed with personal inscriptions to Doriot.

Bodman kicked off the tribute with a poignant remembrance. As he spoke, it became clear that Doriot was the type of person who invariably left an indelible impression on the people who crossed his path. "He had the capacity to cut through to the core of the individual," Bodman explained in his remarks. "He knew each of us in a very personal way." By way of example, Bodman said there were only three people in his life that called him "Sammy": his wife, General Doriot, and President Bush. "The president calls me that a little less often as oil prices declined and hit $60," said Bodman, to the laughs of the crowd.

Bodman closed his remarks by pointing out some of the lessons that General Doriot taught him over the years. One of the lessons was that problems should not be ignored or avoided but confronted. "From problems and challenges we can learn and grow," said Bodman. Another lesson was that products are less important than ideas, and ideas are less important than people. Bodman recalled vivid memories of Doriot treating all the waitresses and busboys at the John Hancock cafeteria with the utmost respect. "I've come to see that it's the people that define an organization," said Bodman. And the final lesson that General Doriot taught him was that a commander leads by action. On that note, Secretary Bodman held up a copy of the U.S. Army Leadership Manual. "The General loved to pass out this manual," he said.

After two more heartfelt speeches by former Doriot students Marvin Traub and Sumner Feldberg, the guests repaired to the Fairmont Copley for cocktails and dinner. The highlight of dinner was a speech by Jean-David Levitte, then the French ambassador to the United States. The cool air of the dining room was filled with tension. In the fall of 2005, French-American relations had reached one of their lowest points in the post-war period, thanks to the invasion of Iraq. But the skilled diplomat partly defused the tension by focusing on a common area of interest between the French and the American people. Opening his remarks, Ambassador Levitte told the story of his first meeting with Secretary Bodman, who confided to him that due to his relationship with General Doriot, the Secretary had become "very impressed with the French people and France." Levitte was pleasantly shocked by this remark. "Whenever someone from the Bush Administration tells me he is very impressed with the French people I take notice," said Ambassador Levitte, drawing peals of laughter from the crowd. "Suddenly we were best friends, thanks to General Doriot."

In fact, Ambassador Levitte credited General Doriot—and the way he brought two contentious countries together even after his death—for a landmark agreement that France signed in early 2005 with the United States and several other nations to develop next-generation nuclear energy technology. France, which derives about 80 percent of its electric power from nuclear energy, wanted to hold a ceremony to celebrate the agreement, and Secretary Bodman graciously recommended the French Embassy. "It was because of General Doriot that we signed another agreement on nuclear plants," said Ambassador Levitte. "It's very important to cultivate the memory of great people."

In the summer of 2007, France's new President, Nicolas Sarkozy, selected Ambassador Levitte to become his national security adviser. Doriot, I suspect, would have voted for Sarkozy, who seems to represent the best of the old Europe and the new—a Europe that is more attuned to the benefits of a free market. And Doriot would have been proud to know that he helped close one more deal that helped push the boundaries of an innovative technology. In death, as in life, the spirit, imagination, and influence of Georges Doriot knew no bounds.

NOTES

Abbreviations Used in Notes

GFD: M.I.T. Entrepreneurship Center Library, Georges F. Doriot papers
LOC: Manuscript Division, Library of Congress, Georges F. Doriot papers

Introduction

xiii. *Venture capital has existed:* The first documented use of the words "venture capital" came in 1920 when an executive from the New York investment bank Morgan Guaranty Trust Company used the term at the 1920 Investment Banking Association conference, according to Martha Louise Reiner. "The enlistment of venture capital is necessary for the development and growth of the country, as well as for the safety of all investment securities," he argued.

xiii. *"He is the founder of the modern VC industry":* Josh Lerner, interview by author.

xiii. *"He was very important":* Arnold Kroll, interview by author.

xiv. *"It was almost like knowing someone":* Charles Dyer, interview by author.

xiv. *the "velvet glove":* Nicholas DeWolf, interview by author.

xiv. *"Sport coats are for newspaper boys":* John A. Shane, interview by author.

xiv. *"Doriot was arresting":* Ralph Hoagland, interview by author.

xv. *"A real courageous man is a man":* Gene Bylinsky, "General Doriot's Dream Factory," *Fortune,* August 1967, 103–136.

xv. *"A lot of the things that were attributed":* Charles P. Waite, interview by author.

xv. *"The general's view of the world":* Georges Doriot, *Man with a Vision,* (Cambridge, MA: Peace River Films, 1987), DVD.

xvii. *"He always thought ARD":* Daniel J. Holland, interview by author.

xvii. *"He gave a dignity or a substance":* Kroll, interview by author.

xvii. *"When you have a child":* Bylinsky, "General Doriot's Dream Factory," 104.

xviii. *"A creative man merely has ideas":* Personal notes, GFD.

xviii. *"ARD led the advent of technology companies":* F. Warren Hellman, interview by author.

xviii. *"He was definitely part of a social revolution":* Parker G. Montgomery, interview by author.

xix. *"When he went on a trip":* Georges Doriot, *Man with a Vision.*

Chapter One

1. *On a sunny afternoon:* This anecdote is based on material contained in Soda's notes of his unpublished book on Doriot, which is based on interviews with Doriot, Dorothy Rowe, and other close associates. Ralph Soda papers.

1. *A student at Coubert 7:* In France the first stage of secondary school is referred to as "college" but it is akin to junior high school in the United States as children attend from ages 11 to 14.

3. *When Auguste Frederic Doriot:* Auguste Doriot, "He is 89 years old; He entered into our factories in 1873," interview in *Peugeot News* (newsletter of the Peugeot Company), 1952.

3. *Originally part of the Holy Roman Empire:* Georges Doriot, interview by Aulikki Olsen, April 1980. The portrait of Valentigney and Doriot's recollections of the village come from a long interview conducted by Aulikki, the wife of Ken Olsen.

4. *Auguste, the next-to-youngest child:* Doriot family tree, created by Eveline Poillot in 2007.

4. *born on October 24, 1863:* Résumé of Georges F. Doriot, April 1980, GFD.

4. *Auguste's father:* Doriot, *Peugeot News.*

4. *Photographs of him:* Poillot family photo album.

5. *"My Father was a very wonderful person"*: Doriot, interview by Olsen.

5. *The Peugeot clan had first settled:* "The Company Saga," Peugeot International Web site, http://www.peugeot.com/tradition/histoire/en/.

5. *they alone possessed the secret:* Enzo Angelucci and Alberto Bellucci, *The Automobile: From Steam to Gasoline* (New York: McGraw-Hill, 1974), 49.

5. *the underappreciated philosopher-economist:* Friedrich A. Hayek, "Richard Cantillon," *Journal of Libertarian Studies* 7, no. 2 (Fall 1985): 217–247; Robert F. Hebert, "Was Richard Cantillon an Austrian Economist?" *Journal of Libertarian Studies* 7, no. 2 (Fall 1985): 269–280.

6. *there were a multitude of individuals:* Fernand Braudel, *The Wheels of Commerce: Civilization & Capitalism 15th–18th Century*, vol. 2 (New York: Harper & Row, 1982), 386–388.

6. *banks began offering loans:* Ibid., 390–392.

6. *the Rothschild family rose to power:* Niall Ferguson, *The House of Rothschild: Money's Prophets, 1798–1841* (New York: Penguin, 1999).

7. *"A commercial bank lends":* "Profile of Shawmut Director Georges F. Doriot," *Shawmut News Bulletin*, January 20, 1961.

7. *The first major modern communications technology:* "History of the Telegraph," Smithsonian Institution's HistoryWired Web site, http://historywired.si.edu/detail.cfm?ID=324.

7. *a Scottish immigrant who developed:* Charlotte Gray, *Reluctant Genius: The Passionate Life and Inventive Mind of Alexander Graham Bell* (New York: HarperCollins, 2006), 76–81.

8. *Hubbard organized the Bell Telephone Company:* Ibid., 160–166.

8. *the unscrupulous Orton:* Ibid., 184.

8. *Western Union had the considerable advantage:* Ibid., 193.

8. *Thomas Sanders had poured $110,000:* Ibid., 189.

8. *"The position of an inventor":* Ibid., 185–186.

8. *Western Union signed an out-of-court settlement:* Ibid., 197.

8. *its stock zoomed:* Ibid., 203.

9. *In 1889, at the World's Fair in Paris:* Angelucci and Bellucci, *The Automobile: From Steam to Gasoline*, 49.

9. *The German engineer Karl Benz:* David Burgess Wise, William Brody, and Brian Laban, *The Automobile: The First Century* (New York: Greenwich House, Inc., 1983), 1–10.

9. *Auguste finished his apprenticeships:* Ibid.

9. *He immediately set about:* Doriot, "He is 89 years old." Ibid.

9. *"The beginnings were rather arduous":* Peugeot News.

10. *In September of 1891:* Angelucci and Bellucci, *The Automobile: From Steam to Gasoline*, 50.

10. *At ten o'clock in the morning:* Pierre Souvestre, *Histoire de l'Automobile* (Paris, 1907). My account of the Paris-Brest race is adapted from the wonderful telling of the story in this book.

12. *the Paris-Rouen Trial of 1894:* Wise, Brody, and Laban, *The Automobile: The First Century*, 86–87; Angelucci and Bellucci, *The Automobile: From Steam to Gasoline*, 80–81.

13. *Berthe, known as Camille to her family:* Eveline Poillot, interview by author.

13. *came from Voujeaucourt, another village:* Résumé of Georges F. Doriot, GFD.

13. *Her father, Jean Baehler:* Poillot, interview by author.

13. *A family photo taken when Camille was thirty-eight:* Poillot family photo album.

13. *she even traveled to Canada:* Gerald D. Sutton, "Canadian Enterprise Development Corporation Limited," in *A Little Bit of Luck* (unpublished memoir) 138.

14. *On September 27, 1894:* Marriage certificate from Department du Doubs Commune, furnished by the Poillot family.

14. *Armand Peugeot sent Auguste to Paris:* Doriot, *Peugeot News.*

14. *lived on the first floor:* Doriot, interview by Olsen.

14. *"Peasants would chase them with whips":* Ibid.

Chapter Two

15. *Georges Frederic Doriot was born:* Georges Doriot, interview by Aulikki Olsen, April 1980.

15. *"I am delighted that you finally":* Marianne Peugeot, letter to Camille Doriot, September 1899 (obtained from Eveline Poillot).

15. *"I hope your hens":* Germaine Peugeot, letter to Camille Doriot, September 27, 1899 (obtained from Eveline Poillot).

15. *"I'm so happy you have"*: Madeleine Peugeot, letter to Camille Doriot, September 27, 1899 (obtained from Eveline Poillot).

16. *"I was enchanted to receive"*: Unknown author to Auguste Doriot, October 13, 1899 (obtained from Eveline Poillot).

16. *A picture taken in July 1900*: Poillot family photo album.

16. *on August 15, 1902, Auguste made*: Eveline Poillot, interview by author.

16. *"For the many years I have known him"*: Armand Peugeot, letter of recommendation for Auguste Doriot (obtained from Eveline Poillot).

17. *Peugeot introduced another line*: G. N. Georgano, *The Complete Encyclopedia of Motorcars: 1885 to the Present* (Boston: E.P. Dutton and Company, 1973), 545.

17. *He spent most of his time*: Doriot, interview by Olsen.

17. *"In the summer"* Ibid.

17. *there was a wonderful smell*: Ibid.

18. *"bankruptcy was a catastrophic event"*: James F. Morgan, interview by author, June 2006.

18. *Auguste teamed up with a colleague*: Georgano, *The Complete Encyclopedia of Motorcars*, 250.

18. *"I don't know anyone on Wall Street"*: "Money's the Least of It," *Forbes* September 1, 1972.

18. *helped finance the creation*: Neil Baldwin, *Edison: Inventing the Century* (Chicago: University of Chicago Press, 2001), 61, 103.

19. *The ultraconservative strategy of J. P. Morgan*: Ron Chernow, *The House of Morgan: An American Banking Dynasty and the Rise of Modern Finance* (Boston: The Atlantic Monthly Press, 1990), 37–38.

19. *"The Kind of Bonds which I want"*: Ibid., 38.

19. *J. P. Morgan who led that transformation*: Ibid., 66–68.

20. *accounting for 60 percent of all issues*: Ibid., 67.

20. *The number of mergers jumped*: Ibid., 81.

20. *the formation of U.S. Steel*: Ibid., 82–85.

20. *On August 11, 1906*: Poillot, interview by author.

20. *A photograph taken in 1908*: Poillot family photo album.

21. *"I remember my youth"*: Doriot, interview by Olsen.

21. *In 1908, Doriot and Flandrin brought*: Wikipedia, http://dewikipedia.org/wiki/DFP-Automobile.

21. *For their slogan*: D.F.P. stock certificate, March 1908 (obtained from Eveline Poillot).

21. *they began selling bigger cars*: Georgano, *The Complete Encyclopedia of Motorcars*, 250.

21. *D.F.P. held a public offering*: D.F.P. stock certificate.

21. *By 1911, D.F.P. began*: Georgano, *The Complete Encyclopedia of Motorcars*, 250.

22. *he entered one of*: Doriot, interview by Olsen.

22. *when Georges was eleven*: Personal history statement, U.S. Army, LOC.

23. *"When he came back from England"*: Poillot, interview by author.

23. *He began school at half past eight*: Doriot, interview by Olsen.

23. *Auguste built a new house*: Poillot, interview by author.

23. *It was a solid brick*: Observation of author, May 2006.

23. *Georges converted this chamber*: Marie-Hélène Poillot, interview by author.

23. *Auguste would let him*: Doriot, interview by Olsen.

24. *Flipping through the pages*: *American Machinist Memories: Selected Articles from Early Issues of American Machinist Magazine: 1913–1915* (XXXX: Publications Inc., 2003).

25. *The factory was turned*: Doriot, interview by Olsen.

25. *"people worked twenty-four hours"*: Ibid.

25. *not old enough to be drafted*: Clayton, *Paths of Glory*, 234.

25. *he continued his studies*: Eveline Poillot, letter to author, 2006.

26. *Georges got his driver's license*: Doriot, interview by Olsen.

26. *Paris was hunkered down*: Anthony Clayton, *Paths of Glory: The French Army 1914–1918* (London: Cassel Military Paperbacks, 2005), 45.

26. *French Army suffered*: Ibid., 115–116.

26. *was convulsed by massive strikes*: Jean-Jacques Becker, *The Great War and the French People* (Providence: Berg Publishers, Inc., 1993), 127, 206.

26. *strikes broke out*: Ibid., 205–206.

26. *"most factories in Courbevoie"*: Ibid., 265.

27. *Georges enlisted in the French Army*: Biographical sketch, U.S. Army, LOC.

27. *A photograph taken that year*: Poillot family photo album.

27. *All of Georges's first cousins:* Doriot, interview by Olsen.

27. *Georges joined the R.A.L.T.:* Résumé of Georges F. Doriot, GFD.

27. *Georges was asked to replace:* Doriot, interview by Olsen.

27–28. *it was France that suffered more:* Clayton, *Paths of Glory,* 220–224.

28. *One of Auguste's friends:* Ibid., XXX.

28. *national debt exploded:* Ibid., 224.

28. *Bentley brothers, decided to end:* Honest John, *The Daily Telegraph Book of Motoring Answers* (London: Constable and Robinson, 1998).

28. *Georges would study machines:* Doriot, interview by Olsen.

Chapter Three

29. *On January 4, 1921:* Georges Doriot, memo, Patricia A. Clark papers, Lexington, MA.

29. *he kept a letter of introduction:* Georges Doriot, interview by Aulikki Olsen, April 1980.

29. *carried a small French coin:* James F. Morgan, interview by author, June 2006.

29. *"One of things that profoundly affected":* Ibid.

30. *La Touraine was built:* http://www.greatoceanliners.net/latouraine.html

30. *New York's harbor was as busy:* "The Connected City," America on the Move Web site, National Museum of American History, http://americanhistory.si.edu/ONTHEMOVE/exhibition/exhibition_6_4.html.

30. *Doriot checked into room 1721A:* Doriot, interview by Olsen.

31. *Albeit imposing, Lowell was kind:* Ibid.

31. *Doriot was the first Frenchman:* Official Register of Harvard University, Graduate School of Business Education, 1921–1922, 103; Official Register of Harvard University, Graduate School of Business Education, 1922–1923, 110.

32. *visit to the Rolls Royce factory:* Recording secretary of Harvard Business School to Rolls Royce Motor Company, October 31, 1921, Office of the Dean (Wallace B. Donham) Records, 1919–1942. Baker Library, Harvard Business School.

32. *A photograph taken in March of 1921:* Poillot family photo album.

32. *Doriot was listed as a "special student":* Official Register of Harvard University, Graduate School of Business Education, 1922–1923, 110.

32. *"I had come to France":* Doriot, interview by Olsen.

32. *"stone buildings that the human mind":* Rebecca West, "Letter From New York," *New Republic,* December 24, 1924, 68.

33. *Founded in 1867 by Abraham Kuhn and Solomon Loeb:* Kuhn, Loeb & Co.: A Century of Investment Banking (New York: Kuhn, Loeb & Co., 1967).

34. *"Let the Jews have that one":* Ken Auletta, *Greed and Glory on Wall Street* (New York: Random House, 1986), 28.

34. *The House of Morgan, by contrast:* Ron Chernow, *The House of Morgan: An American Banking Dynasty and the Rise of Modern Finance* (Boston: The Atlantic Monthly Press, 1990), 37–38.

34. *In 1911, the Computing Tabulating Recording Corporation:* Thomas J. Watson Jr. and Peter Petre, *Father, Son & Co.: My Life at IBM and Beyond* (New York: Bantam, 2000).

34. *a closely affiliated firm named:* Résumé of Georges F. Doriot, April 1980, GFD.

35. *More significant was Doriot's relationship:* Richard Pfau, *No Sacrifice Too Great: The Life of Lewis L. Strauss* (Charlottesville, VA: University Press of Virginia, 1984).

36. *he was a director of New York Foreign and Development:* Thos. J. Bray, letter to Lewis L. Strauss, February 25, 1924, Lewis L. Strauss papers, Herbert Hoover Presidential Library.

36. *The two worked together on a deal:* Managing Committee of International Gear Company, letter to subscribers of company stock, November 27, 1924, Lewis L. Strauss papers, Herbert Hoover Presidential Library and Museum.

36. *"unquestionably the outstanding achievement":* M. E. Charles H. Logue and Reginald Trautschold, *American Machinist Gear Book* (New York: McGraw Hill, 1922).

37. *"there is no definite connection":* Georges Doriot, letter to Lewis Strauss, March 18, 1924, Lewis L. Strauss papers, Herbert Hoover Presidential Library and Museum.

37. *"mainly and primarily a myth":* Beaulieu, "The Dawes Plan Myth," *The New Republic,* September 24, 1924, 90–92.

37. *"the administration of the plan":* Beaulieu, "The Dawes Plan and the Peace of Europe," *The New Republic,* December 10, 1924, 68–70.

38. *he hated writing:* "Remarks on My Notes," 1975, GFD.

38. *"There is no doubt as to the fact":* Georges Doriot, letter to R. R. Santini, December 7, 1925, Lewis L. Strauss papers, Herbert Hoover Presidential Library and Museum.

38. *In a subsequent memo:* Georges Doriot, letter to Lewis Strauss, March 1926, Lewis L. Strauss papers. Herbert Hoover Presidential Library and Museum.

39. *Doriot demonstrated an ability:* Arnaud de Vitry, interview by author.

Chapter Four

41. *the firm had admitted only one unrelated partner:* Theresa M. Collins, *Otto Kahn: Art, Money, & Modern Time* (Chapel Hill & London: The University of North Carolina Press, 2002), 19.

42. *Dean Donham wrestled with all sorts of growing pains:* Details on the early history of Harvard Business School came primarily from two books: Melvin T. Copeland, *And Mark an Era: The Story of the Harvard Business School* (New York: Little, Brown & Co., 1958); and Jeffrey L. Cruikshank, *A Delicate Experiment: The Harvard Business School 1908–1945* (Boston: Harvard Business School Press, 1987).

42. *Doriot shared an office with Donald K. David:* Georges Doriot, interview by Aulikki Olsen, April 1980.

42. *"I enjoyed living there":* Doriot, interview by Olsen.

42. *His first job as assistant dean:* Personal notes, GFD. Doriot maintained so many personal notes that it felt as if he documented nearly his entire life.

43. *On November 9, 1925, Doriot wrote:* Georges Doriot, letter to Andre Siegfried, November 9, 1925, Office of the Dean (Wallace B. Donham) Records, 1919–1942, Baker Library, Harvard Business School.

43. *Doriot suggested to Dean Donham:* Doriot, interview by Olsen.

43. *"Well, I didn't know if I could teach":* Ibid.

44. *Major H. K. Rutherford of the U.S. War Department:* Georges Doriot, letter to Major H. K. Rutherford, March 17, 1926, Office of the Dean (Wallace B. Donham) Records, 1919–1942, Baker Library, Harvard Business School.

44. *Doriot was one of a number of outside teachers:* Major John C. H. Lee, "The Army Industrial College," *The Military Engineer* 25, no. 14 (March–April 1933), 167–171.

44. *In a letter to Secretary of Defense Robert McNamara:* Georges Doriot, letter to Robert McNamara, date not known, LOC.

45. *The stress of learning to teach:* Georges Doriot, letter to Lewis Strauss, April 7, 1926, Lewis L. Strauss papers, Herbert Hoover Presidential Library and Museum.

45. *Doriot compiled the school's first bibliography:* "Remarks on My Notes," 1975, GFD.

46. *Dean Donham handed Doriot a treat:* Wallace B. Donham, letter to E. Van Dien, May 20, 1926, Office of the Dean (Wallace B. Donham) Records, 1919–1942, Baker Library, Harvard Business School.

46. *Doriot spent a week:* Office of the Dean (Wallace B. Donham) Records, 1919–1942, Baker Library, Harvard Business School.

46. *word got back to Harvard:* J. T. Madden, letter to Wallace B. Donham, 28 July 1926, Office of the Dean (Wallace B. Donham) Records, 1919–1942. Baker Library, Harvard Business School.

46. *Doriot started his own course:* Personal notes, GFD.

46. *D.F.P. went out of business:* Georgano, *The Complete Encyclopedia of Motorcars*, 250.

47. *Doriot was one of several staff members:* Letter from Tenney and Oliver [contractors] to McKim, Mead & White [architects], October 1, 1925, Lewis L. Strauss papers.

47. *he had seen every one of his ninety-six students:* Georges Doriot, letter to Samuel O. Dunn, March 22, 1927, Office of the Dean (Wallace B. Donham) Records, 1919–1942, Baker Library, Harvard Business School.

47. *In a letter to a friend of a colleague:* Ibid.

47. *"how business problems come up":* Ibid.

48. *"I haven't had a day's rest for four months":* Georges Doriot, letter to Lewis Strauss, December 15, 1927, Lewis L. Strauss papers.

48. *"Other nations respected France":* Georges F. Doriot, "Creation of the CPA in Paris," September 1975, Patricia A. Clark papers, Lexington, MA.

48. *During his annual summer break:* Ibid.

49. *Her name was Edna Blanche Allen:* Résumé of Edna Allen, GFD.

49. *She was a "very nice person":* Robert McCabe, interview by author..

49. *"very intelligent" and "spoke French fluently":* Patricia A. Clark, interview by author.

49. *she was a "magnificent woman":* Charles P. Waite, interview by author.

49. *Georges would see that she is tall:* Descriptions of Edna are based on several photos of her contained in the GFD collection and French Library.

50. *Doriot's Manufacturing class attracted 140 students:* Georges Doriot, letter to Lewis Strauss, May 18, 1928, Lewis L. Strauss papers.

50. *Doriot asked the students to read an advertisement:* Georges F. Doriot, "Assignments for Business Policy and Manufacturing Course," 1930–1931, Office of the Dean (Wallace B. Donham) Records, 1919–1942. Baker Library, Harvard Business School.

51. *"infuriating students into positive brilliance":* Cruikshank, *A Delicate Experiment,* 171.

51. *Doriot received a call:* Georges Doriot, letter to Major H. K. Rutherford, April 25, 1928, Office of the Dean (Wallace B. Donham) Records, 1919–1942, Baker Library, Harvard Business School.

51. *the Major sought "the benefit":* Major C. A. Schimelfenig, letter to Georges Doriot, April 27, 1928, Office of the Dean (Wallace B. Donham) Records, 1919–1942, Baker Library, Harvard Business School.

51. *Doriot walked into Pierce Hall:* This extraordinary moment is documented in two sources: Georges Doriot, letter to Lewis Strauss, May 18, 1928, Lewis L. Strauss papers; and in an addendum to that letter, which is a copy of the speech the students gave.

52. *"This past year may have been hard":* Ibid.

52. *Doriot began the summer of 1928:* Doriot, "Creation of the CPA in Paris."

52. *Dean Donham asked him to put out another fire:* Personal notes, GFD.

52. *"during lectures they considered boring or irrelevant":* Cruikshank, *A Delicate Experiment,* 134.

53. *Doriot vented the frustration:* Georges Doriot, letter to Lewis Strauss, October 2, 1928, Lewis L. Strauss papers.

53. *"happy solution quite in line":* Major C. A. Schimelfenig, letter to Georges Doriot, October 5, 1928, Office of the Dean (Wallace B. Donham) Records, 1919–1942, Baker Library, Harvard Business School.

54. *Doriot also helped host the Assistant Secretary of War:* Major C. A. Schimelfenig, letter to Georges Doriot, October 26, 1928, Office of the Dean (Wallace B. Donham) Records, 1919–1942. Baker Library, Harvard Business School.

54. *some work to do in connection with purchasing methods:* Georges Doriot, letter to Colonel T. L. Ames, March 12, 1929, Office of the Dean (Wallace B. Donham) Records, 1919–1942, Baker Library, Harvard Business School.

54. *Doriot spent practically every day:* Doriot, "Creation of the CPA in Paris."

54. *"This may well have been":* Jean-Louis Barsoux, *Insead: From Intuition to Institution* (New York: St. Martin's Press, 2000), 6.

56. *"Mr. Catchings and his colleagues":* Georges Doriot, "The Investment Trust Racket," unpublished paper, Lewis L. Strauss papers, 31.

56. *"I'm afraid it can't be published":* Georges Doriot, letter to Lewis Strauss, November 6, 1929, Lewis L. Strauss papers.

56. *"I feel it would be best":* Lewis Strauss, letter to Georges Doriot, November 13, 1929, Lewis L. Strauss papers.

57. *Back at his Business Policy course:* Edmund R. Kind, notes on lectures in Business Policy, 1928–1930, Office of the Dean (Wallace B. Donham) Records, 1919–1942, Baker Library, Harvard Business School.

57. *How much of an advance is the company:* Ibid.

58. *Keep a fresh viewpoint:* Ibid.

58. *Doriot received a Western Union telegram:* Joel T. Boone, telegram to Georges Doriot, December 3, 1929, LOC.

58. *Doriot continued to finalize the last details:* Doriot, "Creation of the CPA in Paris."

58. *Georges introduced Edna to his family that summer:* Doriot, interview by Olsen.

59. *"I asked for not more than 150 students":* Georges Doriot, letter to Lewis Strauss, September 30, 1930, Lewis L. Strauss papers.

59. *Dean Donham delivered a speech:* "Dean Donham Honored by France: Delivers Speech at French School Dedication," *Harvard Business School Alumni Bulletin,* Office of the Dean (Wallace B. Donham) Records, 1919–1942, Baker Library, Harvard Business School.

60. *Doriot's relationship with Edna came to a head:* Doriot, interview by Olsen.

60. *Lewis and Alice Strauss were kind enough:* Minot Simons, letter to Lewis Strauss, December 8, 1930, Lewis L. Strauss papers.

60. *"I am very much in love":* Georges Doriot, letter to Lewis Strauss, December 23, 1930, Lewis L. Strauss papers.

61. *Eighteen close friends attended the ceremony:* Doriot marriage announcement, Lewis L. Strauss papers.

61. *the happy couple spent the evening:* Doriot, interview by Olsen.

Chapter Five

64. *"He often said the only advantage":* Claude Janssen, interview by author.

64. *Doriot served on the boards of twenty companies:* Georges F. Doriot "Directorships, 1932–1952," Patricia A. Clark papers, Lexington, MA.

64. *Doriot was elected to take over:* "McKeesport Tin Plate Corp.'s New President," *Barron's Weekly,* September 9, 1940. Describing how he got the presidency, Doriot quipped off the record: "One day my predecessor got drunk at nine instead of eleven as usual."

64. *They soon found an apartment:* Georges Doriot, interview by Aulikki Olsen, April 1980.

65. *But that security was compromised:* During the 1930s and 1940s, Doriot would send money home to France, according to one coworker of his. Moreover, in the personal history statement Doriot filled out for the U.S. military in September 1949, Doriot admitted as much when he wrote: "I help many people but I can claim tax exemption for none." LOC.

65. *Georges and Edna studied:* Doriot, interview by Olsen.

66. *At the time there were few automobiles:* Ibid.

66. *Doriot boldly called for the internationalization:* Georges F. Doriot, "Internationalization of Transportation System Cited as Means for Peace," *Montana Standard,* November 8, 1931.

67. *"were booked for important positions":* "French Business School Prospers, Doriot Declares," *Harvard Crimson,* September 23, 1931.

67. *"We must formulate and perfect":* "Preparedness to Be Keynote of Next War," *Boston Transcript,* January 21, 1932.

67. *"There is one thing about Professor Doriot":* "Colonel Jordan's Remarks Introducing Professor Georges F. Doriot," LOC.

68. *"This does not mean I have decided":* Georges Doriot, letter to Lewis Strauss, November 7, 1931, Lewis L. Strauss papers, Herbert Hoover Presidential Library and Museum

68. *"American businessmen are now handicapped":* Harry Goldberg, "All Aboard For The New Business Era," *Cincinnati Enquirer,* April 10, 1932.

69. *"Would you be willing to open an account":* Georges Doriot, letter to Lewis Strauss, March 1, 1933, Lewis L. Strauss papers.

69. *one of the key legislative proposals of the New Deal:* David M. Kennedy, *Freedom From Fear: The American People in Depression and War, 1929–1945* (New York: Oxford University Press, 1999), 177–189.

70. *"There is no fear of war":* Georges Doriot, letter to Lewis Strauss, July 15, 1933, Lewis L. Strauss papers.

70. *"Doriot in many ways was the most":* James F. Morgan, interview by author.

71. *"France has done everything she could":* A translation of the story was reprinted here: Georges F. Doriot, "France Has Disgusted Us," *N.Y. American,* December 14, 1933.

71. *Edna met a gentleman:* Doriot, interview by Olsen.

71. *a "rather disinterested mood":* Georges Doriot, letter to Lewis Strauss, December 15, 1934, Lewis L. Strauss papers.

71. *"The New Deal will go down":* "Throngs Acclaim Curley: Huge Rallies Hear Call to Vote Ticket of New Deal," *Boston Post,* November 2, 1934.

72. *"This is a most unusual statement":* Ibid.

72. *a second wave of New Deal legislation:* Kennedy, *Freedom from Fear,* 252–258.

73. *dozens of companies sought his guidance:* Georges F. Doriot Directorships, Patricia A. Clark papers.

73. *Budd Manufacturing cabled Doriot:* Georges Doriot, letter to Lewis Strauss, December 10, 1935, Lewis L. Strauss papers.

73. *Doriot had taken over the required:* Personal notes, GFD.

74. *Doriot adapted the approach:* Melvin T. Copeland, *And Mark an Era: The Story of the Harvard Business School* (New York: Little, Brown & Co., 1958), 160.

74. *the New Deal failed:* Kennedy, *Freedom from Fear,* 350–361.

75. *a "risk-less economy":* Martha Louise Reiner, *The Transformation of Venture Capital: A History of Venture Capital Organizations in the United States* (PhD diss., University of California, Berkeley, 1989), 52.

75. *On top of the Revenue Act of 1932:* Ibid., 6–8.

75. *the undistributed profits surtax:* Ibid., 26–36.

75. *"If investors throughout the land":* Ibid., 38–39.

75. *One of the most prominent organizations:* The history of this important group is detailed in this excellent paper: Henry Etzkowitz, "MIT Goes into Business: High-Tech Regional Economic Development and the Invention of the Venture Capital Firm; 1930–1960," academic paper.

76. *Compton proposed an ambitious program:* Karl T. Compton, "Science Still Holds a Great Promise," *New York Times Magazine,* December 16, 1934.

76. *the New England Council formed a committee:* Etzkowitz, "MIT Goes Into Business," 11–12.

76. *a mechanical engineer who rose:* Ralph E. Flanders, *Senator from Vermont* (New York: Little, Brown & Co., 1961).

77. *Doriot joined forces with another group:* The history of Enterprise Associates is detailed in this Doriot memo: "Notes used by GFD: Evening with first meeting of New England Venture Capital Association, Union Club, February 9, 1976," Patricia A. Clark papers.

77. *"[The Enterprise] experience made Merrill Griswold:* Ibid.

Chapter Six

79. *fascism was on the march:* Background on World War II comes from John Keegan's excellent book *The Second World War* (New York: Penguin Books, 1989).

79. *the paltry state of military aircraft production:* Doris Kearns Goodwin, *No Ordinary Time: Franklin and Eleanor Roosevelt: The Home Front in World War II* (New York: Touchstone, 1995), 44–57.

79. *he stopped by the French Embassy:* Claude Janssen, interview by author.

80. *"I'm sure that's why General Gregory":* "Outfitted to Fight in World War II," Lemelson Center of Smithsonian Institution, videotape of reunion of Military Planning Division of the Office of the Quartermaster General, August 1995.

80. *"Doriot started his venturing during the war":* Ray Hoagland, interview by author.

81. *asked Doriot to meet with President Roosevelt:* Arnaud de Vitry, interview by author.

81. *Doriot strolled into a federal court:* Personal history statement of Georges Doriot, LOC.

81. *"I believe the time has come":* E. B. Gregory, letter to Georges F. Doriot, December 28, 1940, LOC.

81. *Doriot was a hot property:* E. B. Gregory, letter to Georges Doriot, January 21, 1941, LOC.

81. *"I had several offers from different parts":* Georges F. Doriot, letter to Major General George A. Horkan, November 21, 1951, LOC.

82. *after he consulted with an attorney:* Ralph G. Boyd, letter to Georges Doriot, March 3, 1941, LOC.

82. *he passed his physical:* Georges Doriot, personal history file, LOC.

82. *he purchased $10,000 of life insurance:* Georges Doriot, personal history file for the military, LOC.

82. *Doriot was commissioned as a Lieutenant Colonel:* Captain Harold H. Salzer, letter to Lt. Col. Doriot, August 15, 1941, LOC.

82. *he and Edna discovered they needed:* Doriot, interview by Olsen.

82. *"That seemed to be a very extravagant":* Ibid.

83. *the Army was still relying on stockpiles:* Geoffrey Perett, *There's a War to Be Won: The United States Army in World War II* (New York: Random House, 1991), 35.

83. *"They didn't want to invest":* David M. Kennedy, *Freedom From Fear: The American People in Depression and War, 1929–1945* (New York: Oxford University Press, 1999), 477.

83. *when he joined the Procurement Branch:* Doriot's military assignments are detailed in these two documents: Georges Frederic Doriot, Army History, July 1, 1946, LOC; and Officer Qualifications Record, Armed Service Forces, LOC.

83. *Detroit was anticipating strong:* Kennedy, *Freedom From Fear,* 477.

83. *Doriot undertook a survey:* Georges Doriot, memo to Chief of Production Control Branch, September 10, 1941, LOC.

83. *"using a substantial part of the existing truck":* Ibid.

84. *The so-called Victory Program:* R. Elberton Smith, *U.S. Army in World War II: The Army and Economic Mobilization* (Washington, DC: Center of Military History U.S. Army, 1991), 133–137.

84. *The war's eventual cost was $304 billion:* Ibid., 4.

84. *some carmakers were failing to reach half:* Georges Doriot, telephone conversation with Major Thompson, November 13, 1941, LOC.

84. *gave rise to heavy demands:* Smith, *U.S. Army in World War II,* 29.

84. *"It is essential that our procurement"*: Robert P. Patterson, memo to the Chiefs of the Supply Arms and Services, December 8, 1941, LOC.

85. *"The situation is a very bad one"*: Georges Doriot, telephone conversation with Lt. Kuenning, December 27, 1941, LOC.

85. *he pestered a General Motors executive*: Georges Doriot, telephone conversation with Mr. Hoglund of General Motors, December 27, 1941, LOC.

85. *the Quartermaster General was able*: History of Quartermaster Research and Development in World War II (unpublished paper, University of Pittsburgh), 140. Doriot commissioned the university to write a history of the Quartermaster Corps because "he wanted a different perspective" from the official military history, according to Isabelle C. Pounder, the Quartermaster's liaison to the University of Pittsburgh.

86. *Doriot told Edna to come down:* Doriot, interview by Olsen.

86. *"After I removed the ferns"*: Georges F. Doriot, "Organization of Military Planning Division, OQMG," lecture delivered at the Army Industrial College February 13, 1946, LOC.

86. *the single most important factor shaping Quartermaster Corps*: Erna Risch, U.S. Army in World War II: The Quartermaster Corps: Organization, Supply and Services, vol. 1 (Washington, DC: Center of Military History U.S. Army, 1995), 58.

86. *rubber would be "exhausted by the middle of 1943"*: Production Branch, Planning and Control Division, memo on "Rubber Program" to Chief of Planning and Control Division, February 25, 1942, LOC.

87. *government implemented virtually every recommendation:* Details of the rubber program come from these two documents: "Special Report of the Rubber Director," July 25, 1944, GPO, War Board 12058, 2; and War Production Board, Office of Rubber Director, Progress Reports No. 1, GPO, War Board 2650, 3–5. Both found in LOC.

87. *President Roosevelt initiated a nationwide rubber drive:* Goodwin, No Ordinary Time, 357.

87. *the government invested about $700 million:* Kennedy, Freedom From Fear, 647–648.

87. *the War Department underwent a major reorganization:* Smith, U.S. Army in World War II, 112.

88. *were all combined in one place:* History of Quartermaster Research and Development in World War II, 140–150.

88. *war "is in reality applied science"*: Georges Doriot, "Quartermaster Corps Research in War and Peace," address to the National Academy of Sciences, April 24, 1944, LOC.

88. *Doriot organized an advisory board:* Risch, U.S. Army in World War II, 84.

88. *Researchers and executives from leading firms:* pamphlet issued by the Advisory Board to the Research and Development Branch of the Military Planning Division of the Office of the Quartermaster General, revised May 1, 1943.

88. *this was a "brilliant" idea:* Hobson, from "Outfitted to Fight in World War II," videocassette of reunion of the Military Planning Division of the Office of the Quartermaster General, Lemelson Center of Smithsonian Institution, 1995.

88. *Doriot enlisted a number of university laboratories:* Risch, U.S. Army in World War II, 84–85.

89. *Doriot heard from General Joseph W. Stilwell:* "In Memoriam: General Georges F. Doriot," DECWORLD, October 1987, 8–9.

89. *"We made jungle boots"*: McClean, from "Outfitted to Fight in World War II."

89. *"Between the fact that there was nobody available"*: Doriot, "Organization of Military Planning Division, OQMG."

89. *The Quartermaster Corps had three recruiting options:* Erna Risch and Chester L. Kieffer, U.S. Army in World War II: The Quartermaster Corps: Organization, Supply and Services, vol. 2 (Washington, DC: Center of Military History U.S. Army, 1995), 207.

89. *flipped open his extensive address book:* Doriot, "Organization of Military Planning Division, OQMG,"

90. *"I don't do the work"*: Kathleen Kennedy, "Did you Happen to See—Col. George Doriot?" publisher and date unknown, LOC.

90. *developing "Quartermaster items to meet the changing needs"*: History of Quartermaster Research and Development in World War II, 140–150.

90. *the military needed to be "prepared to fight in Maine"*: Georges Doriot, letter to General of the Army, Dwight D. Eisenhower, February 19, 1945, LOC.

90. *"He is probably the best manager"*: Heller, from "Outfitted to Fight in World War II."

91. *"The Army has no interest in the soldier"*: Doriot, "Organization of Military Planning Division, OQMG."

91. *Doriot once had a tank:* Marcia L. Lightbody, "Building a Future: World War II Quartermaster Corps," Military Review, January–February 2001.

91. *"It was such a feeling":* Isabelle C. Pounder, interview by author.

91. *"Everybody had to get past Harry":* Ray Hoagland, interview by author.

91. *"One of the wonderful peculiarities":* Orr, "Outfitted to Fight in World War II."

91. *an ambitious testing program run by the Special Forces:* Harlan Manchester, "Inventors and Fighters," *Atlantic Monthly,* July 1943, 43-47.

92. *the first ascent of Mt. McKinley since 1932:* Details of this wonderful story come from this article: Robert H. Bates, "Mt. McKinley 1942," *The American Alpine Journal* 5, no. 1 (1943)

93. *more than two thousand men and women: History of Quartermaster Research and Development in World War II,* 155.

93. *Edna was doing her part:* Doriot, interview by Olsen.

93. *except for one memorable night:* Ibid.

93–94. *the most critical and urgent problems:* Georges Doriot, "Quartermaster Corps Research in War and Peace," address to the National Academy of Science, April 24, 1944.

94. *had heretofore been attributed to "causes unknown":* Ibid.

94. *they found more useful as stove cleaner or hair rinse:* Geoffrey Perret, *There's A War to Be Won: The United States Army in World War II* (New York: Random House, 1991), 301.

94. *we made biscuits:* Ibid.

94. *the Quartermaster Corps developed eleven special rations:* "Quartermaster Corps Subsistence Research and Development Laboratory," manual published by the Office of the Quartermaster General, July 12, 1945, LOC.

95. *"Wot! No Camels?":* Perret, *There's a War To Be Won,* 301.

95. *shoes "were unfit for field use":* Major General W. D. Styer, memo to the Quartermaster General, "Suitability of Shoes at Present Furnished for Armed Forces," February 1, 1943, LOC.

95. *As shortages of leather, brass:* Risch, *U.S. Army in World War II,* 103.

95. *the Quartermaster had already initiated development:* Steps taken to design various Army shoes are outlined here: "Leather Footwear Specifications," April 12, 1945, LOC.

96. *"Your shoes only last 13 days in combat":* The story is described in Marcia L. Lightbody, "Building a Future: World War II Quartermaster Corps," *Military Review,* January–February 2001.

96. *A decision was made to shift production:* Risch, 104.

96. *deliveries of the 700,000 Type III service shoe:* "Leather Footwear Specifications," April 12, 1945, LOC.

96. *it was recommended that the boot include:* Ibid.

96. *the shoe industry began producing the combat boot:* Risch, *U.S. Army in World War II,* 104.

97. *or about 20 percent of its staff:* Georges Doriot, memo to General Barnes, "Curtailment of Non-Essential Development Projects and Reduction of Development Activities," September 3, 1943, LOC.

97. *recommended the name of "Doron":* Edmond C. Fetter, "Doron Armor: An Achievement and a Promise in Plastics," *Chemical & Metallurgical Engineering,* February 1946, 154–157.

97. *ordnance experts were bitterly opposed:* Edwin Hobson, letter to Georges Doriot, October 26, 1947, LOC.

97. *Rear Admiral Harold G. Bowen noticed:* "Plastic Body Armor Was To Be Worn by Marines in Invasion of Japan," press release by Navy Department, January 24, 1946, LOC.

98. *Colonel Doriot ordered his Plastics Section:* Ludlow King, "Lightweight Body Armor," *Ordnance,* January–February 1953, 694–695.

98. *the Army Air Force approved the establishment:* "Joint Army-Navy Plastic Armor Technical Committee," September 29, 1943, Records of the Office of the Quartermaster General, RG92, Formerly Classified General Correspondence, Box 6, National Archives.

98. *Doriot was elected chairman:* "Joint Army-Navy Plastic Armor Technical Committee Meeting," November 13, 1943, Records of the Office of the Quartermaster General, RG92, Formerly Classified General Correspondence, Box 6, National Acrhives.

98. *"But the Navy was kind enough":* Maurice Sagoff, "Gen. G. F. Doriot Outlines Armor Clothing's Beginning," date and publisher unknown, LOC.

98. *the Navy conducted a spectacular:* "Plastic Body Armor Was To Be Worn By Marines in Invasion of Japan," press release by Navy Department.

98. *"As a result of that, for one day":* Clowe, from "Outfitted to Fight in World War II."

99. *The Marine Corps equipped a whole battalion:* King, "Lightweight Body Armor."

99. *a spate of reports appeared:* Jack Bell, "G.I.s Seen Poorly Clad and Freezing; Eisenhower Admits 'Isolated Cases,'" *Daily News Foreign Service,* January 26, 1945; B. J. McQuaid, "Yanks Suffering from Cold, Lack of Proper Shoes," *Daily News Foreign Service,* February 2, 1945; Edward T. Folliard, "Trench Foot Scourge Ends, but Many Yanks Are Still Hospitalized," *Washington Post,* March 4, 1945.

99. *he pointed the finger:* Major General Robert Littlejohn, letter to Lt. General Brehon B. Somervell, March 2, 1945, papers of Stephen Anders U.S. Army Quartermaster Center and School, Ft. Lee, VA.

99. *Colonel Garside delivered a report:* A summary of the report is contained here: Colonel Charles Garside, letter to Brig. General Albert Browning, May 12, 1945, Anders papers.

100. *"American soldiers are suffering needlessly":* "Shoe Manufacturers Balk on Army Boots, Officer Tells Chamber," *Boston Daily Globe,* May 27, 1944,

100. *"has caused no end of unfavorable":* Col. W. J. Calvert, letter to Major General E. B. Gregory, June 1, 1944, LOC.

101. *"I believe [Doriot's] statements were correct":* Major General E. B. Gregory, letter to Col. W. J. Calvert, June 5, 1944, LOC.

101. *sent a secret radiogram:* Major General E. B. Gregory, letter to Asst. Chief of Staff, Operations Division, War Dept. General Staff, and Commanding General, Army Service Forces, May 25, 1944, LOC.

101. *would leave troops "without any garment":* Ibid.

101. *Troops had begun clamoring:* Perrett, *There's a War To Be Won,* 302.

101. *the General Staff reissued the order:* Col. Lee Denson, memo to Quartermaster General, "Change in Clothing Requirements for European Theater of Operations," June 9, 1944, LOC.

101. *European commanders reversed their decision:* "Summation of Action Taken With Reference to Winter Clothing & Equipment," part of a Special Report prepared for General E. B. Gregory by the Technical Information Branch of the Quartermaster Corps, November 1945, LOC.

101–102. *the European theatre advised the Quartermaster Corps:* Ibid.

102. *He was down to 138 pounds:* Personal history statement of Georges Doriot, LOC.

102. *the Military Planning Division limited its downward:* Georges Doriot, memo to Director of Procurement Division, "Constant Revisions of Master Production Schedules and the Effect on Supply," November 28, 1944, LOC.

102. *instead pushing through a huge requirement:* "Summation of Action Taken With Reference to Winter Clothing & Equipment."

102. *put pressure on the War Production Board:* Major William H. McClean, memo to Colonel Georges F. Doriot, "Weekly Report for Research & Development Branch for Week Ending 8/19/44," National Archives, RG92, Box 412.

102. *Doriot refused to approve:* Georges Doriot, memo to General Corbin, September 19, 1944, LOC.

102. *it was possible to fill:* "Summation of Action Taken With Reference to Winter Clothing & Equipment."

102. *Doriot received a stunning promotion:* Georges Frederic Doriot, Army history statement, July 1, 1946, LOC.

102. *General Eisenhower sent Doriot a note:* Georges Doriot, letter to General of the Army, Dwight D. Eisenhower, February 19, 1945, LOC.

103. *"We in the Military Planning Division":* Georges F. Doriot, memo to All Personnel, Military Planning Division, May 8, 1945, LOC.

103. *Doriot received the Distinguished Service Medal:* Georges Frederic Doriot, Army history statement.

103. *"His professional knowledge":* "Citation for Distinguished Service Medal," presented by the Quartermaster General, October 30, 1945, LOC.

103. *Doriot received dozens of letters:* Secretary of War Robert Patterson to Brig. General Georges Doriot, April 26, 1946, LOC. In this letter, Sec. Patterson said Doriot's contribution of "improved equipment, materials and supplies" to the Army "cannot be exaggerated" and that the "soldiers at the front fought better because of your work."

103. *"I want to congratulate you personally":* Major General R. B. McClure to Brig. General Georges Doriot, Headquarters Chinese Combat Command, United States Forces, China Theater, Office of the Commanding General, August 20, 1945, LOC.

Chapter Seven

105. *Doriot received a call from the Secretary:* Georges Doriot, interview by Aulikki Olsen, April 1980.

106. *distributed a visionary four-page:* Dwight D. Eisenhower, memo to Directors and Chiefs of War Department General and Special Staff Divisions and Bureaus and the Commanding Generals of Major Commands, War Department, Office of Chief of Staff, April 20, 1946, LOC.

106. *Doriot told Secretary Patterson:* Doriot, interview by Olsen.

106. *Doriot received another urgent call:* Ibid.

107. *MIT President Karl Compton dusted off his plans:* Karl T. Compton, letter to Georges Doriot, April 24, 1946, MIT Institute Archives and Special Collections, Office of the President, 1930–1959, AC4, Box 74.

107. *On June 6, 1946, the American Research and Development Corporation:* American Research & Development, 1946 Annual Report, GFD.

107. *Early in 1946 two wealthy East coast families:* "Dynasties Unify" *BusinessWeek*, June 15, 1946, 21–22.

108. *Flanders, in the midst of running:* Karl T. Compton, letter to Georges Doriot, May 10 1946, MIT Institute Archives and Special Collections, Office of the President, 1930–1959, AC4, Box 74.

109. *"We have the [greatest] number of possibilities for new investments":* Patrick R. Liles, *Sustaining the Venture Capital Firm* (Cambridge, MA: Management Analysis Center, 1977), 28.

109. *"trying desperately to become poor businessmen":* Jim Mossman, *Panorama*, n.d., Harvard, James Aisner papers.

110. *it had to obtain a number of exemptions:* "Research Venture Gets SEC Blessing," *New York Times*, August 9, 1946, 31.

110. *one of its board members, attorney Warren Motley:* Joel Seligman, *The Transformation of Wall Street: A History of the Securities and Exchange Commission and Modern Corporate Finance* (Boston: Northeastern University Press, 1995), 229.

110. *This would have precluded the Massachusetts Investors Trust:* Martha Louise Reiner, *The Transformation of Venture Capital: A History of Venture Capital Organizations in the United States* (PhD diss., University of California, Berkeley, 1989), 171–173.

110. *The most important exemptions permitted ARD:* Francis Bello, "The Prudent Boston Gamble," *Fortune*, November 1952.

110. *with at least half of that coming from institutions:* Liles, *Sustaining the Venture Capital Firm*, 35.

110. *mounted a successful campaign to relax the laws of these states:* Donald K. David, letter to Merrill Griswold, September 19, 1945, Office of the Dean (Donald K. David) Records, 1919–1942, Baker Library, Harvard Business School; Merrill Griswold, letter to Donald K. David, September 26, 1945, Office of the Dean (Donald K. David) Records, 1919–1942, Baker Library, Harvard Business School.

111. *The formation of ARD was covered:* "Venture Enterprise of Unusual Management," *Boston Herald*, August 14, 1946, "Boston Firm Plans Public Offer As S.E.C. Frees Venture Capital," *New York Herald Tribune*, September 9, 1946; "Adventure Capital," *BusinessWeek*, August 17, 1946.

111. *The extraordinary results of wartime technology:* Reiner, *The Transformation of Venture Capital*, 54–62.

111. *By 1943, the Office of Scientific Research and Development alone:* "Science Dons a Uniform," *BusinessWeek*, September 14, 1946, 19–22.

112. *ARD's stock offering nearly failed:* Liles, *Sustaining the Venture Capital Firm*, 37.

112. *were it not for a last-minute subscription by Lessing Rosenwald:* "Venture Capital," *Fortune*, 1949.

112. *By the end of December 1946:* Liles, *Sustaining the Venture Capital Firm*, 38.

112. *Projects should have passed the "test-tube" stage:* American Research & Development, 1946 Annual Report, GFD.

112. *"ARD does not invest in the ordinary sense":* Ibid.

112. *"People ask me how we can do the work we do":* Personal notes, GFD.

113. *ARD's staff rejected proposals:* "Enterprise: Yankee Dollar," *Newsweek*, February 3, 1947.

113. *"It made his notes and comments":* Marvin S. Traub, interview by author.

113. *ARD had done enough work to plow money:* American Research & Development, 1947 Annual Report, GFD.

113. *on the verge of bankruptcy when ARD came to its rescue:* "Atomic Offspring," *Time*, September 12, 1949.

114. *ARD ended its first year in the red:* American Research & Development, 1947 Annual Report, GFD.

114. *"It wasn't a question of who has control":* Gene Bylinsky, "General Doriot's Dream Factory," *Fortune*, August 1967, 103–136.

114. *ARD invested nearly $880,000 in five new companies:* American Research & Development, 1948 Annual Report, GFD.

115. *he remained an active participant in the highest levels:* Tours of Active Duty, General Georges F. Doriot, personal papers, LOC.

115. *The overall aim of the JRDB:* Karl T. Compton, memo to L. J. Henderson Jr., "The Joint Research and Development Board Committee on Guided Missiles," February 4, 1947, LOC; Georges Doriot, memo to Arthur E. Raymond, "Study and recommendations as to the most suitable system for active defense of the U.S. against attack," February 25, 1947, LOC.

116. *when he was appointed Brigadier General:* Major General Edward F. Witsell, memo to Brigadier General Georges Frederic Doriot, "Appointment," Adjutant General's Office, War Department, February 27, 1947, LOC.

116. *Reading the writing on the wall:* Vannevar Bush, letter to Brigadier General Georges Doriot, June 20, 1947, LOC

116. *Doriot became entangled in the most bizarre:* An excellent synopsis of the history of the Quartermaster Research Lab is found in the Congressional Record, 82nd Cong., House Armed Forces Committee, March 25, 1952, "Quartermaster Research Laboratory in Natick, Mass."

116. *"The last time we knew of anything comparable":* Merrill Griswold, letter to Georges Doriot, October 25, 1945, MIT Institute Archives and Special Collections, Office of the President, 1930–1959, AC4, Box 103.

117. *would be placed upon [Doriot's] personal recommendation:* Letter from Georges Doriot to Merrill Griswold and William C. Hammond Jr., October 25, 1945, MIT Institute Archives and Special Collections, Office of the President, 1930-1959, AC4, Box 103.

117. *"Boston was selected due to your":* Major General T. B. Larkin, letter to Georges Doriot, July 3, 1947, Office of the Quartermaster General, War Department, LOC.

117. *Hugh D. Scott said the Boston plan should be labeled:* "Philadelphia Fights Boston Army Laboratory, Sees Its Weather Rugged as New England's," *Boston Herald*, February 19, 1948.

117. *Doriot confronted Congressman Scott:* Georges Doriot, letter to Senator Ralph Flanders, June 8, 1948, LOC; Bradley Dewey, telephone conversation with Secretary of Defense James V. Forrestal, June 9, 1948, LOC.

118. *the firm found a new venture it deemed worth backing:* American Research & Development, 1948 Annual Report, GFD.

118. *struck up a conversation with a friend:* Walter Juda, interview by author.

118. *"Our new method focused on removing":* Ibid.

119. *Tracerlab sales more than doubled to $700,000:* American Research & Development, 1948 Annual Report, GFD.

120. *After investing $100,000 in Mississippi car parts maker:* American Research & Development, 1949 Annual Report, GFD.

120. *"In less than three years":* *BusinessWeek*, February 19, 1949, 3.

120. *The offering enabled Tracerlab:* "Atomic Offspring."

120. *ARD could still not find an investment bank:* Liles, *Sustaining the Venture Capital Firm*, 47–50.

120. *"I am afraid that, as usual, people believe in venture capital":* Georges Doriot, letter to Senator Ralph Flanders, May 11, 1949, GFD.

121. *Doriot's office was small but finely furnished:* Harold Evans with Gail Buckland and David Lefer, *They Made America* (New York: Little, Brown & Company, 2004), 302.

121. *"The hardest task is to help a company through its growth pains":* GFD.

122. *ARD acquired voting control of the company:* Bello, "The Prudent Boston Gamble,"

122. *ARD ended its third full year of operations:* American Research & Development, 1949 Annual Report, GFD.

123. *The first of these boards was formed:* American Research & Development, 1950 Annual Report, GFD.

123. *"Most of the young men who came to ARD":* William Elfers, interview by author.

124. *"It looked to me like an adventure":* Ibid.

124. *Elfers found himself as Flexible Tubing's new director:* William Elfers, *Greylock: An Adventure Capital Story* (Boston: Greylock Management Corporation, 1995), 4–5.

124. *"The successful fulfillment of this assignment":* Ibid.

125. *"Doriot wanted the political connections that Harry had":* Ray Hoagland, interview by author.

125. *Doriot didn't think a thing of California:* Ibid.

125. *No. 251 envisioned a "rocket auto":* Bello, "The Prudent Boston Gamble."

125. *ARD picked five companies to back:* American Research & Development, 1950 Annual Report, GFD.

126. *"Never go into venture capital":* Georges F. Doriot, address before the Life Insurance Association of America, June 2, 1950, Atlantic City, NJ.

126. *The first harvest came for ARD:* American Research & Development, 1951 Annual Report, GFD.

126. *"I realize that you were the subject":* Major General George A. Horkan, letter to Georges Doriot, April 11, 1952, LOC.

126. *"This laboratory can be very outstanding":* Georges Doriot, letter to Ass. Sec. of Army Karl R. Bendetsen, April 28, 1952, LOC.

127. *By the end of 1951, combined sales:* American Research & Development, 1951 Annual Report, GFD.

127. *the bid prices for ARD shares drifted:* Liles, *Sustaining the Venture Capital Firm*, 58.

Chapter Eight

129. *professor, showing everyone who was boss:* John A. Shane, interview by author.

129. *"I shall do all the talking": Georges Doriot, Man with a Vision* (Cambridge, MA: Peace River Films, 1987), DVD.

129. *"If you ask most any Harvard Business School graduate":* Marvin S. Traub, interview by author.

130. *Some of Doriot's colleagues derisively referred:* Author unknown, obtained from anonymous review comments on this book.

130. *"It was a true energy sink":* John A. Shane, interview by author.

130. *"The word 'administration' to me indicates something static":* Jim Mossman, *Panorama,* n.d., Harvard, James Aisner papers.

131. *"U.S. Steel does not know what business they are in":* Peter Fuhrman, "A Teacher Who Made a Difference," *Forbes,* July 13, 1987.

131. *"write a report on a subject of your own choosing":* "General Doriot's Topic Reports," *HBS Bulletin,* June 1963, 12.

131. *"These things allowed you to see":* Ralph P. Hoagland, interview by author.

132. *"In the first half of the year, they study these companies":* Jim Mossman, *Panorama,* n.d., Harvard, James Aisner papers.

132. *"Doriot was the only one who brought students outside the school":* Arnaud de Vitry, interview by author.

132. *Marvin Traub teamed up with two of his best buddies:* Marvin Traub, speech delivered at a tribute to Georges Doriot, French Library, Boston, October 8, 2005.

132. *"The only brewery in the United States":* Sumner Feldberg, Marvin Traub, and Wilbur Cowett, "The Croft Brewing Company," 1948, Wilbur Cowett papers, New York.

132. *"We ended up saying as nicely":* Marvin Traub, speech.

133. *"dignity or a substance to the process":* Arnold Kroll, interview by author.

133. *This year, MIT president Karl Compton spoke:* Georges Doriot, letter to Senator Ralph Flanders, February 25, 1952, MIT Institute Archives and Special Collections, Office of the President, 1930–1959, MC495, Box 1.

133. *"We all loved going to these meetings":* Parker G. Montgomery, interview by author.

134. *"The only aspect of Women's Lib":* Gloria Nagel, "Women in Business—Dorothy E. Rowe," *Boston Evening Globe,* June 21, 1972.

134. *"Business was her whole thing":* Brian Brooks, interview by author.

134. *Ionics took full advantage:* William L. Laurence, "New Process Desalts Seawater; Promises to Help Arid Areas," *New York Times,* February 21, 1952.

135. *Senator Flanders received a visit from Sheridan Downey:* Senator Ralph Flanders, letter to Georges Doriot, February 29, 1952, MIT Institute Archives and Special Collections, Office of the President, 1930-1959, MC495, Box 1.

135. *ARD ended 1952 reporting a 50 percent jump:* American Research & Development, 1952 Annual Report, GFD.

136. *skeptics, particularly stockbrokers, believed:* Francis Bello, "The Prudent Boston Gamble," *Fortune,* November 1952.

136. *the ARD board was conflicted over the topic of dividends:* Georges Doriot, letter to Merrill Griswold, December 23, 1952, GFD, Book 2, 6.

136. *in February of 1953 Doriot created:* "They're Products of the Future," *BusinessWeek,* February 28, 1953, 99–101.

137. *In the middle of 1953, Harry Hoagland set off:* Christopher Hartman, *Advance Man: The Life and Times of Harry Hoagland* (Boston: Newberry Street Press, 2005), 69–70.

137. *ARD that year had only invested in two other new situations:* American Research & Development, 1953 Annual Report, GFD.

138. *Doriot set down his thoughts on the state of the industry:* "Re venture capital," November 1953, GFD, 7c.

138. *It is interesting to see how the great interest that existed:* Ibid.

138. *ARD's stock price hit an all-time low:* Patrick R. Liles, *Sustaining the Venture Capital Firm* (Cambridge, MA: Management Analysis Center, 1977), 62.

138–139. *ARD also reported the second biggest write-off:* American Research & Development, 1954 Annual Report, GFD.

139. *We do not know of any interesting new projects:* Georges Doriot, note to himself, May 1954, GFD.

139. *ARD received an average of 382 projects per year:* "Project analysis," Project Summaries, GFD.

139. *But in the beginning of 1954, Doriot mused:* Georges Doriot, letter to Ralph H. Demmler, March 24, 1954, GFD.

139. *the SEC's enforcement and policy-making powers:* Joel Seligman, *The Transformation of Wall Street: A History of the Securities and Exchange Commission and Modern Corporate Finance* (Boston: Northeastern University Press, 1995), 265–272.

140. *"I wonder if our personnel and directors":* Georges Doriot, letter to Ralph H. Demmler, March 24, 1954, GFD.

140. *Doriot grew worried over proposed changes:* Georges Doriot, letter to Senator Ralph Flanders, May 4, 1954, GFD.

140. *"When I first started teaching":* Ibid.

140. *"In the passing of Dr. Karl T. Compton":* American Research & Development, 1954 Semi-Annual Report, GFD.

141. *"the original investments are somewhat more seasoned":* C. E. Unterberg, Towbin Co., research note, "American Research and Development Corporation," March 1954, MIT Institute Archives and Special Collections, Office of the President, 1930–1959, MC495.

141. *"Although continued growth is likely":* H. Hentz & Co., "American Research and Development Corporation," April 15, 1954, MIT Institute Archives and Special Collections, Office of the President, 1930–1959, MC495.

142. *In late July, representatives from the Chamber of Commerce:* The history of INSEAD is expertly told in Jean-Louis Barsoux, *Insead: From Intuition to Institution* (New York: St. Martin's Press, 2000). Another important source was "Notes on the Creation of INSEAD," April 1976, GFD.

142. *Doriot granted a temporary leave of absence:* Leonard Hall, letter to Georges Doriot, October 19, 1954, LOC.

142. *Both men took Doriot's Manufacturing class:* A list of Doriot's 6,000+ students is detailed in "The Former Students of Professor Georges F. Doriot," Ralph Soda papers.

143. *ARD ended 1954 on a positive note:* American Research & Development, 1954 Annual Report, GFD.

143. *"I believe that the support which you have given":* General Leslie R. Groves, letter to Georges Doriot, February 16, 1955, LOC.

143. *"It was nice to hear from you":* President Dwight D. Eisenhower, letter to Georges Doriot, February 16, 1955, LOC.

143. *"come to an informal stag dinner":* President Dwight D. Eisenhower, letter to Georges Doriot, February 21, 1955, LOC.

143. *In 1947, Edna became a secretary of the French Library:* Résumé of Edna Allen, August 1, 1978, GFD.

144. *"I was always very fond":* Janet Testa, interview by author.

144. *After questioning Edna's decision:* Georges Doriot, interview by Aulikki Olsen, April 1980.

144. *it looked and felt like a castle:* Details based on tour of home given by James M. Stone in October 2005.

144. *"This is where he came to sit":* James M. Stone, interview by author.

145. *Georges took the squares of blue paper:* Patricia A. Clark, interview by author.

145. *Sell when "hope seems gone":* "When to Sell," March 1959, GFD.

145. *In 1955, ARD received nearly $1.4 million:* American Research & Development, 1955 Annual Report, GFD.

145. *In 1955, after nine long years, MIT:* "MIT Report of the Treasurer," 1946–1956, MIT Institute Archives and Special Collections.

145. *Doriot wrote that Ford was a "weak and uninteresting man":* Personal notes, GFD.

146. *In the first half of 1956, ARD:* American Research & Development, 1956 Annual Report, GFD.

Chapter Nine

147. *"We felt electronics was going to revolutionize industry":* Ken Olsen, oral history interview by David Allison, Division of Information Technology & Society, National Museum of American History, Smithsonian Institution, September 28, 29, 1988. While working on the book, Ken Olsen became ill and his memory began to fade. Thus, this superb interview was crucial in my telling of the Digital story.

148. *as "a guy who gets things done":* Some of the early history of MIT's Lincoln Laboratory comes from this excellent book by Glenn Rifkin and George Harrar, *The Ultimate Entrepreneur: The Story of Ken Olsen and Digital Equipment Corporation* (Chicago: Contemporary Books, 1993), 16–24.

148. *"There was a lot of trust, a lot of freedom":* Olsen, interview by Allison.

148. *"The books written before those years":* Ibid.

149. *"The reason for building the TX-O":* Ibid.

149. *In the end, "nobody cared":* Ibid.

149. *"A number of companies had started":* Ibid.

149. *"They turned us down flat":* Harlan Anderson, oral history interview by Gardner Hendrie, Computer History Museum, May 15, 2006.

149. *"We were pretty naïve":* Harlan Anderson, interview by author. There are several accounts of how Digital and ARD initially came to know each other. Some ARD alumni claim that ARD staffers reached out to Olsen and Anderson, while other accounts, such as *The Ultimate Entrepreneur*, claim Olsen and Anderson read about ARD in an electronics trade publication. I chose to use the story told to me by Harlan Anderson. In any case, the far more important issue is what happened *after* the two groups came together.

149. *The General turned over the proposal:* Rifkin and Harrar, *The Ultimate Entrepreneur*, 12.

149–150. *submit a more formal business plan:* Ibid.

150. *on April 22, they wrote Congleton:* Kenneth H. Olsen and Harlan E. Anderson, letter to William H. Congleton, April 22, 1957, Collection of the Computer History Museum, Mountain View, CA.

150. *ARD invited Olsen and Anderson:* Rifkin and Harrar, *The Ultimate Entrepreneur*, 13.

150. *"They clearly wanted to discuss it":* Anderson, interview by author.

151. *"I told the General":* Arnaud de Vitry, interview by author.

151. *"We thought we could succeed":* Anderson, interview by Hendrie.

151. *Seven hundred of the one thousand founding shares:* Rifkin and Harrar, *The Ultimate Entrepreneur*, 14.

151. *he insisted on meeting privately with the wives:* Anderson, interview by author.

151–152. *"You never had much in the Depression":* Olsen, interview by Allison.

152. *"The vital problem facing the nation":* William L. Laurence, "Soviet Success in Rocketry Draws Attention to Need for More Students in the Sciences," *New York Times*, October 13, 1957, Week in Review section.

152. *"Sputnik was a wake-up call":* Anderson, interview by author.

152. *Sputnik also galvanized public support:* Martha Louise Reiner, *The Transformation of Venture Capital: A History of Venture Capital Organizations in the United States* (PhD diss., University of California, Berkeley, 1989), 276.

153. *By 1967, 791 licensed SBICs had invested:* Ibid., 281.

153. *"It formed the seed":* Ibid., 332–333.

153. *"We miss projects":* "Additional Capital," note, 1957, GFD.

153. *To raise more money, Doriot proposed:* Ibid.

154. *"The General said he liked":* Dina McCabe, interview by author.

154. *"We got along well":* Robert McCabe, interview by author.

154. *"I am glad":* Robert Lehman, letter to Georges Doriot, January 6, 1958, LOC.

154–155. *"It was all kind of subtle":* Vernon Alden, interview by author.

155. *"I was astonished":* Ibid.

155. *"This was all news":* Ibid.

155. *"They gave their time":* "Notes on the Creation of INSEAD," April 1976, GFD.

156. *"Doriot considered me":* Claude Janssen, interview by author.

156. *"I had easy access to him":* Ibid.

156. *"I had just started my business career":* Ibid.

156. *"Olivier's brother":* Ibid.

156. *"The school was a virtual entity":* Jean-Louis Barsoux, *Insead: From Intuition to Institution* (New York: St. Martin's Press, 2000), 25.

157. *Olsen and Anderson ran a shoestring operation:* Rifkin and Harrar, *The Ultimate Entrepreneur*, 29.

158. *"We had so much confidence in MIT":* Olsen, interview by Allison.

158. *"The potential customers":* Ibid.

158. *"I was one of his best students":* Ted Johnson, interview by author.

158. *Johnson had made an immediate impression:* Ibid.

158. *"People would not work for small companies":* Ibid.

158. *"Harlan Anderson turned around":* Ibid

159. *so he visited Doriot:* Ibid.

159. *"I'm sorry to see this":* Rifkin and Harrar, *The Ultimate Entrepreneur*, 32.

159. *"Our troubles have been principally human ones"*: Everett M. Smith, "AR&D Risk Pioneering Told," *Boston Science Monitor*, March 17, 1959.

160. *many ARD affiliates were attracting increasing interest*: American Research & Development, 1958 Annual Report, GFD.

160. *"we will make an informal"*: Edward C. Gray, letter to Georges F. Doriot, August 26, 1959, GFD.

161. *Doriot headed back to France*: Barsoux, *Insead* 39–49.

162. *"It was terrible"*: Janssen, interview by author.

162. *Janssen and his two associates cabled Doriot*: Barsoux, *Insead*, 49.

162. *Doriot raised $122,650, or 18 percent*: "Notes on the Creation of INSEAD," April 1976, GFD.

162. *"The President extends"*: Barsoux, *Insead*, 54.

162. *"One of the ideas of INSEAD"*: Janssen, interview by author.

163. *"He was moved"*: Ibid.

163. *ARD set off on an investment spree*: American Research & Development, 1959 Annual Report, GFD.

163. *"The concept of an interactive computer"*: Olsen, interview by Allison.

164. *The company accepted an offer*: R. G. Letourneau Inc., letter to Zapata Off-Shore Company, Contract for "Mobile Offshore Platform," January 22, 1957, George Bush personal papers, Zapata Oil Files, George Bush Presidential Library.

164. *"The majority of the Zapata Petroleum board"*: George H. W. Bush, memo to Robert Goodyear, March 20, 1959, George Bush personal papers, Zapata Oil Files, Business Correspondence Files, Box 3.

164. *"shrewd utilization of offshore subsidiaries"*: Kevin Phillips, *American Dynasty: Aristocracy, Fortune, and the Politics of Deceit in the House of Bush* (New York: Viking, 2004), 121–124.

164. *"I have heard a good deal"*: George H. W. Bush, letter to Georges Doriot, November16, 1959, George Bush personal papers, Zapata Oil Files, Business Correspondence Files, Box 3.

165. *the military informed him*: Colonel Dan Gilmer, letter to Brigadier General Georges Doriot, September 11, 1959, Headquarters XIII, U.S. Army Corps (Reserve), LOC.

165. *ARD had considered forming a second investment company*: "Proposed Smith Barney–American Research Period II Fund," GFD.

165. *"I think the best way to get across the story of Zapata"*: George H. W. Bush, letter to General Doriot, January 27, 1960, George Bush personal papers, Zapata Oil Files, Business Correspondence Files, Box 4.

166. *"He was very nervous before teaching"*: Charles P. Waite, interview by author.

166. *"It used to make a lot of people mad"*: Ibid.

166. *"It was a remarkable experience"*: Ibid.

166. *"That's how I got started"*: Ibid.

166. *"When I came to ARD in 1960"*: "Charles Waite: Greylock Management," in *Done Deals: Venture Capitalists Tell Their Stories*, ed. Udayan Gupta (Boston: Harvard Business School Press, 2000), 224.

167. *"It was a fourth-rate company"*: Waite, interview by author.

167. *"They played a pretty important role"*: Ibid.

167. *"These computers were so captivating"*: Olsen, interview by Allison.

168. *"Fundamentally, I was sold"*: Gordon Bell, interview by author.

168. *"There was something really nice"*: Ibid.

168. *He built a snow blower*: William P. Murphy, interview by author.

169. *"I came to admire Doriot enormously"*: Ibid.

169. *"Charlie Waite pointed out"*: Ibid.

169. *The story of this "Back Bay parvenu"*: David A. Loehwing, "Investment Pioneer," *Barron's*, September 26, 1960.

170. *"I always thought I was pretty wild"*: Alex d'Arbeloff, interview by author.

170. *DeWolf hatched a plan*: Nick DeWolf, interview with author.

170. *The rest came from friends and family*: Ibid.

170. *"Most of us were very young"*: Ibid.

170. *Doriot invited them over to the ARD office*: Ibid.

171. *"Our balance sheet looked awful"*: Ibid.

171. *"We had an amazingly warm faith"*: Ibid.

171. *ARD invested $2 million in nine companies*: American Research & Development, 1961 Annual Report, GFD.

172. *"It was a good housekeeping seal"*: John A. Shane, interview by author.

172. *I started to parade down to ARD*: Ibid.

172. *"I liked the people":* Ibid.

172. *he delivered an extraordinary address:* "Creative Capital," a speech delivered by Georges Doriot, March 9, 1961, GFD.

173. *"spectacular rise" of "growth and glamour stocks":* "Yankee Tinkerers," *Time,* July 26, 1960.

173. *it was posted there to "scare":* Personal notes, GFD.

174. *ARD's holdings are "valued very high":* "Re Valuation—board meeting" April 12 1961, GFD.

174. *Doriot was not sure it could "cope with the problems":* Ibid.

174. *Congress added 250 new employees to the SEC's staff:* Joel Seligman, *The Transformation of Wall Street: A History of the Securities and Exchange Commission and Modern Corporate Finance* (Boston: Northeastern University Press, 1995), 291.

174. *"these glamorous sounding companies":* "S.E.C. Head Urges Wall Street Inquiry," *New York Times,* June 27, 1961.

Chapter Ten

175. *he asked only the fiancées and wives of his students to attend: Georges F. Doriot Manufacturing Class Notes Harvard Business School 1927–1966* (Boston: Board of Trustees, French Library in Boston, 1993), 162–166.

175. *"Everybody was sort of a bit petrified":* Molly Hoagland, interview by author.

176. *"It was all these mannerly things":* Ibid.

176. *"How was it?" he asked his wife:* James F. Morgan, interview by author.

177. *"We chatted about things," says Sutton:* Gerald D. Sutton, interview by author.

177. *"He would put an accent on a word":* Ibid.

177. *When Sutton returned to Canada:* Gerald D. Sutton, *A Little Bit of Luck* (unpublished memoir), 142–146.

178. *"We went back with some enthusiasm":* Derek Mather, interview by author.

178. *Digital had become ARD's most valuable affiliate:* American Research & Development, 1962 Annual Report, GFD.

179. *buy "twenty-cylinder Cadillacs":* Gene Bylinsky, "General Doriot's Dream Factory," *Fortune,* August 1967.

179. *"Doriot said don't just lay a circuit board on a desk":* Anderson, interview by author.

179. *"The General had more influence":* Jack Shields, interview by author.

179. *"He was always there as a mentor and a help":* Ken Olsen, oral history interview by David Allison, Division of Information Technology & Society, National Museum of American History, Smithsonian Institution, September 28–29, 1988.

179. *"I think the General had a very profound":* Ted Johnson, interview by author.

180. *"[ARD] wouldn't buy and sell companies":* Ibid.

180. *"Production shipments of our new computer":* Ken Olsen, letter to Georges Doriot, February 27, 1962, Olsen papers, Gordon College, Wenham, MA.

180. *In August of 1961, Doriot had begun sounding out:* "Notes with reference to proposed European Research and Development" and "Exhibit A: Proposed Company in Europe," GFD.

181. *"He felt that venture capital":* John A. Shane, interview by author.

181. *"One talks about 'Europe as such'":* "Notes with reference to proposed European Research and Development," GFD.

181. *As long as the "underwriting activities of ERD are* de minimis": Alan R. Gordon, letter to John Barnard, August 7, 1962, GFD.

181. *"Creative ability knows no boundaries":* "Annual Meeting, March 6, 1963," GFD.

182. *"EED was surrounded by a board of bankers":* Arnaud de Vitry, interview by author.

182. *Time magazine ran a story:* "The Profit-Minded Professor," *Time,* May 8, 1963.

183. *"The SEC was the General's bête noire":* Patricia A. Clark, interview by author.

183. *"It appears that there would be conflicts":* Allan F. Conwill, letter to Georges Doriot, November 7, 1963, GFD.

183. *"I often wish that options had never been invented":* Georges Doriot, letter to Allan F. Conwill, November 29, 1963, GFD.

184. *"Companies come to ARD for financing":* Dorothy Rowe, letter to Joel Harvey, December 3, 1963, GFD.

184. *he typed up a blistering three-page memo:* "Proposed memo to SEC, May 1964, not sent," GFD.

185. *"He took the time to study our problems"*: Personal notes, GFD.

185. *"They fully expected that we were here"*: Details of the SEC surprise audit come from this letter: Georges Doriot, letter to Robert J. Routier, October 22, 1965, GFD.

186. *"He was always meowing about the SEC"*: Brian Brooks, interview by author.

187. *It was fighting through another wave of growing pains*: Glenn Rifkin and George Harrar, *The Ultimate Entrepreneur: The Story of Ken Olsen and Digital Equipment Corporation* (Chicago: Contemporary Books, 1993), 51–57.

187. *"You are right in your assumption"*: Nathan M. Pusey, letter to Georges Doriot, March 22, 1965, LOC.

187. *"His ideas on doing business"*: "Idealist—with a Realistic Touch," *BusinessWeek*, March 20, 1965, 166–169.

188. *"The Commission has instructed me to advise you"*: Solomon Freedman, letter to John W. Belash, March 26, 1965, GFD.

188. *"never did work out very well"*: Shane, interview by author.

188. *"Jim and I stood there waiting for the General's arrival"*: Address by Samuel W. Bodman at the tribute to Georges Doriot, October 2005.

189. *"The examination of the books and records"*: Robert J. Routier, letter to Georges Doriot, October 1, 1965, GFD.

190. *Elfers was sure the directors*: William Elfers, *Greylock: An Adventure Capital Story* (Boston: Greylock Management Corporation, 1995), 4.

190. *"Doriot did not like to make decisions"*: Charles P. Waite, interview by author.

190. *"There was nobody more qualified than Bill Elfers"*: Shane, interview by author.

190. *"The perfect one to have run ARD"*: Waite, interview by author.

191. *Elfers left ARD to form his own venture capital partnership*: Details on the founding of Greylock come from Elfers, *Greylock*.

191. *"I knew Doriot wasn't perfect"*: William Elfers, interview by author.

191. *"Why is there need for revaluation?"*: Georges Doriot, letter to Robert J. Routier, October 22, 1965, GFD.

192. *"Young people at our firm"*: Robert McCabe, interview by author.

192. *"That basically made the deal"*: Morgan, interview by author.

192. *"I am delighted to know"*: Robert Lehman, letter to Georges Doriot, October 11, 1965, LOC.

192. *Digital unveiled the PDP-8*: Rifkin and Harrar, *The Ultimate Entrepreneur*, 70–72.

193. *thanks to a new organizational structure*: Ibid., 57.

193. *But after General Doriot pressed him for four hours*: Ibid., 63–64.

193. *"Our biggest hurdle usually is convincing them"*: David A. Loehwing, "Investment Pioneer," *Barron's*, September 26, 1960.

194. *one investor did not buy it*: "Holder Assails Policies of American Research," *Wall Street Journal*, March 3, 1966, 9.

194. *"A new board of directors"*: Ibid.

194. *McCabe chose two other bankers*: McCabe, interview by author.

194. *"I was a young associate"*: Arnold Kroll, interview by author.

195. *"It was incredibly important"*: Shields, interview by author.

195. *"Clearly, General Doriot was a visionary"*: Andrew G. C. Sage II, interview by author.

195. *"I came away with the feeling"*: Kroll, interview by author.

195. *"People got very intrigued by it"*: Robert Shapiro, interview with author.

196. *"It was near death"*: Waite, interview by author.

196. *"It didn't seem like it was that big a deal"*: Winston Hindle, interview by author.

196. *the shares fell in over-the-counter trading*: National Quotation Bureau, *The National Monthly Stock Summary*, April 1, 1967.

196. *"Some of the people"*: Johnson, interview by author.

196. *"The General joked with me"*: McCabe, interview by author.

197. *"The first meeting with security analysts"*: Morgan, interview by author.

197. *By March of 1967 Digital shares topped $50*: Standard & Poor's Daily Stock Price Record, 4th quarter 1966 to 4th quarter 1980.

197. *"There's no question"*: Waite, interview by author.

197. *"I'd say it was a sea change"*: Morgan, interview by author.

198. *"Doriot was very important"*: Kroll, interview by author.

Chapter Eleven

199. *"Remember that our happiness"*: Georges F. Doriot Manufacturing Class Notes Harvard Business School *1927–1966* (Boston: Board of Trustees, French Library in Boston, 1993), 177.

200. *ARD met Doriot's goal of generating superior performance*: Patrick R. Liles, *Sustaining the Venture Capital Firm* (Cambridge, MA: Management Analysis Center, 1977), 83.

200. *the sixty-five-mile highway surrounding:* : Henry R. Lieberman, "Technology: Alchemist of Route 128," *New York Times*, January 8, 1968, 139. This article cites a 1967 Commerce Department study, which concluded that Boston was "at the head of the list of American cities credited with generating many new technologically based companies. The other cities were Palo Alto, Calif., Washington and Pittsburgh."

201. *"I had made a very substantial contribution"*: "Charles Waite: Greylock Management," in *Done Deals: Venture Capitalists Tell Their Stories*, ed. Udayan Gupta (Boston: Harvard Business School Press, 2000), 232.

201. *he asked Doriot for permission*: William Elfers, *Greylock: An Adventure Capital Story* (Boston: Greylock Management Corporation, 1995), 24.

202. *"It didn't matter when it was dimes and nickels"*: John A. Shane, interview by author.

202. *Congress, however, wrote an exception*: "America Research and Development Corporation Explanatory Statement Relative to Federal Income Tax Status," GFD, January 1967.

202. *"It presently is unclear"*: Ibid.

202. *"It is strange to believe that ARD stockholders should suffer"*: Personal notes, GFD August 1967.

202. *Lybrand, Ross Brothers & Montgomery recommended*: Lybrand, Ross Brothers & Montgomery, letter to Georges Doriot, August 31, 1967, GFD.

202. *"in an era of breathtaking change"*: U.S. Select Committee on Small Business in the United States Senate, The Status and Future of Small Business in the American Economy, 90th Congress, 1st session, March 1, 2, 3, 6, 8, 9, 14, 1967.

203. *"We do have some problems there"*: Ibid., 162.

203. *Doriot devoted the bulk of his statement*: Ibid., 163–170.

203. *"The General interviewed"*: Janet Testa, interview by author.

203. *ARD formed American Enterprise Development Corporation*: Richard J. Testa, letter to Dorothy Rowe, May 22, 1968, GFD.

204. *Doriot invited a few dozen friends*: Robert McCabe, interview by author.

204. *Doriot took action to stem*: Notes for ARD Board Meeting, January 1968, GFD.

205. *"Those two companies and ARD"*: Transcript of ARD Annual Meeting, March 1969, GFD.

205. *"the climate is favorable for passage"*: William T. Barnes, letter to Georges Doriot, August 13, 1968, GFD.

206. *the SEC turned up the heat on Doriot*: Notes for ARD Board Meeting, October 9, 1968, GFD.

206. *"The SEC never understood"*: Notes on ARD's Position, November 9, 1968, GFD.

206. *William H. Wendel, proposed a union*: Notes from ARD Board Meeting, December 8, 1968, GFD.

206–107. *Donaldson, Lufkin & Jenrette proposed*: Agenda for ARD Board Meeting, July 9, 1969, GFD.

207. *G. William Miller then submitted*: ARD-Textron Merger, April 15, 1969, GFD.

207. *Two more proposals came in*: Agenda for ARD Board Meeting, July 9, 1969, GFD.

207. *"I had a tremendous respect"*: Thomas J. Perkins, interview by author.

208. *"Packard was an entrepreneur"*: Ibid.

208. *"There was no way to make significant money"*: Ibid.

208. *"We felt wealthy enough"*: Ray Hoagland, interview by author.

209. *"They had a little VC fund"*: Ibid.

209. *"It is quite an honor, General"*: Daniel J. Holland, interview by author.

209. *"He said early on that I could rectify"*: Ibid.

209. *The committee decided to hire the consulting firm Arthur D. Little*: Details of the contract are contained in this Arthur D. Little memo: Robert O. Saunders Jr., memo to Judge Byron K. Elliott, November 19, 1969, GFD.

209. *Arthur D. Little submitted its report*: Robert O. Saunders Jr., memo to Compensation Committee of Directors of American Research and Development Corporation, November 26, 1969, GFD.

210. *"we have done poorly on new projects"*: Georges Doriot, memo to Judge Byron K. Elliott, December 29, 1969, GFD.

210. *Samuel Bodman submitted his resignation*: Address by Samuel W. Bodman at the tribute to Georges Doriot, French Library and Cultural Center, Boston, MA, October 2005.

210. *ARD's directors tried to accelerate:* ARD Annual Board of Directors Meeting minutes, March 4, 1970, GFD.

211. *"To go to work for ARD":* Charles J. Coulter, interview by author.

211. *"General, I've got a family":* Ibid.

211. *"Everyone else was amazed":* Ibid.

211. *Doriot wrote a memo to ARD director:* Georges F. Doriot, memo to Judge Byron Elliott, September 24, 1970, GFD.

211. *"[Perkins] came to see me":* Ibid.

212. *"He probably thought I was more interested":* Perkins, interview by author.

212. *the Committee finally proposed:* Georges F. Doriot, memo to Judge Byron Elliott, March 1971. GFD.

212. *"I feel fairly confident":* JBH [sic], memo to Georges Doriot, November 6, 1970, GFD.

212. *"We are alone, very alone":* Notes for Affiliate Dinner, March 2, 1971, GFD.

212. *"Before any options are granted":* Notes for Annual Meeting, March 3, 1971, GFD.

213. *the board rejected:* Notes on Project 70, March 7, 1971, GFD.

213. *"As we continue to seek consensus":* G. William Miller, letter to Georges Doriot, July 22, 1971, GFD.

213. *G. William Miller "has what it takes":* Personal note, September 5, 1971, GFD.

214. *Schacht told Doriot he was "very surprised":* Committee of 70, memo to Judge Byron K. Elliott, September 16, 1971, GFD.

214. *Olsen forcefully argued:* Notes on ARD Executive Committee Meeting, October 8, 1971, GFD.

214. *"I do not believe we should make":* Notes on ARD Executive Committee Meeting, October 8, 1971, GFD.

215. *Olsen cut off the ARD employees:* Confidential memo by Georges Doriot, October 23, 1971, GFD.

215. *"Outside directors know nothing":* Ibid.

215. *he wished to resign:* Georges F. Doriot, Resignation Statement to EED Board, November 26, 1971, GFD.

215. *the ARD board gathered in a special meeting:* Quotes are taken from a transcript of this meeting: ARD Board Meeting, November 30, 1971, GFD.

217. *Textron submitted a merger proposal:* Textron, memo to ARD Board of Directors, Proposal for ARD–Textron Merger, January 11, 1972, GFD.

217. *"It would have been hard to turn down":* Perkins, interview by author.

218. *"The reason ARD folded":* Shane, interview by author.

218. *"Dick observed this whole process":* Francis J. Hughes, interview by author.

218. *"He was not a man":* Claude Janssen, interview with author.

218. *"It should have been done in 1965":* Charles P. Waite, interview by author.

218. *"The General was such an extraordinary":* McCabe, interview by author.

218. *"It would have been a very, very complicated":* Ibid.

219. *its board of directors "endorsed in principal":* Press release, American Research and Development Corporation, January 12, 1972, GFD.

219. *"ARD gives us a hedge":* "A Risk Capitalist Bids a Golden Adieu," *BusinessWeek,* January 22, 1972, 18.

219. *"The association between ARD-Textron should have great strength":* Notes for Affiliate Dinner, March 14, 1972, GFD.

219. *"If the ARD stockholders approve":* Notes for Annual Meeting, March 15, 1972, GFD.

219. *"I feel as though I am watching a loved one":* "American Research Wins Board Approval to Merge into Textron," *Wall Street Journal,* March 16, 1972, 12.

219. *a handful of picketers protested:* "Holders of Textron, American Research Approve Merger Plan," *Wall Street Journal,* May 18, 1972, 4.

Chapter Twelve

221. *ARD's merger with Textron "was a mess":* James F. Morgan, interview by author.

221. *a dinner was arranged at 12 Lime Street:* Ibid.

222. *"I was convinced":* John A. Shane, interview by author.

222. *"It was obvious that in the new partnership structures":* Ibid.

222. *"It was classic Doriot":* Robert McCabe, interview by author.

222. *"Yardsticks, measurements to be used in judging":* Quotations are taken from this personal note: "Large Companies in Venture Capital," personal notes, GFD.

222. *"used to the General doing those things":* McCabe, interview by author.

223. *"You know ARD better than anyone"*: Georges Doriot, memo to Dorothy Rowe, May 1972, GFD.

223. *Morgan agreed to fly out*: Morgan, interview by author.

224. *"It seems that Jean Gueroult is very able"*: Georges Doriot, memo to Arnaud de Vitry and Claude Janssen, July 27, 1970, GFD.

225. *Shane and Congleton formed the Palmer:*Shane, interview by author.

225. *ARD associate Daniel J. Holland got a call:* Daniel J. Holland, interview by author.

226. *"After a layoff of less than"*: "Textron Unit's Chairman, G. Doriot, Takes Over Again as Chief Executive," *Wall Street Journal*, October 13, 1972, 16.

226. *"Doriot and others were poring over"*: Holland, interview by author.

226. *"Fortunately we had this big corporation"*: Morgan, interview by author.

226. *"We were 50 percent of the entire venture capital"*: Charles J. Coulter, interview by author.

227. *"I think Doriot was disappointed"*: Ibid.

227. *But since Doriot had been a director:* Textron Annual Reports, 1962–1975.

227. *"It was time for him to quit"*: Coulter, interview by author.

228. *The son of Lewis Terman:* Frederick Emmons Terman papers, Stanford University Archives, SC160, Stanford, CA.

229. *"Here for the first time"*: Stuart W. Leslie, "From Backwater to Powerhouse," *Stanford Magazine*, March 1990, online version.

229. *Hewlett and Packard set up a company:* details on the founding of HP come from this excellent book. Michael S. Malone, *Bill & Dave: How Hewlett and Packard Built the World's Greatest Company* (New York: Penguin Portfolio, 2007), 31–77.

230. *"There was no such thing in those days"*: Arthur Rock, interview by Rob Walker, November 2002, in *Silicon Genesis: An Oral History of the Semiconductor Industry* (Stanford University), http://library.stanford.edu/depts/hasrg/histsci/siligen.html.

230. *"We thought maybe we could form a company"*: Ibid.

230. *"young people are able to step up"*: Donald T. Valentine, interview by author.

231. *A Cincinnati blue blood:* Thomas J. Davis, Jr., *One Man's War: A Boston Lawyer on the Jungle Trails of Burma* (Self-published, 1989), 39–67, 223.

231. *"I got a call from Noyce"*: Rock, interview by Walker.

232. *the entire venture capital community in California "would meet"*: Gib Myers, interview by author.

232. *the region's venture movement reached critical mass:* Martha Louise Reiner, *The Transformation of Venture Capital: A History of Venture Capital Organizations in the United States* (PhD diss., University of California, Berkeley, 1989), 326–341.

232. *The structure of Kleiner, Perkins was influenced by ARD:* Perkins, interview by author.

232. *"It was very clear to me"*: Valentine, interview by author.

233. *their first few investments blew up:* Perkins, interview by author. The chipmaker went under because of some undisclosed liabilities.

233. *"They were very embarrassing"*: Ibid.

233. *"Gene Kleiner and I said, 'Look, this isn't working'"*: Ibid.

233. *Tom Perkins, Valley Boy: The Education of Tom Perkins* (New York: Gotham, 2007), 74–76.

233. *I wanted to start:* Jimmy Treybig, interviewed by author.

233. *Treybig and Perkins cooked up the idea:* Ibid.

233. *I had the product idea:* Jimmy Treybig, interviewed by author.

234. *"In both of those companies"*: Valentine, interview by author.

234. *Valentine was approached by:* Ibid.

234. *Nolan Bushnell and Ted Dabney, founded:* Scott Cohen, *Zap: The Rise and Fall of Atari* (New York: McGraw-Hill, 1977), 23–24.

235. *The game was a smash:* Ibid.

234. *In 1976, Bushnell turned to Valentine:* Ibid.

234. *So Bushnell and his colleagues decided to sell:* Ibid.

234. *asked Bushnell to invest:* Ibid.

236. *"Neither one knew anything about marketing"*: Michael Moritz, *The Little Kingdom: The Private Story of Apple Computer* (New York: William Morrow & Co., 1984), 175. This is a superb book that details the rise of Apple Computer better than anything I've ever read.

236. *he eagerly put skin in the game:* Ibid.

236. *In January of 1978, Markulla raised $517,500:* Ibid.

236. *Markulla and Scott asked the investors:* Ibid.

237. *"It's a simple concept"*: Ibid.

237. *"It became very obvious"*: Ibid.

237. *"Eugene had been impressed"*: Perkins, interview by author.

238. *"Their names were on the door"*: Details on the founding of Genentech come from this superb interview: Robert A. Swanson, "Co-founder, CEO, and Chairman of Genentech, Inc., 1976–1996," an oral history conducted in 1996 and 1997 by Sally Smith Hughes, Regional Oral History Office, The Bancroft Library, University of California, Berkeley, 2001.

238. *This is really an important event:* Ibid.

238. *"My half of an apartment"*: Ibid.

238. *"I was very impressed with Boyer"*: Thomas J. Perkins, "Kleiner Perkins, Venture Capital, and the Chairmanship of Genentech, 1976–1995," an oral history conducted in 2001 by Glenn E. Bugos, Regional Oral History Office, The Bancroft Library, University of California, Berkeley, 2002.

239. *"The day we announced [the gene]"*: Ibid.

239. *"Biotechnology jumpstarted the public's fascination"*: Frederick Frank, interview by author.

Chapter Thirteen

241. *"[ARD] had to go back to the parent"*: Shane, interview by author.

241–242. *"We do not have the freedom"*: Georges Doriot, memo to ARD staff, "Sources of Funds," March 5, 1974, GFD.

242. *"The corporate world has a thing"*: Coulter, interview by author.

243. *"Some thought there was no need"*: Kenneth H. Olsen, letter to G. William Miller, April 23, 1975, Olsen papers, Gordon College, Wenham, MA.

243. *"Unfortunately the market was not the same"*: Jean Gueroult, interview by author.

243. *"I tried to get rid of him"*: Arnaud de Vitry, interview by author.

243. *"Doriot was a bit distant"*: Janssen, interview by author.

243. *"The bankers wanted ARD to guarantee"*: de Vitry, interview by author.

243. *"The board assessed the situation"*: Janssen, interview by author.

243. *"Doriot was really a forward looking person"*: Frank, interview by author.

243. *"Never did a more brilliant guy"*: Morgan, interview by author.

244. *"Many deals which I have been able to accomplish"*: B. W. M. Twaalfhoven to unknown recipient.

244. *"What we were doing was buying"*. Georges Doriot, interview by Aulikki Olsen, April 1980.

245. *The Doriots made up for their spartan accommodations:* Ibid.

245. *"Don't tell Georges. I'm going out to Manchester"*: Patricia A. Clark, interview by author.

245. *"It was more than I could afford"*: Charles Dyer, interview by author.

245. *"When he painted he used to hold"*: Dina McCabe, interview by author.

245. *Edna yearned to build a new home:* Doriot, interview by Olsen.

245. *Doriot and his wife owned 13,192 shares:* Proxy for American Research and Development, March 1972.

246. *"You had said once that you would like"*: Doriot, interview by Olsen.

246. *"Is it not just wonderful to know"*: Edna Doriot, letter to Georges Doriot, November 13, 1975, Ralph Soda papers.

246. *she began to reap the rewards:* Résumé of Mrs. Edna Allen Doriot, August 1, 1978, GFD.

246–247. *"The art of communication is lacking in me"*: "Notes found in Edna's Diaries," transcribed by Georges Doriot, 1977, Ralph Soda papers.

247. *Georges and Edna drove out to Manchester:* Georges Doriot pocket diary, June 4, 1978, Ralph Soda papers.

247. *"Be not afraid"*: "Notes found in Edna's Diaries." 1978.

247. *Edna wrote a poem:* Ibid., July 1978.

247. *Edna's remains were cremated:* de Vitry, interview by author.

248. *a memorial service was held for Edna:* Photocopy of program for memorial service for Edna Allen Doriot, Ralph Soda papers.

248. *"When you have only your wife"*: Janssen, interview by author.

248. *"I tell her what I did"*: Marian Christy, "Love and Life: For General Doriot, The Two Are One," *Boston Globe*, August 21, 1985, 3rd ed., 65.

248. *"I still keep her handbag"*: Ibid.

248. *"When she passed away"*: de Vitry, interview by author.

248. *"I never looked at those sheets"*: Christy, "Love and Life."

248. *"It was a Doriot salon":* Morgan, interview by author.

249. *I haven't for a moment forgotten you:* Lucille Ball, letter to General Georges F. Doriot, June 5, 1979, LOC.

250. *one-third of that new money:* Paul A. Gompers and Josh Lerner, *The Money of Invention* (Boston: Harvard Business School Press, 2001), 92–94.

250. *five hundred former students, spouses, friends:* "An 80th Birthday Celebration for Professor Doriot," *HBS Bulletin,* November/December 1979; and Robert Lerner, "Captains of Industry Go Back to Class—with Doriot," *Boston Globe,* September 25, 1979.

250. *"I remember the stairs":* McCabe, interview by author.

251. *"He always talked about love":* Ted Johnson, interview by author.

252. *"The software opportunities":* Morgan, interview by author.

252. *the General stopped sitting beside Olsen:* Jacobs, interview by author.

253. *one of the company's other directors turned:* Coulter, interview by author.

253. *"By the 80s it got to the point":* Francis J. Hughes, interview by author.

253. *worth an estimated $35 million:* "Textron's Drive to Pay Down Its Debt," *Business Week,* August 5, 1985, 38.

253. *Textron "shed a highly profitable unit":* "The Capitalists," *Venture,* October 1985, 28.

253. *The team started a new fund:* Hughes, interview by author.

253. *"ARD was one of the first five venture firms":* Ibid.

254. *"I simply wanted to send along":* George H. W. Bush, letter to Georges Doriot, February 26, 1985, LOC.

254. *"I believe that I shall be reunited":* Georges Doriot, "Reveries," March 1985, Ralph Soda papers.

254. *"She was dressed in black":* Ibid.

254. *The General dropped down to 140 pounds:* Georges Doriot pocket diary, Ralph Soda papers.

254. *prescribed him a medical cocktail:* Ibid.

255. *"I went to see him at his office":* James M. Stone, interview by author.

255. *Doriot started radiation treatment:* Georges Doriot pocket diary, Ralph Soda papers.

255. *"I used to walk him over":* Stone, interview by author.

255. *"She was there every second":* Ibid.

255. *Olsen "has taken Digital from nothing":* Peter Petre, "America's Most Successful Entrepreneur," *Fortune,* October 27, 1986, 24–32.

255. *trying to make Digital obsolete:* After missing the PC revolution, Digital Equipment was acquired by Compaq Computer on January 27, 1998 for $9.6 billion—then the largest takeover in the history of the computer industry.

255. *"The General tried to whisper something":* Jacobs, interview by author.

256. *"There are two outstanding":* Janssen, interview by author.

256. *died peacefully in his sleep at 5:45 a.m.:* Death certificate for Georges F. Doriot, Commonwealth of Massachusetts, Department of Public Health.

256. *Ida called the police:* Stone, interview by author.

256. *"We got there":* Ibid.

256. *The trust's main asset was 31,298 shares:* "The Values of Doriot," *The Economist,* June 20, 1987, 75.

256. *Georges told the executor:* Last Will and Codicil of Georges F. Doriot, Registry of Probate, Suffolk County, Massachusetts, filed June 4, 1987.

256. *Arnaud de Vitry gave a eulogy:* de Vitry, interview by author.

Epilogue

259. *a landmark agreement that France signed:* "Bush Administration Moves Forward to Develop Next Generation Nuclear Energy Systems," Department of Energy press release, February 28, 2005.

259. *which derives about 80 percent of its electric power:* Remarks by Ambassador Jean-David Levitte on the signature of the framework agreement for international collaboration on research and development of Generation IV nuclear systems by the Governments of Canada, France, Japan, the United Kingdom, and the United States, February 28, 2005, Washington, DC.

INDEX

Advanced Research Projects Agency, 152
AEDC (American Enterprise Development
  Corporation), 203–204
Aellig, Ida, 245, 247–248, 255, 256
Airborne Instruments Laboratory, Inc., 125
"aircraft carrier" investing method, 237
Aircraft Radio Corporation, 160
Alden, Vernon, 154–155
Alex Brown & Sons, 167
Algerian War, 161
Allen, Edna Blanche. *See* Doriot, Edna
Allied Reparations Committee, 37
American Alpine Club, 92
American Can, 157
American Enterprise Development Corporation
  (AEDC), 203–204
American Express, 251
American Machinist magazine, 24–25
American Mathis, Inc., 50
American Radiator Company, 38
American Research and Development Corpora-
  tion (ARD), xiii–xix, 18, 199–200, 232, 250
  annual losses, 115, 119
  annual meetings of, 133–135, 153, 181–182,
    193
  assistance and advice by, 114, 121–122
  attacks on
    by IRS, 140, 200, 203
    over military research facility location, 117,
      118
    by SEC (*see* Securities and Exchange
      Commission)
  board of directors
    blame for succession problem, 218
    discussion of Textron merger, 215–217
    Olsen elected to, 204, 205
    vote to disband, 242
  compensation plan for staff, 205, 209–210,
    212–213
  compensation problems, 191, 200–201
  Digital Equipment Corporation and (*see*
    Digital Equipment Corporation)
  disclosure of proprietary financial data in
    reports, 184, 189, 192
  dividend offerings, 136, 138

Doriot as head of, xvi–xvii
  blamed for ARD's failure to remain
    independent, 217–218
  resignation of, 226–227
  early years of, 105–127
  failure to capitalize on high-tech industries,
    241
  favorable publicity, 134–135, 136
  first technology trade show, 136
  foreign venture partners
    CED, 177–178, 180, 181, 188, 193, 205
    EED, 180–182, 188, 193, 205
  government regulation of, 110
  incorporation of, 107–108
  increase in value of, 119, 127, 169, 172,
    173–174
  investment guidelines and philosophy, 112,
    113, 172–173
  investment in technology companies,
    118–119
  on "investment sprees," 163–165, 168–171
  listed on NYSE "Big Board," 160–161,
    171 172
  move to new headquarters, 121
  new leadership talent in, 123–127
  operating profits, 127, 135, 143
  pioneering business practices, 232–233,
    238–239
  problems of affiliate companies, 178–180
  raising capital for, 153–155, 160–161,
    165–168
  "Regional Committees," 123, 188
  shrinking capital base of (1949), 120–123
  staffing problems, 142–143, 159–160
  status as regulated investment company,
    201–202, 205–206
  stock of
    compensation plan for staff, 205, 209–210,
      212–213
    stock dividends, 146
    stock offerings, 112, 141, 144–146, 153–154,
      159
    stock prices, 138–139, 141, 143, 159, 217
  surprise inspection of offices by SEC,
    185–186

N. W. Ayer & Son, 67–68, 74, 123
Nadler, Marcus, 75
Narragansett Brewing Company, 133
Natick Labs, 126–127, 162
National Academy of Sciences, 94
National Association of Investment Companies, 110
National Association of Security Commissioners, 109
National Defense Research Committee, 228
National Guard, 67
National Industrial Recovery Act of 1933, 69–70
National Labor Relations Act, 72
National Recovery Administration (NRA), 69–70
National Research Co., 77
National Rubber, 107, 133
National Semiconductor, 234, 236
National Venture Capital Association, xix
Natural Gas Odorizing Company, 146
Naval Research Laboratory, 97, 98
Navy Bureau of Aeronautics, 97–98
Nesbitt, Deane, 177
Nesbitt, Thomson and Co., 177
New Deal. *See also* Great Depression
    Doriot's denunciations of, 71–72
    effectiveness of, 72–73, 74
    egalitarian ethos of, 76
    National Industrial Recovery Act of 1933, 69–70
    onerous tax system, 68–69, 74–75, 109
New England Council, 75, 76
    New Products Committee of, 76, 107
    Venture Capital Subcommittee, 108
New England Industrial Foundation, 77
New England Venture Capital Association, 257
New Outlook, 68
New Products Committee, 76, 107
The New Republic, 37–38
Newsweek magazine, 120
New York Central Railroad, 19
New York & Foreign Development Corporation, 34–37, 38, 39, 41, 73
New York Herald Tribune, 111
New York Stock Exchange (NYSE), 20, 145, 160–161, 169, 171
New York Times, 99, 134–135, 152, 174
New York University, 75
Nobel Prize, 168, 230
Noyce, Robert, 231
NRA (National Recovery Administration), 69–70
nutrition experiments, 94
NYSE. *See* New York Stock Exchange

Office of Strategic Services, 81
Office of the Quartermaster General, 80
oil industry, 163–165
Old Colony Trust Company, 42

Olsen, Kenneth H., xviii, 159, 167, 203, 210, 212, 255
    deal with ARD signed, 151–152
    development of interactive computer, 163
    as director of Ford Motor Co., 251
    disdain for "organization man," 148–149
    disorganization in Digital and, 187
    elected to board of ARD, 204, 205
    at Lincoln Laboratory, 147–148
    as miserly, 157
    on morale of ARD staff, 242
    new organizational structure for DEC, 193
    opposition to merger with ARD, 213
    options in Digital stock, 206
    proposal submitted to ARD, 149–151
    relationship with Doriot, 178–180, 214–215, 251, 252–253, 255
    share of Digital IPO, 196
OPEC, 226
Optical Scanning, 195–196, 201
The Organization Man (Whyte), 148
Orr, (Capt.) Robert D., 80, 91–92, 254
Orton, William, 7–8
Osborne, Bill, 194
Owsley, Augustus, 208

Packard, Dave, 207, 208, 229, 233
Palmer Service Corporation, 225
Panhard-Levassor, 11, 13, 26
Panic of 1873, 19
Parant, Alexandre, 21
Parant, Jules René, 21
Paris-Brest et Retour (bicycle race), 10–12
Paris Chamber of Commerce, 52, 54, 142, 156, 161
Paris-Rouen Trial of 1894, 12–13
Patterson, Mrs. Robert, 93
Patterson, Robert P., 84, 105, 106, 117
Pearl Harbor bombing, 84, 86
Pechiney, 155
Pennsylvania Railroad, 30
Pennsylvania Station, 30, 31
Pepperidge Farms, 130, 162
Perkins, Thomas J., 207, 208, 211–212, 214, 217, 232, 233, 238–239
Petre, Pete, 255
Peugeot, Armand, 8–10, 11, 14, 15, 16–17
Peugeot, Germaine, 15
Peugeot, Jean-Frédéric, 5
Peugeot, Jean-Pierre, 5
Peugeot, Madeleine, 15–16
Peugeot, Marianne, 15, 16
Peugeot Motor Company, xiv, 3, 4
    Auguste's resignation from, 16–17
    in automobile racing, 10–13
    beginning of automobile manufacture, 9–12
    formation of, 5
"Phony War," 77

Sears, Roebuck & Co., 33, 112, 123, 235
Sears, Winslow, 132
Seattle Cablevision, Inc., 205
Securities and Exchange Commission (SEC), xix,
    110, 116
  creation of (1934), 72
  Doriot's battles with, 138, 188
    ARD's secrecy about, 200
    over business practices, 189–192
    over stock option issue, 183–186, 206,
      212–213
    over valuation of investments, 139–140
    Senate committee testimony, 202–203
  exemptions for ARD, 112, 201
  inquiries to, regarding European venture
    capital firm, 181
  "Special Study of the Securities Markets," 174
"The Security I Like Best" (Towbin), 141
Select Committee on Small Business (Senate),
    202–203
Semi-Automatic Ground Environment (SAGE)
    Defense System, 148
semiconductor industry, 169–171, 229–231
Senate Armed Services subcommittee, 117
Sequoia Capital, 232, 234, 236, 237
Serpollet, Leon, 9, 10
Shane, John A., 130, 172, 181, 188, 190, 201, 204,
    222, 224, 225, 241
Shapiro, Robert, 195
Shawcross, (Lord) Hartley William, 243
Shields, Jack, 179, 195, 196
Shockley, William, 149, 230
Shockley Semiconductor Laboratory, 230
shoe industry, 100–101
Sidney Farber Cancer Center, 246, 247
Siegfried, Andre, 43
Silicon Valley, 227–239
  attractive to creative talent, 228
  computer gaming industry, 234–235
  creation of markets and industries, 234,
    237–238
  role of Frederick Terman, 228–230
  venture capital industry in, 231–239, 250
Simmons College, 48, 246
Simon, Paul, 210
Simons, Minot, 60–61
Sloan School of Management (MIT), 237, 257
Small Business Administration, 149
Small Business Investment Act of 1958, 153
Small Business Investment Company (SBIC)
    program, 153, 160, 207, 232
Smathers, George A., 202–203, 205, 206
Smith Barney, 165
Snow-Job, 233
Snyder, John W., 106–107
Snyder Chemical Corporation, 114
social change, caused by World War II, 111

Social Security Act, 72
Society of Plastics Engineers, 98
Somervell, (Lt. Gen.) Brehon B., 88, 99, 101
Sorenson, Charles E., 85
Special Forces, equipment testing by, 92
"Special Study of the Securities Markets" (SEC),
    174
Spectra-Physics, 208
Spiratube Division, 114
Sprague, Oliver, 49
Sputnik, 152–153, 158
S.S. Touraine, 29, 30
Standard Oil Company, xix, 134, 255
Standard Power & Light Corporation, 73
Stanfill, Dennis, 207
Stanford University, 48, 212, 228–229
Starbucks, xix
"Start-up Nation," xix
state "blue sky" laws, 110
Statler, Ellsworth, 30
Stevens, Lewis M., 123
Stilwell, (Gen.) Joseph W., 89
stock(s)
  ARD stock (*see* American Research and
    Development Corporation)
  DEC stocks (*see* Digital Equipment Corpora-
    tion)
  Doriot's battles with SEC on stock options,
    183–186, 206, 212–213
stock market
  1962 crash, 182
  fall after DEC IPO, 196–197
  high-tech stock boom, 173
  NYSE, 20, 145, 160–161, 169, 171
  origins of 1929 crash, 55–56
stock offerings
  in ARD, 112, 141, 144–146, 153–154, 159
  in D.F.P., 21
  initial public offerings
    of biotechnology companies, 239
    in DEC, 192–198, 200
    of Optical Scanning, 195–196, 201
Stone, James M., 144, 255, 256
Strauss, Alice (Hanauer), 35, 41, 45, 53, 60–61
Strauss, Lewis L., 48, 58
  advice to Doriot, 56
  communications from Doriot, 52, 53, 59, 68,
    69, 70
  hosts Doriot's wedding, 60–61
  marriage to Alice Hanauer, 41
  relationship with Doriot, 35–37, 45
student-teacher bond, in Doriot's classes, 47
"study groups" on basic business, 42
Styer, (Gen.) W. D., 95
Subsistence Research Laboratory, 94
Sun Life, 177–178
Sutter Hill Ventures, 207, 212, 232

ABOUT THE AUTHOR

SPENCER E. ANTE is an editor at *BusinessWeek*, where he has been covering technology and finance since 2000. Previously, he was a staff reporter for TheStreet.com, a contributing writer at *Wired News*, a columnist for *Business 2.0*, and a producer/consultant for the Netscape NetCenter. Ante was also a founding associate editor at *The Web* magazine and a cofounder of the International Academy of Digital Arts and Sciences. His stories have won awards from the Deadline Club of the Society for Professional Journalists and the American Society of Business Publication Editors. Ante received a bachelor's degree from the Kelley School of Business at Indiana University and a master's in journalism from the University of California at Berkeley. He lives in New York City with his wife and daughter, and can be reached at http://creativecapital.wordpress.com.